Advanced Practical Approaches to Web Mining Techniques and Application

Ahmed J. Obaid
University of Kufa, Iraq

Zdzislaw Polkowski
Wroclaw University of Economics, Poland

Bharat Bhushan
Sharda University, India

A volume in the Advances in Web
Technologies and Engineering
(AWTE) Book Series

Published in the United States of America by
  IGI Global
  Engineering Science Reference (an imprint of IGI Global)
  701 E. Chocolate Avenue
  Hershey PA, USA 17033
  Tel: 717-533-8845
  Fax: 717-533-8661
  E-mail: cust@igi-global.com
  Web site: http://www.igi-global.com

Library of Congress Cataloging-in-Publication Data

Names: Obaid, Ahmed, 1983- editor. | Polkowski, Zdzislaw, editor. |
  Bhushan, Bharat, 1989- editor.
Title: Advanced practical approaches to web mining techniques and
  application / Ahmed Obaid, Zdzislaw Polkowski, and Bharat Bhushan,
  editor.
Description: Hershey PA : Engineering Science Reference, [2022] | Includes
  bibliographical references and index. | Summary: "This book brings
  together all techniques and practical approaches in Web Mining
  Categories which includes Web Content Mining, Web Structure Mining, and
  Web Usage Mining, introducing the practical approach of analyzing
  various web data sources and extracting knowledge by taking into
  consideration the unique challenges present in the Web Environment"--
  Provided by publisher.
Identifiers: LCCN 2021054759 (print) | LCCN 2021054760 (ebook) | ISBN
  9781799894261 (hardcover) | ISBN 9781799894278 (paperback) | ISBN
  9781799894285 (ebook)
Subjects: LCSH: Data mining. | Web databases.
Classification: LCC QA76.9.D343 A3323 2022 (print) | LCC QA76.9.D343
  (ebook) | DDC 006.3/12--dc23/eng/20211128
LC record available at https://lccn.loc.gov/2021054759
LC ebook record available at https://lccn.loc.gov/2021054760

This book is published in the IGI Global book series Advances in Web Technologies and
Engineering (AWTE) (ISSN: 2328-2762; eISSN: 2328-2754)

British Cataloguing in Publication Data
A Cataloguing in Publication record for this book is available from the British Library.

For electronic access to this publication, please contact: eresources@igi-global.com.

Advances in Web Technologies and Engineering (AWTE) Book Series

ISSN:2328-2762
EISSN:2328-2754

Editor-in-Chief: Ghazi I. Alkhatib, The Hashemite University, Jordan; David C. Rine, George Mason University, USA

MISSION

The **Advances in Web Technologies and Engineering (AWTE) Book Series** aims to provide a platform for research in the area of Information Technology (IT) concepts, tools, methodologies, and ethnography, in the contexts of global communication systems and Web engineered applications. Organizations are continuously overwhelmed by a variety of new information technologies, many are Web based. These new technologies are capitalizing on the widespread use of network and communication technologies for seamless integration of various issues in information and knowledge sharing within and among organizations. This emphasis on integrated approaches is unique to this book series and dictates cross platform and multidisciplinary strategy to research and practice.

The **Advances in Web Technologies and Engineering (AWTE) Book Series** seeks to create a stage where comprehensive publications are distributed for the objective of bettering and expanding the field of web systems, knowledge capture, and communication technologies. The series will provide researchers and practitioners with solutions for improving how technology is utilized for the purpose of a growing awareness of the importance of web applications and engineering.

COVERAGE

- Web systems engineering design
- Knowledge structure, classification, and search algorithms or engines
- Integrated Heterogeneous and Homogeneous Workflows and Databases within and Across Organizations and with Suppliers and Customers
- IT readiness and technology transfer studies
- Case studies validating Web-based IT solutions
- Data and knowledge capture and quality issues
- Web user interfaces design, development, and usability engineering studies
- Mobile, location-aware, and ubiquitous computing
- Information filtering and display adaptation techniques for wireless devices
- Human factors and cultural impact of IT-based systems

IGI Global is currently accepting manuscripts for publication within this series. To submit a proposal for a volume in this series, please contact our Acquisition Editors at Acquisitions@igi-global.com or visit: http://www.igi-global.com/publish/.

Titles in this Series

701 East Chocolate Avenue, Hershey, PA 17033, USA
Tel: 717-533-8845 x100 • Fax: 717-533-8661
E-Mail: cust@igi-global.com • www.igi-global.com

Table of Contents

Detailed Table of Contents

Chapter 1

    T. Ramathulasi, Mother Theresa Institute of Engineering and
       Technology, Chittoor, India

    U. Kumaran, Mother Theresa Institute of Engineering and Technology,
       Chittoor, India

    K. Lokesh, Mother Theresa Institute of Engineering and Technology,
       Chittoor, India

The text summing method is obsolete due to recent advances in news articles, official documents, textual interpretation in scientific studies, manual text extraction, and many archives. Dealing with large amounts of text data requires the deployment of effective solutions. It is also impossible to capture text material due to high cost and labor. As a result, the academic community is increasingly interested in developing new ways to capture text automatically. Researchers have been working to improve the process of creating summaries since the invention of text summaries with the aim of creating machine summary matches with man-made summaries. Meaningful sentences are selected from the input document and added to the summaries using the hybrid technique. As a result, researchers are increasingly focusing on concise summaries to provide more coherent and relevant summaries. They use an artificial text summary to gather knowledge and information about recent research. A complete overview of abstraction methods is provided by a recent text summary created over the past decade.

    Avinash Kumar, Sharda University, India
    Bharat Bhushan Kumar, School of Engineering and Technology, Sharda
      University, India
    Saptadeepa Kalita, School of Engineering and Technology, Sharda
      University, India
    Rajasekhar Chaganti, Department of Computer Science, University of
      Texas at San Antonio, USA
    Parma Nand, School of Engineering and Technology, Sharda University,
      India

Monitoring and surveillancing of large amounts of data is a matter of prime concern in the current scenario for major organisations as well as small-scale and large-scale industries. Presently, the increasing need to collect, analyse, and store the data in a real-time environment as well as ensure the qualitative and quantitative analysis of real-time data has become a challenge. In addition, traditional data acquisition and monitoring systems lead industries to face multiple constraints and limitations, which affect their functioning, such as physical infrastructure setup and cost constraints. In this chapter, the surveillance of various applications has been discussed. The chapter also focuses on use of cloud-based model to perform the real-time monitoring with the help of the web. The chapter deeply discusses the use of web for on-site and off-site monitoring of various industries and organizations.

    Mohammad K. Daradkeh, University of Dubai, UAE & Yarmouk
      University, Jordan

While the hype around data science and its key role in driving business and industry change is pervasive, there is scant insight into the factors underlying its successful and widespread adoption in organizations. This chapter presents a systematic approach that integrates text analytics with technology-organization-environment (TOE) framework to analyze the digital voice of practitioners and identify the factors driving data science adoption in organizations. The authors collected 4100 user-generated reviews for 13 prominent data science platforms from Gartner.com and then categorized them into different topics using Latent-Dirichlet Allocation (LDA) model. From the identified topics, 48 factors were derived and synthesized into a model for data science adoption using the TOE framework. The results reveal that alongside technological capabilities, several organizational and environmental factors can significantly influence data science adoption. The results also provide evidence on the potential impact of data science adoption on various aspects of business performance.

Chapter 4

B. M. Arifuzzaman, North South University, Bangladesh
S. M. Niaz Mahmud, North South University, Bangladesh
Ayman Muniat, North South University, Bangladesh
A. K. M. Bahalul Haque, LUT University, Finland

Web-based services are common targets for hackers, and the need for ensuring their security keeps on rising. Attackers often take advantage of the vulnerabilities of different web applications using several mechanisms and thus steal and manipulate valuable information. Therefore, the attack vectors are also increasing since there is a wide variety of internet users. Exploitations caused by different types of cyberattacks results in data loss, identity theft, financial loss, and various other adversaries on both humans and infrastructure. Therefore, investigating various attack vectors and countermeasures can facilitate and encourage future research and create awareness among web application users and developers.

Chapter 5

Tyler W. Soiferman, Stevens Institute of Technology, USA
Paul J. Bracewell, DOT Loves Data, New Zealand

Natural language processing is a prevalent technique for scalably processing massive collections of documents. This branch of computer science is concerned with creating abstractions of text that summarize collections of documents in the same way humans can. This form of standardization means these summaries can be used operationally in machine learning models to describe or predict behavior in real or near real time as required. However, language evolves. This chapter demonstrates how language has evolved over time by exploring historical documents from the USA. Specifically, the change in emotion associated with key words can be aligned to major events. This research highlights the need to evaluate the stability of characteristics, including features engineered based on word elements when deploying operational models. This is an important issue to ensure that machine learning models constructed to summarize documents are monitored to ensure latent bias, or misinterpretation of outputs, is minimized.

Chapter 6

Sonia Tasmin, North South University, Bangladesh
Asma Khanam Sarmin, North South University, Bangladesh
Mitul Shalehin, North South University, Bangladesh
A. K. M. Bahalul Haque, LUT University, Finland

The phishing attack targets the client's email and any other connection medium to illicitly get the user credentials of e-commerce websites, educational websites, banks, credit card information, and other crucial user information. Exploitations caused by different types of cyberattacks result in data loss, identity theft, financial loss, and various other adversaries on both human and infrastructure. Therefore, investigating the threats and vulnerabilities on web applications and analysis of recent cyberattacks on web applications can also provide a holistic scenario about the recent security standpoint. Therefore, in this chapter, phishing attack techniques and their current scenario will be discussed extensively. Moreover, recent phishing techniques will be discussed to understand the severity of this type of attack. Finally, this chapter will outline the proposed and existing countermeasures for protecting users' identities and credentials from the phishing technique.

Chapter 7

Avinash Kumar, School of Engineering and Technology, Sharda
University, India

Bharat Bhushan, School of Engineering and Technology, Sharda
University, India.

Nandita Pokhriya, School of Engineering and Technology, Sharda
University

Raj Chaganti, Department of Computer Science, University of Texas at
San Antonio, USA

Parma Nand, School of Engineering and Technology, Sharda University,
India

The current century has seen a huge amount of data being produced every day by various computational platforms. These data are very large in amount when compared to the past. These data have emerged in form of big data (BD), and it's vital to manage these data for processing as well as extracting. The big data are emerging from Facebook, Instagram, and various other social as well as private platforms. Web mining has the capabilities to mine or extract data from a very huge set of data. The mining of useful information is essential for optimal functioning of various systems. In this chapter, the usage of web mining and one of its sub categories, web usage mining, for various human-driven applications has been discussed. This chapter focuses on the background that leads to the emergence of web mining. The chapter also deeply explores various subdomains that are essential for tackling data extraction using web mining.

Chapter 8

*Abhijit Dnyaneshwar Jadhav, Dr. D. Y. Patil Institute of Technology,
Pimpri, India*
Santosh V. Chobe, Dr. D. Y. Patil Institute of Technology, Pimpri, India

The interactions with web systems is huge because of COVID-19, where every system is run through online interactions. The world wide web is continuously expanding, and users' interactions with websites generate a vast quantity of data. Web usage mining is the use of data mining techniques to extract important and hidden information about users. It allows you to see the most frequently visited sites, imagine user navigation, and track the progress of your website's structure, among other things. The web mining techniques help us to analyze the user's behavior and accordingly create the required web designs, which will appear in the relevant searches of the users. In this scenario, one of the important processes is web document preprocessing, which will help us to extract the particular quality data inputs for analyzing the behaviors which helps in effective web design. Here, the authors discuss preprocessing of web documents. From the four different phases of the web mining, web document pre-processing is a very important phase.

Chapter 9

Safa Teboulbi, Monastir University, Tunisia
Seifeddine Messaoud, Monastir University, Tunisia
Mohamed Ali Hajjaji, Monastir University, Tunisia
Abdellatif Mtibaa, Monastir University, Tunisia

Since the infectious coronavirus disease (COVID-19) was first reported in Wuhan, it has become a public health problem around the world. This pandemic is having devastating effects on societies and economies. Due to the lack of health resources in a short period, all countries and continents are likely to face particularly severe damage that could lead to a large epidemic. Wearing a face mask that stops the transmission of droplets in the air can still be helpful in combating this pandemic. Therefore, this chapter focuses on implementing a face mask detection model as an embedded vision system. The six pre-trained models, which are MobileNet, ResNet-50, MobileNet-V2, VGG-19, VGG-16, and DenseNet, are used in this context. People wearing or not wearing masks were detected. After implementing and deploying the models, the selected models achieved a confidence score. Therefore, this study concludes that wearing face masks helps reduce the virus spread and fight this pandemic.

As the size of the micro-array disease databases increase, finding an essential feature set for the classification problem is complex due to the large data size and sparsity problems. Traditional feature subset models are based on static clustering and classification models due to the fixed sized dimensions cluster-based disease prediction process. Sparsity, missing values, and imbalance are the major issues that affect the selection of essential feature clusters for data classification process. In this chapter, a hybrid cluster-based Bayesian probability estimation model is proposed in order to predict the disease class label on high dimensional databases. The proposed cluster-based classification model selects optimal clusters for feature ranking and classification problems to improve the true positive rate and accuracy. Experimental results are simulated on different training datasets for accuracy prediction. The results proved that the gene-disease-based patterns have better optimization than the conventional methods in terms of statistical metrics and classification models.

Detection of bearing faults have become crucial in electrical machines, particularly in induction motors. Conventional monitoring procedures using vibration sensors, temperature sensors, etc. are costly and need more tests to estimate the nature of fault. Hence, the current monitoring attracts the concentration of many industries for continuous monitoring. Spectral analysis of stator current to estimate motor faults, FFT analysis, is commonly preferred. But the problems associated with normal FFT analysis will mislead the fault diagnosis. Therefore, advanced spectral methods like wavelet transforms, matrix pencil method, MUSIC algorithm, s-transforms have been proposed. But each technique requires special attention to get good results. On the other hand, faults experienced by the induction motor can be categorized into bearing-related, rotor- and stator-related, and eccentricity. Among these faults, bearing damage accounts for 40-90% and requires additional concentration to estimate.

P. V. D. S. Eswar, Koneru Lakshmaiah Education Foundation, India

N. Siva, Koneru Lakshmaiah Education Foundation, India

A. V. Harish, Koneru Lakshmaiah Education Foundation, India

Arunmetha Sundaramoorthy, KL University, India

K. Praghash, Koneru Lakshmaiah Education Foundation, India

We observe fire hazards causing life loss and property loss frequently in domestic and industrial scenarios. In industries we usually have many blocks or buildings, and it is impossible to check every building every second of the day. So, the authors' model continuously checks for fire and gives a signal: either buzzer or light depending on the requirement. This is an embedded way of hardware application and software. They also used different machine learning models and algorithms to predict the future time of the fire, using regression. For prototype applications, they use linear regression, and for real-time applications, they use k-means clustering or any other model for better accuracy.

Sekar R., Koneru Lakshimaiah Education Foundation, India

Hema Likhitha Godavarthi, Koneru Lakshmaiah Education Foundation, India

Satya Deepika Bandi, Koneru Lakshmaiah Education Foundation, India

Sri Vandhana Dadi, Koneru Lakshmaiah Education Foundation, India

K. Praghash, Koneru Lakshmaiah Education Foundation, India

In India, around 70% of the populace depends on agribusiness. The identification of plant infections is significant to forestall misfortunes inside the yield. It's problematic to notice plant illnesses physically. It needs a colossal amount of work, skill inside the plant infections, and conjointly needs an unreasonable time stretch. Subsequently, picture handling models can be utilized for the location of plant illnesses. In this venture, the authors have depicted the procedure for the discovery of imperfections of plant illnesses with the assistance of their leaves pictures. Here they are utilizing the rice plant for recognizing the deformities. Picture handling is a part of sign handling, which can separate the picture properties or valuable data from the picture. The shade of leaves, measure of harm to leaves, space of the leaf, surface boundaries are utilized for arrangement. In this task, the authors have examined diverse picture boundaries or highlights to recognize distinctive plant passes on infections to accomplish the best accuracy.

Chapter 14

    M. Ravi Kumar, Department of Electronics and Communication
        Engineering, Koneru Lakshmaiah Education Foundation, India
    K. Mariya Priyadarshini, Department of Electronics and
        Communication Engineering, Koneru Lakshmaiah Education
        Foundation, India
    Chella Santhosh, Department of Electronics and Communication
        Engineering, Koneru Lakshmaiah Education Foundation, India
    J Lakshmi Prasanna, Department of Electronics and Communication
        Engineering, Koneru Lakshmaiah Education Foundation, India
    G. U. S. Aiswarya Likitha, Department of Electronics and
        Communication Engineering, Koneru Lakshmaiah Education
        Foundation, India

Galois finite field arithmetic multipliers are supported by two-element multiplication of the finite body thereby reducing the result by a polynomial p(x) which is irreducible with degree m. Galois field (GF) multipliers have a variety of uses in communications, signal processing, and other fields. The verification methods of GF circuits are uncommon and confined to circuits of critical information sources and yields with realized piece locations. They also require data from the final polynomial P(x), which affects the execution of the final equipment. Here the authors introduce a math method that is based on a PC variable that easily verifies and figures out GF (2m) multipliers from the use of the initial level and compares with Vedic multiplier and Wallace tree multiplier. The technique relies on the parallel elimination of extraordinary final polynomial and proceeds in three phases: 1) decision of the yield bit – the situation is made; 2) decision of the info bit – the situation is made; and 3) the invariable polynomial used in the structure is segregated.

Chapter 15

    Joshua Ojo Nehinbe, Federal University, Oye, Nigeria

Recent surveys have revealed that about 199 million of active and over 1.2 Billion of inactive websites exist across the globe. The categories of websites have also increased beyond espionage networks of spies, computer networks for corporate organizations, networks for governments' agencies, networks for social interactions, search engines and networks for religious bodies, etc. These diversities have generated complex issues regarding the morphology and classification of webs and web mining. Thus, the validity of the generic web classification, web mining taxonomy, and contemporary studies on the regularities of web usage, web content, web semantic, web structures, and the process of extracting useful information and interesting patterns from the intricate of the Internet are frequently questionable. The existing web mining taxonomy can also lead to misinformation, misclassification, and crisscrossed issues such that numerous webs' patterns could be marked with crossing and inexplicable lines. By using qualitative virtual interviews of 26 skilled web-designers and a focus group-conference of 7 experts in web-usage to brainstorm on the above issues, this chapter comprehensively discusses the above concepts and how they relate to web classification and web mining taxonomy. The themes obtained elucidate the techniques that commonly underpin basic web mining taxonomy. New concepts like existence of esoteric web data, exoteric web data; mysterious, inexplicable, and mystifying patterns; and cryptic vocabularies are discussed to assist web analytics. Finally, the author suggests eight classification attributes for web mining patterns (illustrative, expositive, educative, advisory, interpretative, demonstrative, revealing, and informatory) and proposes a new web mining taxonomy to minimize the impacts of the above concerns on global settings.

Preface

The main objective of this book is to foster transformative, multidisciplinary, and novel approaches that introduce the practical approach of analyzing various web data sources and extracting knowledge by taking into consideration the unique challenges present in the Web Environment. This book attracts contributions in all aspects pertaining to this multidisciplinary paradigm. The authors are expected to investigate state-of-art achievements, applications, and research issues in the field of Web mining and the related categories. in recent years, we did not final some reference books focus on Web Mining, or exploring the techniques, and practical approaches in the Web, all available sources from textbooks or others focus on Data Mining techniques and applications and the science of data mining differ from Web mining in which we need to apply adjusted and new algorithms to work with different data types that reside in Web sources. we have seen some books since 2001 and 2007 focus only on Web Content Mining and Usage mining and these books left the other subject related to structure mining as well as do not list the new challenges in recent years by explosive growth of Web data. This book aims to bring together all techniques and practical approaches in Web Mining Categories which includes Web Content Mining, Web Structure Mining, and Web Usage Mining.

A SURVEY ON TEXT-BASED TOPIC SUMMARIZATION TECHNIQUES

The text summing method is obsolete due to recent advances in news articles, official documents, textual interpretation in scientific studies, manual text extraction and many archives. Dealing with large amounts of text data requires the deployment of effective solutions. It is also impossible to capture text material due to high cost and labor. As a result, the academic community is increasingly interested in developing new ways to capture text automatically. Researchers have been working to improve the process of creating summaries since the invention of text summaries with the aim of creating machine summary matches with man-made summaries. Meaningful sentences are selected from the input document and added to the summaries using the hybrid technique. As a result, researchers are increasingly focusing on concise summaries to provide more coherent and relevant summaries. Uses an artificial text summary, to gather knowledge and information about recent research. A complete overview of abstraction methods is provided by a recent text summary created over the past decade.

CONTROLLING AND SURVEYING OF ON-SITE AND OFF-SITE SYSTEM USING WEB MONITORING

Monitoring and surveillancing of large amounts of data is a matter of prime concern in the current scenario for major organisations as well as small-scale and large-scale industries. Presently, the increasing need to collect, analyse and store the data in a real time environment as well as ensuring the qualitative and quantitative analysis of real time data has become a challenge. In addition, traditional data acquisition and monitoring systems lead industries to face multiple constraints and limitations, which affect their functioning, such as physical infrastructure setup and cost constraints. In this paper, the surveillance of various applications has been discussed. The paper also focuses on use of cloud-based model to perform the real time monitoring with the help of web. The paper deeply discusses the use of web for on-site and off-site monitoring of various industries and organizations.

DETERMINANTS OF DATA SCIENCE ADOPTION IN ORGANIZATIONS: INSIGHTS FROM ANALYZING THE DIGITAL VOICE OF PRACTITIONERS

While the hype around data science and its key role in driving business and industry change is pervasive, there is scant insight into the factors underlying its successful and widespread adoption in organizations. This Chapter presents a systematic approach that integrates text analytics with technology-organization-environment (TOE) framework to analyze the digital voice of practitioners and identify the factors driving data science adoption in organizations. We collected 4100 user-generated reviews for 13 prominent data science platforms from Gartner.com, and then categorized them into different topics using Latent-Dirichlet Allocation (LDA) model. From the identified topics, 48 factors were derived and synthesized into a model for data science adoption using the TOE framework. The results reveal that alongside technological capabilities, several organizational and environmental factors can significantly influence data science adoption. The results also provide evidence on the potential impact of data science adoption on various aspects of business performance.

SECURING WEB APPLICATIONS: SECURITY THREATS AND COUNTERMEASURES

Web-based services are common targets for hackers, the need for ensuring their security keeps on rising. Attackers often take advantage of the vulnerabilities of different web applications using several mechanisms and thus steal and manipulate valuable information. Therefore the attack vectors are also increasing since there are a wide variety of internet users. Exploitations caused by different types of cyberattacks results in data loss, identity theft, financial loss, and various other adversaries on both human and infrastructure. Therefore, investigating various attack vectors and countermeasures can facilitate and encourage future research and create awareness among web application users and well developers.

SIGN OF THE TIMES: SENTIMENT ANALYSIS ON HISTORICAL TEXT AND THE IMPLICATIONS OF LANGUAGE EVOLUTION

Natural Language Processing is a prevalent technique for scalably processing massive collections of documents. This branch of computer science is concerned with creating abstractions of text that summarize collections of documents in the same way humans can. This form of standardization means these summaries can be used operationally in machine learning models to describe or predict behavior in real or near real time as required. However, language evolves. This chapter demonstrates how language has evolved over time, by exploring historical documents from the USA. Specifically, the change in emotion associated with key words can be aligned to major events. This research highlights the need to evaluate the stability of characteristics, including features engineered based on word elements, when deploying operational models. This is an important issue to ensure that machine learning models constructed to summarize documents are monitored to ensure latent bias, or misinterpretation of outputs, is minimized.

COMBATING THE PHISHING ATTACKS: RECENT TRENDS AND FUTURE CHALLENGES

The phishing attack targets the client's email and any other connection medium to illicitly get the user credentials of e-commerce websites, educational websites, banks, credit card information, and other crucial user information. Exploitations caused by different types of cyberattacks results in data loss, identity theft, financial loss, and various other adversaries on both human and infrastructure. Therefore, investigating the threats and vulnerabilities on web applications and analysis of recent cyberattacks on web applications can also provide a holistic scenario about the recent security standpoint. Therefore, in this paper, phishing attacks techniques and their current scenario will be discussed extensively. Moreover, recent phishing techniques will be discussed to understand the severity of this type of attack. Finally, this paper will outline the proposed and existing countermeasures for protecting users' identities and credentials from the phishing technique.

WEB MINING AND WEB USAGE MINING FOR VARIOUS HUMAN-DRIVEN APPLICATIONS

The current century has seen huge amount of data being produced everyday by various computational platforms. These data are very large in amount when compared to the past. These data are has emerged in form of Big Data (BD) and its very vital to manage these data for processing as well as extracting. The big data are emerging from Facebook, Instagram and various other social as well as private platforms. The web mining has the capabilities to mine or extract data from a very huge set of data. The mining of useful information is essential for optimal functioning of various systems. In this paper, the usage of web mining and one of its sub categories, web usage mining for various human driven applications has been discussed. This paper focuses on the background that leads to the emergence of web mining. The paper also deeply explores various subdomains that are essential for tackling data extraction using web mining.

WEB USER BEHAVIOR ANALYSIS USING PRE-PROCESSING OF WEB DOCUMENTS TO CREATE EFFECTIVE WEB DESIGNS

Now a days, the interactions with web systems is huge in numbers, because of the pandemic era of COVID-19, where every system is run through online interactions. The World Wide Web is continuously expanding, and users' interactions with web sites generate a vast quantity of data. Web Usage Mining is the use of data mining techniques to extract important and hidden information about users. It allows you to see the most frequently visited sites, imagine user navigation, and track the progress of your website's structure, among other things. The web mining techniques help us to analyze the user's behavior and accordingly create the required web designs which will appear in the relevant searches of the users. In this scenario, one of the important process is web document preprocessing which will help us to extract the particular quality data inputs for analyzing the behaviors which helps in effective web design. Here, we will discuss about preprocessing of Web documents. From the four different phases of the web mining, web document pre-processing is very important phase.

FACE MASK CLASSIFICATION BASED ON DEEP LEARNING FRAMEWORK

Since the infectious coronavirus disease (COVID-19) was first reported in Wuhan, it has become a public health problem around the world. This pandemic is having devastating effects on societies and economies. Due to the lack of health resources in a short period, all countries and continents are likely to face particularly severe damage that could lead to a large epidemic. Wearing a face mask that stops the transmission of droplets in the air can still be helpful in combating this pandemic. Therefore, this research paper focuses on implementing a Face Mask Detection model as an embedded vision system. The six pre-trained models which are MobileNet, ResNet-50, MobileNet-V2, VGG-19, VGG-16 and DenseNet are used in this context. People wearing or not wearing masks were detected. After implementing and deploying the models, the selected models achieved a confidence score. Therefore, this study concludes that wearing face masks help reduce the virus spread and fight this pandemic.

A HYBRID EM-BASED BOOSTING CLASSIFICATION MODEL FOR MICROARRAY SOMATIC DISEASE PREDICTION

As the size of the micro-array disease databases is increasing, finding an essential feature sets for classification problem is complex due to large data size and sparsity problems. Traditional feature subset models are based on static clustering and classification model due to fixed sized dimensions cluster based disease prediction process. Sparsity, missing values and imbalance are the major issues that affect the selection of essential feature clusters for data classification process. In this paper, a hybrid cluster based Bayesian probability estimation model is proposed in order to predict the disease class label on high dimensional databases. Proposed cluster-based classification model selects optimal clusters for feature ranking and classification problem to improve the true positive rate and accuracy. Experimental results are simulated on different training datasets for accuracy prediction. Proposed results proved that the gene-disease based patterns have better optimization than the conventional methods in terms of statistical metrics and classification models.

PROGRESSIVE BEARING FAULT DETECTION IN A 3 PHASE INDUCTION MOTOR USING S-TRANSFORM VIA PRE-FAULT FREQUENCY CANCELLATION

Detection of bearing faults become very crucial in electrical machines particularly in induction motors. Conventional monitoring procedure susing vibration sensors, temperature sensors etc are costly and needs more tests to estimate the nature of fault. Hence the current monitoring attracts the concentration of many industries for continuous monitoring. Spectral analysis of stator current to estimate motor faults, FFT analysis is commonly preferred. But the problems associated with normal FFT analysis will mislead the fault diagnosis. Therefore, advanced spectral methods like wavelet transforms, Matrix pencil method, MUSIC algorithm, s-Transforms have proposed. But each technique requires special attention to get good results. On the other hand, faults experienced by induction motor can categorize into bearing related, rotor and stator related and eccentricity. Among these faults, bearing damage accounts 40 to 90 percentage and requires additional concentration to estimate. In this, progressive faults like bearing misalignment and generalized roughness faults are frequency occurred. Therefore, in this paper, these faults are detected in a 3 phase induction motor using S-Transform via pre-fault frequency cancellation using Wiener filter. Proposed topology is experimentally verified by conducting several tests on a 2 HP motor.

DESIGN OF WIRELESS IOT SENSOR NODE AND PLATFORM FOR FIRE DETECTION

We observe fire hazards causing life loss and property loss frequently in domestic and industrial scenarios. In industries we usually have many blocks or buildings it is impossible to check every building for every second. So, our proposed model continuously checks for fire and gives a signal either buzzer or light depending on the requirement. This is an embedded way of hardware application and software.

We also used different machine learning models and algorithms to predict the future time of the fire, using regression. For prototype applications, we use linear regression and for real-time applications, we may use k-means clustering or any other model for better accuracy.

AN EXPERIMENT TO FIND DISEASE DETECTION FOR RICE PLANTS USING RESNET

In India, around 70% of the populace depends on agribusiness. The Identification of the plant infections is significant to forestall the misfortunes inside the yield. It's problematic to notice plant illnesses physically. It needs a colossal amount of work, skill inside the plant infections, and conjointly needs the unreasonable time stretch. Subsequently, picture handling models can be utilized for the location of plant illnesses. In this venture, we have depicted the procedure for the discovery of imperfections of plant illnesses with the assistance of their leaves pictures. Here we are utilizing the rice plant for recognizing the deformities. Picture handling is a part of sign handling which can separate the picture properties or valuable data from the picture. The shade of leaves, measure of harm to leaves, space of the leaf, surface boundaries are utilized for arrangement. In this task, we have examined diverse picture boundaries or highlights to recognize distinctive plant passes on infections to accomplish the best accuracy.

ANALYSIS OF ENCRYPTION AND COMPRESSION TECHNIQUES FOR HIDING SECURED DATA TRANSMISSION

Galois finite field arithmetic multipliers are supported by two-element multiplication of the finite body thereby reducing the result by a polynomial p(x) which is irreducible with degree m. Galois field (GF) multipliers have a variety of uses in communications, signal processing, and other fields. The verification methods of GF circuits are uncommon and confined to circuits of critical information sources and yields with realized piece locations. They also require data from the final polynomial P(x), which affects the execution of the final equipment. Here we introduce a math method that is based on a PC variable that easily verifies and figures out GF (2m) multipliers from the use of the initial level and compares with Vedic multiplier and Wallace tree multiplier. The technique relies on the parallel elimination of extraordinary final polynomial and proceeds in three phases: 1) Decision of the yield bit - the situation is made; 2) Decision of the info bit - the situation is made, and 3) The invariable polynomial used in the structure is segregated. GF (2m) multipliers in m strings were demonstrated by this strategy. Analysis carried out on synthesized multipliers with different P(x) polynomials, demonstrate the proposed strategy's high efficiency.

A NEW INSIGHT ON THE MORPHOLOGY OF WEB MINING

Recent survey has revealed that there are over 199 million active and over 1.2 billion inactive websites across the globe. The categories of websites have also increased from the espionage networks of spies, computer networks for corporate organizations, networks for governments' agencies, networks for social interactions, search engines and networks for religious bodies, etc. These diversities have generated complex issues regarding the morphology and classification of webs and web mining. Thus, the validity of the generic web classification, web mining taxonomy and contemporary studies on the regularities of web usage, web content, web semantic, web structures and the process of extracting useful information and interesting patterns from the intricate of the Internet are frequently questionable. Most web mining algorithms and web mining tools are restricted to the identification of web patterns from the above generic taxonomy and some indices that can be specific or occasionally fluctuate across different websites' groups. Consequently, the contextual information extracted from websites is limited to association analysis and clustering techniques during web data analytics. Besides, with the inevitable inclusion of the websites of the crime syndicates, terrorist's consortium, webby and espionage networks on the web, the existing web mining taxonomy can lead to misinformation, misclassification and crisscrossed issues such that numerous web's patterns could be marked with crossing and inexplicable lines. By using qualitative interview of 26 skilled web-designers and a focus group-conference of 7 experts in web-usage over Skype to brainstorm on the above issues, this chapter comprehensively discusses the above concepts and how they relate to web classification and web mining taxonomy. The results obtained elucidate the strengths and weaknesses of data mining techniques that commonly underpin basic web mining taxonomy. New concepts like existence of esoteric web data, exoteric web data; mysterious, inexplicable and mystifying patterns and cryptic vocabularies are discussed to assist web analytics. Finally, we suggest and adopt eight criteria such as the degree of illustrative, expositive, educative, advisory, interpretative, demonstrative; revealing and informatory of providing and conveying information to categorize and propose anew web mining taxonomy in other to minimize the impacts of the above concerns on global settings.

Chapter 1
A Survey on Text–Based Topic Summarization Techniques

T. Ramathulasi
iD https://orcid.org/0000-0003-1797-5499
Mother Theresa Institute of Engineering and Technology, Chittoor, India

U. Kumaran
Mother Theresa Institute of Engineering and Technology, Chittoor, India

K. Lokesh
Mother Theresa Institute of Engineering and Technology, Chittoor, India

ABSTRACT

The text summing method is obsolete due to recent advances in news articles, official documents, textual interpretation in scientific studies, manual text extraction, and many archives. Dealing with large amounts of text data requires the deployment of effective solutions. It is also impossible to capture text material due to high cost and labor. As a result, the academic community is increasingly interested in developing new ways to capture text automatically. Researchers have been working to improve the process of creating summaries since the invention of text summaries with the aim of creating machine summary matches with man-made summaries. Meaningful sentences are selected from the input document and added to the summaries using the hybrid technique. As a result, researchers are increasingly focusing on concise summaries to provide more coherent and relevant summaries. They use an artificial text summary to gather knowledge and information about recent research. A complete overview of abstraction methods is provided by a recent text summary created over the past decade.

DOI: 10.4018/978-1-7998-9426-1.ch001

INTRODUCTION

Network resources on the internet (for example, sites, consumer ratings, news, writing, social network platforms, and so on) are vast textual data sources. Furthermore, there is a prosperity of textual information in the many files of news stories, books, authorized papers, medicinal papers, scientific reports, and other textual content. The volume of word material on the Internet and other archives expands at an exponential rate every day. As a consequence, customers waste a ration of time attempting to get the evidence they require. They didn't unfluctuating read and realize all of the textual content in the search results. Numerous parts of the writings produced are redundant or uninteresting. As a result, text resources must be condensed and compressed more frequently. Summarizing by hand is a time-consuming and labor-intensive process. Manual summarizing such a massive amount of textual material is incredibly challenging for humans (Vilca & Cabezudo, 2017). TTS is the most essential solution to this problem. The purpose of a TTS arrangement is to harvest a synthesis that condenses the most important thoughts first from the main raw material together into a short amount of room while avoiding repetition (Moratanch & Chitrakala, 2017). Users can easily grasp the essential ideas with TTS systems without having to read the entire file (Nazari & Mahdavi, 2019).

Consumers will profit from the automatically created digests because it will accept their time and attempt. "A successful summary distills the most relevant information from multiple sources (or streams) to offer an abbreviated copy of the old albums for a specified user(s) and task(s)," (Maybury, 1995) defined an autonomous synopsis. A summary is a text created by one or more readers that conveys the essential meaning of the source concisely and understandably. It is now upwards of 50% of the original text(s), and it is typically much less "according to number (Radev et al., 2002). It can be used with speech, multimodal papers, hypertext, and other types of content." Only the most important information will be included in the produced synopsis, which should be smaller than the input text (Gambhir & Gupta, 2017).

TTS systems are divided into two types: solitary-document and multiple-document summing systems. The prior constructs the synopsis beginning the textual content, whereas the latter constructs it from a collection of documents. TTS systems are created using exploration and production, abstractions, or hybrid text summarising approaches. The extractive approach develops the summary by selecting the most fundamental sentences from the core raw material. The summarization method turns the input text into such an attempt to bridge the gap before providing a summary based on words and phrases that are different from the previous text phrases. A hybrid technique is created by combining the abstractive summarising processes. As shown in Figure 1, the following procedures make up the overall framework of a TTS system. (Gupta & Lehal, 2010) provides sorting data of the actual letter using linguistic approaches such as sentence splitting, word smart contracts, stop-word elimination, part-of-speech labeling, stemming, and others. Processing: employing one or more processes, transform the source file(s) to the synopsis using one of the text summary approaches. Postprocessing: Before obtaining the final overview, resolve numerous issues in the data generated, such as ambiguity resolving and phrase arrangement.

Figure 1. A general architecture of text summarization

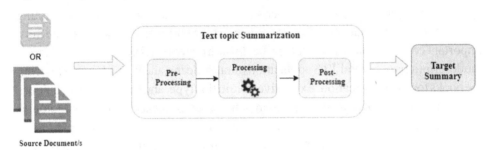

TTS is among the most challenging positions in NLP and AI. TTS research was instigated in 1958 through Luhn's research (Luhn, 1958), which mechanically excerpts abstracts from lads mags and technical periodicals. Continue to desire for a good TTS system that will provide a reporting that 1) includes all of the important subjects in the utterance, 2) is clear of superfluous or repeating information, and 3) is intelligible and consistent for the users. Since the mid-1950s, they've been attempting to build techniques and processes for making summaries, and they're still working on it so that desktop recaps can match intelligent synopses (Gambhir & Gupta, 2017). By now, many evaluations on TTS strategies and processes had been published. Because summarization needs a significant amount of NLP, most surveys concentrate on extractive outline approaches, such as (Nazari & Mahdavi, 2019). (Kirmani et al., 2019) which identify different extraction approaches as well as common statistical characteristics. Using fuzzy inference system approaches, ten survey extractive TTS methods are used. Researchers should use swarm-based optimization for TTS, particularly for brief text summaries, according to their findings. A study of extracting depth text summarization by eleven people. Abstractive approaches (Gupta & Gupta, 2019) and (Lin & Ng, 2019) and computer vision summarization methods have been linked in several studies (Tandel et al., 2019), (Gupta et al., 2019), (Mahajani et al., 2019) additionally provide a summary of some simplification and extraction methods.

The majority of state-of-the-art assessments inspiration by a subset of TTS characteristics, such as one methodology (extraction summation), unity approach for removal fuzzy inference methodology, and one specific TTS system (regulatory document summarizes), and so on. Furthermore, as (Dutta et al., 2019) points out, distinct TTS algorithms produce conflicting results from the same raw texts; hence, integrating the outputs of multiple TTS algorithms to build stronger summaries appears to be a promising strategy. In addition, hybrid TTS was proposed as a way to get the benefit of all extraction summarization techniques. As a result, the fundamental goal of this research is to provide a comprehensive review of numerous TTS features to assist academics in perhaps improving their abstracts by integrating multiple approaches and methods, as compared to traditional abstractions. The most important contribution of this study is the illustrations of TTS system categories and the descriptions of several TTS applications alongside instances of TTS systems from the books for each application. Extractive, role in this type, and hybrid TTS techniques are all thoroughly examined. Each approach is used in a variety of methodologies in the literature. The survey reveals 1) human expert text summarization processes, 2) commonly used statistical and grammatical traits that indicate essential phrases and grammar, and 3) text categorization components. The structure components comprise 1) generalized text illustration systems, 2) multilingual scrutiny and guidelines, then 3) computational techniques. Based on the restrictions and issues of existing TTS systems, they are producing a list and categorizing future study pathways for the study population.

The construction of this work reflects its primary contributions: Section 2 discusses the many approaches to TTS, and Section 3 discusses TTS methodologies and goes deeper into the methods mentioned. Section 4 puts the study to a close-by detailing TTS research's next directions.

APPROACHES FOR TEXT SUMMARIZATION

Text summarization can be done in three ways: extractive, abstraction, or hybrid. As shown in Table 1, every strategy is implemented in a variety of ways. This section will go through each of these techniques in-depth, as well as the methodology employed in the publications for each method.

Table 1. Document text summarization approaches and corresponding related methods

Text Summarization Approach	Related Methods
Extractive	Statistical-Based Topic-Based Clustering-Based Semantic-Based Machine-Learning-Based Deep-Learning-Based Fuzzy-Logic-Based
Abstractive	Template-Based Ontology-Based Semantic-Based Deep-Learning- Based
Hybrid	Extractive to Abstractive Extractive to Shallow Abstractive

EXTRACTIVE AND ABSTRACTIVE TEXT SUMMARIZATION APPROACHES

Figure 2 depicts the extractive and abstractive automatic summarization system architecture, which includes 1) input text preprocessing 2) postprocessing (e.g., reordering mined sentences, swapping prepositions with their forebears, substituting relative temporal interpretation with definite dates, etc., also 3) data dispensation (Gupta & Lehal, 2010). Abstractive summarization necessitates a more thorough examination of the incoming text. Abstractive transcript summarizers create an instant by utilizing natural language processing (NLP) to recognize the important concepts in the input material, then paraphrase the text to represent individuals' notions in scarcer words and with simple words (Al-Abdallah & Al-Taani, 2017), (Chitrakala et al., 2018). For a summary generation, this slant doesn't facsimile words from the source text, but rather involves the ability to create new phrases. Preprocessing, postprocessing, and processing tasks in an abstractive text summarizer include: 1) creating an intrinsic vector meaning, as well as 2) engendering a summary by language processing practices to produce an instantaneous that is nearer to human-generated precise (Aggarwal et al., 2012). Various extraction text summarising methods, such as statistical-based, concept-based, and so on, are shown in Table 1.

Methods for Extractive and Abstractive Text Summarization

Statistical-Based: These methods use data study of many characteristics to extract relevant phrases and words from the foundation text. The "most significant" word is distinct as the one that is "most attractively positioned," "most frequent," and so on 18. A statistical-based extractive summarizer's sentence scoring phases are as follows (Gambhir & Gupta, 2017): 1) giving a final score to each phrase in the text that is obtained using a preview algorithm.

Figure 2. The architecture of text summarization using both Extractive and abstraction approaches

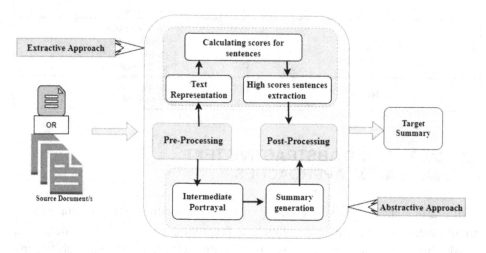

Topic-Based: These methods focus on determining the topic of a document, which is its principal topic. Term Frequency, TF-IDF files, lexical networks, topic word techniques where the topic presentation consists of a series of tables and their related values (Aggarwal et al., 2018), and so on are some of the most popular forms for topic representations. A topic-based extractive summarizer's processing steps include 1) trying to convert the input text to an alternative manner that captures the input text's discussed topics, and 2) assigning a measure measures of firm performance to each of the paragraphs in the effort document based on this illustration.

Clustering-Based: A multi-document extract summarizer is used in these methods to identify the most central and relevant sentences in a cluster, ensuring that they cover the vital information connected to the cluster's main theme. The centrality of a phrase is determined by the significance of its words. The center of the content cluster in subspaces is a standard approach to measure word centrality. A cluster's centroid is a pseudo-document made up of words with TF-IDF scores over a predefined level. In a centroid-based summarizer, the sentence scoring steps are: 1) computing the TFIDF depictions of each paragraph in the document to build a representative centroid, and 2) contemplating a punishment as central when it did contain more words from the cluster centroid as a measure of its connectedness to the cluster centroid (Mehta & Majumder, 2018). The more essential a sentence is, the closer is to the cluster centroid. In the resulting summary, clustering-based summarization incorporates both relevance and duplication elimination. The sets off a chain steps for ATS are: 1) using a clustering method to cluster the input phrases, 2) ranking as well as purchasing clusters such that a grouping gets a high rank and that it has quite important words, and 3) selecting fair representation sentences for the conclusion from these clusters (Nazari & Mahdavi, 2019).

Semantic-Based: LSA (Latent Semantic Analysis) is a semantic-based extraction ATS method that has been widely utilized. LSA is an unsupervised method for representing text semantics based on observed word co-occurrence. Any LSA-based extractive summarizer's sentence scoring phases are: 1) constructing the matrix (word matrix), and 2) implementing Singular Value Decomposition (SVD) towards the input matrix to find the links between terms and sentences. Semantic Role Labeling (SRL) and Explicit Semantic Analysis are two more semantic-based methodologies employed in ATS (ESA). (Mohamed & Oussalah, 2019) introduces a semantic-based extraction ATS structure based on the SRL and ESA, as well as the Wikipedia knowledge base, in (Mohamed & Oussalah, 2019).

Machine-Learning-Based: Machine-Learning-Based At the word and sentence, these methods translate the summarization problem into a supervised classification challenge. Using training documents, the network learns by example to identify each phrase of the text document as "summary" or "non-summary". The sentence scoring phases for the machine-learning-based parser are as follows (Moratanch & Chitrakala, 2017) 1) extracting characteristics from the heavily processed document (based on numerous aspects of words and sentences), and 2) passing the collected features to a perceptron that generates a data point as an outcome score.

Template-Based: Human summaries contain shared phrase structures that can be specified as templates in particular fields (e.g. meeting summaries). The sentence summary can be generated based on the provided text genre while using the data with in-text corpus to fill the gaps in the appropriate which was before patterns (Lin & Ng, 2019). The text samples that fill the template slots are determined using extraction procedures and linguistic patterns.

Ontology-Based: These methods create a semantic representation of the input document(s) (e.g., informational objects, conditional structures, or semantic graphs), which is then given to a natural language generation system, which generates the final abstractive summary using a verb and noun phrases (Gupta & Gupta, 2019) propose a multi-document sentence summarizer that: 1) represents input documents with predicate-argument frameworks using SRL, 2) clusters semantically similar transitive structures all across text using some semantic similarity metric, 3) ranks conditional structures features - based weighted and optimized using an Algorithm, and 4) uses language production to generate phrases.

Semantic-Based: These methods create a semantic representation of the input document(s) (e.g., information items, conditional structures, or semantic graphs), which is then given to a natural language generation system, which generates the final abstractive summary using a verb and noun phrases (Gupta & Gupta, 2019) consider a multi abstractive gives higher that: 1) represents input documents with transitive constructions using SRL, 2) clusters semantically similar transitive structures all across text using a definitional similarity metric, 3) ranks the syntactic structures using features weighted and optimized using an Optimization Technique, and 4) uses language generation to develop sentences.

Fuzzy-Logic-Based: For ATS, these procedures employ the fuzzy ruling notion. Because not everybody in the universe can be characterized as zero and one, fuzzy set theory resembles the human thinking systems and provides a good technique to encode the extracted features of sentences 10. The following are the sentence scoring steps (Nazari & Mahdavi, 2019): 1) picking a collection of features for each phrase, such as long sentences, term weight, and so on, and 2) utilizing the fuzzy inference arrangement to get a rating for an individual sentence that indicates the sentence importance. As a result, each word in the output is assigned a notch from 0 to 1 dependent on the language structures and the knowledge base's preset criteria.

Deep-Learning-Based: Abstractive summarization is now conceivable thanks to the recent accomplishment of sequential learning. Seq2seq has excelled at a variety of NLP tasks, including translation, speech recognition, and dialog platforms. For short text summarization, a collection of RNN models on attention transceiver yields auspicious results; nonetheless, deep learning techniques still have issues with 1) creating repetitive words, and 2) dealing with out-of-vocabulary terms. The steps in (Hou et al., 2017)'s summarization system include: 1) trying to convert the dataset into straightforward writings and saving the historical copy (e.g. news stories) and their synopses separately, 2) applying depending on a particular and using a syntactic model to process the data, and 3) smearing word segmentation and through a subword model to analyze the information. 3) preparing the word vectors with the Gensim tool[1], which would be further learned in the suggested model 4) Making use of Tensorflow[2] proposes using one unidirectional Long Short-Term Memory layer for the encoder besides a directional LSTM sheet for the decoder for implementation. The loss is calculated using cross-entropy, and the loss is optimized using the Adam optimizer.

Hybrid Text Summarization

The hybrid text instantaneous is exposed in Figure 3 extractive To shallow abstractive approaches, go from abstractive and extractive procedures. Following that, both strategies are briefly explained. Approaches that go from extractive to abstractive:

These methods start with one of the extraction TTS techniques and then apply one of the abstractive summaries methods to the recovered rulings. The "EA-LTS" hybrid model for long message summarization. There are two phases to the system: 1) the extraction segment, which employs a graph to extract essential phrases, and 2) an abstraction segment, which builds an RNN-based encoder-decoder and generates summaries using a pointer and awareness methods. Extractive to Shallow Abstractive Methods: These methods start with an extractive TTS method, then apply some or all of the following strategies to the mined sentence fragments: information firmness techniques, evidence fusion methods (Lloret et al., 2013), synonym replacement methodologies, etc.

Figure 3. The architecture of text summarization using a hybrid approach

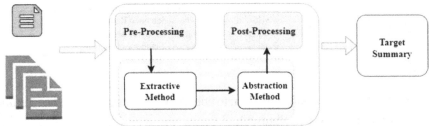

TECHNIQUES TO IMPLEMENT TTS SYSTEMS

This chapter provided an overview of the various components and techniques used in the design and implementation of TTS Systems. The operations for text summarization are defined first. Such operations are defined by analyzing the operations of human Experts. The statistical & linguistic characteristics are obtainable in the second section. These characteristics are commonly used to differentiate important phrases and grammar. The text categorization building blocks are then presented in the following order: text depiction models, which are generally used to characterize input texts, textual investigation, and processing performances, which are used in various TTS stages, and soft computing practices, which are convenient in TTS employments.

Operations for Text Summarization

There are two types of text summarising operations (Shaalan et al., 2018): single-sentence processes and multi-sentence actions. A single-sentence process is performed on a single verdict, while a multi-sentence process is performed on at least two sentences. Text categorization operations can be separated into two categories: 1) atomic operation (e.g., word insertion and deletion) that cannot be subdivided into other operations, and 2) complicated action that can be subdivided into additional processing. The text summarising procedures are categorized as single-sentence or multisentence processes in Table 2.

Table 2. Text summarization operations on single or multiple sentence documents

Text Document	Operations for Summarization
with Single sentence	Sentence Compression/Reduction Syntactic Transformation Lexical paraphrasing Generalization Specification
with Multiple sentences	Sentence Fusion/Combination Sentence Reordering Sentence assortment Sentence clustering

1   Sentence Compression/Reduction: to abbreviate the original sentence, remove irrelevant portions (e.g. Phrases).

2   Syntactic Transformation: the process of modifying the syntactic structure of a sentence. Both sentence reduction and sentence addition operations can benefit from this process.

3   Lexical paraphrasing: phrases are replaced with their paraphrases.

4   Generalization: the use of more general descriptions to replace phrases or clauses.

5   Specification: more explicit explanations are used to replace words or clauses.

6   Sentence Fusion/Combination: combining two otherwise even more innovative sentences into the unique instantaneous phrase.

7   Sentence Reordering: Changing the sequence of summary phrases is called sentence reordering.

8   Sentence assortment: Sentence selection is the process of choosing one sentence from a group of two or added comparable verdicts.

9   Sentence clustering: Sentence Clustering is the process of organizing sentences hooked on distinct groups. This process comes in handy when summarising many documents (e.g., identifying the topic and clustering the phrases by topic (Zhong et al., 2017). Each TTS system employs one or more of the operations listed above.

CONCLUSION

Manual transcript summarizing is indeed a time-overwhelming and expensive process with numerous processes. To manually translate a single document, for example, the stages are as follows 1) attempting to comprehend the contents of the text, 2) attempting to excerpt the "most important" elements from it, in addition 3) attempting to produce a summary that meets the following criteria: Legibility and language eminence of the summary. The formed summary's non-redundancy. Although there are several artificial language summarizers in the field, their results are far from those of human text summaries. The machine still has a hard time understanding and identifying the "most significant" parts. Since the 1950s, researchers have been working to dazed these obstacles and find innovative solutions. After a while, the science communal has primarily fixated on the text resource extraction categorization methodology.

It has implemented this approach's concise summary methodologies for various applications, including customer reviews, news items, blogs, emails, scientific articles, official papers, biomedicine documents, etc. In reality, extractive TTS systems generate summaries that are very different from those produced by humans. The goal of the researchers is to automate the development of human-like summaries. In comparison to extracting text summarization, summarization has a much smaller amount of literature. The majority of inquiry articles were published since the summary approach is far more difficult and less mature than the extraction procedure. The study's goal and provide a comprehensive analysis of TTS's many aspects. The survey's main contributions are as follows: Explaining the many categories and implementations of ATS systems, as well as completing a comprehensive examination of the literature on TTS approaches (resource extraction, abstractive, and composite) and methodologies that leverage these approaches. Detailing and classifying the many aspects and processes that go into developing and implementing TTS arrangements, such as 1. Text summary operations. 2. Quantitative and linguistics characteristics.

REFERENCES

Al-Abdallah, R. Z., & Al-Taani, A. T. (2017). *Arabic single-document text summarization using particle swarm optimization algorithm. Procedia Computer Science.*

Belkebir. (2018). TALAA-ATSF: A global operation-based Arabic text summarization framework. In K. Shaalan, A. E. Hassanien, & F. Tolba (Eds.), *Intelligent natural language processing: Trends and applications.* Springer International Publishing.

Chitrakala, S., Moratanch, B., & Ramya, C. G. (2018). Concept-based extractive text summarization using graph modelling and weighted iterative ranking. *Emerging research in computing, information, communication and applications, 2016*, 149–160.

Dutta, S., Chandra, V., Mehra, K., Ghatak, S., Das, S., & Ghosh, S. (2019). *Summarizing microblogs during emergency events: A comparison of extractive summarization algorithms*. Paper presented at the International Conference on Emerging Technologies.

Gambhir, M., & Gupta, V. (2017). "Recent automatic text summarization techniques," *A survey. Artificial Intelligence Review*, 1–66.

Gupta, S., & Gupta, S. K. (2019). Abstractive summarization: An overview of the state of the art. *Expert Systems with Applications*, 49–65.

Gupta, V., Bansal, N., & Sharma, A. (2019). *Text summarization for big data: A comprehensive survey*. Paper presented at the International Conference on Innovative Computing and Communications, Singapore.

Gupta, V., & Lehal, G. S. (2010). A survey of text summarization extractive techniques. *Journal of Emerging Technologies in Web Intelligence*, 258–268.

Hou, L., Hou, P., & Bei, C. (2017). *Abstractive document summarization via neural model with joint attention*. Paper presented at the Natural Language Processing and Chinese Computing, Dalian, China.

Kirmani, M., Manzoo, H., & Mohd, M. (2019). *Hybrid text summarization: A survey*. Paper presented at the Soft Computing: Theories and Applications, Singapore.

Krishnakumari, K., & Sivasankar, E. (2018). Scalable aspect-based summarization in the hadoop environment. In V. B. Aggarwal, V. Bhatnagar & D. K. Mishra (Eds.), *Big data analytics: Proceedings of CSI 2015*. Academic Press.

Lin, H., & Ng, V. (2019). *Abstractive summarization: A survey of the state of the art*. Paper presented at the Thirty-Third AAAI Conference on Artificial Intelligence (AAAI-19).

Lloret, E., Romá-Ferri, M. T., & Palomar, M. (2013). Compendium: A text summarization system for generating abstracts of research papers. *Data & Knowledge Engineering*, 164–175.

Luhn, H. P. (1958). The automatic creation of literature abstracts. *IBM Journal of Research and Development*, 159–165.

Mahajani, A., Pandya, V., Maria, I., & Sharma, D. (2019). *A comprehensive survey on extractive and abstractive techniques for text summarization.* Paper presented at the ambient communications and computer systems, Singapore.

Maybury, M. T. (1995). Generating summaries from event data. *Information Processing & Management*, 735–751.

Mehta, P., & Majumder, P. (2018). Effective aggregation of various summarization techniques. *Information Processing & Management*, 145–158.

Mohamed, M., & Oussalah, M. (2019). SRL-ESA-TextSum: A text summarization approach based on semantic role labeling and explicit semantic analysis. *Information Processing & Management*, 1356–1372.

Moratanch, N., & Chitrakala, S. (2017). *A Survey on Extractive Text Summarization.* Paper presented at the 2017 International Conference on Computer, Communication and Signal Processing (ICCCSP), Chennai, India.

Nazari, N., & Mahdavi, M. A. (2019). A survey on automatic text summarization. *Journal of Artificial Intelligence and Data Mining*, 121–135.

Nenkova, A., & McKeown, K. (2012). A survey of text summarization techniques. In C. C. Aggarwal & C. Zhai (Eds.), *Mining text data, Boston, MA.*

Radev, D. R., Hovy, E., & McKeown, K. (2002). Introduction to the special issue on summarization. *Computational Linguistics.*

Tandel, J., Mistree, K., & Shah, P. (2019). *A review on neural network based abstractive text summarization models.* Paper presented at the 2019 IEEE 5th International Conference for Convergence in Technology (I2CT).

Vilca, G. C. V., & Cabezudo, M. A. S. (2017). *A study of abstractive summarization using semantic representations and discourse level information.* The 20th International Conference on Text, Speech, and Dialogue, Prague, Czech Republic.

Zhong, Y., Tang, Z., Ding, X., Zhu, L., Le, Y., & Li, K. (2017). An improved LDA multi-document summarization model based on TensorFlow. *IEEE 29th International Conference on Tools with Artificial Intelligence (ICTAI).*

ENDNOTES

[1]   https://pypi.org/project/gensim/
[2]   https://www.tensorflow.org/

Chapter 2
Controlling and Surveying of On–Site and Off–Site Systems Using Web Monitoring

Avinash Kumar
Sharda University, India

Bharat Bhushan Kumar
https://orcid.org/0000-0002-9345-4786
School of Engineering and Technology, Sharda University, India

Saptadeepa Kalita
School of Engineering and Technology, Sharda University, India

Rajasekhar Chaganti
Department of Computer Science, University of Texas at San Antonio, USA

Parma Nand
School of Engineering and Technology, Sharda University, India

ABSTRACT

Monitoring and surveillancing of large amounts of data is a matter of prime concern in the current scenario for major organisations as well as small-scale and large-scale industries. Presently, the increasing need to collect, analyse, and store the data in a real-time environment as well as ensure the qualitative and quantitative analysis of real-time data has become a challenge. In addition, traditional data acquisition and monitoring systems lead industries to face multiple constraints and limitations, which affect their functioning, such as physical infrastructure setup and cost constraints. In this chapter, the surveillance of various applications has been discussed. The chapter also focuses on use of cloud-based model to perform the real-time monitoring with the help of the web. The chapter deeply discusses the use of web for on-site and off-site monitoring of various industries and organizations.

DOI: 10.4018/978-1-7998-9426-1.ch002

INTRODUCTION

The Internet, referred to as a system of interconnected networks, has connected people across the world together and has revolutionised communication systems since the end of 20th century. It is a plethora of information about almost everything. Other than communication, the internet is a storehouse of information based on what is requested by the user surfing the internet. The advent of the internet can be credited to the Advanced Research Projects Agency (ARPA), which belongs to the United States Defence (USD). ARPA was into research for time-sharing systems, resource sharing, and packet switching. This led to the incorporation of a data communication network in ARPA which came to be known as ARPA Network (ARPANET) (McKelvey & Driscoll, 2018). Gradually with more research and advancements in the field of networking, the Internet service providers (ISP) emerged commercially and allowed the civil people to use the Internet or World Wide Web (WWW) for personal or related uses. The Internet is based on the framework of the Internet Protocol suite which includes the Transmission Control Protocol/ Internet Protocol (TCP/IP) (Goralski, 2017). This framework consists of IP addresses, routing and subnetting. The Internet can be classified as public, private or organization-specific, called intranet, based on the type of usage and the type of users. It is sometimes interchangeably used with the term WWW, which includes the use of frontend and backend programming languages such as the Hyper-Text Markup Language (HTML), Cascading Style Sheets (CSS), eXtensive Markup Language (XML), JavaScript along with other tools and multimedia technology by designing the web pages and linking pages with the help of hyperlinks and delivering information to users in a more user-friendly manner. Now, it is able to serve a lot of applications as well as services to its users in such a way that one cannot imagine a life without it. Be it the electronic mails, browsing the web, social media applications or entertainment, business and education softwares, all of this is a boon of the internet.

As the internet serves myriad applications to the users, and connects the users to the other parts of the world as well, it is important to safeguard the security of devices and information. It is also important to monitor the browsing activity and ensure safe browsing. Since the Internet serves both home and business activities, surveillance becomes a matter of prime concern. Thus, an important application of the internet can be found in designing and implementing surveillance systems (Isravel et al., 2020). As per the term, surveillance systems are responsible to monitor the activities on the devices, and alert the authorised users using the devices about the same if any suspicious behaviour or anomaly is detected. It can be considered similar to an alert or alarm system and can be both wired or wireless. The choice of a wired or wireless surveillance system depends on the area to monitor and bandwidth factor. The most common example of a surveillance system is a Closed Circuit Television

(CCTV) camera, which monitors physical activities in the area where it is deployed. The physical activities detected in the CCTV camera can be monitored with the help of a computer system by the authorized user using it, thereby assisting surveillance. In general, a surveillance system can have either type of recording device based on their method of recording activities, mainly; Digital Video Recorder (DVR) or Network Video Recorder (NVR). A DVR actually records the activity in analog format and then processes it by converting it into digital footage. On the other hand, an NVR only operates with the digital data and processes it even before transmitting it to the monitoring device (Lee et al., 2019; Stolojescu-Crisan et al., 2021). There are multiple ways to track and monitor activities, some of them can be mentioned as classical computer systems, biometric methods, wireless tracking mechanisms such as Remote Frequency Identification (RFID) tagging, Internet of Things (IoT)-based methods, telephonic methods and aerial device-based surveillance such as surveillance through drones. Telephonic methods for surveillance are used to ensure security for Voice-over Internet Protocol (VoIP) communications (Hsieh & Leu, 2017). On large-scale, surveillance systems can be designed using cloud computing frameworks, which can strengthen the storage, processing and dissemination of the data captured by IoT sensors.

In recent years, cloud computing has come to be known as one of the most efficient computing paradigms in the sector of information technology (IT). This happened as the result of the paradigm shifts IT sector has been experiencing from the past few decades, distributed, grid, parallel computing, etc. (Jouini & Rabai, 2019). This new paradigm allowed users to access the computing resources in such a manner that users are now able to carry out upscaling and downscaling operations with minimal third party intervention. Cloud computing offers its users three basic models to choose from, Software as a service (SaaS), Platform as a service (PaaS) and Infrastructure as a service (IaaS). In SaaS the softwares are centrally hosted and are available for the end users to use on a pay per use or subscription basis (Alam & Benaida, 2018). The PaaS focuses on delivering hardware and software tools which can be used by developers for developing applications. The IaaS is primarily intended to provide high level Application Programming Interface (APIs) that help in tinkering and working with the underlying network architecture. The cloud operator is the one who bears the responsibility for the maintenance and management of the information stored in the cloud. Providing security as a part of the many services cloud provides is one of the most important focus points for these operators (Alam & Rababah, 2020). The security aspect of cloud's features, like with any other technology, hold the potential to either popularize it to an extreme extent or completely undermine it. Therefore, various standards, and countless rules and protocols have been set in place (Alam, 2020). Some of the major features offered by the cloud includes infrastructure virtualization. Moreover, it provides a virtualized technology platform that allows for the virtualization of both hardware and software resources, which is irrespective of the final deployment structure the cloud solutions aim at making the most out of the already available solutions by making them available at large (Arasaratnam, 2011), dynamic procuring where this enables the providers to fulfil requirements and deliver solutions based on the ongoing demands and market trends. It is achieved in a fairly automatic manner as it goes in proportion with the advancement occurring in the technological sector. The challenges faced with respect to this includes maintaining the security, integrity and reliability while expanding, easy access to the network that allows the users to access the internet from a wide range of devices, such as PCs, tablets, laptops and other mobile devices. The cloud-based solutions carry answers to everything from business related applications to the latest devices with embedded softwares and the control allows for the easy control and automation of the infrastructure (Nieuwenhuis et al., 2018). The new technologies like smart systems are widely using cloud computing for various purposes like storage, services and monitoring using web.

Smart systems can be traced back to the time when extensive work was done on devices that could somehow imitate the idiosyncrasies of a human being. It was being found if there were certain materials that could be used to emulate the nervous system and the muscular system that was exclusive to humans. The main goal is to devise a non-biological system such that it can satisfactorily mimic a biological system such that it is as close as possible to a human's ability to adapt and similar in the overall design as well. A smart system may contain parts like actuators and sensors. These parts can either be attached or embedded and form a very integral part of the smart system (Arsan, 2016). The smart system, along with its constituent parts, form a unit. This unit will perform in a manner that has been previously predicted. These predicted functions are based on how a biological system acts and reacts. So if a similar pattern is followed by the smart system, it will ultimately be successful in emulating a biological system. The human body can be seen as the ideal smart system. Many kinds of materials were used to devise smart systems. Many attempts were made that included using materials that were specifically made to execute the functions that an electromechanical device would perform (Lynch, 2017). Ever since then, there have been a number of sensors and actuators. These advancements have helped immensely to measure and excite a smart system. The technology still is being worked upon and is said to have a lot of room for improvement. However, once it reaches its full potential, it is proved to be highly beneficial to the workings of society. Innovation, these days, is highly needed and the development of new technologies and their applications have spiked. Every field of science is making use of these advancements. This has also raised the bar for what is expected from the applications that are being developed. Additionally, the need for new and innovative technologies has increased. Requirements for efficiency, reliability, and sustainability when it comes to implementation in the system are high. All this has made the field of smart systems to be very promising in the coming times (Li et al., 2019).

This paper puts in efforts to describe web monitoring and web surveillance by using cloud-based techniques and explains various applications of the same. The paper emphasises web-based real time monitoring surveillance and a existing model for its implementation. The major contributions in the paper can be summarised below.

- The paper describes real time web monitoring and its implementation using cloud technologies.
- The paper addresses a remote system model for web monitoring of assets.
- The paper presents existing systems which provides state-of-art mechanism for real time monitoring of live data.
- The paper explains monitoring of cellular phone using web surveillance.
- The paper deeply discusses embedded dynamic web for monitoring of smart systems.

The remainder of this paper has been organised as follows; Section 2 describes real time web monitoring using cloud-based approach and states existing model for implementing the same. Section 3 discusses the areas of applications of web monitoring and web surveillance in detail. Finally, section 4 presents the conclusion and future research directions.

REAL TIME WEB MONITORING USING CLOUD

Compared to the traditional monitoring technologies, cloud-based real time web monitoring has emerged as a boon for large-scale as well as small-scale industries and companies. Real time web monitoring can be described as the method of monitoring and visualising real time or live data from remote locations or remotely-located devices using a web interface. Using cloud technology to facilitate web monitoring for live data can help improve collection, analysis and storage of data by improving metrics, data processing and visualisation (Pereira et al., 2018). Cloud-based web monitoring can provide reliable and accurate results about a network, website, device or any other system. Supervisory Control and Data Acquisition (SCADA) is a popular centralised system, which is used for real time monitoring of data as well as help with controlling critical components within the network which is monitored (Gonzalez et al., 2019). SCADA performs the following functions; data collection or acquisition, networked communication of data, presentation of data and data control. It can be deployed with the help of components such as data inputs, Remote

Telemetry Units (RTU), Human-Machine Interface (HMI) and a communication network. Real time web monitoring is still being improved and enhanced through research and development.

Background Work

For carrying out and ensuring a qualitative operation offshore taking safety and efficiency into consideration, real time web monitoring becomes a crucial player. The necessity of collecting and processing live data with the help of simplified technologies and methods is emerging. However, till date, use of real time web monitoring is not yet adopted as a standard method in practice in the industries of oil and gas production (Selvaraju et al., 2019). In the present scenario, the monitoring of operations in the industries are carried out on the physical sites, and a very small number of them are monitored with the help of remote tools. There are special centers owned by the contractors or bigger organisations to specifically conduct remote monitoring and analysis of data from industrial sites, known as the Real Time Monitoring Centers (RTMCs) (Liu et al., 2019). However, implementing real time web monitoring services require that real time data should be sent directly from the industrial sites to a central repository or server within periodical frequencies without compromising delay. Access to the centralised server should only be preserved with the technically specialised users. Obviously, remote access demands the devices for monitoring to be connected to the internet. Moreover, in order to show as well as analyse the live data from the industrial sites into the server, specialised softwares for statistical and qualitative analysis are also required. If there is a need to process the live data intensively and deeply, the specialised softwares ought to be equipped with sufficient Random Access Memory (RAM) for ensuring reduced delay. The above requirements can be rarely fulfilled in a complete manner using mobile or simple web-based devices. It is so because the requirements need to address a massive amount of data without compromising speed of access, security, transmission and data processing technique, in a live environment.

However, with the advent of advanced technologies and rapid developments in them, real time web monitoring for live industrial data can be seen practically. These technologies include mainly cloud computing and IoT. With the help of cloud computing, data along with network and computation-related resources can be accessed anytime and anywhere, using cloud servers (Namasudra et al., 2020). Since cloud computing is based on a pay-as-you-go model and thus provides necessary services as per the users' demand, it tends to be an optimal and feasible solution to carry out tasks in a network. While dealing with smaller data, the operations can be remotely monitored using the cloud computing frameworks and does not require a dedicated fixed system for data retrieval, processing and analysis, and thus reduces the cost of implementation and usage for smaller companies conducting industrial operations. Cloud computing can be accompanied by web applications, which can be used by the users to visualise and analyse live data (Singh et al., 2019). The web applications can be accessed via web browsers and one can install and run them directly in the cloud in a hassle-free manner. Also, conventional applications can be migrated to the cloud by converting them into web-supported packages and then made accessible to end users (Jeong et al., 2019).

A New Remote Real Time Monitoring Model

The existing system for real time monitoring of on-site data is highly expensive and thus can be hardly afforded by small-scale companies and industries. The cost increases since they may require a fixed infrastructure and monitoring setup on a physical location to store the data in a centralised server. A general web monitoring diagram in real time is represented in figure 1 where monitoring is done with the help of various components involved in it.

Figure 1. Web monitoring diagram

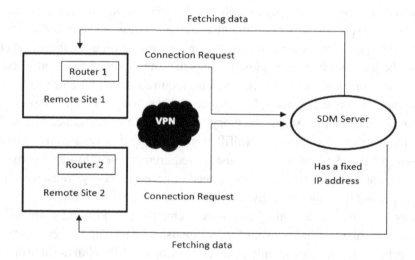

The system functions initially by collecting the live data from the site using specialised devices. The collected data is then processed with the help of Site Data Manager (SDM) server followed by storing the data on a cloud-based platform. A web-based application migrated on the cloud-based platform is used to access, analyse and visualise the stored data. In this manner, the data can be easily accessed by any connected web-based device in remote manner. Computations and related tasks can also be assisted by cloud-enabled Virtual Machines (VMs) (Bharati, 2017). Post analysis of live data, the outputs and results achieved from the analysis can be further stored on the cloud or on the local devices as well. A web application also facilitates additional important data to be added to the cloud by loading it from a web-based device as well as by acting as an intermediary between the cloud platform and the web-based devices. There exist multiple technologies for transmission of live data from sites for industries and organisations. Some of those prominent technologies include satellite transmission, microwaves, Optical Fibre Cables (OFC) and radio waves, which are used according to specified factors such as bandwidth, cost and complexity (Alimi et al., 2019). The data collection is generally facilitated through a local device connected to the sensors with a wired connection. In order to transmit data to a remote SDM server, the local device is also locally connected to an ethernet. Moreover, the security is ensured in the diagram by mandatorily implementing Virtual Private Network (VPN) for both local devices as well as the SDM server (Liyanage et al., 2018). Each site has a wireless router which owns a valid client certificate which is used for validation of connections among the devices. In the case of small-scale industries, SDM can act as a device manager to process as well as store the live data, thereby reducing the implementation costs for a backup server.

In figure 1, using cloud storage will be cost-effective as well as an ideal solution to assist reliable as well as faster data access and processing from any location. Thus, the SDM server then transmits the data to a cloud-based platform for storage which is generally commercial, and can be used to send the preferred data to any customer as per the demand directly from the cloud. In addition, the diagram also simplifies web monitoring by eliminating the need of installing the web applications on devices. Injection techniques can be used to directly deliver the applications to end users using browsers. The web-based application can act as an integrated module for simulation using VM, data analysis and monitoring (Rath, 2017). It can also ease data integration and task workflows in industries. Overall, the model works on the basis of request and response with the help of interconnected devices and applications.

Small Scale Real Time Monitoring Project

Expensive and critical operations rely on real-time monitoring for ensuring a constructive, safe and efficient execution. This is one of the reasons why live data is often collected and processed on site. However, the remote use of this data hasn't yet become as common in the gas and oil industries (Gonzalez et al., 2018). Accessing field data remotely, at real-time needs really high data transfer rates without any significant delays, to transmit the said data to centralized data server repositories from where it could then be accessed by the technical professionals. The many requirements of real-time monitoring systems such as transmitting massive amounts of data at extremely fast speeds, high capacity storage, short access time, and computational tools required for proper analysis, limit the areas of applications of remote real-time monitoring systems while elevating the capital involved at the same time.

Currently remote real time monitoring based operations are carried out at fixed geographical locations. The Real Time Mutual Control (RTMC) centers are specially used since real-time data or analytical softwares cannot be accessed from web-enabled devices. Cloud computing has seen extensive and fast paced developments in the past few decades, which has allowed users to utilize a number of services and resources at anytime from anywhere on the globe. The field of cloud computing provides an effective solution for the problems faced in the implementation of real-time monitoring systems. Cloud solutions have also proved to be highly cost effective. This allows even smaller companies to shift their operations on to the remote web monitoring side of the sphere without incurring the overhead of dedicated networks data servers and databases that were used in traditional client-server architecture. Although cloud computing has emerged to be one of a solution to the numerous issues faced in the remote real-time monitoring domain, it is still not a complete solution as it cannot help in the complete realization of the idea of using web-enabled devices to access the monitoring system. Even with the use of the cloud, the local machines would need a traditional desktop installation to visualise and analyse data (Sani et al., 2020). In order to avoid installation related inconveniences, one could go for performing the visualizing and analysing using web applications, which unlike the traditional desktop applications can be accessed through web browsers and can be used in relation with the cloud. These applications tend to be independent of hardware related restrictions, and can easily be accessed from any web-enabled devices with internet access. Because of how the web browser is the tool utilized by most end users, many conventional desktop-based applications have been web-enabled and migrated to cloud to not only reduce costs but also to ease down the managing and updating of these applications.

A feasibility study was conducted for the Karnes injection project followed by the injection parameters that were adjusted based on the prediction data collected from various simulations for monitoring (Zhuang et al., 2014). The occurrence of failures though was still a possibility because of the uncertainties that are innate to the data and also because of the intricate nature of the whole operation (Bautista & Dahi Taleghani, 2016). These potential risks sometime occur because of over or under estimation of the stress limit, concealed faults that existed before the analysis been carried out and integrity issues of passive data. Live data however, was detected as the answer to most of those issues, since it would help in the monitoring and finding of potential risks at early stages thereby helping in the timely mitigation of the risk. Despite the growing importance of real-time monitoring systems in all fields of critical implementation, its applications so far are limited while most existing remote models on the other hand are expensive and hence, not affordable for many small operators. Guo et al. (Guo et al., 2018) proposed a model that makes use of the cloud as discussed above to deliver not only an affordable but an efficient and sturdy solution, in which the real time data collected from the site was stored on Azure rather than a dedicated server.

APPLICATIONS OF WEB SURVEILLANCE

The systems which are existing in the digital world mostly rely on the communicating channel for inter communication between their different devices to deliver designated tasks. These systems are driven by the internet for interactions between different nodes of the section including human interactions. These systems include some of the latest technologies such as smart system, embedded system, mobile based system and various others that completely relies on the web for their proper processing and controlling. Since various systems are firmware in nature and hence, they require proper surveillance or monitoring in order to avoid machine failure, damage to humans due to industrial accidents and various other related activities. The monitoring of cellular phones is one of the critical uses that is required to be surveillanced or monitored for user's convenience. Also, the emerging systems smart healthcare, smart homes, smart offices and others which are based upon the concept of IoT needs proper surveillance either for the benefit of the user or law bodies for optimal and fruitful use of these IoT based systems. Many industries heavily rely on the data for delivering their services to the customers. This data ranges from Mega Byte (MB) to Tera Byte (TB) and hence, requires powerful database and web servers for their storage and processing. Therefore, these servers need proper monitoring for their temperature and humidity management where they are physically installed. Also, in case of systems that are based upon a combination of software for controlling hardware needs proper monitoring to avoid hazards in these systems such as in case of embedded systems where software controls the entire system could lead to financial loss and human loss. The below subsections deeply present the vitality of Web Monitoring (WB) for various real-life applications.

Web-Based Monitoring of Cellular Phones

'Redefining security' has recently emerged as result of technological venture. Most efforts are made in order to ensure and enforce security are concerned with redefining agendas, passing proposals, making laws, passing amendments and so on. With the continuous shift from the real to the digital world such as education, politics, or finance, the shift in this trend of redefining security extending to an individual's virtual security does not only make choice but has also emerged as the most pressing need of the hour (Buzan & Hansen, 2018). It therefore seems only natural to extend the concepts of Information and Communication Technology (ICT) into the domain of security. Many articles illustrate the efficient usage of image processing in security solutions (Collins et al., 2001; Haq et al., 2010). Moreover, there exist researches underlining the vital indulgence of cameras for their video, audio feed in web-based surveillance systems (Gelbord & Roelofsen, 2002; Sharma & Garg, 2019). The client-server-based models has emerged as probable solutions in the implementation of effective information-based systems where the client-side device in these types of surveillance systems holds a decisive solution in the system's overall performance (Barnes & Huff, 2003). Using cell phones to serve the purpose of surveillance for the client machines can have a revolutionizing impact on the domain of security owing to its features of portability and mobility (Wiredu & Sørensen, 2006). Georis et al. (Georis, 2003) proposed a Visual Surveillance System (VSS), that gathered and processed gray scale images from many camera units that were used for monitoring a specific area. Moreover, the gathering was done via a Local Area Network (LAN) where the system was capable of combining and comprehending the information obtained from different cameras to arrive at a decision. This helped to detect intrusions and gave the minimum number of false intrusion alerts. The Multimedia Surveillance System (MSS) proposed by Aggarwal et al. (Aggarwal & Cucchiara, 2006) on the other hand gave suggestions on providing an automatic analysis along with a real time web-based monitoring. The video information and the sensors integrated together in a single system served as the fundamental structure. With Cellular Surveillance Systems (CSS), a number of image files can be periodically taken by cameras connected via LAN to the system, transmitted to a central repository. The data is stored after resizing have been performed on collected images. Storing the images in the repository is done by a process called buffering that means storing data at one location before sending it off to other final locations as and when demanded. These buffered images are then sent to the client's browser and are displayed as either stationary or quasi moving picture blocks. The mobile communication is one of the needs for modern web monitoring system.

The evolution of surveillance systems leads to monitoring using mobile devices because the wireless portable devices such as laptops, cell phones and other mobile devices have become essential part of the daily use for both personal and corporate use that stores various multimedia information. Features introduced through the involvement of portable devices in the field of web surveillance system provides remote monitoring and control, which have proved to be increasingly useful and beneficial in maintaining and improving the system's reliability and security. Bandini et al. (Bandini & Sartori, 2005) focused on improving the efficacy of monitoring and control systems using Artificial Intelligence (AI) to improve the performance of the system. Imai et al. (Imai et al., 2008) proposed a web-based surveillance system with cell phones at the client side. This surveillance system is very useful not only for traditional organisations and companies rather for emerging organisation which includes smart system where the smart system generally consists of cellular as well as mobile devices in most of the cases.

Web Monitoring for Smart System

In recent years, drastic change in technological development has revolutionized the way of our living. With the advancement in technology, the Internet of Things (IoT) has made it much easier to control and monitor everything remotely with the help of web. One such application is the smart systems that consolidate human cognition with machine accuracy. Smart systems have the capabilities of self-learning, making decisions and contextual data awareness. The power of sensors and various smart system components integrating together has paved the way for deployment of smart systems in areas like healthcare, transportation, safety and security, smart homes, smart offices, manufacturing units and logistics. Most commonly preferred by the majority of the people are smart homes where they can remotely monitor their homes using web to control doors, windows and other home attributes like lighting, entertainment systems and appliances. In addition, the web monitoring also provides one of the vital features to be achieved that is safety for home automation. So, Web monitoring for smart systems has extreme significance in safety and crime prevention in various real-life applications. For a wide range of security-based applications, the most reliable and appropriate implementation is biometric authentication that includes fingerprint, palmprints, facial, iris and footprints where these relies on the web for remote implementation. The most widely used authentication method after fingerprint recognition is facial recognition that highly rely on web for remote authentication.

Consistently, sensor-based home security systems are in high demand. The various IoT sensors and Raspberry pi together have played a vital role in developing smart security systems. With the commencement of IoT and cloud computing, the voice activated smart speakers are turning out to be progressively famous. Domb et al. (Domb, 2019) proposed a low-cost cloud-based surveillance system for home providing a wide range camera to monitor entry of people at the door. The technologies used to build up security based smart home automation are cloud computing, Raspberry pi and Amazon Echo Dot. It works on Amazon Web Services (AWS) facial recognition system (Bermudez et al., 2014). AWS is an evolving cloud computing service offered by Amazon that allows end users to request resources, data storage in database servers and virtual cloud servers. The RPi camera attached with Raspberry Pi is utilized as closed-circuit television (CCTV) for monitoring people at the door using AWS Kinesis Video Stream and capturing the facial images. Amazon Echo Dot is used for taking voice input from users. In the cloud side there are mainly four services, S3 Bucket used for image storage, Amazon Rekognition offers facial recognition service by extracting facial features, DynamoDB a NoSQL database for storing facial features and AWS Lambda runs applications rather than hosting applications on the server.

The system starts with triggering the bell button leading to capturing an image of the visitor and uploading it in S3 Bucket by the RPi. When the owner interacts with the Amazon Echo Dot i.e., Alexa then AWS Lambda function is triggered in the AWS cloud. This function reads the image in the S3 Bucket and sends a request for face search in the AWS Rekognition. If the captured image matches with the storage image, the lambda function searches the name of the person from the DynamoDB and returns the name back to Alexa. Alexa finally informs the user about the face (unknown face /known face / no face) and depending on the voice request to Alexa to open or close the door, the lambda sends a signal to Raspberry Pi to take necessary action. The operation of the opening or closing of the lock is done by servo motor as per the request. Anitha T. et. al (Anitha & Uppalaiah, 2016) framed a home network system consisting of actuators as well as detectors for monitoring the home environment with the use of Raspberry Pi. It further communicates with users' android applications via web servers. Devdas, G. et al. (Devdas et al., 2017) proposed a home monitoring system at low cost and flexibility. The system is consolidated with a micro web server along with IP networking that helps the users to control remotely using computers and Android phones. These all help in monitoring using web technology as they drive on the internet.

Data-Center Temperature Monitoring Using Web

In these recent years, technology has been evolving drastically. The commencement of IoT having its feature of communication with different objects to decide outcome based upon interaction with each other helps people to control these objects remotely. Sensors play a vital role in this context. They are integrated with different objects mostly with electronics like ovens, Air Conditioning (AC), refrigerator and others. Open-source devices that help in implementing applications of IoT are Raspberry Pi and Arduino. This acts as an access center or intermediate between sensors and the internet for accessing data generated from field sensors. Moreover, regulation of physical objects is possible if these devices are mounted with a microcontroller. There are various environmental factors that affect the overall efficiency of the

IoT system such as, temperature and humidity. Temperature and humidity are two factors that can affect the working of any device inside a room. The reason that causes servers to become hot is highly dependent upon the temperature and humidity of the room. The rise in temperature can cause damage to hardware and sudden fall in temperature can cause a lot of electricity consumption. Humidity is another factor where rise of humidity could result in damaging the hardware of the servers and low humidity can lead to static electrical signals in the server room that could degrade the functionality. Thus, monitoring of maintaining a proper temperature and humidity of the server rooms are utmost important.

Poonam et al. (Poonam & Mulge, 2013) made a prototype using wireless sensor networks to monitor room temperature to avoid fire incidents. In this system LM35 sensor is used to sense the room's temperature and the recorded temperature is sent to the phone via General Packet Radio Service (GPRS). A flash or a beep message is received to android users in case of fire. For transferring data between the smartphone and the application layer, the LM35 sensor is connected via Universal Serial Bus (USB) cable using Google's C2DM service (Poonam & Mulge, 2013). This will help in tackling cases of fire emergencies in companies, organizations as well as individual homes. Nkenyereye et al. (Nkenyereye et al., 2021) proposed a system where anyone can remotely monitor the temperature and humidity of Point of Presence (PoP). The most common way to provide connectivity to the outer world to a user is done via ISP. The wireless LAN is one of the most general methods for providing services to the user by ISP. This Wireless LAN has both pros and cons. It has fairly high speed but limited coverage. Therefore, the PoP is used as the of the solutions that acts as a repeater station by adding more access points at specified locations to increase the coverage. PoP are generally locked inside a room and overheating may cause serious damage to these servers. Leakage of cooling systems is a frequently occurring problem in PoP. Therefore, the temperature of the PoP's room must be monitored at regular intervals. This system has two parts which are the hardware module consisting of Remote Control (RC) and Temperature Humidity Data Sender (THDS) whereas, the other part is the web service that uses a microcontroller for sending data to the database. The Arduino UNO and IR LEDs transmitter together form the remote-control module and monitors the air conditioning of the PoP room. The raw data is transmitted to the Air Conditioner IR LEDs Receiver (ACIRLR). The microcontroller WeMos R1D2 ESP8266 obtains the temperature and humidity data from the DHT22 sensor. Each device in the PoP room is assigned a unique ID so that they can distinguish themselves from one another. The web service receives the data from each unique ID. Every data saved in the database will be displayed to the users in Web Monitoring (WM) so that they can control the temperature of the PoP room from anywhere at any time.

V. M. Davande et al. (Davande et al., 2016) proposed an architecture to automate different electrical appliances such as fans, AC etc. by monitoring the real time temperatures. The real time temperature is provided by the thermistor in terms of voltage. In case it exceeds the assigned threshold value, the system then controls the LED as well as the DC motor. This helps in monitoring the real time factors of a room that is temperature and humidity for preventing the electrical appliances as well as servers from damage.

Monitoring Smart System Based on Embedded Dynamic Web

These days, industrial applications all around the world have been extensively using the web in almost every aspect of their working. It has led to a discussion that entails implementing web technology in the bottom layer of the field of industrial monitoring. If the embedded web server used in the field controlling device is executed in the bottom most layer of the device monitoring the industry, it will greatly help in accessing and monitoring the control devices that are spread out over a large area just by the use of the internet and a web browser. The current state of the field device can be easily and dynamically reflected on the layout of the web (Park, 2021). This is especially helpful for collecting feedback after the monitoring task is performed. Real time data is also collected from the field in the most accurate manner and the data is analysed and checked accordingly to remove any possibilities of errors. The field devices are controlled and maintenance is performed for the system routinely. There is a defined architecture for a monitoring system that is networked. For instance, in a gas station, there are certain field devices in its forecourt that include tank-level gauges and dispensers (Mendiboure et al., 2021). All these field devices are connected using the embedded web server and are connected to the internet. After this, the devices make use of a wireless port or an ethernet port to ultimately be connected to the web-based browsing monitoring station (Gupta & Mathew, 2017). The realization of the data monitoring and communication, if done in real time is proved to be extremely favourable for such an architecture. Other things that are deemed to be favourable are an encrypted system and network security. Adopting an embedded technology that is web based in its approach towards integrated management and dynamic web monitoring is also extremely useful (Mhalla et al., 2019). There are multiple benefits, which includes convenience, configuration, and controllability. It is very convenient to help get a better understanding of intelligent communication with the help of dynamic web monitoring done by law bodies for integrity and confidentiality of data and information. It also helps in making sure that the data transfer doesn't hamper the security of the data. The embedded dynamic web is an implementation of the software system. There are three parts to the software system, which comprises of application software, web server and operating system

(Zikria et al., 2018). The web server has many purposes including monitoring of real time data, configuration of devices, and ensuring that all the constituent jobs are being performed the way they were intended to perform. The other purposes include monitoring of the log file of the server that is running, analyse the data that is being collected statistically and ensure that there are no errors being made. It also functions to prevent a security breach. It is imperative that when the data is transferred, must stay safe from third party intrusion. This can be done by closely controlling the different parameters and monitoring by legal authority. An embedded computer that has extremely high performance essentially comprises of a web server. It contains a flash ROM that is generally of 32MB size and a Synchronous Dynamic RAM (SDRAM) of size 128MB (Alkamil & Perera, 2020). It contains a number of serial ports. Moreover, an ethernet port with 10/100 mbps, a communication of Personal Computer Memory Card Internal Association (PCMCIA) that is wireless in nature, a data input that is 8 channels, an output data of similar configuration and a Compact Flash (CF) with an interface that is extended, all make up a web server (de Carvalho et al., 2020). All of these parts play an integral role in making sure that the web server is able to perform all of its intended functions efficiently without any issues arising. Therefore, the surveillance of these systems for proper control and process of resources is a must. The web monitoring does not only help in monitoring proper working of any system rather it also ensures security.

CONCLUSION AND FUTURE RESEARCH DIRECTIONS

The burgeoning of new technology which highly depends upon communication either in the form of LAN or WAN drives on huge amount of data. Many organizations and companies heavily depend upon passive and active data for their functioning. Starting from traditional client-server architecture to modern systems such as cloud computing heavily rely on data and web for their processing. The industries such as gas and oil industry require adequate surveillance for proper working and avoidance as well as detection of intruder in the system. Also, smart systems whose decision making depends upon live data requires web support for proper monitoring of important assets involved in it. In this paper, a deep analysis is conducted to suggest web monitoring or web surveillance as one of the major solutions for identifying proper working of the system as well as proper monitoring for security of the system. The paper begins with background work and advances to various methods for web surveillance or web monitoring. This paper also explains various applications of web surveillance that includes some of the most vital and recent technologies such as cellular phones, data centers and smart systems.

Finally, the paper has also suggested future guidelines for effective use of web monitoring for various applications. This work will act as a reference for various future research work that could contribute to web surveillance or web monitoring. The companies, organizations as well as individuals are now highly dependent on web for their daily life activities and corporate works. Therefore, it requires more research for monitoring real time data in coming future. This paper would be helpful for carrying out future research work such web monitoring and web surveillance.

REFERENCES

Aggarwal, J. K., & Cucchiara, R. (2006). Special issue on multimedia surveillance SYSTEMS: Guest editorial. *Multimedia Systems*, *12*(3), 165–167. doi:10.100700530-006-0072-7

Alam, T. (2020). IoT-Fog a communication framework using blockchain in the Internet of things. doi:10.36227/techrxiv.12657200.v1

Alam, T., & Benaida, M. (2018). The role of cloud-manet framework in the internet of things (iot). *International Journal of Online and Biomedical Engineering*, *14*(12), 97. doi:10.3991/ijoe.v14i12.8338

Alam, T., & Rababah, B. (2020). Convergence of MANET in communication among smart devices in IoT. doi:10.22541/au.159164757.78780485/v2

Alimi, A. I., Tavares, A., & Pinho, C. (2019). Enabling Optical Wired and wireless technologies for 5G and beyond networks. Telecommunication Systems - Principles and Applications of Wireless-. *Optics Technology*. Advance online publication. doi:10.5772/intechopen.85858

Alkamil, A., & Perera, D. G. (2020). Towards dynamic and partial reconfigurable hardware architectures for cryptographic algorithms on embedded devices. *IEEE Access: Practical Innovations, Open Solutions*, *8*, 221720–221742. doi:10.1109/ACCESS.2020.3043750

Anitha, T., & Uppalaiah, T. (2016). Android Based Home Automation using Raspberry Pi. *International Journal of Innovative Technologies.*, *4*(1), 2351–8665.

Arasaratnam, O. (2011). Introduction to cloud computing. *Auditing Cloud Computing*, 1–13. doi:10.1002/9781118269091.ch1

Arsan, T. (2016). Smart systems: From design to implementation of embedded Smart Systems. *2016 HONET-ICT.* . doi:10.1109/HONET.2016.7753420

Bandini, S., & Sartori, F. (2005). Improving the effectiveness of monitoring and control systems exploiting knowledge-based approaches. *Personal and Ubiquitous Computing, 9*(5), 301–311. doi:10.100700779-004-0334-3

Barnes, S. J., & Huff, S. L. (2003). Rising sun. *Communications of the ACM, 46*(11), 78–84. doi:10.1145/948383.948384

Bautista, J. F., & Dahi Taleghani, A. (2016). The state of the art and challenges in geomechanical modeling of Injector Wells: A review paper. *Polar and Arctic Sciences and Technology, 8*. doi:10.1115/OMAE2016-54383

Bermudez, I., Traverso, S., Munafo, M., & Mellia, M. (2014). A distributed architecture for the monitoring of clouds and CDNs: Applications to Amazon AWS. *IEEE eTransactions on Network and Service Management, 11*(4), 516–529. doi:10.1109/TNSM.2014.2362357

Bharati, K. F. (2017). Effective task scheduling and dynamic resource optimization based on heuristic algorithms in cloud computing environment. *Transactions on Internet and Information Systems (Seoul), 11*(12). Advance online publication. doi:10.3837/tiis.2017.12.006

Buzan, B., & Hansen, L. (2018). *Defining–redefining security.* Oxford Research Encyclopedia of International Studies. doi:10.1093/acrefore/9780190846626.013.382

Collins, R. T., Lipton, A. J., Fujiyoshi, H., & Kanade, T. (2001). Algorithms for cooperative multisensor surveillance. *Proceedings of the IEEE, 89*(10), 1456–1477. doi:10.1109/5.959341

Davande, V. M., Dhanawade, P. C., & Sutar, V. B. (2016). Real Time Temperature Monitoring Using LABVIEW and Arduino. *International Journal of Innovative Research in Computer and Communication Engineering, 4*(3), 3409–3415.

de Carvalho, J. A., Veiga, H., Pacheco, C. F., & Reis, A. D. (2020). Extended Performance Research on IEEE 802.11 a WPA multi-node laboratory links. *Transactions on Engineering Technologies,* 175–186. . doi:10.1007/978-981-15-8273-8_14

Devdas, G., Dhanaji, B., Vaibhav, M., Saurabh, H., & Pravin, P. (2017). Home Automation System using Android Application. *Trends in Electrical Engineering, 7*(1), 19–24.

Domb, M. (2019). *Smart Home Systems based on Internet of Things.* IoT and Smart Home Automation. doi:10.5772/intechopen.84894

Gelbord, B., & Roelofsen, G. (2002). New surveillance techniques raise privacy concerns. *Communications of the ACM, 45*(11), 23–24. doi:10.1145/581571.581586

Georis, B. (2003). Ip-distributed computer-aided video-surveillance system. *IEE Symposium Intelligent Distributed Surveillance Systems*. 10.1049/ic:20030044

Gonzalez, E., Stephen, B., Infield, D., & Melero, J. J. (2019). Using high-frequency SCADA data for wind turbine performance monitoring: A sensitivity study. *Renewable Energy, 131*, 841–853. doi:10.1016/j.renene.2018.07.068

Gonzalez, M., Seren, H. R., Ham, G., Buzi, E., Bernero, G., & Deffenbaugh, M. (2018). Viscosity and density measurements using mechanical oscillators in oil and gas applications. *IEEE Transactions on Instrumentation and Measurement, 67*(4), 804–810. doi:10.1109/TIM.2017.2761218

Goralski, W. (2017). TCP/IP protocols and devices. *The Illustrated Network, 47*–69. . doi:10.1016/B978-0-12-811027-0.00002-3

Guo, Y., Mohamed, I., Abou-Sayed, O., & Abou-Sayed, A. (2018). Cloud computing and web application-based remote real-time monitoring and data analysis: Slurry injection case study, onshore USA. *Journal of Petroleum Exploration and Production Technology, 9*(2), 1225–1235. doi:10.100713202-018-0536-2

Gupta, S., & Mathew, L. (2017). LabVIEW implementation of WSN for real time monitoring in Precision Agriculture. *International Journal of Computers and Applications, 171*(4), 36–40. doi:10.5120/ijca2017915023

Haq, A., Gondal, I., & Murshed, M. (2010). Automated multi-sensor color video fusion for nighttime video surveillance. *The IEEE Symposium on Computers and Communications*. 10.1109/ISCC.2010.5546791

Hsieh, W.-B., & Leu, J.-S. (2017). Implementing secure VoIP communication over SIP-based networks. *Wireless Networks, 24*(8), 2915–2926. doi:10.100711276-017-1512-3

Imai, Y., Hori, Y., & Masuda, S. (2008). Development and a brief evaluation of a web-based surveillance system for cellular phones and other mobile computing clients. *2008 Conference on Human System Interactions*. 10.1109/HSI.2008.4581494

Isravel, D. P., Silas, S., & Rajsingh, E. B. (2020). Reliable surveillance tracking system based on software defined internet of things. *The Cognitive Approach in Cloud Computing and Internet of Things Technologies for Surveillance Tracking Systems*, 1–16. . doi:10.1016/B978-0-12-816385-6.00001-5

Jeong, H.-J., Shin, C. H., Shin, K. Y., & Lee, H.-J. (2019). Seamless offloading of web app computations from mobile device to edge clouds via HTML5 web worker migration. *Proceedings of the ACM Symposium on Cloud Computing.* 10.1145/3357223.3362735

Jouini, M., & Rabai, L. B. (2019). A security framework for secure cloud computing environments. *Cloud Security*, 249–263. doi:10.4018/978-1-5225-8176-5.ch011

Lee, J., Kang, J., Jun, M., & Han, J. (2019). Design of a symmetry protocol for the efficient operation of IP cameras in the IOT environment. *Symmetry*, *11*(3), 361. doi:10.3390ym11030361

Li, B., Lu, R., Xiao, G., Bao, H., & Ghorbani, A. A. (2019). Towards insider threats detection in Smart Grid Communication Systems. *IET Communications*, *13*(12), 1728–1736. doi:10.1049/iet-com.2018.5736

Liu, X., Yao, L., & Zeng, X. (2019). *Fusion of multi-time section measurements for state estimation of power system. In 2019 IEEE Innovative Smart Grid Technologies - Asia.* ISGT Asia. doi:10.1109/ISGT-Asia.2019.8881481

Liyanage, M., Ahmad, I., & Okwuibe, J. (2018). Software defined security monitoring in 5G Networks. *A Comprehensive Guide to 5G Security*, 231–243. . doi:10.1002/9781119293071.ch10

Lynch, C. (2017). Welcome to smart materials and structures 2017. *Smart Materials and Structures*, *26*(2), 020401. doi:10.1088/1361-665X/aa572d

McKelvey, F., & Driscoll, K. (2018). ARPANET and its boundary devices: Modems, Imps, and the inter-structuralism of infrastructures. *Internet Histories*, *3*(1), 31–50. doi:10.1080/24701475.2018.1548138

Mendiboure, L., Chalouf, M. A., & Krief, F. (2021). Toward new intelligent architectures for the internet of vehicles. *Intelligent Network Management and Control*, 193–215. . doi:10.1002/9781119817840.ch8

Mhalla, A., Chateau, T., Gazzah, S., & Amara, N. E. (2019). An embedded computer-vision system for multi-object detection in traffic surveillance. *IEEE Transactions on Intelligent Transportation Systems*, *20*(11), 4006–4018. doi:10.1109/TITS.2018.2876614

Namasudra, S., Chakraborty, R., Kadry, S., Manogaran, G., & Rawal, B. S. (2020). Fast: Fast accessing scheme for data transmission in cloud computing. *Peer-to-Peer Networking and Applications*, *14*(4), 2430–2442. doi:10.100712083-020-00959-6

Nieuwenhuis, L. J. M., Ehrenhard, M. L., & Prause, L. (2018). The shift to cloud computing: The impact of disruptive technology on the enterprise software business ecosystem. *Technological Forecasting and Social Change*, *129*, 308–313. doi:10.1016/j.techfore.2017.09.037

Nkenyereye, L., Hwang, J. Y., Pham, Q.-V., & Song, J. S. (2021). Meix: Evolving Multi-Access Edge Computing for Industrial Internet-of-things services. *IEEE Network*, *35*(3), 147–153. doi:10.1109/MNET.011.2000674

Park, Y. M. (2021). A GPS-enabled portable air pollution sensor and web-mapping technologies for field-based learning in Health Geography. *Journal of Geography in Higher Education*, 1–21. doi:10.1080/03098265.2021.1900083

Pereira, R. I. S., Dupont, I. M., Carvalho, P. C. M., & Jucá, S. C. S. (2018). IOT embedded linux system based on Raspberry Pi applied to real-time cloud monitoring of a decentralized photovoltaic plant. *Measurement*, *114*, 286–297. doi:10.1016/j. measurement.2017.09.033

Poonam, Y. M., & Mulge, Y. (2013). Remote temperature monitoring using LM35 sensor and intimate android user via C2DM service. *International Journal of Computer Science and Mobile Computing*, *2*(6), 32–36.

Rath, M. (2017). Resource provision and QoS support with added security for client side applications in cloud computing. *International Journal of Information Technology*, *11*(2), 357–364. doi:10.100741870-017-0059-y

Sani, A. S., Yuan, D., Ogaji, S., & Dong, Z. Y. (2020). Cyreume: A real-time situational awareness and decision-making blockchain-based architecture for the energy internet. Handbook of Real-Time Computing, 1–49. doi:10.1007/978-981-4585-87-3_48-1

Selvaraju, S., Ramba, V., Subbiha, S., & Dubey, P. K. (2019). An innovative system architecture for real-time monitoring and alarming for cutting transport in oil well drilling. *Day 3 Wed*. doi:10.2118/197870-MS

Sharma, L., & Garg, P. K. (2019). Block-based adaptive learning rate for detection of motion-based object in visual surveillance. *From Visual Surveillance to Internet of Things*, 201–214. doi:10.1201/9780429297922-14

Singh, P., Gupta, P., Jyoti, K., & Nayyar, A. (2019). Research on auto-scaling of web applications in cloud: Survey, trends and Future Directions. Scalable Computing. *Practice and Experience*, *20*(2), 399–432. doi:10.12694cpe.v20i2.1537

Stolojescu-Crisan, C., Crisan, C., & Butunoi, B.-P. (2021). Access control and surveillance in a smart home. *High-Confidence Computing, 100036.* Advance online publication. doi:10.1016/j.hcc.2021.100036

Wiredu, G. O., & Sørensen, C. (2006). The dynamics of control and mobile computing in distributed activities. *European Journal of Information Systems, 15*(3), 307–319. doi:10.1057/palgrave.ejis.3000577

Zhuang, Y., Sampurno, Y., Wu, C., Wu, B., Mu, Y., Borucki, L., Philipossian, A., & Yang, R. (2014). (invited) comparison of slurry film distribution between a novel slurry injection system and conventional slurry application method. *ECS Transactions, 60*(1), 625–631. doi:10.1149/06001.0625ecst

Zikria, Y. B., Yu, H., Afzal, M. K., Rehmani, M. H., & Hahm, O. (2018). Internet of things (IOT): Operating system, applications and protocols design, and Validation Techniques. *Future Generation Computer Systems, 88,* 699–706. doi:10.1016/j.future.2018.07.058

Chapter 3
Determinants of Data Science Adoption in Organizations:
Insights From Analyzing the Digital Voice of Practitioners

Mohammad K. Daradkeh
University of Dubai, UAE & Yarmouk University, Jordan

ABSTRACT

While the hype around data science and its key role in driving business and industry change is pervasive, there is scant insight into the factors underlying its successful and widespread adoption in organizations. This chapter presents a systematic approach that integrates text analytics with technology-organization-environment (TOE) framework to analyze the digital voice of practitioners and identify the factors driving data science adoption in organizations. The authors collected 4100 user-generated reviews for 13 prominent data science platforms from Gartner.com and then categorized them into different topics using Latent-Dirichlet Allocation (LDA) model. From the identified topics, 48 factors were derived and synthesized into a model for data science adoption using the TOE framework. The results reveal that alongside technological capabilities, several organizational and environmental factors can significantly influence data science adoption. The results also provide evidence on the potential impact of data science adoption on various aspects of business performance.

DOI: 10.4018/978-1-7998-9426-1.ch003

INTRODUCTION

The proliferation of digital technologies such as social media platforms, smartphones, cloud-based data storage and the Internet of Things (IoT) have enabled companies to accumulate a wealth of data of various types and characteristics. As a result, most companies do not suffer from a lack of data on their customers, products, business operations or competitors. On the contrary, the ever-growing data silos that organizations are accumulating present them with a significant challenge in deriving knowledge and actionable insights from this data in a timely manner. This is particularly important now, as products, services, and business cycles become shorter; therefore, faster, better, and more informed decision making has become a competitive imperative (Chatterjee, Chaudhuri, & Vrontis, 2021; Daradkeh, 2019a). In this competitive environment, characterized by increasing demand for evidence-based decision-making and the proliferation of big data, data science has quickly become a mainstream practice used by many organizations to unlock the value of big data, support decision-making at the strategic and operational levels, and improve various aspects of business performance and operations (Cybulski & Scheepers, 2021; Medeiros, Hoppen, & Maçada, 2020; Oussous, Benjelloun, Ait Lahcen, & Belfkih, 2018; Sharda, Delen, & Turban, 2021).

The potential value and impact of data science has been extensively demonstrated in various business and industry applications and has been promoted by many academic and research communities (Cybulski & Scheepers, 2021; Donoho, 2017; Medeiros et al., 2020; Vicario & Coleman, 2020). While this constitutes a leap forward in the realm of data science, the challenge for researchers and industry is that the development of data science tools and technologies has not adequately addressed the subtleties and factors that are critical to the successful and effective adoption of data science in enterprises (Cybulski & Scheepers, 2021; Wimmer & Aasheim, 2019). At the same time, data science tools are becoming more sophisticated and important for business applications and decision making (Brous & Janssen, 2020; Latif et al., 2020), making the issue of adoption and acceptance even more pressing (Wimmer & Aasheim, 2019). Medeiros et al. (2020) emphasized that it is critical to understand enterprise users and the factors that could influence the adoption process when bringing data science solutions into widespread use. Understanding these factors is not only of great value to the successful adoption of data science capabilities in the workplace, but also helps reduce the risk of rejection or resistance to the adoption of new and potentially disruptive data science solutions (Brous & Janssen, 2020; Vicario & Coleman, 2020; Waller & Fawcett, 2013).

This chapter aims to develop a model that prioritizes and provides insights into the underlying factors that contribute to the success of developing data science maturity and practices in organizations. To this end, we present a systematic approach that combines topic modeling with the technology organization environment (TOE) to analyze the voices of data science professionals and identify the distinctive factors that influence the adoption of data science in organizations. We collected 4100 online reviews from gartner.com for 13 popular data science platforms. The collected and pre-processed reviews were then examined and categorized into different topics using the Latent Dirichlet Allocation (LDA) model (Blei, Ng, & Jordan, 2003). Based on the application of LDA, 48 factors were identified as important enablers/ barriers to the adoption of data science at the enterprise level. These factors were ranked according to their relative weight and frequency of occurrence in the collection of online reviews. Then, using the TOE context, they were grouped into four categories: organizational characteristics, technological characteristics, environmental characteristics, and organizational impact. Finally, we combined the factors into a data science adoption model to provide a contextual understanding and granular view of their interrelationships and impacts on organizational performance and operations.

Collectively, the results of this chapter suggest that the decision to adopt a data science practice at a company does not depend solely on its technical and inventive capabilities. Instead, a variety of organizational and environmental determinants may have a significant impact on the adoption of data science. The findings likewise suggest that effective adoption of data science tools has a significant impact on different components of business outcomes, including decision-making, customer relationships and services, revenue growth, business process agility, compliance and risk management, strategic and financial planning, and supplier and partner relationships. These findings not only add to the body of knowledge on the acceptance of data science, but also provide an important reference for organizations and practitioners involved in researching the possible antecedents and consequences of integrating data science into business processes.

The remainder of this chapter is organized as follows. The next section discusses the theoretical background of this chapter, as well as the benefits and business value of data science applications. In addition, it presents an overview of the research on data science adoption and the importance of understanding the voice of data science professionals. The subsequent section discusses the textual analysis methods used in this chapter to analyze the digital voice of professionals and identify the salient factors driving data science adoption. Then, in the next section, the results of the chapter and the model developed for data science adoption are presented. Finally, implications for research and practice are presented, as well as a discussion of limitations and future research directions.

RESEARCH BACKGROUND

Data Science Adoption

Notwithstanding the increasing scholarly attention paid to the scope, discipline, and issues of data science, there is still no unified definition of the field, or it fluctuates among analysts. For example, Waller and Fawcett (2013) define data science as "the application of quantitative and qualitative methods to solve relevant problems and predict outcomes." Another commonly accepted definition comes from Provost and Fawcett (2013), who provide a high-level definition of data science as "a set of basic principles and, by extension, general concepts that support and guide the principled extraction of information and knowledge from data." A more detailed definition can be found in Dhar (2013), who describes data science as "the study of data acquisition, data analysis, metadata, rapid retrieval, archiving, sharing, mining to find unexpected knowledge and data relationships, visualization in two and three dimensions, including movement and management." The latter definition implies a data lifecycle; a set of processes to transform raw data into actionable intelligence and decisions for effective business outcomes, using principles, techniques, and methods from mathematics, statistics, machine learning, and information systems, along with a variety of data and domain expertise. From a disciplinary development perspective, recent advances in computational and storage capabilities, combined with advances in areas such as data warehousing, descriptive, predictive, and prescriptive analytics, data visualization, machine learning, and big data analytics, have had a particularly strong impact on the growth of data science applications and widespread adoption in organizations (Dhar, 2013; Donoho, 2017; Latif et al., 2020; Medeiros et al., 2020; Oussous et al., 2018).

Although data science is a relatively new paradigm of data analysis and methodology, it has now reached sufficient maturity that several data science platforms are widely available, with more innovative research in the pipeline. Gartner (2021) defines the data science platform as "a cohesive software application that provides a mix of basic building blocks needed to create all types of data science solutions and integrate those solutions with business processes, surrounding infrastructure, and products." Many vendors in the data science and analytics market, such as Microsoft, Tableau, SAS, Alteryx, TIBCO Software, KNIME, and RapidMiner, have expanded their portfolios to offer a wide range of solutions with modeling and analytics capabilities such as predictive modeling, machine learning, and interactive exploration and visualization. The primary goal of these platforms is to enable a broad range of data science professionals, including data scientists, data engineers, business analysts, application developers, and business decision makers, to perform tasks across the data science and analytics pipeline via user-friendly and intuitive user interfaces (Gartner, 2021). This includes tasks related to accessing and ingesting data, performing data preparation, interactively exploring and visualizing data, building functionality and advanced modeling, and testing, delivering and sharing analytics results and business insights with relevant stakeholders and decision-makers (Cybulski & Scheepers, 2021; Vicario & Coleman, 2020).

Despite the immense capabilities and potential benefits of data science solutions for businesses, the development of innovative and sophisticated data science platforms is by no means the end goal. To fully realize the potential advantages of a data science platform, it is paramount to ensure that the platform can be effectively and successfully leveraged by end users for their modeling, analytics, and decision-making demands (Vicario & Coleman, 2020). Cybulski and Scheepers (2021) discussed several enablers or impediments to the effective adoption of data science platforms by potential adopters. These factors include the availability of appropriate infrastructure to support the new data science platform, the alignment of training for users, the integration of the data science platform into existing business processes, and ensuring that time, management support, and resources are available to support the adoption process. Similarly, Brous and Janssen (2020) note that migrating data science tools into broad analytic use involves addressing privacy and security challenges, supporting interoperability so that the data science tool fits into current business processes, and empowering business users to use the data science tool in their workflows.

Wimmer and Aasheim (2019) argue that there remains a dearth of research that empirically validates the factors that influence data science adoption. To address this gap, they merged constructs from the Theory of Planned Behavior (TPB) (Ajzen, 1991) and the IS Success Model (Delone & McLean, 2003) to develop a theoretical framework that determines the underlying determinants of the perceived benefits of data science and the ultimate intention to adopt data science. They found that system quality is influenced by data science knowledge; both social norms and behavioral control are influenced by information and system quality. Net benefits are influenced by social norms and behavioral control, which in turn influence people's intent to adopt data science platforms. Medeiros and Maçada (2021) suggest that organizations need to develop their data science capabilities (i.e., the organization's competence to effectively use data science resources along with other related technologies and enablers) to drive improved, sound, and responsive decision making and create value through data science platforms. Moreover, the adoption of data science platforms within an organization and the benefits achieved are evolutionary in nature, distributed throughout the organization, and dependent on entrepreneurial management practices (Alloghani, Al-Jumeily, Mustafina, Hussain, & Aljaaf, 2020).

During the process of data science adoption, the potential benefits and capabilities must first be communicated to business decision makers before they can be widely adopted during the deployment phase. Potential users must also create a deep awareness of their individual data science goals and requirements, as well as positive or negative assessments of their value and benefits (Medeiros et al., 2020). From a business viewpoint, data science is considered a disruptive technological advance, largely defined by its information processing capabilities (Louro, Brandão, & Sincorá, 2020). It can add value to the enterprise by enabling knowledge workers to extract value from enterprise data through knowledge and actionable insights that would not be possible with traditional statistical methods and analytical techniques (Cybulski & Scheepers, 2021; Daradkeh, 2019a). In addition, the adoption of data science technologies can lead to significant changes in an organization's internal and external operations, decision-making culture, and capabilities (Chatterjee et al., 2021; Daradkeh, 2019c; Medeiros & Maçada, 2021).

From an organizational perspective, the decision to adopt and fully utilize a data science platform is influenced by the intrinsic structure of the organization, the extrinsic characteristics of the organization, and the attitude of managers toward change (Medeiros & Maçada, 2021). Specifically, the innovative capabilities, organizational characteristics, and environmental conditions surrounding the organization all contribute to the successful and widespread adoption of data science platforms, which can be explained by the technology-organization-environment (TOE) framework (Daradkeh, 2019c).

Technology-Organization-Environment (TOE) Framework

The technology-organization-environment (TOE) model proposed by Tornatzky and Fleischer (1990) provides a useful foundation for understanding enterprise-level technology adoption and its impact on organizational performance. The core of the TOE model is to identify the technological, organizational, and environmental perspectives that drive end-user adoption of organization-level IT innovations. The three contextual perspectives influence technological innovation, decision making, and several other performance indicators (Al Hadwer, Tavana, Gillis, & Rezania, 2021; Awa, Ukoha, & Emecheta, 2016). The organizational perspective encompasses an organization's internal determinants, such as prior experience with technology, innovation capability, high-level management support, organization size, information status, and organizational readiness (Daradkeh, 2019c, 2019d). The environmental perspective includes factors that influence day-to-day operations, such as competitive and industry pressures, regulatory and government communications, and governance practices (Ergado, Desta, & Mehta, 2021).

Because of its methodological rigor and representativeness, the TOE model has consistently demonstrated its usefulness as a theoretical lens for understanding organizational adoption of new technologies in a variety of technological, industrial, and cultural contexts and studies (e.g., Awa, Ojiabo, & Orokor, 2017; Awa et al., 2016; Daradkeh, 2019c, 2019d; Daradkeh & Sabbahein, 2019; Ergado et al., 2021; Orji, Kusi-Sarpong, Huang, & Vazquez-Brust, 2020; Pateli, Mylonas, & Spyrou, 2020; S. Sun, Cegielski, Jia, & Hall, 2018). An important advantage of the TOE model is that its scope is not limited to a specific industry or company size (Al Hadwer et al., 2021); therefore, it provides an integrated understanding of technology adoption by companies, expected challenges, impact on value chain activities, diffusion in companies after adoption, factors influencing the decision to adopt innovations in companies, and building better capabilities in organizations that leverage innovations through the use of technology (Daradkeh, 2019c; Ghaleb, Dominic, Fati, Muneer, & Ali, 2021; Setiyani & Rostiani, 2021). However, the TOE framework has been criticized for having unclear main constructs (Al Hadwer et al., 2021) and for being too generic (Daradkeh, 2019c). It is therefore argued that the TOE framework requires further elaboration to make it applicable to specific contexts. While TOE has been used in the context of several other technological innovations (e.g., visual analytics and project management) (such as visual analytics and project management) (Daradkeh, 2019c), it has not yet been used in the field of data science, which provides an interesting context for the TOE model to explore organizational adoption of data science platforms.

The Voice of Data Science Practitioners

A cost-effective way to understand the factors influencing adoption of data science platforms is to study practitioners' experiences and practices in using data science platforms to solve a variety of business and analytics problems. Recently, advances in Internet and Web technologies, particularly Web 2.0 applications, and the proliferation of electronic word-of-mouth (eWOM) forums have opened up a wider range of opportunities for data scientists to publish and share their experiences, ratings, and reviews of various data science tools online (Fang, Tang, Li, & Wu, 2018). Zhang, Fan, Zhang, Wang, and Fan (2021) describe online reviews as peer-generated reviews that provide detailed, fine-grained information about the competence and expected benefits of a particular product or service. Such user-generated reviews are typically found on product and service review websites such as trustradius.com, itcentralstation. com, and gartner.com. Online user-generated reviews are often created and shared by end users who have experience with the product. Therefore, peer users in online review communities often embrace such information sharing to mitigate anonymity regarding the merits and shortcomings of technologies in the decision-making process (M. Sun, Chen, Tian, & Yan, 2021; Vana & Lambrecht, 2021).

Although user-generated reviews are considered trustworthy and credible indicators of knowledge and intelligence for all parties involved in expanding the scope and reach of data science applications, capturing the experiences and reviews of data science tool users in a detailed and thorough manner is a difficult undertaking. Typically, data science tools have hundreds or even thousands of reviews on an evaluation platform. As a result, the sheer volume of online reviews creates an information overload problem (Bi, Liu, Fan, & Cambria, 2019). Due to limited elaboration capacity and processing capabilities, potential consumers may not be able to comprehensively and correctly process all reviews, leading to uninformed or even biased purchase decisions (Zhang et al., 2021). To address this limitation, researchers have recently applied text mining and topic modeling techniques to automatically uncover the latent structures in large texts, extract product features or capabilities, and identify key factors for technology adoption and user satisfaction from online reviews (Bi et al., 2019; Daradkeh, 2019c, 2019d; Daradkeh & Sabbahein, 2019; Fang et al., 2018; Orji et al., 2020; M. Sun et al., 2021; Vana & Lambrecht, 2021; Zhang et al., 2021). Nevertheless, existing scientific knowledge on the application of text mining and topic modeling techniques in the context of enterprise-level data science adoption is relatively sparse.

RESEARCH METHODOLOGY

The primary objective of this chapter is to investigate and develop a model of the determinants that influence the adoption of data science platforms in organizations from the perspective of data science practitioners. To this end, a systematic approach integrating topic modeling with the TOE framework was developed to analyze the voice of data science practitioners and identify the factors that may influence their decision to adopt data science platforms when performing their modeling, analysis, and decision-making tasks. The research methodology used in this chapter consisted of five main phases: 1) collection and pre-processing of online reviews; 2) identification of factors using LDA method; 3) labeling and ranking of factors; 4) categorization of factors using the TOE framework; and 5) incorporation of factors into a model for data science adoption. Figure 1 provides an overview of the research methodology.

Figure 1. Research methodology to identify determinants of data science adoption from online reviews

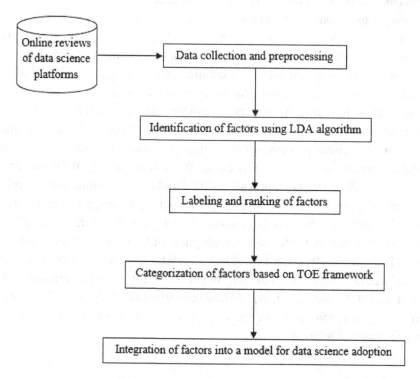

Data Collection and Preparation

The online reviews used in this chapter were collected from gartner.com (https://www.gartner.com/reviews/home), a global IT consulting and research firm that provides an Internet-based arena for professionals to freely share their opinions, reviews, and comments on various data science and machine learning platforms evaluations (Gartner, 2021). A sample of 4,100 reviews was collected on 13 prominent data science platforms, including MATLAB, SAS Enterprise Miner, Alteryx Designer, RapidMiner Studio, Anaconda Enterprise, IBM SPSS Statistics, and KNIME exam platforms. The top data science platforms evaluated were MATLAB (nearly 50% of audits), followed by Base SAS (nearly 25% of surveys), Alteryx Designer (nearly 20%), RapidMiner Studio (15%), and SAP BusinessObjects Analysis and TIBCO Spotfire (nearly 5%). While a wide variety of data science platforms exist, the selection was narrowed down to the most well-known ones, according to Gartner's Magic Quadrant for Data Science and Machine Learning Platforms 2021 (Gartner, 2021).

Due to their ubiquity among data science professionals, these data science platforms typically receive a large number of online reviews compared to other platforms.

To ensure quality and representativeness, a number of criteria were used as the basis for inclusion or exclusion of online reviews. The first criterion is the clarity and appropriateness of the content of the review to the objective of this chapter. Second, previous research has shown that the depth of the review (i.e., the amount of information in the review) can influence the quality and quantity of the information (Daradkeh, 2019c). Longer reviews often contain more information about products and explain in more detail how and where the product was used in a particular context. Therefore, only reviews with at least 50 words were included in the analysis process. Third, the inclusion of online reviews was also limited to those created and posted by real practitioners with experience in using data science platforms, which is already ensured and verified by Gartner's policy. The reviewers in this chapter had a variety of job titles, including data scientists, data analysts, data engineers, analytics managers, business analysts, and application developers. They also came from a variety of industries, including finance, education, communications, healthcare, transportation, manufacturing, construction, services, retail and supply chain, energy and utilities, and government (Gartner, 2021).

To avoid omitting review comments that could contribute to the research objectives of this chapter, all reviews were extracted and aggregated into a review corpus, with each sentence in an original review retained as one sentence in the constructed aggregated review corpus. Structured information associated with the online reviews, such as job titles, geographic location, and industry type and company size, was also derived and then combined with the textual information during the data collection process. The online reviews were selected separately by two coders and then aggregated into a corpus through a consensus process to ensure agreement among the coders and the relevance of the selected reviews to the objectives of this chapter. Among these reviews, any comments, statements, or opinions about the factors that might influence the adoption of data science platforms from the perspective of data science professionals formed an important content focus and were therefore selected for text analysis and topic modeling using Latent Dirichlet Allocation (LDA).

After collecting and aggregating online reviews into a corpus, a key preprocessing step in LDA consists of eliminating content-free phrases within the corpus to obtain topics that are particularly interpretable. The retrieved documents (i.e., online reviews) from the corpus were processed using natural language processing, which includes operations such as tokenization of periods or phrases, stopword filtering, token filtering, capitalization, stemming, and pruning. We then represented each score using the Term Frequency and Inverse Document Frequency (TF-IDF) weighting scheme. The final result of this preprocessing step is a dataset-period matrix that contains the phrase distributions within the documents (Blei, 2012). The document term matrix is then used in subsequent steps as described in the framework shown in Figure 1.

When collecting and aggregating online reviews into a corpus, an important preprocessing step in LDA is to screen out content-less words from the corpus to obtain more interpretable results. The reviews retrieved from the corpus were processed using standard language processing, which includes, for example, tokenization of terms or words, removal of stop words, capitalization, stemming, and pruning. Then, each review was treated with the Term Frequency and Inverse Document Frequency (TF-IDF) weighting scheme. The result of this preprocessing step is a document term matrix that represents the word distributions in the corpus (Blei, 2012). The document term matrix is then used in the following steps according to the methodology explained in Figure 1.

Identification of Factors Using LDA

The main purpose of this step is to discover all the topics (i.e., factors) addressed by reviewers on data science platforms from the corpus of online reviews. After constructing a relevant and adequate document term matrix, LDA was run with its typical parameter settings using the Gensim Python Library. The basic idea of LDA is to group similar expressions and words within the same topic. It treats each document as a mixture of topics and each topic as a mixture of words; therefore, documents may overlap in content (Blei, Ng, & Jordan, 2003). Given the dynamic nature and increasing volume of online reviews, LDA can be an effective means to periodically categorize online reviews into topic groups and reduce the time complexity of analyzing the textual content of online reviews. Considering this potential advantage, LDA is considered suitable for this chapter because it enables the automatic and detailed discovery of various factors that influence the adoption of data science platforms from online reviews. It also ranks the discovered factors according to their distribution in the corpus of online reviews.

The number of topics is a required parameter for the estimation of the LDA model. However, determining the number of topics is not a simple process as it largely depends on the researcher and the chapter at hand (Basilio, Brum, & Pereira, 2020). In most cases, documents are grouped by topic so that researchers can filter and select documents based on these topics if they are meaningful to them. This can only be achieved by comparing different numbers of topics and deciding which are the most meaningful. Moreover, different levels of granularity of topics may be required, while in some situations a few coarse topics may be sufficient. Technically, different algorithms can be used to determine the number of topics, e.g., Perplexity and ELBOW methods (Daradkeh, 2021a). Thus, since there is no prior knowledge about the appropriate number of factors that could be obtained from online reviews, a cyclic procedure with further iterations is performed until the LDA model is tuned to achieve the best possible number of topics (i.e., factors) (Daradkeh, 2021b). The procedure involved iterative experiments in which the number of topics was increased and the obtained model was evaluated until the final agreed number of 48 topics (factors) was reached, as shown in Table 4, which represents the best distribution of the online reviews dataset.

Labeling and Ranking of Factors

The factors identified using LDA were then labeled by assigning relevant and meaningful names according to the terms describing each factor and the content of each review based on the information in the word-topic matrix. Manual labeling of topics is a standard procedure in LDA-based topic identification (Al-Ramahi, Elnoshokaty, El-Gayar, Nasralah, & Wahbeh, 2021; Basilio et al., 2020). The label of a topic is usually selected by researchers by taking the most representative top words of the topic classification and using these words to assign a meaningful label for the topic (Daradkeh, 2019d). For this chapter, the top 10 words for each factor (topic) are presented according to their probabilities. These factors were then ranked according to their relative weight and frequency of occurrence within the collection of online reviews to determine the importance of each factor and the reviews representing each factor.

Incorporation of Factors into a Model for Fata Science Adoption

After labeling and ranking the factors, the two coders grouped them into four categories based on the TOE framework, namely technological characteristics (TC), organizational characteristics (OC), environmental characteristics (EC), and organizational impact (OI). The obtained results were tested for inter-coder reliability and agreement using Krippendorff's alpha (Krippendorff, 2012). In general, a Krippendorff's alpha (α) of 0.80 is considered an acceptable level of inter-coder agreement [ref]. The final set of factors was then incorporated into a model for data science adoption. The resulting model shows the interrelationship of the factors and their impact on the adoption of data science platforms. It also shows the impact of data science platform adoption on organizational outcomes from the perspective of data science practitioners.

RESULTS

Based on analyzing the voice of data science practitioners using LDA, 48 factors emerged that have the potential to enable and/or hinder the adoption of data science platforms in organizations. Table 4 shows the factors identified, the category code, the weight for each factor, and the rank of each factor.

The results show that the technology characteristics (TC) category consists of predictive analytics and modeling, data exploration and visualization, data access, preparation and manipulation, text and image analysis, ease of use, ease of implementation and configuration, ease of learning, adaptation to data and BI infrastructure, adaptation to existing enterprise and cloud applications, support for open source capabilities, platform reliability, platform interoperability, platform compatibility, scalability, extensibility and openness, autonomy, security and privacy, comprehensibility and interpretability of the results, data presentation and format, governance and metadata management, accuracy of information and analytics, presentation and format of information.

The organizational characteristics (OC) include organizational needs and requirements, organizational resources, organizational decision-making culture, organizational strategy and future vision, financial readiness. The environmental characteristics (EC) include quality of customer service/experience, quality of technical support, pricing and licensing flexibility, availability of quality third-party resources (integrators, service providers, etc.), timeliness of vendor response, quality of peer user community, quality and availability of end-user training, pre-existing relationship with vendor, product roadmap and future vision, vendor viability, and competitive pressures.

Finally, organizational impact (OI) includes improving decision making, improving customer relationships/service, driving revenue growth, improving business process outcomes, improving business process agility, improving compliance and risk management, driving innovation and new product development, creating internal/operational efficiencies, and strategic and financial planning. The factors discovered by LDA are highly consistent with those identified by human experts in the existing literature (Daradkeh, 2019a, 2019b, 2019c), demonstrating the validity and effectiveness of this methodology. Moreover, the LDA model is capable of discovering fine-grained factors, thus providing a fairly detailed picture of the potential factors that could influence the adoption of data science platforms.

Table 1. Topics names (determinants) and top ten terms describing the determinants of data science adoption

No.	Topic label	Category*	Freq.	Rank	Top-10 terms
T1	Predictive analysis and modeling	TC	653	1	model, predictive, build, develop, data, mining, machine, learning, workflow, automation
T2	Data exploration and visualization	TC	647	2	visual, explore, statistical, analysis, report, dashboard, design, interactive, design, insight
T3	Data access, preparation and manipulation	TC	617	3	data, preparation, access, multiple, extract, transform, integrate, clean, manipulate, source
T4	Ease of use	TC	611	4	complex, difficult, use, easy, intuitive, user, friendly, interface, tool, experience
T5	Ease of implementation and configuration	TC	598	5	implement, install, configuration, deploy, admin, department, partner, complex, easy, enterprise
T6	Ease of learning	TC	588	6	learn, easy, steep, curve, experience, lack, programming, skill, education, qualification
T7	Quality of customer service/experience	EC	564	7	customer, service, experience, vendor, help, support, excellent, bad, cooperation, partner
T8	Quality of technical support	EC	564	7	technical, support, solve, difficult, problem, complicated, issue, experience, implementation, product
T9	Pricing and license flexibility	EC	550	8	price, cost, license, flexible, high, expensive, competitor, investment, purchase, subscription
T10	Alignment with data and BI infrastructure	TC	533	9	align, data, business, intelligence, infrastructure, team, middleware, warehouse, connect, integrate
T11	Alignment with existing enterprise and cloud applications	TC	523	10	cloud, infrastructure, application, enterprise, integrate, align, system, support, service, provide
T12	Support for open-source capabilities	TC	523	10	open, source, software, language, easy, integration, support, python, script, adapt
T13	Platform reliability	TC	501	11	reliability, robust, analytics, capability, scale, big, data, bug, model, result
T14	Platform interoperability	TC	470	12	ability, exchange, different, information, system, application, communicate, connect, infrastructure, enterprise
T15	Platform compatibility	TC	470	12	fit, consistent, need, experience, skill, level, decision, analysis, style, workflow, process
T16	Organizational needs and requirements	OC	440	13	need, requirement, enterprise, business, align, fit, meet, decision, making, analysis
T17	Availability of quality 3rd-party resources (integrators, service providers, etc.)	EC	433	14	third, party, partner, integration, service, provider, relationship, resources, support, monitor
T18	Timeliness of vendor response	EC	420	15	time, answer, question, technical, issue, resolve, poor, response, problem, communicate
T19	Quality of peer-user community	EC	410	16	user, community, forum, consult, share, post, issue, answer, complicated, help
T20	Improve decision-making	IO	400	17	improve, decision, making, business, data, driven, support, management, problem, solve

continues on following page

Table 1. Continued

No.	Topic label	Category*	Freq.	Rank	Top-10 terms
T21	Improve customer relations/service	IO	400	17	retention, customer, service, experience, relationship, understand, management, analytics, engagement, support
T22	Quality and availability of end-user training	EC	380	18	training, user, need, support, resources, documentation, online, use, product, skill
T23	Drive revenue growth	IO	320	19	drive, revenue, growth, sale, innovation, business, value, insight, competition, market
T24	Organizational resources	OC	301	20	data, scientist, tool, team, skill, infrastructure, enterprise, resources, capability, available
T25	Organizational decision-making culture	OC	288	21	data, analytic, driven, decision, team, culture, process, build, transform, enterprise
T26	Organization strategy and future vision	OC	270	22	strategic, objective, change, vision, planning, prepared, align, invest, future, industry
T27	Pre-existing relationship with the vendor	EC	253	23	relationship, vendor, great, partner, work, support, long, time, reliable, exist
T28	Scalability	TC	250	24	scale, big, data, different, model, division, unit, enterprise, level, performance
T29	Extensibility and openness	TC	250	24	easy, extensible, flexible, platform, open, source, language, machine, learning, library
T30	Product roadmap and future vision	EC	244	25	product, roadmap, update, vision, build, open, future, market, self, service
T31	Improve business process outcomes	IO	230	26	improve, business, process, performance, analysis, outcomes, execution, success, project
T32	Improve business process agility	IO	221	27	business, process, agility, flexible, need, management, change, analysis, fast, decision
T33	Improve compliance & risk management	IO	201	28	improve, risk, compliance, fraud, monitor, control, mitigate, analysis, management, process
T34	Drive innovation and new product development/R&D	IO	171	29	drive, force, innovation, research, product, design, development, discover, identify, opportunity
T35	Create internal/operational efficiencies	IO	171	29	improve, internal, operation, efficient, performance, process, build, data, workflow, process
T36	Vendor viability	EC	157	30	viable, credible, long, established, stable, strong, position, lead, market, industries
T37	Strategic and financial planning	IO	138	31	strategic, finance, plan, analysis, management, tool, method, resource, allocation, business, partner
T38	Security and privacy	TC	135	32	security, privacy, concern, collect, access, manage, information, risk, protect, permission
T39	Financial readiness	OC	98	33	financial, readiness, invest, analytic, tool, infrastructure, train, recruit, staff, data
T40	Comprehensibility and interpretability of the results	TC	93	34	understand, interpret, easy, time, complicated, model, analytic, results, visualization, hypotheses
T41	Improve supplier or partner relationships	IO	88	35	partner, relationship, efficient, process, management, discover, pattern, supply, chain, management
T42	Text and image analysis	TC	82	36	text, mining, predictive, image, process, natural, language, analytic, data, algorithm

continues on following page

Table 1. Continued

No.	Topic label	Category*	Freq.	Rank	Top-10 terms
T43	Data presentation and format	TC	77	37	present, format, result, interactive, visual, web, clear, enable, analysis, insight
T44	Ease of consuming and sharing models and analytics	TC	61	38	share, communicate, reuse, model, analysis, consume, report, visual, web, deploy
T45	Governance and metadata management	TC	50	39	multiple, sources, ownership, problems, data, quality, integration, governance, metadata, practice
T46	Information and analytics accuracy	TC	42	40	analyze, information, accuracy, prediction, clean, prepare, test, model, reliable, trust
T47	Autonomy	TC	33	41	self, service, reliant, dependent, analysis, modeling, level, data, scientist, skill
T48	Competitive pressure	EC	12	42	competitive, pressure, advantage, industry, compare, high, increase, market, customer, rival

* Notes: TC (Technological Context); OC (Organizational Context); EC (Environmental Context); IO (Organizational Impact).

As shown in Table 1, all factors were ranked based on their weights, indicating the overall popularity of the factors in the online reviews. For example, predictive analytics and modeling were highlighted as the most important factor in the decision to adopt data science tools. Other factors such as data exploration and visualization, data access, preparation, and manipulation, complexity (ease of use), ease of implementation and configuration, ease of learning, quality of customer service, and quality of technical support were also ranked highly and perceived as important factors by data science practitioners. Conversely, factors such as presentation and format of data, agility of the system, ease of use and sharing of models and analytics, governance and metadata management, accuracy of information and analytics, autonomy, and competitive pressures were perceived as less influential on the decision-making process to adopt data science platforms in organizations. These findings help us understand which factors organizations need to consider and which factors should be assigned the highest priority to ensure successful and widespread adoption of data science tools among data science professionals.

To synthesize all the factors identified through the topic modeling process, an integrated model of data science adoption was developed based on the TOE framework. Figure 2 illustrates the factors and their relationship to data science adoption. The model includes factors that are believed to have a significant impact on the data science adoption decision-making process from the perspective of data science practitioners. According to the model in Figure 2, the technological context includes the largest number of factors compared to other contexts, indicating that the technological factors include more uncertain aspects. These factors can be from the concerns of the capabilities that the data science tool should provide. Organizational and environmental contexts include new factors that are emerging in the current business ecosystem, such as privacy and security, peer user community quality, governance, and metadata management and autonomy. The final agreement between coders in this process, as measured by the Krippendorffs alpha coefficient, was 83.11%; indicating an acceptable level of inter-coder agreement and reliability (Krippendorff, 2012).

Figure 2. Model for data science adoption in organizations

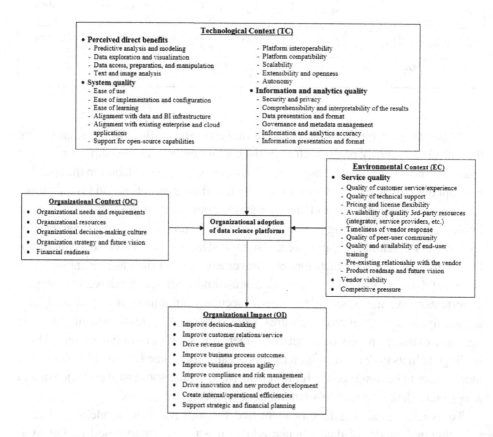

DISCUSSION

As the adoption of data science platforms becomes widespread across most industries, it is important for researchers and practitioners to understand the intricacies and factors that influence their effective and successful adoption in organizations. This chapter addresses this key, yet under-researched, issue by developing a model that captures various factors that influence the adoption of data science technologies from the perspective of practitioners. Compared to other IT adoption studies, this chapter leverages online software reviews of various data science platforms as a data source. Moreover, it addresses the research problem from the perspective of a relatively large number of real practitioners working in different roles and different industries. Thus, the findings from this chapter not only provide a theoretical foundation for further exploration of the critical issue of data science adoption, but also offer actionable guidance for practical implementation.

Implications for Research

This chapter extends previous work on IT adoption by presenting a theoretical model that highlights several technological, organizational, and environmental factors that enable or inhibit adoption of data science platforms. The theoretical background section of this chapter highlights several factors that have been validated in other IT adoption contexts such as data mining and business intelligence (BI) applications (Chatterjee et al., 2021; Louro et al., 2020; Medeiros et al., 2020; Medeiros & Maçada, 2021). Many of these factors also emerged in the data science adoption context. However, unlike previous IT adoption studies, other unique factors were identified by analyzing the voice of data science practitioners. For example, security, privacy, interoperability, and data governance were identified as critical factors that can influence an organization's decision to adopt new and disruptive data science platforms. These factors have not previously appeared in studies of IT adoption, but may appear here because of the unique characteristics of data science. It is worth noting that these newly identified factors and other factors from the IT adoption literature have not yet been adequately discussed and empirically tested in the context of data science adoption. Therefore, the model proposed in this chapter can serve as a theoretical basis for further investigation of possible antecedents and consequences of data science adoption at the enterprise level.

This chapter also demonstrates the applicability and effectiveness of text analytics and topic modeling techniques for analyzing the rich content of online reviews and providing a detailed view of the factors that influence organizational adoption of data science platforms. Traditionally, IT adoption studies use research-centric tools such as surveys, focus groups, or self-reported usage documents to collect data on user experiences and perceptions. They also rely predominantly on manual identification, analysis, and categorization of text sources to discover relevant adoption factors. A clear limitation of this process is that it can be costly, time consuming, and resource intensive (Basole, Seuss, & Rouse, 2013). Consequently, researchers often limit the scope and scale of the data analysis process to a selective subset of keywords and phrases in the text data (Orji et al., 2020). The unsupervised nature of online software reviews provides valuable information for understanding users' multifaceted perceptions and usage patterns without interference from prompts. The current chapter can be used as an example of a practical application of topic modeling to understand user behaviors and perceptions, and it addresses concerns about declining enthusiasm for the use of text analytics in IT adoption studies. It also illustrates the advantages of using text analytics and topic modeling techniques over manual coding in analyzing a large corpus of user-generated comments. Therefore, the research methodology proposed in this chapter can be easily extended to other IT adoption contexts and topics.

The results of this chapter confirm the merit of the TOE framework and its applicability to understand the emerging issue of data science adoption at the organizational level. This chapter has shown that the adoption decision for data science platforms is dependent on distinct innovation characteristics. Specifically, the results of this chapter support previous work that the relative advantage, complexity, and compatibility of an innovation are key factors in accelerating adoption rates (Al-Ramahi et al., 2021; Daradkeh, 2019a, 2022; Orji et al., 2020). Following the topic modeling of online reviews, data science platforms have been valued by practitioners for their interactive and intuitive capabilities to synthesize information and extract insights from heterogeneous data sources. They were also recognized for their flexibility in creating interactive reports and dashboards to explore and analyze enterprise data and support BI and decision-making activities.

Besides technological characteristics, the results of this chapter show that organizational and environmental factors are important predictors that influence the decision to adopt data science technologies. These results represent an important contribution to theory and indicate that organizational factors should be included in models that examine the acceptance and use of data science technologies by users in the organizational environment (Cybulski & Scheepers, 2021). From an organizational perspective, financial readiness and technological readiness were identified as key determinants influencing data science adoption. Regardless of the perceived benefits of data science technology, if there is not enough budget and resources to support the adoption process, it is meaningless to the organization. The results of this chapter have shown that top management support is a critical factor influencing data science adoption and usage. Supporting evidence for these findings can be found in a variety of data science studies (e.g., Alloghani et al., 2020; Cybulski & Scheepers, 2021; Wimmer & Aasheim, 2019). However, more empirical evidence is needed to verify and evaluate their relevance to the adoption decision process of data science technologies in organizations.

Implications for Practice

This chapter highlights several factors that organizations should consider for successful and widespread adoption of data science technologies among data science practitioners. In practice, the results of this chapter have shown that innovation characteristics alone are not compelling enough to drive acceptance and widespread adoption of data science technologies at the organizational level. There are many other factors that emanate from the organization and the environment in which the organization operates. These factors either directly or indirectly contribute to supporting the adoption decision process of data science technologies and thus developing an analytics-driven culture among enterprise users. The theoretical framework proposed in this chapter provides actionable guidance for organizations as it encompasses pre-adoption and post-adoption factors. For example, in the early stages of the adoption process, the organization should provide adequate training and user support to facilitate the initial adoption of data science technologies. After the adoption of data science technologies, organizations should build an analytics-oriented culture among business users to promote broader adoption of data science technologies.

As demonstrated in this chapter, there are significant barriers that still raise major concerns, such as data security, privacy, and governance. In particular, when scaling the capabilities of data science technologies to multi-user environments, privacy, security, and governance considerations must be proactively addressed by adhering to privacy and security policies at all stages of research, development, and deployment (Medeiros et al., 2020; Wimmer & Aasheim, 2019). These factors also have financial implications that must be planned for prior to the decision to adopt data science technologies. The difficult part of adopting a new data science tool is understanding how it fits into the user's overall analytical software environment and how it fits into the user's processes. This underscores the different specific context of using data science technologies versus operating IS, namely that data science technologies are predominantly used in unstructured business processes, compounded by the fact that the instructions for using the data science tool are less developed and systematized. Sharda et al. (2021) has already suggested that the role of training may be even more important in the context of data science systems, which are inherently more disruptive and more likely to generate resistance. Effective training improves understanding and gives confidence to business users, developing a positive perception of data science technologies. In addition, successful training paths help business users understand how best to use a new data science tool and integrate it into their work processes. They build their confidence along with their skills, improve their self-efficacy, and motivate them to engage in using data science technologies, especially in a more exploratory and innovative way.

LIMITATIONS AND FUTURE RESEARCH

Notwithstanding the important contribution of the research findings, this chapter contains a number of limitations that should be considered when interpreting the results and planning future research. First, topic modeling is a data-driven, unsupervised text analysis technique; therefore, the results of this chapter are dependent on the data set used in the analysis process. Factors influencing the adoption of data science platforms were primarily identified from online reviews contributed by practitioners and posted on only one website, namely Gartner.com. In addition, this chapter focused primarily on commonly used data science platforms, such as RapidMiner, KNIME, Base SAS, Anaconda and Amazon Web Services (AWS). Therefore, the results of this chapter may not provide a complete picture of user perceptions and experiences. This limitation may hamper the generalizability of the findings, as there may have been some bias in the responses that was not shared by practitioners familiar with other data science platforms that were not included in this chapter. Indeed, there are many other factors that could influence the adoption/decision-making process of data science platforms in organizations. Future research should be devoted to understanding these factors from a theoretical perspective and should be examined within different industries.

Second, the purpose of the current chapter was to examine the factors that influence organizational adoption of data science platforms using the TOE context. Despite maintaining inter-coder agreement and reliability, due to the fact that multiple coders were involved in data analysis, coding, classification, and scoring biases may occur as a result of the coders' subjective judgment. The text analysis process used in this chapter was intended to make the results more objective; however, biases in the analysis phase could not be eliminated due to the inherent ambiguity of word meanings and the coding rules imposed. Hence, the results reported in this chapter reflect only the overall picture from a practical point of view. To address these bias limitations, prospective studies could increase the sample size by including online reviews from multiple online portals to gain more insights. In addition, both case studies and empirical studies could provide useful information, which in turn should contribute to existing efforts to better understand the adoption of data science platforms at the enterprise level.

Finally, this chapter relied only on the online opinions of practitioners, which are largely shaped by their own individual perceptions and personal experiences. In reality, however, there are many other factors that can influence the decision-making process to adopt data science platforms and solutions at the enterprise level. Future studies should focus on understanding these factors from a vendor perspective and should be examined across a broad range of industries. Given the increasing popularity of online platforms managed by professionals and software vendors, a comparative chapter could also examine the differences and similarities in online reviews by professionals and software vendors and explore their impact on the factors influencing adoption of data science platforms. As discussed earlier, the main purpose of the current chapter is to provide a comprehensive framework for further exploratory research. Figure 2 illustrates the factors that influence the adoption of data science at the organizational level and their interrelationships. Since few empirical studies on these factors have been conducted and reported in the existing literature, it is imperative that these factors be empirically investigated in future research.

CONCLUSION

In today's fast-paced and disruptive business environment, the prominence of data science is rapidly increasing across all industries as it provides analytics and data discovery capabilities that can provide organizations with both actionable intelligence and knowledge to make informed decisions. While many efforts are made to advance the technical capabilities of data science technologies, the nuances and factors that determine the ultimate success and operational benefits of enterprise-level data science solutions have received little attention in previous research. This chapter extends existing research on the adoption of data science solutions by examining the factors that drive adoption of data science platforms from the perspective of practitioners. The results of this chapter show that several organizational, technological, and environmental factors can inform a company's decision to adopt data science technologies. These findings also confirm the importance of data science in driving various aspects of business performance.

This chapter makes several important contributions. Theoretically, on the one hand, it provides insight into the broader context of enterprise adoption of data science and how it is driven by organizational, technology, and environment-related factors. From a methodological perspective, this chapter provides evidence of the applicability and usefulness of topic modeling for discovering knowledge from online reviews to automatically uncover relevant factors related to information technology (IT) adoption. The research method described in this chapter is applicable to other contexts of IT adoption and can serve as a synthetic means to assess the burgeoning and growing multidisciplinary body of knowledge. As a basis for future research on data science deployment, this chapter provides an important foundation for future empirical investigations.

REFERENCES

Ajzen, I. (1991). The theory of planned behavior. *Organizational Behavior and Human Decision Processes, 50*(2), 179–211. doi:10.1016/0749-5978(91)90020-T

Al Hadwer, A., Tavana, M., Gillis, D., & Rezania, D. (2021). A Systematic Review of Organizational Factors Impacting Cloud-based Technology Adoption Using Technology-Organization-Environment Framework. *Internet of Things, 15*(1), 100407. doi:10.1016/j.iot.2021.100407

Al-Ramahi, M., Elnoshokaty, A., El-Gayar, O., Nasralah, T., & Wahbeh, A. (2021). Public Discourse Against Masks in the COVID-19 Era: Infodemiology Study of Twitter Data. *JMIR Public Health and Surveillance, 7*(4), e26780. doi:10.2196/26780 PMID:33720841

Alloghani, M., Al-Jumeily, D., Mustafina, J., Hussain, A., & Aljaaf, A. (2020). A Systematic Review on Supervised and Unsupervised Machine Learning Algorithms for Data Science. In In M. Berry, A. Mohamed, & B. Yap (Eds.), Supervised and Unsupervised Learning for Data Science. Unsupervised and Semi-Supervised Learning. Springer. doi:10.1007/978-3-030-22475-2_1

Awa, H., Ojiabo, O., & Orokor, L. (2017). Integrated technology-organization-environment (T-O-E) taxonomies for technology adoption. *Journal of Enterprise Information Management, 30*(6), 893–921. doi:10.1108/JEIM-03-2016-0079

Awa, H., Ukoha, O., & Emecheta, B. (2016). Using T-O-E theoretical framework to study the adoption of ERP solution. *Cogent Business & Management, 3*(1), 1196571. doi:10.1080/23311975.2016.1196571

Basilio, M., Brum, G., & Pereira, V. (2020). A model of policing strategy choice. *Journal of Modelling in Management, 15*(3), 849–891. doi:10.1108/JM2-10-2018-0166

Basole, R., Seuss, C., & Rouse, W. (2013). IT innovation adoption by enterprises: Knowledge discovery through text analytics. *Decision Support Systems, 54*(2), 1044–1054. doi:10.1016/j.dss.2012.10.029

Bi, J., Liu, Y., Fan, Z., & Cambria, E. (2019). Modelling customer satisfaction from online reviews using ensemble neural network and effect-based Kano model. *International Journal of Production Research, 57*(22), 7068–7088. doi:10.1080/00207543.2019.1574989

Blei, D. (2012). Probabilistic topic models. *Communications of the ACM, 55*(4), 77–84. doi:10.1145/2133806.2133826

Blei, D., Ng, A., & Jordan, M. (2003). Latent dirichlet allocation. *Journal of Machine Learning Research*, *3*(1), 993–1022.

Brous, P., & Janssen, M. (2020). Trusted Decision-Making: Data Governance for Creating Trust in Data Science Decision Outcomes. *Administrative Sciences*, *10*(4), 81–99. doi:10.3390/admsci10040081

Chatterjee, S., Chaudhuri, R., & Vrontis, D. (2021). Does data-driven culture impact innovation and performance of a firm? An empirical examination. *Annals of Operations Research*, *302*(1). Advance online publication. doi:10.100710479-020-03887-z

Cybulski, J., & Scheepers, R. (2021). Data science in organizations: Conceptualizing its breakthroughs and blind spots. *Journal of Information Technology*, *36*(2), 154–175. doi:10.1177/0268396220988539

Daradkeh, M. (2019a). Critical Success Factors of Enterprise Data Analytics and Visualization Ecosystem: An Interview Study. *International Journal of Information Technology Project Management*, *10*(3), 34–55. doi:10.4018/IJITPM.2019070103

Daradkeh, M. (2019b). Determinants of Self-Service Analytics Adoption Intention: The Effect of Task-Technology Fit, Compatibility, and User Empowerment. *Journal of Organizational and End User Computing*, *31*(4), 19–45. doi:10.4018/JOEUC.2019100102

Daradkeh, M. (2019c). Determinants of visual analytics adoption in organizations: Knowledge discovery through content analysis of online evaluation reviews. *Information Technology & People*, *32*(3), 668–695. doi:10.1108/ITP-10-2017-0359

Daradkeh, M. (2019d). Understanding the Factors Affecting the Adoption of Project Portfolio Management Software Through Topic Modeling of Online Software Reviews. *International Journal of Information Technology Project Management*, *10*(3), 91–114. doi:10.4018/IJITPM.2019070106

Daradkeh, M. (2021a). Exploring the Usefulness of User-Generated Content for Business Intelligence in Innovation: Empirical Evidence From an Online Open Innovation Community. *International Journal of Enterprise Information Systems*, *17*(2), 44–70. doi:10.4018/IJEIS.2021040103

Daradkeh, M. (2021b). The Influence of Sentiment Orientation in Open Innovation Communities: Empirical Evidence from a Business Analytics Community. *Journal of Information & Knowledge Management*, *20*(3), 2150029. doi:10.1142/S0219649221500313

Daradkeh, M. (2022). Organizational Adoption of Sentiment Analytics in Social Media Networks: Insights from a Systematic Literature Review. *International Journal of Information Technologies and Systems Approach, 15*(1), 15–45.

Daradkeh, M., & Sabbahein, H. (2019). Factors Influencing the Adoption of Mobile Application Development Platforms: A Qualitative Content Analysis of Developers' Online Reviews. *International Journal of Enterprise Information Systems, 15*(4), 43–59. doi:10.4018/IJEIS.2019100103

Delone, W., & McLean, E. (2003). The DeLone and McLean Model of Information Systems Success: A Ten-Year Update. *Journal of Management Information Systems, 19*(4), 9–30. doi:10.1080/07421222.2003.11045748

Dhar, V. (2013). Data science and prediction. *Communications of the ACM, 56*(12), 64–73. doi:10.1145/2500499

Donoho, D. (2017). 50 Years of Data Science. *Journal of Computational and Graphical Statistics, 26*(4), 745–766. doi:10.1080/10618600.2017.1384734

Ergado, A., Desta, A., & Mehta, H. (2021). Determining the barriers contributing to ICT implementation by using technology-organization-environment framework in Ethiopian higher educational institutions. *Education and Information Technologies, 26*(3), 3115–3133. doi:10.100710639-020-10397-9

Fang, Y., Tang, K., Li, C., & Wu, C. (2018). On electronic word-of-mouth diffusion in social networks: Curiosity and influence. *International Journal of Advertising, 37*(3), 360–384. doi:10.1080/02650487.2016.1256014

Gartner. (2021). *2021 Magic Quadrant for Data Science and Machine Learning Platforms*. Retrieved from https://www.gartner.com/reviews/market/data-science-machine-learning-platforms

Ghaleb, E., Dominic, P., Fati, S., Muneer, A., & Ali, R. (2021). The Assessment of Big Data Adoption Readiness with a Technology–Organization–Environment Framework: A Perspective towards Healthcare Employees. *Sustainability, 13*(15), 8379.

Krippendorff, K. (2012). *Content analysis: An introduction to its methodology*. Sage.

Latif, S., Usman, M., Manzoor, S., Iqbal, W., Qadir, J., Tyson, G., ... Crowcroft, J. (2020). Leveraging Data Science to Combat COVID-19: A Comprehensive Review. *IEEE Transactions on Artificial Intelligence, 1*(1), 85–103. doi:10.1109/TAI.2020.3020521

Louro, A., Brandão, M., & Sincorá, L. (2020). Understanding the Self-Efficacy of Data Scientists. *International Journal of Human Capital and Information Technology Professionals*, *11*(2), 50–63. doi:10.4018/IJHCITP.2020040104

Medeiros, M., Hoppen, N., & Maçada, A. (2020). Data science for business: Benefits, challenges and opportunities. *The Bottom Line (New York, N.Y.)*, *33*(2), 149–163. doi:10.1108/BL-12-2019-0132

Medeiros, M., & Maçada, A. (2021). Competitive advantage of data-driven analytical capabilities: the role of big data visualization and of organizational agility. *Management Decision*. doi:10.1108/MD-12-2020-1681

Orji, I., Kusi-Sarpong, S., Huang, S., & Vazquez-Brust, D. (2020). Evaluating the factors that influence blockchain adoption in the freight logistics industry. *Transportation Research Part E, Logistics and Transportation Review*, *141*(1), 102025.

Oussous, A., Benjelloun, F., Ait Lahcen, A., & Belfkih, S. (2018). Big Data technologies: A survey. *Journal of King Saud University - Computer and Information Sciences, 30*(4), 431-448. doi:10.1016/j.jksuci.2017.06.001

Pateli, A., Mylonas, N., & Spyrou, A. (2020). Organizational Adoption of Social Media in the Hospitality Industry: An Integrated Approach Based on DIT and TOE Frameworks. *Sustainability*, *12*(17), 7132.

Provost, F., & Fawcett, T. (2013). Data Science and its Relationship to Big Data and Data-Driven Decision Making. *Big Data*, *1*(1), 51–59. doi:10.1089/big.2013.1508

Setiyani, L., & Rostiani, Y. (2021). Analysis of E-Commerce Adoption by SMEs Using the Technology - Organization - Environment (TOE) Model: A Case Study in Karawang, Indonesia. *International Journal of Science, Technology & Management, 2*(4), 1113-1132. doi:10.46729/ijstm.v2i4.246

Sharda, R., Delen, D., & Turban, E. (2021). *Analytics, Data Science, & Artificial Intelligence: Systems for Decision Support* (11th ed.). Pearson.

Sun, M., Chen, J., Tian, Y., & Yan, Y. (2021). The impact of online reviews in the presence of customer returns. *International Journal of Production Economics*, *232*(1), 107929.

Sun, S., Cegielski, C., Jia, L., & Hall, D. (2018). Understanding the Factors Affecting the Organizational Adoption of Big Data. *Journal of Computer Information Systems*, *58*(3), 193–203. doi:10.1080/08874417.2016.1222891

Tornatzky, L., & Fleischer, M. (1990). *The Process of Technology Innovation*. Lexington Books.

Vana, P., & Lambrecht, A. (2021). The Effect of Individual Online Reviews on Purchase Likelihood. *Marketing Science, 40*(4), 708–730. doi:10.1287/mksc.2020.1278

Vicario, G., & Coleman, S. (2020). A review of data science in business and industry and a future view. *Applied Stochastic Models in Business and Industry, 36*(1), 6–18.

Waller, M., & Fawcett, S. (2013). Data Science, Predictive Analytics, and Big Data: A Revolution That Will Transform Supply Chain Design and Management. *Journal of Business Logistics, 34*(2), 77–84.

Wimmer, H., & Aasheim, C. (2019). Examining Factors that Influence Intent to Adopt Data Science. *Journal of Computer Information Systems, 59*(1), 43–51. doi :10.1080/08874417.2017.1295790

Zhang, M., Fan, B., Zhang, N., Wang, W., & Fan, W. (2021). Mining product innovation ideas from online reviews. *Information Processing & Management, 58*(1), 102389.

Chapter 4
Securing Web Applications:
Security Threats and Countermeasures

B. M. Arifuzzaman
North South University, Bangladesh

S. M. Niaz Mahmud
North South University, Bangladesh

Ayman Muniat
North South University, Bangladesh

A. K. M. Bahalul Haque
ⓘD https://orcid.org/0000-0002-7942-0096
LUT University, Finland

ABSTRACT

Web-based services are common targets for hackers, and the need for ensuring their security keeps on rising. Attackers often take advantage of the vulnerabilities of different web applications using several mechanisms and thus steal and manipulate valuable information. Therefore, the attack vectors are also increasing since there is a wide variety of internet users. Exploitations caused by different types of cyberattacks results in data loss, identity theft, financial loss, and various other adversaries on both humans and infrastructure. Therefore, investigating various attack vectors and countermeasures can facilitate and encourage future research and create awareness among web application users and developers.

DOI: 10.4018/978-1-7998-9426-1.ch004

INTRODUCTION

The internet has now become an inevitable part of our life and is revolutionizing the world as we have never seen before (Haque et al., 2021a). Along with the internet, web-based applications are also gaining popularity as they offer services such as online shopping, online banking, and online courses. Such applications contain a variety of sensitive information that must be protected (Haque, 2019; Saini, 2019). Otherwise a hacker may exploit the confidential data which is not only a breach of privacy, but can also lead to the impersonation of users.

Unfortunately, cyber-attacks have become increasingly common in recent times. 2016 recorded over 229,000 web attacks every single day (Anonymous, 2016). As per (Eian et al., 2020), there are three factors that work behind the web security attacks. They are - spectacularity, vulnerability and the fear factor. Specularity implies that an attacker wants to gain from the damage incurred in an application. An individual or an organization going through losses can be an example. Namely, if a DoS attack was initiated, large e-commerce organizations such as Amazon, eBay or Walmart will go through massive losses in their sales. The second factor, vulnerability, refers to the loopholes or lack of sufficient system security. Some applications either do not take enough safety measures or may use an outdated framework, making them an easy prey for attacks. Finally, the fear factor insinuates that the attacker wants to terrorize the user. An example of such an attack could be ransomware attacks. Targeting the root factors may help in improving cyber security.

For securing web applications, we have to ensure the security of three major components - data integrity, data confidentiality and web application availability (Al-Khurafi et al., 2015).

There are many existing solutions that can be applied to each attack or more than one type of attack that comprise the aforementioned components. For example, for injection based attacks, mostly in SQLs, the counters include the 'trust no one' approach, avoiding dynamic SQL, reducing attack surface etc. For Cross Site Scripting (XSS) attacks, utilising Content Security Policy (CSP) and modern JavaScript frameworks are useful. In order to mitigate DoS/DDoS attacks, the attacks need to be detected as early as possible. Sahoo (2020), Haider (2020) have both been recently developed for detecting DDoS breaches. In case of ransomware attacks, Davies et al., (2020) illustrate the existing solutions. Other web attacks such as Format String Attack, Buffer Overflow etc. mandate well documented codes. Deep Learning has also been a recent trend for treating security attacks (Sharma et al., 2019).

However, the existing measures do not fully address all the security gaps. The paper aims to provide an overview of Web Application Security in order to bring the security issues to light and create a knowledge base for further research on securing web applications. It briefly discusses similar literature and goes in depth into the fundamentals of web security, various types of web attacks, their respective solutions, recent cyber-attacks. Contributions of this chapter is summarized as follows-

- Fundamentals of Web Security
- Attack Vectors / Types of Cyber Attacks
- State-of-the-art countermeasures
- Recent Cyber Attacks Statistics
- Future Research Agendas based on the current knowledge

The paper is organized in different sections where in Section 2, related works have been discussed. Section 3 outlines the fundamentals of web security and the categories of various attacks. Section 4, 5 and 6 explains the attack vectors, their countermeasures and the recent cyber-attacks respectively. Section 7 provides an insight into scope for future research and the following section concludes the article.

RELATED WORKS

In recent years, research and experimentation has been done on various existing web-based attacks and their solutions. Web services are often targeted for violating the network security and gaining access to sensitive information. E-commerce, banking, mailing etc. have all switched to online platforms and are now more vulnerable to security attacks. Singh et al. (2019) highlighted some of the existing attacks on web applications as well the mechanisms to prevent them. Cross-Site Scripting (XSS), Session Management, SQL Injection (SQLi), Authentication based Attacks, Input Validation attacks and Cross Site Request Forgery (CSRF) were reviewed thoroughly by the authors. A similar study was done by (Fredj et al., 2020), where the authors surveyed the top ten attacks made on web applications along with their protective techniques.The types of XSS attacks and all the tools and techniques used in detecting such attacks have been outlined in (Rodríguez et al., 2020). The authors concluded that there is an increasing preference of traditional methods to counter XSS attacks over the Artificial Intelligence approaches. However, deep learning techniques are also being implemented in hopes of tackling web attacks. A framework based on deep learning was proposed by (Tann et al., 2021) to filter out DDoS Attacks.

Another deep learning based technique to detect the web-server attacks, called ASCII Embedding was seen in (Jemal et al., 2020). The authors used an online real dataset CSIC 2010 and gained a pretty high accuracy in their experiment. As social media gain more popularity, they run the risk of being prone to attacks even more. The authors of (Sahoo et al., 2019) classified the types of security breaches on social networks and how they can be defended against. For the prevention of ransomware attacks on web servers, an explanation on how user search patterns and analysis of query logs can contribute to cyber attacks was provided in (Bansal et al., 2020). The writers provided a machine learning based model to detect such queries. Kaspersky security network and Sophos security threat reports have been highlighted in this study as well. Other notable security attacks such as SQL Injection, XML based attacks, Phishing Attacks etc. have recently been thoroughly studied to find possible solutions in (Alenezi, 2021; Gupta, 2020; Azeez, 2021). A brief summary of them is presented in Table 1.

Table 1. Overview of related works

Reference	Year	Objective
(Singh et al., 2019)	2019	Detailed explanation of prevailing web attacks and their counter mechanisms
(Fredj et al., 2020)	2020	Survey on the current top ten driven web application attacks and their preventive measures
(Rodríguez et al., 2020)	2020	Detection and prevention of all kinds of XSS attacks
(Tann et al., 2021)	2021	Applying Deep Learning for mitigating DDoS attacks on web services
(Jemal et al., 2020)	2020	Deep Learning based framework to detect web attacks
(Sahoo et al., 2019)	2019	Defending the existing attacks on online social networks
(Bansal et al., 2020)	2020	How web searches can lead to ransomware attacks
(Alenezi et al., 2021)	2021	Outlined Countermeasures for all layers of SQL Injections
(Gupta et al., 2020)	2020	Prevention of XML based attacks on web based applications
(Azeez et al., 2021)	2021	Proposed framework on phishing attacks

Most of the recent works on Web based attacks discussed each type of attack and how they can be mitigated. Newer kinds of security breaches keep coming as well as the need to find their countermeasures. Hence, researching cyber security is of great importance.

FUNDAMENTAL OF WEB APPLICATION SECURITY

Web applications that can be accessed from a web browser are created for getting necessary information without any issues. A web application consists of two things, frontend, and backend. The frontend is the web application design that users see, and the backend is the storage mechanism where precious data is stored. The main vulnerability remains in the backend of a web application. Attackers target databases to get those valuable data to blackmail, identity theft, steal money or assets, and sometimes confidential information from different organizations. Attacks differentiate in various categories, command-based attacks, network attacks, authentic-based attacks, and client-side attacks.

- Command-based attacks occur through inputting malicious scripts that allow an attacker to modify or harm the database (Su et al., 2006).
- Network attacks that appear bypassing network security mechanisms, attackers use this technique to disrupt services (Hoque et al., 2014).
- The authentic-based attack is performed by finding actual authentication details via miscellaneous methods (Raza et al., 2012).
- A client-side attack that harms users to gather valuable information. The main reason for these vulnerabilities is code imperfections (Kirda et al., 2006).

A web application contains millions of lines of codes written by several developers. Sometimes, it creates a loophole when they make mistakes or typos, allowing an attacker to access the database or administrator privileges. It may also happen during a software update in a web application. In a software update, developers fix previous bugs and add new features to keep up-to-date with the flow of time. This helps to keep the application from cyber threats, but while doing so, different bugs are created by the developer's faults.

However, all the web attacks do not happen at the developer's fault. Sometimes users do not follow basic security measures. Using poor passwords, not turning on two-step authentication, accessing web applications from public WiFi makes them more vulnerable because they do not understand the dangerous activity they are doing. An attacker may trick them to steal usernames and passwords and to get access to their account. Table 2 provides the idea of several vulnerabilities based on their attack type and the reasons behind those types of attacks.

The given table overviews the categories and causes of web vulnerabilities and thus covers all the fundamentals of web application security. A strongly secured web application can be developed by ensuring these bases.

Table 2. Name of different vulnerabilities according to the categories and reasons

Category	Name of the vulnerabilities	Reasons behind these vulnerabilities
Command executing attack (Khari et al., 2016)	SQL, Format String Attack, Buffer Overflow	Code flaws and bugs
Network attack (Sinha et al., 2017)	DoS/DDoS, Session Hijacking	Vulnerable network architecture
Authentic based (Jesudoss & Subramaniam, 2014)	Brute Force Attack	Ineffectual user security
Client side attack (Srokosz, 2018; Goswami, 2017)	LFI, RFI, CSRF, XSS, RCE	Poor database and web application developer

TYPES OF CYBER ATTACKS

A web application consists of different components that function jointly. Due to adequate coding standards, an attacker may perform attacks finding various vulnerabilities in the web applications. This section examines how the most common web application attacks occur.

SQL Injection

A SQL injection attack attempts to trick a web application into revealing data from its database by inserting some malicious code into the input fields on a web form. A common mistake that website developers make is writing queries that include user input without filtering or sanitizing it. For example, if they're expecting an integer but get text instead, this may allow the attacker to inject additional SQL commands.

Also, many developers write queries that allow the user input to select columns from a database and then use that input in a different question that inserts into or deletes from the database. This is very dangerous - again, imagine if the user enters text and this causes an integer comparison (for example, when you're expecting an integer). Now, let's suppose the attacker injects text into the database field. If this field is passed on to another database query, the SQL server will treat this injection as "equal" to zero (Ping-Chen, 2011, pp.4131-4135).

Local File Inclusion (LFI)

LFI is a security flaw in web applications that can be caused by mistakes made by a programmer if they inaccurately use the wrong character encoding while designing the web application. The most common mistake in a programmer's code is an error in opening a file. The vulnerability occurs when the site or application takes user input and then includes that input into a system command to read or write files on the server. If the website has been poorly programmed, it may also include all of the directories found on its file system, leading to directory traversal vulnerabilities.

When an application uses a local file as an input, it values this as trusted and safe. This means that hackers can easily manipulate the code. An attacker would then use this method to execute a malicious PHP script (Hubczyk et al., 2012).

Remote File Inclusion (RFI)

RFI is a web application vulnerability attack that targets external scripts, pictures, stylesheets, and other dynamically referenced files ("What is RFI | Remote File Inclusion Example & Mitigation Methods | Imperva", 2019). These attacks occur when attackers inject arbitrary code into the executed JavaScript or ImageFile components of web pages without user interaction. Remote File Include allows users to include remote executable commands within a maliciously crafted document via script tag injection by using scripting techniques described above. The result is that if it can invoke local administrative tasks such as run functions through JVM options instead from memory, all this will be done remotely while being hidden because its execution would only succeed after successful connection with the victim computer; further on, there are instructions how an attacker could perform RTF payloads, but we don't believe these have been leaked so far though we may find out soon (Robledo, 2008).

Denial of Service (DoS) and Distributed Denial of Service (DDoS)

DoS arises when the attacker can occupy all the web application's network resources so that other rightful users cannot access them. Different attackers have different motives, while the primary one is to prevent or discontinue the services. A variation of DoS attacks is DDoS, where many more machines are worked together. There are different kinds of DoS/DDoS attacks. Among them, crash attacks and flood attacks are the most common. The attacker examines the network's weakness, discovers the victim, and infects it with malicious code (Peng et al., 2007). The infected machine finds more victim devices and infects them, until a botnet is created. The whole attack consists of the attacker, master and slave shown in Fig. 1.0.

DoS/DDoS controls excess network traffic to fall the packets that surpass some threshold boundaries. Declining packets makes the user send a small number of packets. After that, the attacker increases its packet dropping rate and uses more memory space of the victim. So, the CPU gets conquered and can not do its normal operations, and rejects primary requests from allowed users (Mahjabin et al., 2017).

Figure 1. DDoS Attack

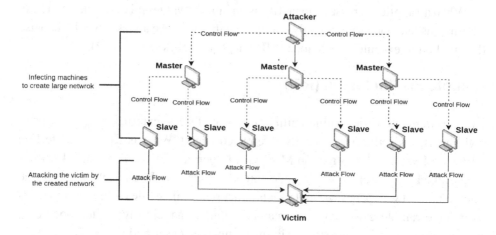

Cross Site Request Forgery (CSRF)

Whenever a user is requesting a web server, cookies are sent automatically. After that, the server can verify the login. A Cross Domain Access Control restricts one website to embedding another one into an iframe by following the same-origin policy. It is a security protocol that prevents an attacker's website from creating a random request to an arbitrary web server. When a user sends a request to an attacker's website, cookies are also sent. But by that protocol, re-request to another domain access created by the attacker is not possible. It will be allowed if it is in the same domain, same port, and same protocol it follows (Nagpal et al., 2017).

CSRF tricks the user into sending a malicious request using social engineering. It happens when one domain successfully forges requests to another domain to modify some value. It targets specific state changes such as username, password, or buying something in a web server. For example, while logging into that web server, a cookie is saved in the browser with the session id and other authentication information. To change a website's password, a user requires to send a request to the web server by clicking change password. It transmits a *POST* request to the web server that a user requested for a password change, and then it will update the password with the new one. But, when the same *POST* request is implanted into a pseudo link like xyz.com, and the user clicks it, the actual server will obtain the *POST* request, and the password will change. However, the user will think he clicked xyz.com to visit that website. Following this, xyz.com forges a password change request to the web server user was using.

Cross Site Scripting (XSS)

XSS permits an attacker to transfer malicious scripts to an undoubting user. This attack happens when the attacker gets control over a website's JavaScript, mainly via a fillable form (Cui et al., 2020). The user has no idea about the attack because he thinks that it came from a trusted website. JavaScript can control a website's view or data. When an attacker gets control over it, it injects some malicious code to get cookies, session tokens, and other precious data maintained by the browser and handled by that website.

Cookies can hold the information of users on how frequently they visit, sometimes their login information also. Suppose an attacker successfully injected a malicious script into a webpage that will give the user cookie information. So, whenever a user visits that web page, the attacker will get that user's information without notifying anything suspicious. There are primarily three varieties of XSS (Ambedkar et al., 2016).

1. **Reflected XSS:** In this type of XSS, the script comes from the victim's browser while visiting the webpage. For example: <script> alert("Hello") </script>
2. **Stored XSS:** In this type of XSS, the malicious script is stored in the database of that particular website, which can harm all the users of that website. For example: <script> alert(document.cookie)</script>
3. **DOM XSS:** This type of attack happens on the client-side. To access some data, the user gives some information in input, and after that, it responds in the browser like document.innerHTML. If it is vulnerable, the attacker can inject JavaScript code in this.

Remote Code Execution (RCE)

RCE is a type of cyberattack in which an attacker may run commands on another person's computer from afar. Browser exploitation, document exploitation, and network exploitation are three of the most frequent ways to do this. A remote user's administrative access to a susceptible system is frequently the goal of remote arbitrary code execution. The assault is frequently preceded by an information gathering attack, in which the attacker employs tools like an automated scanning tool to find the vulnerable software version (Biswas et al., 2018).

The most common way to get access to someone else's computer is by sending them a malicious email attachment or link that will trigger the exploit when they open it. The idea behind some kinds has been to allow attackers control over people who work with their own software before we even sign into their computers. For example, if there is a file in our system known as libopen, anybody could be given privileges based on what sort (or which libraries) those files use. With malware like Flamefish, the attacker will be able to find vulnerabilities within our operating systems.

Broken Authentication / Session Hijacking

The reason for this vulnerability is that developers frequently build custom authentication systems that contain security defects in areas such as password control, account update, logging out, timeouts, etc. To log into a website, a user needs to provide login information such as username and password. The web server creates an encoded session id (SID) and sends it back to the user device. By any chance, if an attacker sniffs the data, he can decode and change the authentication data to get the same access privilege of that user (Huluka et al., 2012).

Furthermore, to work conveniently, a user preserves the authentication data in a browser to avoid repeating putting user information and password. At that time, a web server authenticates the user via a cookie saved in the user device. That cookie also includes a SID, which helps the user recognize the exact user. If an attacker can sniff or predict that cookie while connecting with the web server, he can access the user account without any issue (Pannu & Kaur, 2014). This access can allow the attacker to collect or corrupt any sensitive data.

Format String Attack

The route of an application can change by the format string attacks. It uses the string formatting library of ANSI-C attributes to obtain other memory spaces (Cowan et al., 2001). Format string attack occurs when an attacker can evaluate the submitted data of an input string. An attacker can read data from the stack, cause segmentation problems, and execute code to crash the program (Nagpal et al., 2014).

Buffer Overflow

A buffer is a component of physical memory storage that temporarily holds data to move from one location to another. Buffer overflow attack arises when an attacker attempts to put more data in memory than its capability (Ruwase et al., 2004). A web application can be unavailable to use, crash the program, or corrupt valuable data by this attack. In a web application, sometimes there are some input boxes. The user will input some value to save in the memory. If an attacker can get the length of that input parameter that overflows the application, he can damage it severely.

Brute Force Attack

An attacker uses a brute force attack to access a web application by inputting a list of authentication credentials, such as username and password, until the correct one is identified (Bošnjak et al., 2018). A possible combination of all guesses is stored in a list, and then an intruder tries all the values one by one. After a successful match, the intruder can access that user account and harm in various ways, fow example stealing data, corrupting the data, or malware insertion. This guess can be performed simply if the credentials are not strong.

COUNTERMEASURES

To reduce damages from web attacks, it is necessary to know how to keep secure from those attacks. The following countermeasures can lessen the effectiveness of the attack conducted by the attacker.

SQL Injection

The best approach to avoid SQL injections is to utilize safe programming techniques such as parameterized queries (prepared statements) and stored procedures, making SQL injections impossible. Secure functions are available in every major programming language, and developers should only use them when working with databases (Alsobhi & Alshareef 2020). Data sanitization and validation are the most crucial safeguards in SQL injections, and they should already be in place. Sanitization usually entails passing any submitted data via a function to verify that no potentially harmful characters are given to a SQL query.

Trust No One: Assume that all user-provided data is harmful, and thoroughly examine and sanitize everything.

Avoid Dynamic SQL: Prepared statements, parameterized queries, and stored procedures should be used wherever practical.

Update and Patch: SQL injection vulnerabilities in apps and databases are constantly discovered; as a result, it's vital to apply patches and upgrades as soon as feasible.

Reduce Our Attack Surface: Remove any database capabilities we are not using to prevent hackers from taking advantage of them. For example, the XP cmd shell extended stored procedure in MS SQL opens a Windows command shell and accepts a text for execution, which a hacker would find helpful.

Query Comparison: These techniques make decisions about SQL statements at different stages, such as removing user characteristics from the query and comparing it to a preset one, detecting changes in the query's intent, sanitizing queries or inputs, and so on.

Testing / Attacking System using Automated Tools: These techniques exploit SQL injection vulnerabilities in the target system using automated tools or test case generators. These tools generate reports that help developers fix issues.

Local File Inclusion (LFI)

LFI is harmful, especially when paired with additional flaws, such as the ability of uploading malicious files to the server by an attacker. Even if the attacker cannot upload files, they can obtain sensitive information by combining the LFI weakness with a directory traversal flaw. So, Never trust user input to avoid LFI and many other security flaws. Use a safelist of authorized file names and locations to incorporate local files in the web application or website code. Ascertain that the attacker cannot use file upload functions to replace any of these files.

Here are a few techniques to avoid being a victim of an LFI attack:

ID Assignment: keep the file paths in a secure database and assign an ID to each; this way, users can only see their ID and not see or change the path.

Whitelisting: utilize whitelist files that have been validated and secured, and ignore everything else.

Use Databases: instead of putting files on a web server that may be hacked.

Better Server Instructions: instead of running files in a defined directory, the server automatically transmits download headers.

Remote File Inclusion (RFI)

As in all code injection attacks, RFI occurs when insecure data is allowed into a secure environment. Using arbitrary input data in a literal file, including a request, is the best way to avoid an RFI attack ("What is RFI | Remote File Inclusion Example & Mitigation Methods | Imperva", 2019).

Three key ways to prevent RFI attacks:

1. In a literal file, include requests; never utilize arbitrary input data.
2. To properly cleanse input parameters against potential file inclusions, use a filter.

3.   Create a dynamic safelist.

Denial of Service (DoS) / Distributed Denial of Service (DDoS)

Early threat detection is the most convenient way to limit DoS/DDoS attacks. Every large or small company web applications are a target of this attack; therefore, engineers and network administrators should monitor traffic in the network (Chouhan et al., 2013). Using an intrusion prevention and threat management system, along with some firewalls and anti-spam service, will alleviate the level of a DDoS attack (Naik et al., 2017). Practicing basic network security and maintaining robust network architecture is also essential for reducing harm.

Cross Site Request Forgery (CSRF)

CSRF attacks are successful when attackers can get cookie data or specific tokens via malicious script. So, the comprehensive prevention method of CSRF is to use random tokens that are not easy to guess. Unique tokens need to generate every form, so *POST* requests can not be validated via the same token. Tokens can be included in both cookie header and body to match because an attacker may only get the token of a cookie header, not the token in the user's web browser's body (Jovanovic et al., 2006). A re-authentication module can also prevent this attack. When a user makes essential changes in his account, retype password or one-time password method can prevent the attacker from making these changes. Limiting the authentication cookies lifetime can ensure to prevent this attack. The use of OAuth 2.0 explicitly identifies CSRF attacks. It forces the unauthorized user to perform an authorization via this application (Shernan et al., 2015).

Cross Site Scripting (XSS)

XSS happens when malicious code executes in the client's web server. The consequence of the XSS attack is severe, as it is a code injection attack on the client side. To prevent this, a developer should have basic knowledge about this attack. They should treat all the user input as a threat. Because attackers use those input fields to exploit this attack, for this verification is a must to prevent it. The use of encoding and escaping to prevent executing malicious code is client-side (Steinhauser et al., 2020). The existing library for escaping is enough to counter this. Using Content Security Policy (CSP) which constructs source authorize indexes for client side resources of the web application. CSP is one of the diverse HTTP Response Headers adopted in the latest time for excellent protection of communication over

HTTP and HTTPS protocols (Dolnák & Ivan, 2017). The use of modern JavaScript frameworks also helps to reduce it.

Remote Code Execution (RCE)

RCE attacks are complicated, and as recent findings in the field demonstrate, network vulnerabilities are continually evolving and bringing up new options for exploitation. The most effective cybersecurity approach for mitigating remote code execution risks prevents attackers from patching or installing software updates on time (Biswas et al., 2018).

Broken Authentication / Session Hijacking

To prevent session hijacking, credentials must be hashed or appropriately encrypted. There must be adequately robust cryptography. Key sizes smaller than 64 bits are too vulnerable, at most, 128 bits in size are advised since they are usually viewed as sufficiently strong to be secure for some period in the end (Murphey & Luke, 2005). Generating an arbitrary SID and deleting that after the user logs out from the device can also prevent this attack. Automatic logout after some period of time can also be implemented to provide an extra layer of security. It is also important for the developer to avoid viewing SID's from URLs. A developer should use the *POST* method instead of the *GET* method.

Format String Attack

The root cause of the format string attack is a code error. While building a program, a developer should be conscious of complicated functions and their usage. A programmer should not define a format string as an input but as a part of the program. Almost all of them are solved by setting "%s" as a format string and not using the data string as the format string (Li & Chiueh, 2007).

Buffer Overflow

The most effective way to prevent buffer overflow is to select a language that does not support it, for example, Python, Perl, Java, if possible. Fixing code flaws is also essential; while taking small input, a programmer should limit the buffer size for that input. Use of safe library modules, middleware libraries, source code scanning tools, compiler enhancement tools, patches to disable stack execution can mitigate this threat (Lhee et al., 2003).

Brute Force Attack

To keep safe from brute force attacks, a user has to choose passwords carefully. Sometimes people use identical passwords for various sites, which produces much more damage for the user—selecting a strong password that contains characters, numbers, a combination of upper and lowercase without using any direct word from the dictionary. Limiting login attempts, monitoring IP addresses, using the "Completely Automated Public Turing test to tell Computers and Humans Apart" (CAPTCHA) can prevent this crime from the web server (Powell et al., 2016).

Table 3 summarizes various attacks and countermeasures of web applications. The table illustrates the security difficulties of several web applications, attack strategies, effects, and possible solutions to prevent.

Table 3. Various web attacks analysis and possible solutions

Security Difficulties	Attack Strategies	Effects	Possible Solutions
SQL Injection ("What Is SQL Injection (SQLi) And How To Prevent Attacks.", 2020)	Malicious SQL queries were used to take control of the web application's database server.	Confidential data being deleted, lost, or stolen	Data sanitization, validation and utilize safe programming techniques.
LFI (Hassan et al., 2018)	By misusing the INCLUDE and REQUIRE functions in the web application's code, the attacker can include files or scripts on the web server.	Expose sensitive information	Whitelisting of authorized file names and locations to incorporate local files in the web application or website code.
RFI (Begum et al., 2016)	Web applications that dynamically reference external scripts are targets for attackers.	Remotely control user device	Using arbitrary input data in a literal file.
DoS/DDoS (Mahajan et al., 2013)	Flooding with packets to increase network traffic	Unable to service properly	Different filtering techniques, monitoring network packets, using strong network architecture
CSRF (Semastin et al., 2018)	Bypassing requests through user's browser	Sensitive data corruption	Random value encryption, unique token creation
XSS (Sarmah et al., 2018)	Putting malicious script in a trusted input field	Personal data stealing	Encoding and escaping, using CSP
RCE (Hassan et al., 2020)	An attacker can run server commands on a remote server	remotely execute commands on someone else's computing device	Updates are required for operating systems and third-party applications on a regular basis. To stop RCE attacks before they happen, a Cyber Threat Intelligence platform is essential. Block special characters and function names as much as possible.

continues on following page

Table 3. Continued

Security Difficulties	Attack Strategies	Effects	Possible Solutions
Broken Authentication / Session Management (Baitha, 2018; Dacosta, 2012)	Spoofing in the network to steal information via cookies	Full account privileges, sensitive data gathering	Arbitrary session management, implementing one time cookies
Format String Attack (Kilic et al., 2014)	Exploiting *printf* function by using arbitrary format specifier	Read private data, crash the program	Define the format function as a part of the program
Buffer Overflow (Kuperman et al., 2005)	Putting more data than its size	Program crash, data corruption	Fixing code flaws, using different modules
Bruteforce Attack (Gautam et al., 2015)	Guessing possible username and password	Personal data stealing or corrupting	Using strong password containing letters, numbers and symbols

RECENT CYBER ATTACKS

Web attacks cause service disruptions, shutdowns, and data theft and manipulation, generating an extensive loss of wealth. Cyber attack damage has been effectively out of control in recent years since hackers are increasingly targeting web applications more. Table 4 summarizes the overall attacks that happened over the last few years, along with the harm caused by the attackers.

Table 4. Summary of cyber attacks and damages occurred

Attack Name	Year	Description	Damage happened
AWS DDoS attacks ("Amazon 'thwarts largest ever DDoS cyber-attack'", 2020)	2020	AWS revealed the specifics of a Connectionless Lightweight Directory Access Protocol (CLDAP) Reflection attack that targeted one of their clients. The three-day assault peaked at 2.3 terabytes per second. AWS providing their "surface area of DDoS monitoring" in more detail offers information.	The attack lasted three days and peaked at 2.3 terabytes per second.
Freepik and Flaticon data breach via SQL injection (Gatlan, 2020)	2020	Hackers obtained emails and password hashes for 8.3 million Freepik and Flaticon users during a SQL injection attack on the company's Flaticon website, according to Freepik. Because they only utilized federated logins, 4.5 million of these 8.3 million users had no hashed password (Google, Facebook, and Twitter). These users' email addresses were the only information the attacker obtained from them.	8.3 million Freepik and Flaticon users' emails and passwords were stolen.

continues on following page

Table 4. Continued

Attack Name	Year	Description	Damage happened
British Airways data breach ("British Airways fined £20m over data breach", 2018)	2018	Magecart, a hacking organization, was suspected of being involved in the incident. Magecart is well-known for obtaining private payment card information using card skimming techniques. A malicious library was used to exploit a cross-site scripting vulnerability. For their malicious server, the attackers even purchased a security certificate (SSL).	Affected 380,000 booking transactions between August to September 2018
Brute-force attack WordPress sites (Javier, 2017)	2017	According to Wordfence, the brute-force attacks peaked at 14.1 million requests per hour. Almost 10,000 different IP addresses sent brute-force queries to about 190,000 WordPress websites every hour.	Over 190,000 WordPress sites are being targeted every hour in a brute-force attack.
DDoS via IoT botnets (Balaban, 2016)	2016	For the first time in October 2016, DDoS attackers used poorly secured IoT equipment to launch attacks. This assault was predicted to have a power of more than 1Tbps. It brought down Reddit, Spotify, CNN and the New York Times websites, as well as a slew of other well-known sites.	The attack's power was estimated to be greater than 1Tbps.
DDoS attacks: Thousands of CCTV devices hacked (Constantin, 2016)	2016	More than 25,000 digital video recorders and CCTV cameras have been hacked, and attackers are exploiting them to perform distributed denial-of-service (DDoS) assaults against websites.	25,000 digital video recorders.
Yahoo's security breached (Ngak, 2012; Yap, 2012)	2012	According to Yahoo, a cyber group has stolen 450,000 user credentials from Yahoo!. The logins were allegedly obtained from Yahoo! Voices, a Yahoo! subdomain. The group got over Yahoo's security by using a "union-based SQL injection method.".	Stolen 450,000 login credentials
MySQL.com compromised (Dede, 2011)	2011	A hacker used SQL blind injection to get access to the official MySQL webpage. During the attack, hackers were able to obtain 47 databases on an Apache Web Server that included usernames, database schemas, and passwords, as well as specific table and column names.	The data was being sold in Russian cyber-forums for $3,000 US.
7-eleven breach (Zetter, 2010)	2010	Using SQL injection, a gang of hackers broke into corporate networks at several companies, including the 7-Eleven convenience store chain, and stole 130 million credit card numbers.	130 million credit card details

FUTURE RESEARCH DIRECTIONS

Though there are many preventive mechanisms to alleviate damages from those cyberattacks, there remain many holes. Improvement defensive tools are also facing attacks every day, which brings new defensive policies.

Machine Learning Based Approaches

The machine learning approach in blocking different attacks is increasing nowadays. Researchers are working to improve the accuracy in intrusion detection for blocking DDoS attacks. One of the algorithms tries to classify genuine network traffic with traffic that occurs during a DDoS attack using the D-FAC method (Behal et al., 2021). Another work is going on to detect and mitigate DDoS through IoT servers. They are using SDELM model for detecting the attacks (Ravi et al., 2020). Some researchers are working on SD-IoT controller (Yin et al., 2018), REATO framework (Sicari et al., 2018). to detect and mitigate DDoS. But none of these works actually applied in real applications. More work is going on in detecting CSRF into the Machine Learning (ML) and Deep Learning (DL) approaches. But the outcome of that approach is meager, and experimental evaluation is not ensuring all sorts of security functionalities (Calzavara et al., 2019). Machine learning approaches are also being welcomed to relieve XSS attacks. One of the approaches used different *POST* and *GET* methods by crawling websites. After preprocessing, they trained with CNN and classified the output. Accuracy is 99%; still, it is not applied in any real-world application. However, in real-world application how the program will work needs to be examined by executing (Akaishi et al., 2019).

Blockchain Technology

Blockchain has become a prevalent technology in different aspects of life using various types of applications (Haque, 2020, 2021b). Use of blockchain technology for database security preventing SQL injection. Though theoretically, no virtual attack is possible, practically an attack in the blockchain system in 2017 created trouble for the researchers (Sinha et al., 2021). Many Blockchain based techniques have been studied for the prevention of DDoS attacks (Singh et al., 2020). There are some loopholes and the solutions are still in their infancy but improvements are going on to make a more robust system through blockchain.

Fuzzy Systems

Fuzzy systems are being recently looked onto for possibly providing the solutions to the existing web attacks. A DDoS attack detection technique using fuzzy logic and entropy was presented by the authors of (Ates et al., 2020). The authors used Fuzzy c-means clustering to detect whether the port numbers or IP addresses tend to be in the same cluster or not. Based on this, they have outlined the attack and attack free model. Another fuzzy logic based solution to SQLi attacks was proposed in (Nofal et al., 2020). C-means was used in the paper for the detection and prevention of SQL Injections. Even though the proposed frameworks were pretty impressive, a full-proof implementation is yet to be done.

Deep Learning, Blockchain and Fuzzy Logic are all emerging trends for the solution of numerous web attacks. There is yet to be an accurate model for preventing any attack, but these technologies have shown promise for counteracting the different security threats over the traditional measures. More studies are needed for the mentioned techniques and therefore, they could be a great research area. Besides, as new technologies and new types of web services are developed, brand new kinds of security threats arise. There will be need to do proper experimentation on each new web application in order to prevent more malicious attacks. Thus, web security issues will require further research for a long time to come.

CONCLUSION

As web applications keep on rising to meet the needs of the modern world, there is a need for strongly secured web based platforms. There are still some loopholes for which cyber-attacks are still very much prevalent. All possible measures must be taken for avoiding any attack. It is extremely important to emphasize proper coding practices as well as cover the required techniques to maintain the integrity and confidentiality of the web applications. Users also need to take care of some fundamental security measures on their part. Newer technologies like Blockchain or Fuzzy logic must be researched more for tackling the web application vulnerabilities. Owing to the fact that web applications are privy to the sensitive information of the users as well as huge amounts of transactions, ensuring their security has to be the top most priority. Hence, this paper surveys some of the current web-attacks along with their defense mechanisms and future research scope. Utilizing any of the mentioned methods or working on new frameworks based on the referred studies can definitely help in minimizing the number of security attacks.

REFERENCES

Akaishi, S., & Uda, R. (2019). Classification of XSS attacks by machine learning with frequency of appearance and co-occurrence. In *2019 53rd Annual Conference on Information Sciences and Systems (CISS)* (pp. 1-6). IEEE.

Al-Khurafi, O. B., & Al-Ahmad, M. A. (2015). Survey of web application vulnerability attacks. In *2015 4th International Conference on Advanced Computer Science Applications and Technologies (ACSAT)* (pp. 154-158). IEEE. 10.1109/ACSAT.2015.46

Alenezi, M., Nadeem, M., & Asif, R. (2021). SQL injection attacks countermeasures assessments. *Indonesian Journal of Electrical Engineering and Computer Science, 21*(2), 1121–1131.

Alsobhi, H., & Alshareef, R. (2020). SQL Injection Countermeasures Methods. In *2020 International Conference on Computing and Information Technology (ICCIT-1441)* (pp. 1-4). IEEE.

Amazon 'thwarts largest ever DDoS cyber-attack'. (2020). *BBC News*. Retrieved 3 November 2021, from https://www.bbc.com/news/technology-53093611

Ambedkar, M. D., Ambedkar, N. S., & Raw, R. S. (2016). *A comprehensive inspection of cross site scripting attack. In 2016 international conference on computing, communication and automation (ICCCA)*. IEEE.

Anonymous. (2016). Retrieved 6 November 2021, from https://insights.cynergistek.com/infographics/symantec-s-2016-internet-security-threat-report

Ates, C., Özdel, S., & Anarim, E. (2020). Graph-based fuzzy approach against DDoS attacks. *Journal of Intelligent & Fuzzy Systems*, 1–10.

Azeez, N., Misra, S., Margaret, I. A., & Fernandez-Sanz, L. (2021). Adopting Automated Whitelist Approach for Detecting Phishing Attacks. *Computers & Security*.

Baitha, A. K., & Vinod, S. (2018). Session Hijacking and Prevention Technique. *International Journal of Engineering & Technology, 7*(2.6), 193-198.

Balaban, D. (2016). *The History and Evolution of DDoS Attacks - Embedded Computing Design*. Embedded Computing Design. Retrieved 3 November 2021, from https://www.embeddedcomputing.com/technology/security/network-security/the-history-and-evolution-of-ddos-attacks

Bansal, C., Deligiannis, P., Maddila, C., & Rao, N. (2020). Studying ransomware attacks using web search logs. In *Proceedings of the 43rd International ACM SIGIR Conference on Research and Development in Information Retrieval* (pp. 1517-1520). ACM.

Begum, A., Hassan, M. M., Bhuiyan, T., & Sharif, M. H. (2016). RFI and SQLi based local file inclusion vulnerabilities in web applications of Bangladesh. In *2016 International Workshop on Computational Intelligence (IWCI)* (pp. 21-25). IEEE.

Behal, S., Kumar, K., & Sachdeva, M. (2021). D-FAC: A novel φ-Divergence based distributed DDoS defense system. *Journal of King Saud University-Computer and Information Sciences*, *33*(3), 291–303.

Biswas, S., Sajal, M. M. H. K., Afrin, T., Bhuiyan, T., & Hassan, M. M. (2018). A study on remote code execution vulnerability in web applications. *International Conference on Cyber Security and Computer Science (ICONCS 2018)*.

Biswas, S., Sajal, M. M. H. K., Afrin, T., Bhuiyan, T., & Hassan, M. M. (2018). A study on remote code execution vulnerability in web applications. *International Conference on Cyber Security and Computer Science (ICONCS 2018)*.

Bošnjak, L., Sreš, J., & Brumen, B. (2018). Brute-force and dictionary attack on hashed real-world passwords. In *2018 41st international convention on information and communication technology, electronics and microelectronics (mipro)* (pp. 1161-1166). IEEE.

British Airways fined £20m over data breach. (2018). Retrieved 7 January 2022, from https://www.bbc.com/news/technology-54568784

Calzavara, S., Conti, M., Focardi, R., Rabitti, A., & Tolomei, G. (2019). Mitch: A machine learning approach to the black-box detection of CSRF vulnerabilities. In *2019 IEEE European Symposium on Security and Privacy (EuroS&P)* (pp. 528-543). IEEE.

Chouhan, V., & Peddoju, S. K. (2013). Packet monitoring approach to prevent DDoS attack in cloud computing. *Int. J. Comput. Sci. Electr. Eng.*, *1*(2), 2315–4209.

Constantin, L. (2016). *Thousands of hacked CCTV devices used in DDoS attacks*. Computerworld. Retrieved 3 November 2021, from https://www.computerworld.com/article/3089365/thousands-of-hacked-cctv-devices-used-in-ddos-attacks.html

Cowan, C., Barringer, M., Beattie, S., Kroah-Hartman, G., Frantzen, M., & Lokier, J. (2001). FormatGuard: Automatic Protection From printf Format String Vulnerabilities. In *USENIX Security Symposium* (*Vol. 91*). Academic Press.

Cui, Y., Cui, J., & Hu, J. (2020). A survey on xss attack detection and prevention in web applications. In *Proceedings of the 2020 12th International Conference on Machine Learning and Computing* (pp. 443-449). Academic Press.

Dacosta, I., Chakradeo, S., Ahamad, M., & Traynor, P. (2012). One-time cookies: Preventing session hijacking attacks with stateless authentication tokens. *ACM Transactions on Internet Technology*, *12*(1), 1–24.

Davies, S. R., Macfarlane, R., & Buchanan, W. J. (2020). Evaluation of live forensic techniques in ransomware attack mitigation. *Forensic Science International: Digital Investigation, 33*, 300979.

Dede, D. (2011). *MySQL.com compromised*. Sucuri Blog. Retrieved 3 November 2021, from https://blog.sucuri.net/2011/03/mysql-com-compromised.html

Dolnák & Ivan. (2017). Content security policy (csp) as countermeasure to cross site scripting (xss) attacks. In *2017 15th International Conference on Emerging eLearning Technologies and Applications (ICETA)* (pp. 1-4). IEEE.

Eian, I. C., Yong, L. K., Li, M. Y. X., Qi, Y. H., & Fatima, Z. (2020). *Cyber attacks in the era of covid-19 and possible solution domains*. Academic Press.

Fredj, O. B., Cheikhrouhou, O., Krichen, M., Hamam, H., & Derhab, A. (2020). An OWASP top ten driven survey on web application protection methods. In *International Conference on Risks and Security of Internet and Systems* (pp. 235-252). Springer.

Gatlan, S. (2020). *Freepik data breach: Hackers stole 8.3M records via SQL injection*. BleepingComputer. Retrieved 3 November 2021, from https://www.bleepingcomputer.com/news/security/freepik-data-breach-hackers-stole-83m-records-via-sql-injection

Gautam, T., & Jain, A. (2015). Analysis of brute force attack using TG—Dataset. In *2015 SAI Intelligent Systems Conference (IntelliSys)* (pp. 984-988). IEEE.

Goswami, S., Hoque, N., Bhattacharyya, D. K., & Kalita, J. (2017). An Unsupervised Method for Detection of XSS Attack. *International Journal of Network Security, 19*(5), 761–775.

Gupta, C., Singh, R. K., & Mohapatra, A. K. (2020). A survey and classification of XML based attacks on web applications. *Information Security Journal: A Global Perspective, 29*(4), 183-198.

Haider, S., Akhunzada, A., Mustafa, I., Patel, T. B., Fernandez, A., Choo, K. K. R., & Iqbal, J. (2020). A deep CNN ensemble framework for efficient DDoS attack detection in software defined networks. *IEEE Access: Practical Innovations, Open Solutions, 8*, 53972–53983. doi:10.1109/ACCESS.2020.2976908

Haque, A. B., Bhushan, B., & Dhiman, G. (2021a). Conceptualizing smart city applications: Requirements, architecture, security issues, and emerging trends. *Expert Systems: International Journal of Knowledge Engineering and Neural Networks*. doi:10.1111/exsy.12753

Haque, A. B., Islam, A. N., Hyrynsalmi, S., Naqvi, B., & Smolander, K. (2021b). GDPR compliant Blockchains–A systematic literature review. *IEEE Access: Practical Innovations, Open Solutions.*

Haque, A. K. M. (2019). *Need for Critical Cyber Defence, Security Strategy and Privacy Policy in Bangladesh–Hype or Reality? International Journal of Managing Information Technology*, 11.

Haque, A. K. M., & Rahman, M. (2020). *Blockchain Technology: Methodology, Application and Security Issues.* arXiv preprint arXiv:2012.13366.

Hassan, M. M., Bhuyian, T., Sohel, M. K., Sharif, M. H., & Biswas, S. (2018). SAISAN: An automated Local File Inclusion vulnerability detection model. *IACSIT International Journal of Engineering and Technology*, 7(2-3), 4.

Hassan, M. M., Mustain, U., Khatun, S., Karim, M. S. A., Nishat, N., & Rahman, M. (2020). Quantitative Assessment of Remote Code Execution Vulnerability in Web Apps. In *InECCE2019* (pp. 633–642). Springer.

Hoque, N., Bhuyan, M. H., Baishya, R. C., Bhattacharyya, D. K., & Kalita, J. K. (2014). Network attacks: Taxonomy, tools and systems. *Journal of Network and Computer Applications*, *40*, 307–324.

Hubczyk, M., Domanski, A., & Domanska, J. (2012). Local and remote file inclusion. In *Internet-Technical Developments and Applications 2* (pp. 189–200). Springer.

Huluka, D., & Popov, O. (2012). Root cause analysis of session management and broken authentication vulnerabilities. In *World Congress on Internet Security (WorldCIS-2012)* (pp. 82-86). IEEE.

Javier, A. (2017). *A History of WordPress Security Exploits and What They Mean.* WPMU DEV Blog. Retrieved 3 November 2021, from https://wpmudev.com/blog/wordpress-security-exploits/

Jemal, I., Haddar, M. A., Cheikhrouhou, O., & Mahfoudhi, A. (2020). ASCII embedding: an efficient deep learning method for web attacks detection. In *Mediterranean Conference on Pattern Recognition and Artificial Intelligence* (pp. 286-297). Springer.

Jesudoss, A., & Subramaniam, N. (2014). A survey on authentication attacks and countermeasures in a distributed environment. *Indian Journal of Computer Science and Engineering*, *5*(2), 71–77.

Jovanovic, N., Kirda, E., & Kruegel, C. (2006). *Preventing cross site request forgery attacks. In 2006 Securecomm and Workshops.* IEEE.

Khari, M., & Sangwan, P. (2016). Web-application attacks: A survey. In *2016 3rd International Conference on Computing for Sustainable Global Development (INDIACom)* (pp. 2187-2191). IEEE.

Kilic, F., Kittel, T., & Eckert, C. (2014). Blind format string attacks. In *International Conference on Security and Privacy in Communication Networks* (pp. 301-314). Springer.

Kirda, E., Kruegel, C., Vigna, G., & Jovanovic, N. (2006). Noxes: a client-side solution for mitigating cross-site scripting attacks. In *Proceedings of the 2006 ACM symposium on Applied computing* (pp. 330-337). ACM.

Kuperman, B. A., Brodley, C. E., Ozdoganoglu, H., Vijaykumar, T. N., & Jalote, A. (2005). Detection and prevention of stack buffer overflow attacks. *Communications of the ACM, 48*(11), 50–56.

Lhee, K. S., & Chapin, S. J. (2003). Buffer overflow and format string overflow vulnerabilities. *Software, Practice & Experience, 33*(5), 423–460.

Li, W., & Chiueh, T. C. (2007). Automated format string attack prevention for win32/x86 binaries. In *Twenty-Third Annual Computer Security Applications Conference (ACSAC 2007)* (pp. 398-409). IEEE.

Mahajan, D., & Sachdeva, M. (2013). DDoS attack prevention and mitigation techniques-a review. *International Journal of Computers and Applications, 67*(19).

Mahjabin, T., Xiao, Y., Sun, G., & Jiang, W. (2017). A survey of distributed denial-of-service attack, prevention, and mitigation techniques. *International Journal of Distributed Sensor Networks, 13*(12).

Murphey & Luke. (2005). Secure Session Management: Preventing Security Voids in Web Applications. The SANS Institute, 29.

Nagpal, B., Chauhan, N., & Singh, N. (2017). SECSIX: Security engine for CSRF, SQL injection and XSS attacks. *International Journal of System Assurance Engineering and Management, 8*(2), 631–644.

Nagpal, N. B., & Nagpal, B. (2014). Preventive measures for securing web applications using broken authentication and session management attacks: A study. *International Conference on Advances in Computer Engineering and Applications (ICACEA)*.

Naik, N., Jenkins, P., Cooke, R., Ball, D., Foster, A., & Jin, Y. (2017). Augmented windows fuzzy firewall for preventing denial of service attack. In *2017 IEEE International Conference on fuzzy systems (FUZZ-IEEE)* (pp. 1-6). IEEE.

Ngak, C. (2012). *Yahoo reportedly hacked: Is your account safe?* Cbsnews.com. Retrieved 4 November 2021, from https://www.cbsnews.com/news/yahoo-reportedly-hacked-is-your-account-safe/

Nofal, D. E., & Amer, A. A. (2020). SQL Injection Attacks Detection and Prevention Based on Neuro—Fuzzy. *Machine Learning and Big Data Analytics Paradigms: Analysis, Applications and Challenges, 77*, 93.

Pannu & Kaur. (2014). A Survey on Web Application Attacks. *International Journal of Computational Science.*

Peng, T., Leckie, C., & Ramamohanarao, K. (2007). Survey of network-based defense mechanisms countering the DoS and DDoS problems. *ACM Computing Surveys, 39*(1), 3.

Ping-Chen, X. (2011). SQL injection attack and guard technical research. *Procedia Engineering, 15*, 4131–4135.

Powell, B. M., Kumar, A., Thapar, J., Goswami, G., Vatsa, M., Singh, R., & Noore, A. (2016). A multibiometrics-based CAPTCHA for improved online security. In *2016 IEEE 8th International Conference on Biometrics Theory, Applications and Systems (BTAS)* (pp. 1-8). IEEE.

Ravi, N., & Shalinie, S. M. (2020). Learning-driven detection and mitigation of DDoS attack in IoT via SDN-cloud architecture. *IEEE Internet of Things Journal, 7*(4), 3559–3570.

Raza, M., Iqbal, M., Sharif, M., & Haider, W. (2012). A survey of password attacks and comparative analysis on methods for secure authentication. *World Applied Sciences Journal, 19*(4), 439–444.

Robledo, H. F. G. (2008). Types of Hosts on a Remote File Inclusion (RFI) Botnet Symposium conducted at the meeting of the CERMA'08 Electronics. *Robotics and Automotive Mechanics Conference.*

Rodríguez, G. E., Torres, J. G., Flores, P., & Benavides, D. E. (2020). Cross-site scripting (XSS) attacks and mitigation: A survey. *Computer Networks, 166*, 106960.

Ruwase, O., & Lam, M. S. (2004). A Practical Dynamic Buffer Overflow Detector. In NDSS (Vol. 2004, pp. 159-169). Academic Press.

Sahoo, K. S., Tripathy, B. K., Naik, K., Ramasubbareddy, S., Balusamy, B., Khari, M., & Burgos, D. (2020). An evolutionary SVM model for DDOS attack detection in software defined networks. *IEEE Access: Practical Innovations, Open Solutions, 8*, 132502–132513. doi:10.1109/ACCESS.2020.3009733

Sahoo, S. R., & Gupta, B. B. (2019). Classification of various attacks and their defence mechanism in online social networks: A survey. *Enterprise Information Systems*, *13*(6), 832–864.

Saini, H., Bhushan, B., Arora, A., & Kaur, A. (2019). Security vulnerabilities in Information communication technology: Blockchain to the rescue (A survey on Blockchain Technology). In *2019 2nd International Conference on Intelligent Computing, Instrumentation and Control Technologies (ICICICT)* (Vol. 1, pp. 1680-1684). IEEE.

Sarmah, U., Bhattacharyya, D. K., & Kalita, J. K. (2018). A survey of detection methods for XSS attacks. *Journal of Network and Computer Applications*, *118*, 113–143.

Semastin, E., Azam, S., Shanmugam, B., Kannoorpatti, K., Jonokman, M., Samy, G. N., & Perumal, S. (2018). Preventive measures for cross site request forgery attacks on Web-based Applications. *IACSIT International Journal of Engineering and Technology*.

Sharma, A., Singh, A., Sharma, N., Kaushik, I., & Bhushan, B. (2019). Security countermeasures in web based application. In *2019 2nd International Conference on Intelligent Computing, Instrumentation and Control Technologies (ICICICT)* (Vol. 1, pp. 1236-1241). IEEE.

Shernan, E., Carter, H., Tian, D., Traynor, P., & Butler, K. (2015). More guidelines than rules: CSRF vulnerabilities from noncompliant OAuth 2.0 implementations. In *International Conference on Detection of Intrusions and Malware, and Vulnerability Assessment* (pp. 239-260). Springer.

Sicari, S., Rizzardi, A., Miorandi, D., & Coen-Porisini, A. (2018). REATO: REActing TO Denial of Service attacks in the Internet of Things. *Computer Networks*, *137*, 37–48.

Singh, A., Sharma, A., Sharma, N., Kaushik, I., & Bhushan, B. (2019). Taxonomy of attacks on web based applications. In *2019 2nd International Conference on Intelligent Computing, Instrumentation and Control Technologies (ICICICT)* (Vol. 1, pp. 1231-1235). IEEE.

Singh, R., Tanwar, S., & Sharma, T. P. (2020). Utilization of blockchain for mitigating the distributed denial of service attacks. *Security and Privacy*, *3*(3), e96.

Sinha, K., & Verma, M. (2021). The Detection of SQL Injection on Blockchain-Based Database. In *Revolutionary Applications of Blockchain-Enabled Privacy and Access Control* (pp. 234–262). IGI Global.

Sinha, P., Jha, V. K., Rai, A. K., & Bhushan, B. (2017). Security vulnerabilities, attacks and countermeasures in wireless sensor networks at various layers of OSI reference model: A survey. In *2017 International Conference on Signal Processing and Communication (ICSPC)* (pp. 288-293). IEEE.

Srokosz, M., Rusinek, D., & Ksiezopolski, B. (2018). A new WAF-based architecture for protecting web applications against CSRF attacks in malicious environment. In *2018 Federated Conference on Computer Science and Information Systems (FedCSIS)* (pp. 391-395). IEEE.

Steinhauser, A., & Tůma, P. (2020). Database Traffic Interception for Graybox Detection of Stored and Context-Sensitive XSS. *Digital Threats. Research and Practice*, *1*(3), 1–23.

Su, Z., & Wassermann, G. (2006). The essence of command injection attacks in web applications. *ACM SIGPLAN Notices*, *41*(1), 372–382.

Tann, W. J. W., Tan, J. J. W., Purba, J., & Chang, E. C. (2021). Filtering DDoS Attacks from Unlabeled Network Traffic Data Using Online Deep Learning. In *Proceedings of the 2021 ACM Asia Conference on Computer and Communications Security* (pp. 432-446). ACM.

What Is S. Q. L. Injection (SQLi) And How To Prevent Attacks. (2020). Retrieved 4 November 2021, from https://www.acunetix.com/websitesecurity/sql-injection/

What is RFI | Remote File Inclusion Example & Mitigation Methods | Imperva. Learning Center. (2019). Retrieved 3 November 2021, from https://www.imperva.com/learn/application-security/rfi-remote-file-inclusion/

Yap, J. (2012). *450,000 user passwords leaked in Yahoo breach*. ZDNet. Retrieved 4 November 2021, from https://www.zdnet.com/article/450000-user-passwords-leaked-in-yahoo-breach/

Yin, D., Zhang, L., & Yang, K. (2018). A DDoS attack detection and mitigation with software-defined Internet of Things framework. *IEEE Access: Practical Innovations, Open Solutions*, *6*, 24694–24705.

Zetter, K. (2010). Hacker Sentenced to 20 Years for Breach of Credit Card Processor. *Wired*. Retrieved 4 November 2021, from https://www.wired.com/2010/03/heartland-sentencing/

Chapter 5
Sign of the Times:
Sentiment Analysis on Historical Text and the Implications of Language Evolution

Tyler W. Soiferman
Stevens Institute of Technology, USA

Paul J. Bracewell
DOT Loves Data, New Zealand

ABSTRACT

Natural language processing is a prevalent technique for scalably processing massive collections of documents. This branch of computer science is concerned with creating abstractions of text that summarize collections of documents in the same way humans can. This form of standardization means these summaries can be used operationally in machine learning models to describe or predict behavior in real or near real time as required. However, language evolves. This chapter demonstrates how language has evolved over time by exploring historical documents from the USA. Specifically, the change in emotion associated with key words can be aligned to major events. This research highlights the need to evaluate the stability of characteristics, including features engineered based on word elements when deploying operational models. This is an important issue to ensure that machine learning models constructed to summarize documents are monitored to ensure latent bias, or misinterpretation of outputs, is minimized.

DOI: 10.4018/978-1-7998-9426-1.ch005

INTRODUCTION

Data, as a commodity, is often touted as the new oil. Highly accessible via the World Wide Web, the written word is a type of data that is especially prevalent and potent. However, people can describe similar things with different words, writing styles and documents of varying length. Summarizing this content manually is not scalable.

Technological developments provide the ability to process massive amounts of unstructured data with the intent of automatically and consistently extracting latent patterns. Text mining is the process of transforming unstructured text into a structured format consumable within machine learning frameworks. The imposition of structure upon text then enables features to be engineered which enable meaningful patterns and new insights to be identified.

More specifically, Natural Language Processing (NLP) can be used to summarize the themes quickly and efficiently within a corpus. NLP refers to the branch of computer science concerned with creating abstractions of text that summarize collections of documents in the same way humans can. This form of standardization means these summaries can be used operationally in machine learning models to describe or predict behavior in real or near real time as required.

With the ability to summarize collection of documents at scale, there are myriad applications of this technology. As Vajjala et. al. (2020) outlined, the past decade's breakthroughs in research regarding NLP stem from increased processing power, accessibility of digitized text, as well as algorithmic enhancement to have greater generalizability and interpretability. These advancements have resulted in NLP being increasingly used in a range of diverse domains such as retail, healthcare, finance, law, marketing, human resources and many more.

A common NLP technique is sentiment analysis, which is often used to draw sentiments from text such as customer reviews or social media posts. This functionality enables businesses to efficiently analyze unstructured data that pertains to their company, leading them to conclusions about, for example, their reputation, or the overall reaction to a product.

Sentiment analysis is a family of techniques that assign polarity scores to natural language. Typically, it is treated as a supervised machine learning problem. Example sentences are supplied that have been labelled as "positive" and "negative". Given sufficient training data, learning algorithms can distinguish positive from negative language. Positive language use scores above 0.0, and negative language scores below 0.0. Importantly, digital delivery of news reporting and sports commentary provides a wealth of accurately time-stamped textual data that can be easily indexed via technological means.

Bracewell et. al. (2016) outlined a method for quantifying the collective mood of New Zealanders using mainstream online news content. Mood is quantified using a text mining pipeline built with the Natural Language Toolkit (Bird, 2009) in Python to measure the sentiment of articles and comments. Intervention analysis was applied to identify statistically significant events which cause a permanent shift in the quantified mood. Their two-step process showed a statistically significant, positive shift in the mood of New Zealanders after their national team, the All Blacks, won the 2015 Rugby World Cup, with victory over Australia.

Bracewell et. al. (2019) extended this approach further by linking the sentiment about athletes with on-field performance. They argued that popular opinions of sports teams and players can be shaped by myriad influences, including player performance and media descriptions. The media has a substantial role in describing events for the purpose of informing and entertaining. Previous work in team sports, such as rugby (Simmonds, et. al., 2018) and cricket (McIvor et. al., 2018) demonstrated that the sentiment and themes within written commentary is statistically significantly associated with match outcomes and in-game events. Their intent was to understand the association between mainstream media and individual player performance. Knowledge of this association would be useful for reputation management and player welfare, especially from a mental health perspective. They were able to demonstrate that there is a meaningful relationship between on-field performance and online reactions. Importantly, a player's playing reputation has the greatest impact on a player's online profile, in terms of the number of articles and sentiment.

These examples show the potency of NLP. A simple query with any search engine for *NLP examples* will reveal a multitude of tutorials and exemplar code to enable interested parties to undertake NLP themselves. Furthermore, the number of digitized historical documents has increased rapidly during the last a few decades, spawning research into methods for information retrieval and knowledge extraction (Martinek, 2020). With data and methods for processing that data readily accessible, it is no surprise to see the explosion in use cases for NLP (Vajjala et. al., 2020).

However, this ease of access to data and technology is cause for concern. Of great importance is that the meanings of words can change over time, as can the associated sentiment. This has obvious implications for the application of NLP and sentiment analysis to interpret and derive insight about collections of documents. This places pressure on the potential operational deployment of trained models as language evolution may change the interpretation and applicability of a training NLP model.

Therefore, the intent of this chapter is to demonstrate how language has evolved over time, which serves as a reminder to evaluate the stability of characteristics, including features engineered based on word elements, when deploying operational NLP models. This is an important issue to ensure that machine learning models constructed to summarize documents are monitored to ensure latent bias, or misinterpretation of outputs, is minimized. Despite the advancements in machine learning and artificial intelligence, this chapter reinforces the requirement to understand the source and latent purpose of the data used to construct autonomous models. Indeed, the emergence of new phrasing and evolving sentiment (Martínek et. al., 2020) requires continual updating and training of algorithms that leverage outputs from natural language processing.

A practical application demonstrates the evolution of how words are used using text mined from the web. Interesting insight about how and why words change is contrasted against a backdrop of world events to help connect sentiment with the period in question.

BACKGROUND

Sentiment analysis can be applied to various groupings of text to draw revealing analyses from these data. Historians often must sift through many historical documents to draw conclusions about what these papers may reveal about the times from which they came. Sentiment analysis allows for timely and scalable analyses of large groupings of text, which can prove useful when analyzing historical text over several centuries.

To investigate how sentiment analysis can be used to draw analyses from historical text and, more specifically, how sentiment analysis can reveal changes in language usage over time, this chapter intends to undertake sentiment analysis on American documents from 1600-2009. The process of rating the sentiments associated with a document effectively scales and normalizes documents. The quantitative data that is output enables meaningful comparisons across decades. This then enables how perceptions regarding key words have evolved over time, thereby reinforcing the need to explore the stability of the characteristics embedded in operational NLP models to ensure latent bias is not introduced to the system.

Importantly, while sentiment analysis is used for commercial or marketing purposes today, its uses are not limited to consumer reviews and news articles. Analysis of historical documents is performed in various fields and industries, such as law, politics, and historical preservation, to contextualize the events and language that is used in the text. This analysis and contextualization can provide key insights into the times from which the documents came from; however, this process may take a lengthy amount of time depending on the number of documents. A sentiment analysis of many documents is efficient and can allow one to observe key analyses of historical text, which reveal how language usage and sentiment change over time in correlation with real world events that unfold at the time the documents originate from. While sentiment analysis and natural language processing can be used for historical text just as it is used for modern documents, there could be differences and limitations pertaining to its usage for older corpuses; at the same time, NLP functionalities can be utilized to demonstrate language evolution over time.

NLP can assist historians in sifting through and identifying key information from texts. Pettersson (2018) outlined the example of a historian looking to extract verb phrases from historical texts using tagging and parsing. Tagging and parsing is an NLP functionality that involves representing features of words (for example, parts of speech) and organizing said terms into segments to analyze their structures (Schweinberger, 2020). Pettersson (2018) described how this process is more difficult to execute when it comes to some historical texts, listing some of the aspects of historical texts that may interfere with NLP functionality, such as: "different, and inconsistent spelling, different vocabulary…inconsistent use of punctuation, different syntax and inconsistent word order…differences between texts from different time periods, genres, and authors". Unconventional spelling makes textual analysis difficult as well.

To effectively analyze historical documents using NLP functionality, these issues, and specifically inconsistent spelling, should be resolved if present. As a solution to the issue, Pettersson (2018) suggested two main solutions, those being to train a tagger/parser on historical data, or to undergo spelling normalization, which involves "automatically translating the original spelling to a more modern spelling, before performing tagging and parsing". Spelling normalization involves correcting spelling errors and inconsistencies within text. "Non-standard words occur in many text genres such as advertisements, SMS, texts on social media sites, historical texts and student writings (Hong, 2018)". There are several methods that can be utilized to correct these errors that are not exclusive to historical texts. There are four main methods to correct these spelling inconsistencies (Pettersson, 2018; Hong, 2018). Rule-based normalization involves employing manually crafted normalization standards based on "known language changes and/or empirical findings".

Levenshtein-based normalization uses an edit-distance strategy and compares the historical word to a word in a modern dictionary that is closest to the historical term (Petterson, 2018). Memory-based normalization utilizes a dictionary, with the historical words acting as the keys and the modern words as the values. Finally, SMT-based normalization involves "translation based on character sequences rather than words and phrases". Using NLP functionalities on historical text can be more involved compared to analyzing a modern corpus. Depending on the corpus and the time from which it came, more effort may be required to clean the text when analyzing historical documents and amend inconsistencies in spelling.

While NLP at times has its limitations when applied to historical text, its functionalities can help to reveal how the English language has changed over the years, illuminating how words have taken on different meanings and spellings over time. Hamilton et. al. (2016) focused on "the semantic evolution of more than 30,000 words across 4 languages". As a result of their research, they found that language seems to follow two laws. They proposed that words evolve according to the "law of conformity" and the "law of innovation". The law of conformity states that "words that are used more frequently change less and have meanings that are more stable over time"; while the law of innovation states that "words that are polysemous (have many meanings) change at faster rates". To conduct their study, they used six data sets from four languages that took from various sources and spanned from, at the earliest, 1800, and at the latest, 2009. Different methods were used to construct their historical word embeddings for each period. Word embeddings are vectors that represent how frequently a word occurs with other words (Schweinberger, 2020). A common method for use in calculating word embeddings was the positive pointwise mutual information (PPMI) method, which measures the association between words.

PPMI also replaces negative values with zeros, which leads to better performance and a representation that highlights positive word co-occurrence correlations instead of negative correlations (Hamilton et. al, 2016).

That research demonstrated how several terms' meanings evolved over time and the rate of change of high frequency words and polysemous word PPMI. From a technical perspective, the key finding was that NLP, and more specifically, word embeddings and PPMI, could be utilized to show how language evolves over time.

Hamilton et. al. (2016) summarized the evolution of a sample of words. For example, *awful* has evolved from meaning "impressive\majestic" prior to 1800 to "disgusting\mess" in modern times (Simpson et. al., 1989). *Nice* has moved from "refined\dainty" circa 1890 to being "pleasant\lovely" (Wijaya et. al., 2021). Around 1950 saw the shift in usage of *gay* to mean "happy\showy" to "homosexual\lesbian" (Kulkarni et. al., 2014). *Fatal* has shifted from "fate\inevitable" prior to 1800 to be associated with "illness\lethal" (Jatowt et. al., 2014).

APPLICATION TO HISTORICAL DATA

In this chapter, the work of Hamilton et. al. (2016) is extended to consider the sentiment associated with selected words. The rationale for exploring the sentiment associated with key words is that this becomes a contextual guide regarding the intended meaning and interpretation of that word in that era. Thus, the associated sentiment reveals clues as to how the word should be interpreted in that context.

A sentiment analysis was performed on historical texts from the United States spanning from 1600-2009, where the corpuses were split initially century and then by decade to make alignment with major world events relevant., whilst maintaining sufficient coverage of documents per period.

DATA AND TECHNOLOGY

The text was split into documents within the corpus by paragraphs and headings. These historical documents came from various container websites (The Avalon Project, 2008; Eidenmuller, 2001-2021; Eisenhower Presidential Library, 2021; Miller Center, 1993; Miller Center, 1998; Schulman, 2021; University of Groningen, 1994-2012; WGBH Educational Foundation, 1995-2011; Wilson, 2021).

Each century's corpus was loaded into R from a .txt file containing the documents. Digitization of historical texts enables relatively easy access to topics of interest.

The packages used in R were tidyverse, readr, tidytext, zoo, Hmisc, sentimentr, SnowballC, ggplot2, tm, and dplyr. Each corpus was then cleaned: numbers, punctuation, whitespace, stop words were removed, and the text was transformed to lowercase. A similar approach is outlined by Schweinberger (2021). Indeed, the description of code supplied by Schweinberger (2021) make this type of analysis easily replicable.

RESULTS

The first step cleaned and processed the corpuses; subsequently, a sentiment analysis was performed on the historical texts, and the resulting data frame showed the words, the century they came from, the number of words in the century corpus, and the sentiment of the word (if one was analyzed). The results were then summarized, showing the centuries, the sentiments analyzed in the corpuses, the sentiment frequency (how many words were analyzed to have this sentiment in the century corpus), the number of words in the century corpus, and the "percentage," calculated by dividing the sentiment frequency and the total number of words in the century corpus.

As shown in Figure 1, "Trust" sentiment is the most prevalent in all the corpuses, independent of the century; this may be because the documents analyzed incorporated language and rhetoric that conveyed a sense of formality and assurance to the audience.

Next, the "score" of the three words that contribute the most to each core emotion categories were calculated. The "score" is the proportion between the number of times the tracked word occurs in the century corpus where its sentiment is the tracked sentiment, to the number of words in the corpus whose sentiment is the tracked sentiment; the core emotions tracked were anger, fear, trust, joy, anticipation, surprise, and disgust.

Figure 1. Bar graph showing several words and their percentages (sentiment frequency divided by total number of words in the decade corpus) for each century (1600s-2000s)

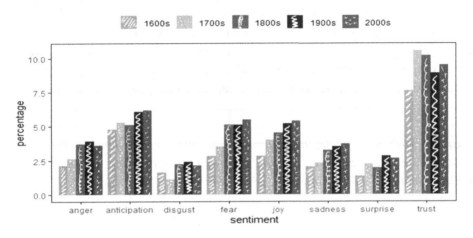

The results show the centuries, their top three words for each emotion category, the sentiment (emotion), the number of times the word occurs in the century corpus, and the score. These trends show how a sentiment analysis can reveal changes in the usage of language, and how these changes correlate with events that occurred during the time of the change. Importantly, the techniques described, and their application are applicable for those performing NLP on data from different time periods. In addition, the changes in the emotion associated with a term serves as a convenient reminder to evaluate the origins of a dataset to ensure appropriate conclusions can be derived.

From Figure 2, "government" had one of the top three scores for the "fear" sentiment in each century, suggesting "government" often had a fearful connotation in these corpuses. Another observation was "money" had one of the top three scores for several different sentiments from the 1600s to the 1900s: in the 1600s for "anger" and "surprise"; in the 1700s for "anger" (with a score of over 50%), "joy," and "surprise"; in the 1800s for "anger"; and in the 1900s for "anger" (with a score of over 60%), "trust," "joy," "anticipation," and "surprise."

The complexity of "money" and the emotions associated with the term are depicted in Figure 2. While some may perceive money to be "joyful," a sentiment analysis of documents from several centuries reveals that money is often strongly associated with "anger." In the 1800s, which included debates over slavery and the Civil War, "congress" had a score of nearly 70% for the "disgust" sentiment, demonstrating the prevalence of the term being used with a connotation of revulsion, most likely due to the heated political climate in America at the time. Additionally, the second highest scoring word for "disgust" in the century was "slavery," once again leading one to see that the issue of slavery was a, if not the, major topic of the century in the United States, where many felt a strong abhorrence towards the matter. In the 2000s, when terrorism was a major topic in the United States, "terrorism" had one of the top three scores for the "anger" sentiment in the century corpus, once again demonstrating how a sentiment analysis can lead one to observe and infer topics within corpuses from different time periods, as well as connotations around various words, and how those topics and connotations have changed with time.

Figure 2. Word profiling depicting the centuries, the top three-four words for each emotion category in each century, the sentiment (emotion), and the score (for an enlarged image of the axis of words, see figure 2a)

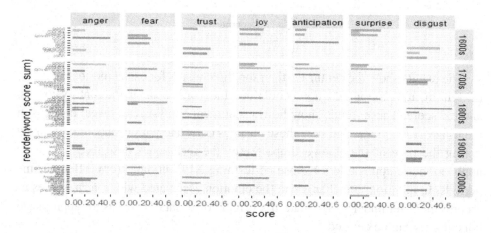

Figure 3. Enlarged image of the axis of words from figure 2

<u>1600s</u>: good, money, present, government, court, time, god, lord, governor, offender, sir, john

<u>1700s</u>: good, money, present, government, court, time, war, lord, treat, possession, assembly, majesty, vote, fire

<u>1800s</u>: good, money, masters, government, court, congress, words, slavery, wealth, law, public, united, labor, true, case, tribunal

<u>1900s</u>: good, money, government, time, congress, war, words, evil, nation, young, boy, enemy

<u>2000s</u>: good, government, time, congress, war, god, freedom, words, terrorist, nation, white, liberty, death, president, fight, hope

To further observe a sentiment analysis' ability to reveal how language usage changes over time, text from 1600-2009 was split into decade corpuses, excluding the 1650s and the 1740s, as no documents were analyzed from those periods. The text was again split into documents within the corpuses by paragraphs and/or headings. The corpuses were processed in the same manner. The scores were recalculated; the results showed the centuries, the words for each emotion category (not just the top three), the sentiment (emotion), the number of times the word occurs in the century corpus, and the score. Additionally, the proportion between the number of times the tracked word occurs in the century corpus where its sentiment is the tracked sentiment and the number of documents in the decade corpus was included, to account for the differing number of documents included in each decade corpus. Figure 3 is a bubble graph which tracks the scores of the words "god," "government," "powerful," and "war", where their sentiment was "fear", by decade.

Figure 4. Bubble graph portraying the score for a subset of words from 1600-2009 where the sentiment analyzed is fear

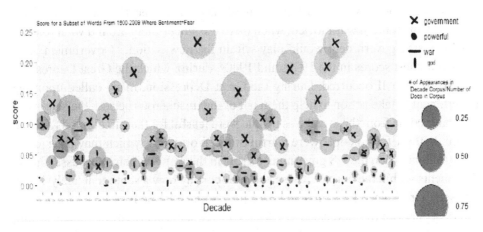

The USA Department of Veterans Affairs has supplied a comprehensive list of casualties by American conflicts (https://www.va.gov/opa/publications/factsheets/fs_americas_wars.pdf). Twardos (2011) describes the timeline of the United States deadliest war. This data provides important context for interpreting emotions associated with war by showing a timeline of when the US was at war. This is a crucial step in understanding the nuances of data that is gathered.

While not a USA conflict, the English Civil War occurred during the 1640s, when the score for "war" was at one of its highest points, depicted by the bubble graph. The other highest point for "war" during the first two centuries analyzed was during the 1750s, when the French and Indian War occurred. The score for "war" increased from the 1760s to the 1770s, which was when the Revolutionary War took place. During the 1800s, "war" had highpoints around the War of 1812 and during the Civil War, while also scoring high around the Mexican-American War. The highest point for "war" during the 1900s was around World War I and increased again during World War II. The score sharply increased during the 2000s as well, when the Iraq War took place.

These trends show how a sentiment analysis can reveal changes in the usage of language, and how these changes correlate with events that occurred during the time of the change. Consider the score for "god", which was at its highest during the 1630s. This was a time when Puritans were colonizing New England. According to an article entitled "People & Ideas: The Puritans" from PBS, Puritans were Calvinists, and "Calvin taught that God was all-powerful and completely sovereign," (People & Ideas). One can infer the Puritans spoke of "god" with a fearful connotation, as evidenced by their beliefs, and the sentiment analysis.

The score for "powerful" was at its highest during 1700-1709, however the term did not appear to be very prevalent throughout the centuries in general.

The score for "government" was at its highest during the 1790s, a period right after the Constitution was ratified, when there was uncertainty around what role the newly created government would play within the new nation. "Government" had its next highest scores in the 1930s and 1940s, during which the Great Depression and World War II occurred. During the Great Depression, many called upon the government to take action to help them out of the treacherous period; the sentiment may have come from these calls, as people were fearful for their livelihoods and the future. In the 1940s, people were fearful of the World War, which may have led to a fearful tone when the US government's role in the war was being discussed in the documents within the corpus. These analyses portray how a sentiment analysis can be used to track specific words and their prevailing sentiment at the time.

Most importantly, this analysis of the associated sentiment and emotion regarding key words found in American historical documents revealed that the perceptions around words evolved. NLP seeks to leverage those perceptions to draw inferences regarding documents at scale. Consequently, as language and perceptions evolve, caution must be used when interpreting and deploying NLP based models. These results highlight the importance of understanding the source and characteristics of data.

FUTURE ANALYSES

To understand the stability of features engineered from text, the intent is to explore the applicability of characteristics such as the population stability index (PSI). The PSI measures how much a variable has shifted in distribution between two samples or over time. It is widely used for monitoring changes in the characteristics of a population and for diagnosing possible problems in model performance. This approach is commonly used within credit risk to determine if there has been significant change between the sample a model was constructed on and the current population of interest. The intent would be to compare the PSI for engineered features from text when models were developed compared with the most recent text presented to an operational model.

CONCLUSION

NLP is a popular and accessible set of techniques for processing data. However, the ease of access to data and technology requires greater consideration about the evolving meaning of words. Lack of regard to language evolution can lead to biased or erroneous conclusions.

As the meanings of words can change over time, as well as the associated sentiment, this has implications for the application of NLP and sentiment analysis to interpret and derive insight about collections of documents. As demonstrated in this chapter, sentiment analysis is a convenient tool for analyzing many historical documents. A practical application exploring historical American documents revealed the evolution of how words are used and potentially interpreted. Interesting insight about how and why words change was contrasted against a backdrop of world events to help connect sentiment with the period in question. Word connotations and sentiment prevalence were used to contextualize historical text within the time it came from. These observations reveal how language usage changes over the course of several centuries, and how words can serve as a sign of the times. The results revealed that there was at times a correlation between the score/prevalence of emotions and historical events happening during the period in which the increased or decreased score/prevalence was observed.

The change in interpretation of words is an important issue to ensure that machine learning models constructed to summarize documents are monitored to ensure latent bias, or misinterpretation of outputs, is minimized. Despite the advancements in machine learning and artificial intelligence, this chapter reinforces the requirement to understand the source and latent purpose of the data used to construct autonomous models. Indeed, the emergence of new phrasing and evolving sentiment requires continual updating and training of algorithms that leverage outputs from natural language processing.

This places pressure on the potential operational deployment of trained models as language evolution may change the interpretation and applicability of a training NLP model. Therefore, this chapter has demonstrated how language has evolved over time, which serves as a reminder to evaluate the stability of characteristics, including features engineered based on word elements, when deploying operational NLP models.

REFERENCES

Bird, S., Klein, E., & Loper, E. (2009). *Natural Language Processing with Python*. O'Reilly Media.

Bouchet-Valat, M. (2020). *SnowballC: Snowball Stemmers Based on the C 'libstemmer' UTF-8 Library*. R package version 0.7.0. https://CRAN.R-project. org/package=SnowballC

Bracewell, P. J., Hilder, T. A., & Birch, F. (2019). Player ratings and online reputation in super rugby. *Journal of Sport and Human Performance*, 7(2).

Bracewell, P. J., McNamara, T. S., & Moore, W. E. (2017). How Rugby Moved the Mood of New Zealand. *Journal of Sport and Human Performance*, 4(4).

Eidenmuller, M. E. (2001-2021). Rhetorical Literacy: 49 Important Speeches in 21st Century America. *American Rhetoric*. https://www.americanrhetoric. com/21stcenturyspeeches.html

Eisenhower Presidential Library. (2021). *Speeches*. Dwight D. Eisenhower Presidential Library, Museum & Boyhood Home. https://www.eisenhowerlibrary. gov/eisenhowers/speeches

Feinerer, I., & Hornik, K. (2020). *tm: Text Mining Package*. R package version 0.7-8. https://CRAN.R-project.org/package=tm

Feinerer, I., Hornik, K., & Meyer, D. (2008). Text Mining Infrastructure in R. *Journal of Statistical Software*, 25(5), 1–54. doi:10.18637/jss.v025.i05

Hamilton, W. L., Leskovec, J., & Jurafsky, D. (2016). Diachronic Word Embeddings Reveal Statistical Laws of Semantic Change. *ACL 2016*. https://arxiv.org/pdf/1605.09096.pdf

Harrell, F. E. (2021). *Hmisc: Harrell Miscellaneous. R package version 4.5-0.* https://CRAN.R-project.org/package=Hmisc

Hong, Y. (2018). *Spelling Normalization of English Student Writings* [Unpublished Master's Thesis]. Uppsala University. http://uu.divaportal.org/smash/get/diva2:1251763/FULLTEXT01.pdf

Jatowt, A., & Duh, K. (2014). A framework for analyzing semantic change of words across time. In *Proceedings of ACM/IEEE-CS Conference on Digital Libraries* (pp 229–238). IEEE Press. 10.1109/JCDL.2014.6970173

Jeffers, R., & Lehiste, I. (1979). *Principles and Methods for Historical Linguistics.* MIT Press.

Martínek, J., Lenc, L., & Král, P. (2020). Building an efficient OCR system for historical documents with little training data. *Neural Computing & Applications, 32*(23), 17209–17227. doi:10.100700521-020-04910-x

McIvor, J. T., Patel, A. K., Hilder, T., & Bracewell, P. J. (2018) Commentary sentiment as a predictor of in-game events in T20 cricket. *Proceedings of the 14th Australian Conference on Mathematics and Computers in Sports*, 44-49.

Miller Center. (1993). *January 5, 1993: Address at West Point.* UVA | Miller Center, Rector and Visitors of the University of Virginia, https://millercenter.org/the-presidency/presidential-speeches/january-5-1993-address-west-point

Miller Center. (1998). *March 25, 1998: Remarks to the People of Rwanda.* UVA | Miller Center, Rector and Visitors of the University of Virginia, https://millercenter.org/the-presidency/presidential-speeches/march-25-1998-remarks-people-rwanda

Pettersson, E. (2018). *NLP for Historical (Or Very Modern) Text.* Uppsala University, Language Technology: Research and Development. https://cl.lingfil.uu.se/~nivre/master/fou-historical.pdf

Rinker, T. W. (2019). *sentimentr: Calculate Text Polarity Sentiment version 2.7.1.* https://github.com/trinker/sentimentr

Schulman, M. (2021). Missouri vs. Holland [1920]. *History Central.* https://www.historycentral.com/documents/MissourivsHolland.html

Schweinberger, M. (2020). *Semantic Vector Space Models in R.* The University of Queensland. https://slcladal.github.io/svm.html

Schweinberger, M. (2021). *Sentiment Analysis in R.* The University of Queensland. https://slcladal.github.io/sentiment.html

Silge, J., & Robinson, D. (2016). tidytext: Text Mining and Analysis Using Tidy Data Principles in R. *Journal of Open Source Software, 1*(3), 37. doi:10.21105/joss.00037

Simmonds, P. P., McNamara, T. S., & Bracewell, P. J. (2018). Predicting win margins with sentiment analysis in international rugby. *Proceedings of the 14th Australian Conference on Mathematics and Computers in Sports*, 137-142.

Simpson, J. A., & Weiner, E. (1989). *The Oxford English Dictionary* (Vol. 2). Clarendon Press.

The Avalon Project. (2008). *Yale Law School Lillian Goldman Law Library.* https://avalon.law.yale.edu/default.asp

Twardos, M. (2011). *Timeline of the United States Most Deadly Wars.* The Information Diet.

University of Groningen - Humanities Computing. (1994-2012). *"Documents" American History from Revolution to Reconstruction and Beyond.* http://www.let.rug.nl/usa/documents/

WGBH Educational Foundation. (1995-2011). *People & Ideas: The Puritans.* PBS, WGBH Educational Foundation, 1995-2011. https://www.pbs.org/wgbh/pages/frontline/godinamerica/people/puritans.html

Wickham, H. (2016). *ggplot2: Elegant Graphics for Data Analysis.* Springer-Verlag.

Wilson, T. (2021). *Barack Obama: 'A common dream born of two continents', Democratic National Convention - 2004.* Speakola. https://speakola.com/political/barack-obama-keynote-dnc-2004

Wickham, H., François, R., Henry, L., & Müller, K. (2021). *dplyr: A Grammar of Data Manipulation. R package version 1.0.6.* https://CRAN.R-project.org/package=dplyr

Wickham, H., & Hester, J. (2020). *Readr: Read Rectangular Text Data. R package version 1.4.0.* https://CRAN.R-project.org/package=readr

Wickham. (2019). Welcome to the tidyverse. *Journal of Open Source Software, 4*(43), 1686.

Wijaya, D. T., & Yeniterzi, R. (2011). Understanding semantic change of words over centuries. In *Proceedings of the Workshop on Detecting and Exploiting Cultural Diversity on the Social Web* (pp. 35–40). ACM.

Vajjala, S., Majumder, B., Gupta, A., & Surana, H. (2020). *Practical Natural Language Processing: A Comprehensive Guide to Building Real-World NLP Systems.* O'Reilly Media. doi:10.1145/2064448.2064475

Kulkarni, V., Al-Rfou, R., Perozzi, B., & Skiena, S. (2014). Statistically significant detection of linguistic change. *Proceedings of International World Wide Web Conference Committee (IW3C2)*, 625–635.

Zeileis, A., & Grothendieck, G. (2005). zoo: S3 Infrastructure for Regular and Irregular Time Series. *Journal of Statistical Software*, *14*(6), 1–27. doi:10.18637/jss.v014.i06

Chapter 6
Combating the Phishing Attacks:
Recent Trends and Future Challenges

Sonia Tasmin
North South University, Bangladesh

Asma Khanam Sarmin
North South University, Bangladesh

Mitul Shalehin
North South University, Bangladesh

A. K. M. Bahalul Haque
ⓘD https://orcid.org/0000-0002-7942-0096
LUT University, Finland

ABSTRACT

The phishing attack targets the client's email and any other connection medium to illicitly get the user credentials of e-commerce websites, educational websites, banks, credit card information, and other crucial user information. Exploitations caused by different types of cyberattacks result in data loss, identity theft, financial loss, and various other adversaries on both human and infrastructure. Therefore, investigating the threats and vulnerabilities on web applications and analysis of recent cyberattacks on web applications can also provide a holistic scenario about the recent security standpoint. Therefore, in this chapter, phishing attack techniques and their current scenario will be discussed extensively. Moreover, recent phishing techniques will be discussed to understand the severity of this type of attack. Finally, this chapter will outline the proposed and existing countermeasures for protecting users' identities and credentials from the phishing technique.

DOI: 10.4018/978-1-7998-9426-1.ch006

INTRODUCTION

Cyber Security refers to the process of defending cyberspace from threats (Iwendi et al., 2020, Rehman et al., 2020). It is concerned with maintaining, limiting, and retrieving all internet-connected resources from cyber-attacks (Javed et al., 2020, Mittal et al., 2021). The complexity of the cybersecurity domain grows by the day, making it difficult to identify, explain, and monitor the relevant risk events. In this process, some cyber professionals are always trying to protect computer systems from cyberattacks. Nowadays, cyberattacks target corporations, private systems, and various attacks are also increasing day by day. According to the former CEO of CISCO, two types of companies are threatened by cyber security. One has already been attacked, and the other one has not been hacked yet. Cyber-attack is one kind of malicious attack where attackers try to gain data, disrupt digital operations or damage sensitive information in an unauthorized way (Tweneboah-Koduah et al., 2017). Among numerous cyberattacks, phishing has become one of the most threatening offenses in the Internet world. The term phishing was first introduced in 1996, and it has evolved since then (Gupta et al., 2018). It refers to a social engineering crime that aims to seize crucial and personal information such as username, password, bank and transaction card details of users.

The approaches to phishing attack techniques that create a trap for the user over email, SMS, social networking sites, and other websites have evolved over the years. The types of phishing are deceptive, malware-based, DNS-based, and content-injection phishing (Ali, 2017, Chaudhry et al., 2016). The most common path is via Email, where attackers provide the hyperlink to update their information (Halevi et al., 2015). In this case, they create an interface that looks real, and users think the message comes from a trusted sender. As users engage with other works, they do not notice the minor significant differences. As a result, they become phishing victims as they often download malware unknowingly on their computers. On the other hand, phishers can get access to a variety of information with our password. In this case, when a user uses unsecured WIFI in a public place, attackers create a barrier between the visitor and the network using malware to install software that helps transmit the personal data to the attacker (Gupta et al., 2018). There is also an underground market where phishers can purchase and sell their phishing tools and users' valuable information (Ramzan, 2010). Phishers use several phishing tools and techniques such as Email Phishing, Clone Phishing, SMS Phishing, Voice Phishing, Software Phishing, and Websites Phishing. The latest techniques of phishing are WI-FI Phishing, Cross-site Scripting, and Domain Phishing (Singh et al., 2019, Sharma et al., 2019).

A single approach does not define phishing; instead, it can be considered a collection of approaches as every attacker works differently and uses different methods. Since there are several phishing techniques, detection must be done efficiently to protect our information. The first step to creating protection against phishing attacks is detection, followed by countermeasures. Detection can be done either by users' awareness or by software-based solutions. The user's detection side can be implemented by training them to recognize phishing attempts and making them aware of spoof links and suspicious URLs (Alabdan, 2020). The software-based solutions work by implementing different approaches such as machine learning, visual similarity. Through these approaches, one can detect the attack, use initial countermeasures to stop the attempt, and inform the user about this attempt simultaneously. In some cases, after the attack happens, it is possible to notify the users to seek the help of service providers and Law Enforcement Agencies. We can find several countermeasures which prove to be effective for preventing phishing attacks in their tracks. However, the most common type of countermeasures is the browser plug-ins, where each plug-in works differently and does different things depending on the type of attack (Khonji et al., 2013).

Phishing has become a security threat towards the information that involves different corporate data as well as our personal and crucial details. Earlier studies indicate that major companies and corporate offices were unprepared to build protection against various phishing attacks. As a result, phishers can easily collect and manipulate information. However, phishing techniques have evolved over the past few years, and there are also well-built safeguards introduced to protect our information. We should know about the harmful sides of the internet world as it has become a part of our daily life. This paper will help users to be aware of the concept of phishing and its techniques. We have also tried to present various solutions that will guide business administration in designing new effective protection against different phishing threats for their enterprise. On the other hand, it will also alert the general users not to share their essential information such as passwords and bank details. Moreover, users will be more conscious of the systems of cyber-attacks by having proper knowledge. It will secure their information and help them not to be a victim of phishing attacks.

This section provides an overview of phishing. At first, we discussed the literature review of phishing operations in Section 2. Next, we describe the fundamentals of phishing in Section 3. Section 4 outlines variations of phishing attacks. After the attacks, we explained different countermeasures, prevention, and awareness of phishing in Section 5. The section rolls us to current challenges and research direction in Section 6. Finally, we have concluded our paper with section 7.

LITERATURE REVIEW

This literature review section discusses phishing threats with prevention systems along with the suggested countermeasures. We also talk about researchers' contributions to the subject, and we bring up some interesting topics that need more research and examination. The most recent advancements in AI-assisted spam detection have generally exacerbated these problems. As a result, analyzing recent work on social spam and spammer identification becomes extremely important in combating this problem and its consequences (Rao et al., 2021). We go over the many strategies that the researchers use to assess their approaches. This gives researchers a greater grasp of the problem and future research opportunities to deal with such attacks effectively (Gupta et al., 2017).

Basit et al., (2021) discussed quite extensively in AI-based techniques for phishing attack detection along with current challenges and future research direction of phishing attacks. Sahoo et al., (2017) provided an ML approach to detect malicious URLs identifying the features for classifying malicious websites. Whereas Chiew et al., (2019) studied phishing approaches—specifying mediums and vectors for these approaches. Later Chiew et al., (2019) presented an ML-based feature-selection framework for phishing detection. Peng et al., (2018) discussed ML and NLP-based phishing attack detection. Jain et al., 2019 and Sahingoz et al., (2019) gave ML-based anti-phishing systems from hyperlinks or URLs with more than 98.4% accuracy and 97.98% accuracy rate consecutively. Marchal et al., (2017) developed a client-side anti-phishing add-on to conserve user privacy, identify the target website, and show a warning. Similarly, Baykara et al., (2018) designed a software to detect phishing and spam mails

Van Der Heijden et al., (2019) gives measurements of cognitive vulnerability triggered in phishing emails to anticipate the success rate of an attack. Later Hakim et al., (2021) discussed a framework to study the cognitive neuroscience of phishing detection. Oest et al., (2020) analyzes the end-to-end life cycle of phishing attacks on large scales. In his other work in 2018, he talked about understanding the anti-phishing ecosystem and phishers by examining phishing kits and URLs. Goel et al., (2018) discussed mobile phishing techniques, defense mechanisms, different issues, and challenges, and Aonzo et al., (2018). Show phishing attacks from instant apps and mobile passwords manager.

Jensen et al., (2017) introduced mindfulness techniques to develop anti-phishing training, and later Williams et al., (2021) talked about phishing prevention investigation and in-depth security awareness training. Alkhalil et al., (2021) also discussed the anatomy of phishing and the lifecycle of a phishing attack to increase awareness and develop an anti-phishing system and countermeasures. Alabdan et al., (2020) give a literature review of phishing attack techniques to build awareness and promote the use of anti-phishing tactics. Gupta et al., (2018) discusses types of phishing attacks, solutions, the impact of phishing attacks in IoTs, issues, and challenges. Aleroud et al., (2017) did a similar survey on phishing attacks, anti-phishing techniques, countermeasures, detection, and prevention in different environments

Several phishing-related review papers are currently accessible. There is, however, a general scarcity of published articles in prevention and awareness. Most papers focus on phishing techniques and types of attacks. Table 1 below shows a few surveys and approaches in attacks, countermeasures, prevention, ecosystem, current challenges, and future research.

Table 1. Phishing-related studies and their contributions

Reference	Contribution
Basit et al., 2021	Here a broad review of AI techniques for phishing attack detection is given. It compares different AI techniques to detect phishing and their features and flaws. They also discussed current challenges and future research directions of phishing.
Hakim et al., 2021	Their work proposed a framework to study the cognitive neuroscience of phishing detection where they study participants' behavior and measure their ability to detect phishing emails.
Alkhalil et al., 2021	This article discussed the anatomy of phishing and the lifecycle of a phishing attack to increase awareness; They also developed an anti-phishing system and countermeasures.
Williams et al., 2021	In this paper, phishing prevention investigation is done from three different angles, including email and web security gateway and in-depth security awareness training.
Oest et al., 2020	In this paper, researchers measure the end-to-end life cycle of phishing attacks on a larger scale. They developed a special framework that can measure victim traffic from phishing pages while securing hundreds of accounts in the process.
Alabdan et al., 2020	This paper talks about phishing attack techniques to build awareness and encourage phishing prevention techniques.
Chiew et al., 2019	This paper proposed an ML feature selection framework for phishing detection. They applied different classifiers and algorithms to get the best results. Finally, they chose the HEFS as it worked best for the feature selection technique.
Jain et al., 2019	This paper presents a language-independent ML-based phishing detection approach from hyperlinks with more than 98.4% accuracy on logistic regression classifier. They evaluated their accuracy on various classification algorithms using datasets of many phishing and non-phishing sites.
Sahingoz et al., 2019	The paper proposes an ML-based anti-phishing system that gives a 97.98% accuracy rate for detecting phishing URLs. The system has distinctive features like language independence, real-time execution, and no third-party services.
Van Der Heijden et al., 2019	This paper measures cognitive vulnerability triggers in phishing emails to predict the degree of success of an attack. To do this, they rely on the cognitive psychology literature and an ML mechanism built around the cognitive features of a phishing email.

continues on following page

Table 1. Continued

Reference	Contribution
Gupta et al., 2018	The paper discusses types of phishing attacks, solutions, and the impact of phishing attacks in IoTs Authors also presents issues and challenges in this domain that still needs to be tackled.
Peng et al., 2018	This paper presents NLP-based techniques to analyze text and detect inappropriate statements which indicate phishing.
Goel et al., 2018	This paper gives a detailed discussion on mobile phishing techniques, defense mechanisms along with different issues and challenges faced by fellow researchers dealing with mobile phishing.
Oest et al., 2018	The paper gives a clear idea of the anti-phishing ecosystem. It also classifies phishers by examining phishing kits and URLs.
Chiew et al., 2018	The author plans to create awareness and encourage the practice of anti-phishing approaches with the help of this paper. They discussed future research directions and the lackings in this field to give fellow researchers a direction.
Aonzo et al., 2018	The paper shows phishing attacks from instant apps and mobile password managers. They proposed a secure API by design that can avoid common errors of phishing.
Baykara et al., 2018	They developed software to detect phishing and spam emails.
Jensen et al., 2017	The paper introduces mindfulness technique to develop an anti-phishing training
Aleroud et al., 2017	This paper survey on phishing attacks, anti-phishing techniques, countermeasures, detection, and prevention in different environments.
Sahoo et al., 2017	This paper discussed malicious attacks and ML approaches to detect malicious URLs—identifying the features for classifying malicious websites. It also discusses future research directions and practical issues in designing a system.
Marchal et al., 2017	This paper provides a client-side anti-phishing add-on that preserves user privacy, identifies the target website, and shows a warning.

Phishing's widespread occurrences and technological advancements present significant challenges for academic and industry researchers. Table 1 above discusses the most recent phishing literature to determine how research has progressed in content and publications. Furthermore, the literature review identifies the importance of phishing trends and summarizes the study gap that still exists in this field of research.

Fundamentals of Phishing

Phishing got the influence from the word fishing. Hackers generally use the letter "PH" instead of "F," Phishing is the term for this type of fraud. Phishing is a technique used to phish information from a user's usernames, passwords, credit card information, and sensitive information from a large number of people.

Phishing is a type of social assault that is used to steal user information such as login credentials, credit card numbers, and personal details. It occurs when an attacker poses as a trustworthy entity and convinces a victim to open an email or text message. By clicking the link of the email or text message's link, the attacker gets the users' information. The first phishing case was brought in 2004 against a California teenager who constructed a website that looked like "America Online" (Kumar et al., 2021). Phishers were able to obtain sensitive information from credit cards and use that information to withdraw funds from a bank account using this website. There are many phishing ideas other than email and websites, which are Voice Phishing, SMS Phishing. The motive of Cyber-attacks is money, but sensitive information including bank account numbers, usernames, passwords, credit card numbers, and other personal information is also targeted.

Type of Phishing

There are several types of phishing, including deceptive, malware-based, DNS-based, and content-injection phishing.

Deceptive Based Phishing

This is a standard method for attackers to send false email, text messages, or random links in which by clicking the link, personal information and data are captured and given to the attacker (Chaudhry et al., 2016). Email Phishing, Clone Phishing, Voice phishing is one kind of deceptive base Phishing where the attacker sends a link to the user and grabs the user's sensitive information.

Malware Based Phishing

An attack creates some way to set up some software which is commonly known as malicious software, on the user's device. The attacker uses it to steal the user's personal information from the device. Key and screen loggers, web Trojans data theft are also a part of malware-based phishing (Chaudhry et al., 2016). Wi-Fi phishing, SMS phishing, Software phishing, and Cross-site Scripting are based on Malware phishing which is mainly used by phishing tools.

DNS Based Phishing

This one is based on a domain name. An attacker builds a new domain by changing some characters in the DNS and creating a fraud website. DNS-based phishing also includes host file poisoning, proxy server penetration, and polluting users' DNS cache. IP addresses interfere with the resolution of the domain name; therefore, a website of the domain name is mapped onto a rogue website's IP address (Andryukhin,

2019). Website phishing, DNS spoofing is one kind of DNS-based phishing where an attacker targets a random famous website and creates a phishing trap for users which is not possible to understand at first glance.

Recent Phishing Attacks

In the years 2007 to 2009, PayPal, and eBay were the most victims of Phishing. They received respectively 2511, 5750, 6240 attacks. Fifth bank, PayPal, Internal Revenue Service received the attack respectively 1180,3795,325, and the third position held eBay and Bank of America received 795,570, 290 attacks (San Martino and Perramon, 2010).

In 2020, 75% of companies worldwide experienced phishing attacks, and 74% of attacks were mainly targeted at US businesses (expertinsights.com, 2021). Many organizations claim to have educated and informed their employees about phishing threats. In 2020, this was not enough to protect from Phishing. Phishers are now using advanced techniques at present. OAuth phishing, third-party Phishing, Multi-factor authentication(MFA), Cross-site Scripting, WI-FI Phishing are the modern techniques of Phishing. OAuth phishing is one kind of authorization type phishing where phishers ask to log in to their site with a social media account. Multi-factor authentication mainly makes a trap where attackers ask for authentication of users' social media or sensitive accounts. Cross-site Scripting and WI-FI Phishing are also used by some tools which are helped by any third-party tools to transfer user data from users to attackers.

Underground Economy of Phishing

The underground Economy facilitates phishing assaults that refer to sellers and buyers involved in cybercrime. Where phishers sell the phishing information to the seller, that is mainly a cybercrime. For example, a phisher can buy a phishing kit like software or a popular domain name with an email ID of several bands. That software helps to upgrade phisher technical skills with one click. The seller also sells a well-known band's website clone copy which is the same as the real one, at a low cost. The average price of a phishing kit is about 10USD. Those phishing sites are not mainly hosted on legitimate sites. Phishing kits are also available for rent, where phishers can rent their needed phishing kits. Phishers can also sell users' sensitive information like ID, bank, and credit card details, gained from phishing. From July 2007 to 2008, about 44milion information was passed from underground economy markers. In 2021 the amount became huge. In the underground Economy, the most demandable information is bank account credentials, about 18% sold from the whole market. Table 2 shows the details of the price and the percentage of sales requested in the underground mark of phishing.

Table 2. Price and details of the underground economy market for the seller and buyer

Service and items	Percentage of sale	Percentage of request	Price range
Bank account credentials	18%	14%	10-1,000$
Credit cards with CVV	16%	13	0.05-12$
Credit information	13%	8%	0.10-25$
Email addresses	6%	7%	0.30-40$
Prime Email and passwords	6%	2%	4-30$
Email passwords	5%	9%	0.90-25$
Cash-out services	5%	8%	8-50% total value
Proxies	4%	3%	0.30-20$
Scams	3%	6%	2.50-100/ week
Mailers	3%	6%	1-25$

(Ramzan, 2010)

ATTACK TECHNIQUES

Email spoofing, instant messaging, and text messaging are common techniques of phishing. This is the standard way to take people's personal information and attack the user's system into ransomware or malware

The phishing phase consists of five processes: attack preparation, attack accumulation, attack configuration, fraud, and follow-up. In figure 1, we try to give the primary concept of the phishing technique.

In this figure on point 1, the attacker tries to send an email to the victim to update the user's username, password, or credit card information, and the victim clicks on the email and the link goes through to the phishing website. A phishing website looks like an original website. Suppose an attacker makes a clone website the same as a popular site, and the user cannot make any difference between those two sites quickly. Without any thought, users provide to the attacker all of their personal information. This is the most common phishing technique that is used to expose users to attackers.

Figure 1. The process of phishing
(Ali, 2017)

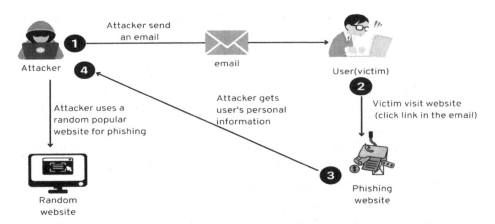

Email Phishing

The most popular Email phishing scenario is malicious mail which is sent to users mimicking an authentic organization. This is also known as spam phishing. In this way, attackers get access to a considerable amount of users registered on a site. By phishing, email attackers get the user's information by clicking the email link (Halevi et al., 2015). For example, attackers target users or random users by sending random mail, requesting to update users' information or bank details. Users have no idea whether the email is a Fraud text or not; they simply click the link and unintentionally provide sensitive information to the attacker.

Clone Phishing

Clone phishing is where the attacker collects some original mail and makes a clone copy for them to send the user. Attackers just replace the link or attachment from the original mail to their clone mail. By clicking the clone mail, users give all their sensitive information to the attacker (Bhavsar et al., 2018).

For example, Suppose the attacker targets XYZPay. When an attacker makes a clone mail for XYZPay, they replace the original link to update the bank information with their clone link and ask the user to update their information by sending mail. They use the Original logo and all the information from XYZPay. As a result, users cannot create a difference between the real one and the fake one.

Domain Spoofing

Domain Spoofing is one kind of phishing which is the perpetrator spoofing a notable organization's domain name. This method makes it look as though you are getting an email from a legitimate company. An attacker creates a website that looks like the original website with the same interference (Maksutov et al., 2017). We know that every website has an IP address with a DNS domain name system. For Example, an attacker creates the same website as a famous E-Commerce, suppose the DNS of famous E-Commerce is www.fshopsite.com. However, an attacker will create the same interphase of that website but replace it with their phishing website. They change or add some letters of DNS name like fshopsitee.com instant of fshopsite. com. Sometimes this kind of change could not be seen by the user carefully therefore the user falls into the trap of the attacker.

If the user does not look closely, there is no way to capture the side where the change is. Using this method, attackers grab the user's personal information from the users. We try to show the way of changing the Domain Name of Any website in figure no 2

Figure 2. Example of domain spoofing site

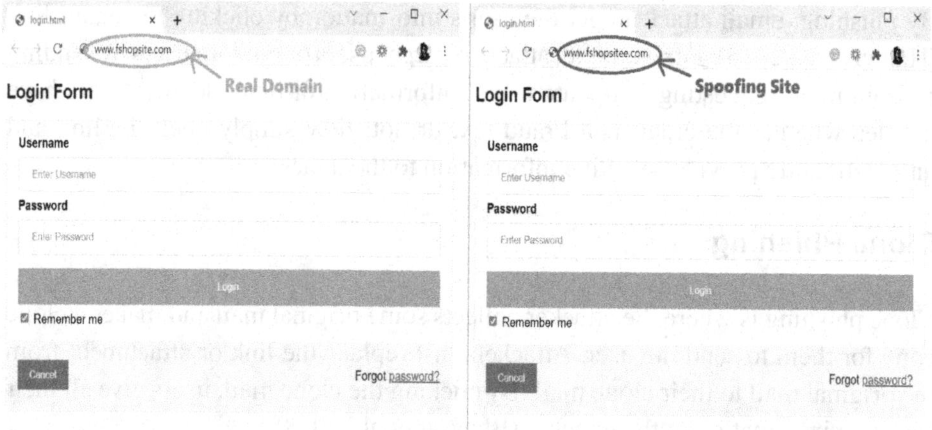

SMS Phishing

Phishing using SMS is called Smishing. This is primarily a type of text message used by scammers to trick users into providing account information or downloading malwares. Smishing is a fraudulent attempt to collect credit card details or other important personal information from a file by impersonating a reputable organization or individual through text message. SMS phishing is a method of attack., where attackers use text messages to obtain personal information from users (Jakobsson, 2018). For example, users get a text message pretending to be from a well-known popular and ask one to update their phone or data with a fake link. Users provide the information and give all their personal information to phishers. By giving malware and spyware links to steal information, the attacker provides a link and asks the user to download an app that helps them get all the information on the user's phone.

Voice Phishing

Vishing is often known as Voice Phishing. There is an old problem named telephone scam with a new name, Vishing. Phisher asked for some information from the user over a voice call. It is a standard phishing method, but sometimes phishers can catch some users to commit fraud (Kim et al., 2018). For example, Phishing calls the user and asks him for information about his bank, credit card, or something like that, acting as if the phisher is the author of the bank's office. Phishers manipulate that they are updating users' information, and this way, they get the information of users. Nowadays, Vishing is not working because people are becoming more aware day by day.

Software Phishing

Phishers use some software to attack personal laptops or phones. Phishers ask users to download software by providing download links. When users set up the software on their personal computers, attackers lockdown or lock the window and grab all users' sensitive files. This file is used on several sites, and sometimes they ask for money to get back the file. For example, many of us want to use pirated software. That is why we need to crack the software. Attackers take this advantage to give their cloned files and control the user's PC to take the information of users. Sometimes, attackers do the same thing on phone users.

Websites Phishing

Websites Phishing is a web-based phishing system that is mainly used to fraud websites. When a victim attempts to log in, these sites look authentic, and phishers are utilized to capture the victim's personal information. There are many methods that an attacker uses. For example, an attacker can create a popular website using the same theme for phishing information from users. It is challenging to find fraud websites nowadays; that is why many users are the primary victims of this phishing method (Alabdan, 2020).

WI-FI Phishing

Wi-Fi phishing usually happens when users are using random hotspots. Attackers create some scripts which help them gain information about what users are doing using Wi-Fi. They also set up some software that saves users' sensitive information. Wi-Fi phishing may come in a variety of forms. The most common technique is for an attacker to create some trick where malware software is set up on the user's device to collect passwords or redirect to fraudulent websites, similar to the other types of Phishing described above. There are more ways for intercepting traffic on these networks to help to get user's devices and sensitive information transferred by users utilizing public unsecured WI-FI zones (Heartfield and Loukas, 2015).

Cross-Site Scripting

Client-side Scripting is often utilized to improve the user experience on modern websites. However, the user is sent to a website form, which is referred to as Scripting and also known as cross-site Scripting. Mainly Cross-site Scripting is an XSS or CSS file format of Scripting. XSS files are the same as SQL files. That is why it supports the function of the database query, whereas the XSS file targets the HTML outputs. This code is used with some languages, which are PHP or NET. With this vulnerability, the attacker gains access to a database of data mapping on the target website or the website's URL. Cross-Site Scripting is two basic methods that are stored and reflected in XSS. Stored XSS is persistent, which has the most impact on stored databases. In this approach, malicious program code is installed as a resource (for example, in a database) on a web applications server, where it may be accessed by anybody who has access to that specific resource. For example, when a user connects to a blog section with a comment or provides information on a sensitive website, the Stored XSS script holds the site. When a user visits the website, their browser runs the script, and while the user's remark is submitted, their personal information is captured and recorded on a server maintained by the attacker.

Another one is reflected XSS cross-site-scripting, where the script is not permanently kept but quickly reflected towards the user. By taking advantage of this opportunity, phishers can send crafted links. By clicking the links, users submit the file where the user's personal data is stolen and transmitted by using this script to the attacker (DAR et al., 2019).

DETECTION AND COUNTERMEASURES

Phishing, in general, is a comprehensive concept, and it has various sides. Though phishing attack techniques are becoming advanced day by day, there are several detection and prevention countermeasures against them to protect our crucial information. For this reason, it is essential to understand all the aspects of phishing mentioned above to create a safeguard as opposed to phishers' intentions. In addition, the best approach towards that will be to visualize the life cycle of phishing attacks as the first step towards its countermeasures (Khonji et al., 2013). That is why detection plays a vital role in stopping phishing attacks.

Detection

For the detection of various phishing attacks, multiple techniques can be incorporated to make the detection even robust. These techniques include detection by service providers, user education programs and software systems detection process. The main challenge of phishing detection is in its approaches that combine user training and software detection solutions that we think should be considered when discussing phishing detection from our review of existing literature.

User Education

Users who are prone to fall victim to phishing can be trained to recognize a phishing attack. This method can prove fruitful as we can actively care against phishing, and end-users do not even have to go through the hassles. There should be security awareness participation through which users can identify phishing tools (Allman et al., 2005). They can save themselves from phishing by recognizing the attack systems. Besides, the manual authentication approach can provide phishing signs to the user. By this approach, they can be aware of the phishing emails by checking the IP addresses (Aleroud and Zhou, 2017, Dwyer and Duan, 2010). Several large companies can arrange a workshop to train their staff about different phishing attacks (Alabdan, 2020, Khonji et al., 2013). While this is a very premature and effective detection method, an essential fact to consider here would be its efficiency. Training users requires more resources and time, as in the case of larger groups prone to attack, user training becomes an impossible option. At this point, the software detection solutions make an appearance with a more effective process.

Software Detection Solutions

Applying software-based detection solutions to safeguard against phishing attacks seems the most helpful approach to phishing detection. This method uses software-designed programs to detect a phishing attempt and terminate it during the process of attacking. It is better than the user training approach since there remains a chance of human error in human-based detection. That is why software-based detection is a perfect alternative to bridge the gap of human error (Khonji et al., 2013).

- **Machine learning approaches**

Phishing detection using machine learning approaches focuses on applying different methods and algorithms to detect phishing attacks. Among various techniques, classification, neural networks, and data-mining are primarily used for the anti-phishing process, such as phishing email detection, recognizing the variation between the website's structure and its HTTP transactions (Alabdan, 2020, Alghoul et al., 2018). These methods, mentioned above, mainly depend on the training dataset and the machine learning approach follows some sequential steps to classify phishing types. At first, the data will be pre-processed, extracted features, and then a model will be designed to classify the data into two categories: phishing data and legal data by detecting particular features (Aleroud and Zhou, 2017). Next, the model will be trained by learning patterns from training samples according to the given directions. We can apply the classifier algorithms (Decision Tree, Support Vector Machine, Logistic Regression, Naive Bayes, K-Nearest Neighbor) based on URL features, textual features, and hybrid features. Here, URL-related features: IP Address, Domain Name have been used for phishing detection (Bergholz et al., 2008, Bulakh and Gupta, 2016). In addition, the Classification approach also inspects any doubtful substance in the textual content to identify whether it is phishing or legal. Moreover, some dynamic classifiers extract features from textual content and URLs in websites to detect phishing using the online support vector machine approach. This Classification methodology and performance mainly depends on the size of the training dataset (L'Huillier et al., 2009). Another machine learning approach is the clustering technique that identifies classes of similar data as they have familiar elements (Chen et al., 2009). An anomaly detection technique is also used to identify phishing attacks as an outliner. For instance, this approach will reveal the usual behavior of a phishing website as each website has a distinctive identity in cyberspace (Nguyen et al., 2014). Machine learning methods can develop strong protection against phishing attempts if sufficient training data is available (Alabdan, 2020, Somesha et al., 2020)

- **Offensive defense approach**

This approach attempts to render a phishing attack ineffective by the process of disruption, and a widespread way is to flood the phishing websites with false information. This method gives a difficult time to the attacker as they have to search for the real credentials amid the fake ones. Two toolbars: BogusBiter and Humboldt, follow this approach (Khonji et al., 2013).

BogusBiter: BogusBiter provides bogus information in HTML forms when a user visits a phishing website. Other tools, according to BogusBiter, are used to detect phishing websites. The purpose of submitting bogus information through HTML forms is to counter various phishing attempts, expecting that the phony data will make it more difficult for attackers to identify actual data. While this is good and all, there are limitations to it also such as the user needs to install a toolbar. Otherwise, the bogus information that needs to be supplied will not be much adequate. BogusBiter also demands increased bandwidth to work correctly. In the case of non-standard HTML forms, BogusBiter malfunctions do not work properly (Khonji et al., 2013, Yue and Wang, 2008).

Humboldt: Humboldt depends on dispersed and committed users through the internet rather than end-user toolbars that can be visited numerous spoofing websites, as well as a technique to prevent DOS floods. Due to the increased frequency of data submitted to phishing pages, Humboldt may become increasingly effective against phishing websites (Knickerbocker et al., 2009). Humboldt is approximately similar to Bogusbites, including the limitations. It also requires bandwidth demand as well as like BogusBiter, Humboldt also does not detect non-standard HTML forms. Although offensive and defensive approaches work best most of the time, finding information is not that high. A phisher can easily build up a script to collect the credentials and use different techniques to determine the credentials' validity (Khonji et al., 2013).

- **Visual similarity approach**

The visual similarity detection approach is also an important method for distinguishing between a suspicious site and a legitimate side. This method is effective in identifying phishing in websites. Users sometimes find visible similarities of web interface designing such as layouts, images, structure (Albadan, 2020). Usually, the attackers copy these visual elements to fool the target users. A number of visual similarity approaches are introduced, such as Segmentation based visual similarity (Afroz and Greenstadt, 2011, Bozkir and Sezer, 2016), Earth Mover's Distance based on images (Fu et al., 2006), and DOM Tree Similarity to recognize phishing attacks

(Fu et al., 2006). The DOM method detects phishing by comparing phishing and legitimate web pages based on graph similarities. Some matching approaches apply more than one type of resemblance and compare the overall features of a webpage (Hsu et al., 2011, Aleroud and Zhou, 2017). However, this detection method is not efficacious as the attackers can easily bypass and successfully achieve their targeted information (Gupta et al., 2018).

- **Blacklist and whitelist**

Other detection techniques are whitelist and blacklist methods which are used to find the threats of phishing websites and prioritize making a database of trustworthy and suspicious domains. Matching against a black list and a whitelist is done when the domain filtering techniques detect any anomalies (Aleroud and Zhou, 2017). This kind of anti-phishing technique is known as one of the most effective phishing detection techniques like browser blacklist provides safe browsing to the clients by constantly checking any suspicious URL on the browser.

In the blacklist method, it lists the domain names and the URL of suspicious and harmful sites, and the user can check if sites are harmful or not. Nowadays, blacklists include browser-based security such as automated detection of risky websites and help users save themselves from being tricked. There are some new tools that find the cloned websites on the internet and block them (Alabdan, 2020). For example, some browsers use Google Safe Browsing like Chrome, some browsers use their own blacklists like edge, and some browsers use borrowed blacklists to detect the threat, like opera. However, not all the approaches of blacklist were effective in handling phishing; sometimes, it misses some emails through which phishers may collect the user's information (Aleroud and Zhou, 2017, Tsalis et al., 2014).

Whitelists refer to a list of URLs that are not suspicious but often, arranging a list of trustworthy sources can take much time. As a result, this method causes a high number of false positives, which allows many phishing sites to get access. For this reason, it does not appear too promising and effective enough to identify present-time phishing attacks. Blacklist and whitelist approaches are weak to detect phishing at a high level with the changing technologies such as ipv4 to ipv5, tiny URLs (Almomani et al., 2013), and this detection failure can lead towards an extensive risk for the regular users.

- **Correction approach**

Another approach that needs discussion is the correction approach, which refers to taking the phishing resources down after detecting a phishing attack. The most known way is to report the attacks to service providers who will take the necessary steps. For instance, service providers can remove the phishing contents and elements from several websites or suspend the email accounts that are used for phishing (James, 2005). Tracing and shutting down botnets can also help towards this method to block phishing attacks (Khonji et al., 2013). Following these necessary acts, there is a chance of completely shutting down phishing attacks, especially email phishing.

Countermeasures

Because of the high risks of phishing, it becomes necessary to build a powerful protection system against phishing techniques. The countermeasures help us not only to save our crucial information but also to avoid being victims of phishing. We can apply countermeasures during different phases of phishing attacks so that the phishers cannot get the chance to commit their attack completely. Countermeasures can be divided into two parts depending on which side we are considering. The user-side countermeasures will focus on acts, including the users' responsibilities and activities. Moreover, the other is the server-side countermeasures which need to be handled by the websites and service providers.

User-side countermeasures

- **Two-Factor Authentication and Firewalls**

Two-factor authentication (TFA) refers to having another authentication method on top of the traditional password-based systems using the access codes sent to phones or email. One Time Passwords (OTP) can also be used via text messages that help protect against phishing trying to access your account. Besides using access codes and OTPs, TFA also refers to the biometrics system that is more secure since the attacker might have some method to access one's texts. Nevertheless, there is no way that an attacker can access one's biometrics (Ramzan, 2010). Firewalls are another type of countermeasure, and they help filter out spam emails and act as an additional layer of protection (Junaid et al., 2016).

- **Antivirus and Anti-Malware**

Since phishing works by having malware at the user's terminal, the antivirus can also help to prevent phishing attacks. The antivirus sweeps the user's machine for such malware and acts as a shield against phishing. Many antivirus software operate procedures to notify users about suspicious websites. Browsers are also more likely to warn users when they enter data into a non-SSL-secured website. As a result, it is harder for attackers to set up such websites to collect information (Junaid et al., 2016, Anderson, 2020).

- **Using Plug-Ins and Toolbars to Prevent Phishing**

Plug-ins and toolbars have always helped guard users against phishing attacks for a very long time. Various plug-ins can serve a variety of purposes by providing a safe system to the users. While some notify the user of potential attack risks, others block users' access to a suspicious website. These mentioned steps can act as the starting phase of defense in opposition to phishing techniques. In addition, some plug-ins supply phishing sites with inaccurate information to make the attacker's job more difficult. Google Safe Browsing API allows user applications to test whether a particular URL belongs in Google's regularly updated blocklists as there will be no match for a changing phishing URL. Sometimes PhishNet (Prakash et al., 2010) addresses the similar restrictions discovered in blocklists. As a result, PhishNet processes deny listed URLs (parents) and produce several forms of the same URL (children) via five distinct URL variation heuristic programs to solve the problem. SpoofGuard (Teraguchi et al., 2004), a Stanford University web browser plug-in, identifies HTTP(S)-based phishing attacks as a web browser toolbar by loading specific anomalies observed in HTML form against a detailed threshold value. Fishguard and PhishWish are also browser plug-ins that can act as phishing countermeasures.

Server-side countermeasures

- **Providing better interfaces**

Having an interface that can prompt users when someone tries to access their account can be a useful countermeasure as the problem with phishing is being left in the dark about unauthorized access. When it is possible to have an interface that notifies the users whenever an account tries to access from a different device or address, in that case, the user can efficiently work on online platforms without any stress. While Google already employs such a method whenever the email gets accessed, this feature is not available for most websites. As a result, when a user account gets accessed from another location, she/he is unaware of it even happening (Hong, 2012).

- **Email authentication**

In order to generate an email that appears authentic, a phisher would nearly fake the "From" address in an email. This way of phishing is conceivable because the Simple

Mail Transfer Protocol (SMTP) that administers how an email is delivered with the help of the internet does not provide enough guarantees on email authenticity (in and of itself). Having an additional layer of email authentication for all the accounts can help users secure their credentials (Ramzan, 2010, Allman et al., 2005).

In the following table, a brief summary of phishing attacks, strategy, effects, and solutions to phishing attacks are shown.

Table 3. Summary of phishing attacks, strategy, effects, and solutions

Attacks	Strategy	Effects	Solution
Email Phishing (Halevi et al., 2015, Jeurissen et al., 2021)	Extract information using deceptive email	Loss of sensitive Accounts, personal information, credit card details and bank details.	Secure email gateway; Cautious of unknown or suspicious, emails, URLs, websites
Clone Phishing (Kolley, 2021)	Replacing real emails with fake ones; Adding fake links/website to email;	Loss of money; Damage to reputation; Disruption of operational activities	Closely check sender Email ID; Check mail carefully for spelling, grammar mistakes or suspicious link
Voice Phishing (Kim et al., 2015)	Fraudulent phone call; Use of automated text to speech system	Personal threat; Loss of money and personal information	Avoid answering unknown calls; Verify number; Use a paid caller ID app
Smishing (Jakobsson, 2018)	SMS phishing; Delivers malicious short links to smartphone users Malware installation on the phone;	Personal threat; Device's file threat; Fear of losing information; Malware attack	Check sender information and hyperlink; Avoid doubtful texts on Social media; Call the office directly to confirm the Given SMS
Domain Spoofing (Maksutov et al., 2017, AlEroud and Karabatis, 2020)	Exchanging real domain name (of a company) with a fake one	Decreased brand safety and consumer trust; Lost revenue;	Add DKIM record; Closely review the domain name; Check spelling mistakes in the name
Software Phishing	Unauthorized software download; Crack tools download from unofficial websites; Malware install on the device;	Threat on a personal device; Loss of personal data; Malware attack	Download software and tools from the official site; Avoid cracked version of a paid software
Websites Phishing (Odeh et al., 2020)	Make fake website; Ask to login with social media account or any information sensitive account	Lost revenue; Reputation damage; Disruption of operational activities of a company; Show Unpaid advertisements on website	Update website often; Use of antivirus software tools; Use designs that are difficult to clone
WI-FI Phishing (Choi et al., 2021)	Fake Wi-Fi access point; Third-party tools; Exchange DNS from the official site	Get an overview of user's activities; Personal information leak	Avoid using public Wi-Fi/ free Wi-Fi;
Cross-site Scripting (DAR et al., 2019)	Malicious script injection into websites and web applications to access end user's device; Attack on the server database	Threat on server database; Information leak from server	Use of web application firewall (WAF); Develop website Scripting; Use of anti-phishing software tools; Update database security

FUTURE RESEARCH DIRECTIONS

Considering the future innovative urbanized environment, which is interconnected through a network, understanding the future research challenges can go a long way to promote the safety and security of the citizens (Haque et al., 2021). In today's world, phishing attacks exist as one of the considerable widespread hazards to the internet community, impacting everyone from particular users to huge businesses and assistance providers. As previously described, there are now available ways to identify and block phishing approaches; nonetheless, there is no complete answer to the phishing issue. (Jain and Gupta, 2017). A full grasp of these tactics will pave the way for developing more effective anti-phishing strategies for future phishing issues. This information will also aid the general public in adopting cautious and preventive steps against phishing assaults, as well as policymakers in implementing legislation to avoid future phishing attempts. In order to understand the limits of this little exploratory research, it is necessary to be realistic. It is possible that the experimental manipulation failed to discriminate between various degrees of cybercrime awareness in the participants. Future studies should examine how phishing and cybercrime knowledge influences people's susceptibility to scams and prevent them from happening. (Broadhurst et al., 2018).

SSL and Antivirus Software

One of the most challenging things to prevent phishing is telling the difference between legitimate and counterfeit websites. Over the last few years, 78 percent of all found phishing sites have been seen using SSL to make websites look authentic. The majority of current browsers are used to notify users when a target was routed to an insecure website, even if the target was sent to a legitimate website. The introduction of SSL, on the other hand, makes phishing far simpler to perpetuate and detection significantly more complex. According to the manufacturer, some antivirus software now includes browser add-ons that analyze a site's reputation and provide warnings if the site is regarded as untrustworthy. Despite the fact that these systems depend on community ratings and may be easily manipulated, they should be able to identify primary phishing sites with relative ease. When used by organizations and people capable of installing them, they are effective. On the other hand, older generations are the most often targeted by phishing attacks since they are less likely to be aware of these technologies.

Mobile Phishing Attacks

It is also vital to have anti-malware protection for some forms of phishing. While many individuals are aware of them and have them installed on their desktops, the number of people who use them on their mobile devices is far fewer (Dupuis et al., 2019). This becomes a big problem since mobile devices are just as prone to phishing attempts as email or other kinds of communication. Desktop phishing attacks are distinct from mobile phishing attacks because they have different architectures. This is due to the changes in design. Furthermore, professionals in this field are worried about the accuracy with which mobile phishing attacks may be carried out. Despite introducing various anti-phishing technologies for mobile devices, a complete solution to this issue has not yet been developed (docs.apwg.org, 2020). Mobile devices are essential to safeguard since they are often used as a second factor in two-factor authentication, which is required or highly recommended by many websites and services. Unfortunately, this is a problem for hackers since one-time passwords are significantly more challenging to break than basic passwords, making them a target. Because of this, new phishing detection and precluding systems must concentrate on mobile appliances and how they might be used in combination with extra classic phishing efforts to be effective.

Loopholes in Phishing Detection Technique

Because the majority of currently available phishing detection systems rely on heuristics or a straightforward blacklisting strategy, phishing attacks may still go unnoticed if the phisher employs appropriate precautions. Examples of these approaches include: incorporating semantic modifications into emails when disseminating spam, using alternative addresses, or using a botnet of infected devices to avoid detection (Goel and Jain, 2018, Gutierrez et al., 2018). In addition, since phishing attacks may be delivered via a multitude of channels and media, anti-phishing technologies exist, incapable of identifying every kind of phishing attack. Because many individuals do not have the necessary skills or financial resources to defend themselves adequately, it is difficult for ordinary people to defend themselves. On the other hand, businesses may have as much protection as they can afford. However, the fact is that all it takes is one person to overlook a warning or blunder it for a phisher to take over the firm and use lateral phishing to increase their control. Furthermore, anti-phishing processes must be executed in real-time; otherwise, it will be too late after the victim has fallen prey to the "bait."

Phishers and their Behavioral Aspect

While researching this project, it evolved unmistakable that the bulk of existing and one-time research on phishing was mainly focused on the specialized strategies utilized by phishing perpetrators and the specific preventative measures that were being created. However, just a few studies attempted to determine the demographics or habits of the most vulnerable individuals to phishing regardless of age and gender. In contrast, most studies focused on age and gender. A dearth of study on the value of different channels, vectors, and technological techniques in relation to target audiences' demographics is also present. There has also been a minimal investigation into the reasons behind phishing raids other than the numerous typical causes for financial gain. Future studies may take an interesting turn by looking at phishing from the attacker's point of view and analyzing their emotions and motives, which could make counter phishing easier. Attackers may be driven by concrete outcomes like economic worth and more abstract ideas such as human or symbolic significance (Hauske, 2018).

ML to Counteract Phishing/ ML in Anti-Phishing Technology

A large portion of the most recent research on technical phishing prevention and detection methods seems to have concentrated chiefly on dispatch range, preferably than different kinds of phishing such as advertising, crouching tactics. Research into Natural Language Processing (NLP) has recently been a critical focus of attention. This technology will detect phishing emails more effectively and block them since they will no longer be able to use semantic modifications to bypass available filtering methods. According to research, this strategy is more effective than prior techniques in filtering out phishing emails (Verma et al., 2020, Kumar et al., 2020), despite the fact that these methods have not been tested on more extensive datasets. Phishing prevention systems using neural networks are also being researched. However, they have been criticized for requiring lengthy training and specialized knowledge to adjust the settings. In order to combat phishing attacks, other aspects of machine learning are being researched as well as deep learning.

More Challenges and Research Areas

Phishers target the internet as their primary medium, with six out of the total of eight vectors associated with it being accessible on the internet at any one moment. However, this does not rule out the use of the other two mediums, short messaging service (SMS) and voice, which have maintained their popularity due to the fast rise of the mobile phone market. Phishing attempts, such as smishing and vishing, are still prevalent due to the fast growth of mobile phone demand. Cloud computing and mobile phones are two sectors that will attract the attention of phishers as their markets continue to develop rapidly. A concerted effort to combat phishing is required, particularly in these two areas (Alabdan, 2020). As previously stated, inadequate protection against phishing is provided by anti-phishing methods that detect phishing websites when they are accessed via websites. As a result of this detection, the user becomes vulnerable to drive-by-download assaults, in which malware, viruses, or shellcode is injected into the victim's computer as soon as the victim visits the page. Because there is no access to the website, it is preferable to identify phishing websites via a link supplied in an email or on social media platforms. To effectively combat phishing assaults, a concerted anti-phishing effort in this direction is required (Chiew et al., 2018).

A future study might concentrate on the human characteristics that allow for the exploitation of phishing as well as the most effective educational options available to students. The literature does not consistently address this topic, with much recent research concentrating on novel detection techniques and tools. As part of future research, the systematic evaluation of phishing strategies will be broadened to include a review of existing anti-phishing measures from the literature, including in the current study. Phishing and its countermeasures will be better understood by researchers and developers as a result of this, enabling them to design more effective anti-phishing systems.

CONCLUDING REMARKS

In the last couple of decades, phishing has become a vital global security problem for individuals and organizations. Though we have numerous techniques available to prevent phishing attacks, whenever any secure solution approaches to overcome attacking techniques, the phishers appear with their more powerful attack systems. Despite the well-built barrier, phishers often become more successful in stealing our private and significant information. They used communication networks such as spoofed emails, fake websites to accomplish their illegal activities. If this situation continues, it will create a negative impact not only for general users but also for owners of multi-level companies. It will also hinder the regular activity of people. People have become more reliable on different online platforms in the modern era of the Internet, especially during the COVID-19 pandemic. To ensure the safe use of online platforms, a multi-level phishing defense strategy should be implemented (Gupta et al., 2018, Jampen et al., 2020) .

Our paper outlined the history, different phishing attack techniques, and several available solutions to protect user information. As time passed, phishers were trying to advance their attacking techniques. As a result, we cannot completely eradicate phishing from the internet world. However, a combination of user awareness and software tools can reduce the overall threats of phishing and secure our information. Future studies could use a more robust approach to assess deceit susceptibility. We should understand the facts that determine susceptibility will guide to reduce the risk of phishing and other forms of cybercrime.

REFERENCES

Afroz, S., & Greenstadt, R. (2011, September). Phishzoo: Detecting phishing websites by looking at them. In *2011 IEEE fifth international conference on semantic computing* (pp. 368-375). IEEE. DOI: 10.1109/ICSC.2011.52

Alabdan, R. (2020). Phishing attacks survey: Types, vectors, and technical approaches. *Future Internet, 12*(10), 168. doi:10.3390/fi12100168

AlEroud, A., & Karabatis, G. (2020, March). Bypassing detection of URL-based phishing attacks using generative adversarial deep neural networks. In *Proceedings of the Sixth International Workshop on Security and Privacy Analytics* (pp. 53-60) DOI: 10.1145/3375708.3380315

Aleroud, A., & Zhou, L. (2017). Phishing environments, techniques, and countermeasures: A survey. *Computers & Security, 68*, 160–196. doi:10.1016/j.cose.2017.04.006

Alghoul, A., Al Ajrami, S., Al Jarousha, G., Harb, G., & Abu-Naser, S.S. (2018). Email Classification Using Artificial Neural Network. *Int. J. Acad. Eng. Res.*

Ali, W. (2017). Phishing website detection based on supervised machine learning with wrapper features selection. *International Journal of Advanced Computer Science and Applications, 8*(9), 72–78. doi:10.14569/IJACSA.2017.080910

Alkhalil, Z., Hewage, C., Nawaf, L., & Khan, I. (2021). Phishing Attacks: Recent Comprehensive Study and a New Anatomy. *Frontiers of Computer Science, 3*, 6. doi:10.3389/fcomp.2021.563060

Allman, E., Callas, J., Delaney, M., Libbey, M., Fenton, J., & Thomas, M. (2005). *Domain keys identified mail.* IETF Internet Draft.

Almomani, A., Gupta, B. B., Atawneh, S., Meulenberg, A., & Almomani, E. (2013). A survey of phishing email filtering techniques. *IEEE Communications Surveys and Tutorials, 15*(4), 2070–2090. doi:10.1109/SURV.2013.030713.00020

Anderson, R. (2020). *Security engineering: a guide to building dependable distributed systems*. John Wiley & Sons. doi:10.1002/9781119644682

Andryukhin, A. A. (2019, March). Phishing attacks and preventions in blockchain based projects. In *2019 International Conference on Engineering Technologies and Computer Science (EnT)* (pp. 15-19). IEEE. DOI: 10.1109/EnT.2019.00008

Aonzo, S., Merlo, A., Tavella, G., & Fratantonio, Y. (2018, October). Phishing attacks on modern android. In *Proceedings of the 2018 ACM SIGSAC Conference on Computer and Communications Security* (pp. 1788-1801). DOI:10.1145/3243734.3243778

Basit, A., Zafar, M., Liu, X., Javed, A. R., Jalil, Z., & Kifayat, K. (2021). A comprehensive survey of AI-enabled phishing attacks detection techniques. *Telecommunication Systems, 76*(1), 139-154. DOI: / doi:10.1007/s11235-020-00733-2

Baykara, M., & Gürel, Z. Z. (2018, March). Detection of phishing attacks. In *2018 6th International Symposium on Digital Forensic and Security (ISDFS)* (pp. 1-5). IEEE. DOI:10.1109/ISDFS.2018.8355389

Bergholz, A., Chang, J. H., Paass, G., Reichartz, F., & Strobel, S. (2008, August). Improved Phishing Detection using Model-Based Features. CEAS. DOI: 10.1.1.216.4317

Bhavsar, V., Kadlak, A., & Sharma, S. (2018). Study on phishing attacks. *International Journal of Computers and Applications, 182*, 27–29. doi:10.5120/ijca2018918286

Bozkir, A. S., & Sezer, E. A. (2016, April). Use of HOG descriptors in phishing detection. In *2016 4th International Symposium on Digital Forensic and Security (ISDFS)* (pp. 148-153). IEEE. 10.1109/isdfs.2016.7473534

Broadhurst, R., Skinner, K., Sifniotis, N., Matamoros-Macias, B., & Ipsen, Y. (2018). *Phishing and cybercrime risks in a university student community*. Advance online publication. doi:10.2139srn.3176319

Bulakh, V., & Gupta, M. (2016, March). Countering phishing from brands' vantage point. In *Proceedings of the 2016 ACM on International Workshop on Security And Privacy Analytics* (pp. 17-24). DOI:10.1145/2875475.2875478

Chaudhry, J. A., Chaudhry, S. A., & Rittenhouse, R. G. (2016). Phishing attacks and defenses. *International Journal of Security and Its Applications, 10*(1), 247–256. doi:10.14257/ijsia.2016.10.1.23

Chen, K. T., Chen, J. Y., Huang, C. R., & Chen, C. S. (2009). Fighting phishing with discriminative keypoint features. *IEEE Internet Computing*, *13*(3), 56–63. doi:10.1109/MIC.2009.59

Chiew, K. L., Tan, C. L., Wong, K., Yong, K. S., & Tiong, W. K. (2019). A new hybrid ensemble feature selection framework for machine learning-based phishing detection system. *Information Sciences*, *484*, 153–166. doi:10.1016/j.ins.2019.01.064

Chiew, K. L., Yong, K. S. C., & Tan, C. L. (2018). A survey of phishing attacks: Their types, vectors and technical approaches. *Expert Systems with Applications*, *106*, 1–20. doi:10.1016/J.ESWA.2018.03.050

Choi, H. S., Carpenter, D., & Ko, M. S. (2021). Risk Taking Behaviors Using Public Wi-Fi™. *Information Systems Frontiers*, 1–18. doi:10.100710796-021-10119-7

Dar, M. U. J., Shah, J. L., & Khanday, G. I. A. (2019). Web abuse using cross site scripting (XSS) attacks. *Journal of Artificial Intelligence Research & Advances*, *6*(1), 69–75.

Dupuis, M., Geiger, T., Slayton, M., & Dewing, F. (2019, September). The Use and Non-Use of Cybersecurity Tools Among Consumers: Do They Want Help? In *Proceedings of the 20th Annual SIG Conference on Information Technology Education* (pp. 81-86). DOI: 10.1145/3349266.3351419

Dwyer, P., & Duan, Z. (2010, July). MDMap: Assisting users in identifying phishing emails. In *Proceedings of 7th Annual Collaboration, Electronic Messaging, Anti-Abuse and Spam Conference (CEAS)* (pp. 1-4). 10.1.1.1/67.3988

Fu, A. Y., Deng, X., & Wenyin, L. (2006). REGAP: A tool for unicode-based web identity fraud detection. *Journal of Digital Forensic Practice*, *1*(2), 83–97. doi:10.1080/15567280600995501

Fu, A. Y., Wenyin, L., & Deng, X. (2006). Detecting phishing web pages with visual similarity assessment based on earth mover's distance (EMD). *IEEE Transactions on Dependable and Secure Computing*, *3*(4), 301–311. doi:10.1109/TDSC.2006.50

Goel, D., & Jain, A. K. (2018). Mobile phishing attacks and defence mechanisms: State of art and open research challenges. *Computers & Security*, *73*, 519–544. doi:10.1016/j.cose.2017.12.006

Gupta, B. B., Arachchilage, N. A., & Psannis, K. E. (2018). Defending against phishing attacks: Taxonomy of methods, current issues and future directions. *Telecommunication Systems*, *67*(2), 247–267. doi:10.100711235-017-0334-z

Gupta, B. B., Tewari, A., Jain, A. K., & Agrawal, D. P. (2017). Fighting against phishing attacks: State of the art and future challenges. *Neural Computing & Applications*, *28*(12), 3629–3654. doi:10.100700521-016-2275-y

Gutierrez, C. N., Kim, T., Della Corte, R., Avery, J., Goldwasser, D., Cinque, M., & Bagchi, S. (2018). Learning from the ones that got away: Detecting new forms of phishing attacks. *IEEE Transactions on Dependable and Secure Computing*, *15*(6), 988–1001.

Hakim, Z. M., Ebner, N. C., Oliveira, D. S., Getz, S. J., Levin, B. E., Lin, T., ... Wilson, R. C. (2021). The Phishing Email Suspicion Test (PEST) a lab-based task for evaluating the cognitive mechanisms of phishing detection. *Behavior Research Methods*, *53*(3), 1342–1352.

Halevi, T., Memon, N., & Nov, O. (2015). Spear-phishing in the wild: A real-world study of personality, phishing self-efficacy and vulnerability to spear-phishing attacks. *Phishing Self-Efficacy and Vulnerability to Spear-Phishing Attacks*.

Haque, A.K., Bhushan, B., & Dhiman, G. (2021). Conceptualizing smart city applications: Requirements, architecture, security issues, and emerging trends. *Expert Systems: International Journal of Knowledge Engineering and Neural Networks*. Advance online publication. doi:10.1111/exsy.12753

Hausken, K. (2018). A cost–benefit analysis of terrorist attacks. *Defence and Peace Economics*, *29*(2), 111–129. doi:10.1080/10242694.2016.1158440

Heartfield, R., & Loukas, G. (2015). A Taxonomy of Attacks and a Survey of Defense Mechanisms for Semantic Social Engineering Attacks. *ACM Computing Surveys*. Advance online publication. doi:10.1145/2835375

Hong, J. (2012). The state of phishing attacks. *Communications of the ACM*, *55*(1), 74–81. doi:10.1145/2063176.2063197

Hsu, C. H., Wang, P., & Pu, S. (2011, September). Identify fixed-path phishing attack by STC. In *Proceedings of the 8th Annual Collaboration, Electronic Messaging, Anti-Abuse and Spam Conference* (pp. 172-175). DOI: 10.1145/2030376.2030396

Iwendi, C., Jalil, Z., Javed, A. R., Reddy, T., Kaluri, R., Srivastava, G., & Jo, O. (2020). Keysplitwatermark: Zero watermarking algorithm for software protection against cyber-attacks. *IEEE Access : Practical Innovations, Open Solutions*, *8*, 72650–72660. doi:10.1109/ACCESS.2020.2988160

Jain, A. K., & Gupta, B. B. (2017). Phishing detection: Analysis of visual similarity based approaches. *Security and Communication Networks, 2017*. Advance online publication. doi:10.1155/2017/5421046

Jain, A. K., & Gupta, B. B. (2019). A machine learning based approach for phishing detection using hyperlinks information. *Journal of Ambient Intelligence and Humanized Computing, 10*(5), 2015–2028. doi:10.100712652-018-0798-z

Jakobsson, M. (2018). Two-factor authentication–the rise in SMS phishing attacks. *Computer Fraud & Security, 2018*(6), 6–8. doi:10.1016/S1361-3723(18)30052-6

James, L. (2005). *Phishing exposed*. Elsevier.

Jampen, D., Gür, G., Sutter, T., & Tellenbach, B. (2020). Don't click: Towards an effective anti-phishing training. A comparative literature review. *Human-centric Computing and Information Sciences, 10*(1), 1–41. doi:10.118613673-020-00237-7

Javed, A. R., Usman, M., Rehman, S. U., Khan, M. U., & Haghighi, M. S. (2020). Anomaly detection in automated vehicles using multistage attention-based convolutional neural network. *IEEE Transactions on Intelligent Transportation Systems*. Advance online publication. doi:10.1109/tits.2020.3025875

Jensen, M. L., Dinger, M., Wright, R. T., & Thatcher, J. B. (2017). Training to mitigate phishing attacks using mindfulness techniques. *Journal of Management Information Systems, 34*(2), 597–626. doi:10.1080/07421222.2017.1334499

Jeurissen, L., Mennink, B. J. M., & Daemen, J. J. C. (2021). *E-mail phishing prevention proposal*. CEPP.

Junaid, C., Shafique, C., & Robert, R. (2016). Phishing attacks and defenses. *International Journal of Security and Its Applications, 10*, 247-256. DOI: doi:10.14257/ijsia.2016.10.1.23

Khonji, M., Iraqi, Y., & Jones, A. (2013). Phishing detection: A literature survey. *IEEE Communications Surveys and Tutorials, 15*(4), 2091–2121. doi:10.1109/SURV.2013.032213.00009

Kim, J. H., Go, J. Y., & Lee, K. H. (2015). A Scheme of Social Engineering Attacks and Countermeasures Using Big Data-based Conversion Voice Phishing. *Journal of the Korea Convergence Society, 6*(1), 85–91. doi:10.15207/JKCS.2015.6.1.085

Knickerbocker, P., Yu, D., & Li, J. (2009). Humboldt: A distributed phishing disruption system. In 2009 eCrime Researchers Summit (pp. 1-12). IEEE. DOI: doi:10.1109/SURV.2013.032213.00009

Kolley, S. (2021). *Phishing attacks: Detection and prevention* (Doctoral dissertation). University of Bradford.

Kumar, A., Chatterjee, J. M., & Díaz, V. G. (2020). A novel hybrid approach of SVM combined with NLP and probabilistic neural network for email phishing. *Iranian Journal of Electrical and Computer Engineering, 10*(1), 486. doi:0.11591/ijece.v10i1

Kumar, H., Prasad, A., Rane, N., Tamane, N., & Yeole, A. (2021). Dr. Phish: Phishing Website Detector. In E3S Web of Conferences (Vol. 297). EDP Sciences. DOI: doi:10.17148/IARJSET.2021.8831

L'Huillier, G., Weber, R., & Figueroa, N. (2009, June). Online phishing classification using adversarial data mining and signaling games. In *Proceedings of the ACM SIGKDD Workshop on CyberSecurity and Intelligence Informatics* (pp. 33-42). DOI: 10.1145/1599272.1599279

Maksutov, A. A., Cherepanov, I. A., & Alekseev, M. S. (2017, April). Detection and prevention of DNS spoofing attacks. In *2017 Siberian Symposium on Data Science and Engineering (SSDSE)* (pp. 84-87). IEEE. DOI: 10.13052/jcsm2245-1439.7114

Marchal, S., Armano, G., Gröndahl, T., Saari, K., Singh, N., & Asokan, N. (2017). Off-the-hook: An efficient and usable client-side phishing prevention application. *IEEE Transactions on Computers, 66*(10), 1717–1733. doi:10.1109/TC.2017.2703808

Mittal, M., Iwendi, C., Khan, S., & Rehman Javed, A. (2021). Analysis of security and energy efficiency for shortest route discovery in low-energy adaptive clustering hierarchy protocol using Levenberg- Marquardt neural network and gated recurrent unit for intrusion detection system. *Transactions on Emerging Telecommunications Technologies, 32*(6), e3997. doi:10.1002/ett.3997

Nguyen, L. D., Le, D. N., & Vinh, L. T. (2014, December). Detecting phishing web pages based on DOM-tree structure and graph matching algorithm. In *Proceedings of the Fifth Symposium on Information and Communication Technology* (pp. 280-285). DOI:10.1145/2676585.2676596

Odeh, A., Keshta, I., & Abdelfattah, E. (2020). *Efficient Detection of Phishing Websites Using Multilayer Perceptron.* DOI: doi:10.3991/ijim.v14i11.13903

Oest, A., Safei, Y., Doupé, A., Ahn, G. J., Wardman, B., & Warner, G. (2018, May). Inside a phisher's mind: Understanding the anti-phishing ecosystem through phishing kit analysis. In *2018 APWG Symposium on Electronic Crime Research (eCrime)* (pp. 1-12). IEEE. DOI:10.1109/ECRIME.2018.8376206

Oest, A., Zhang, P., Wardman, B., Nunes, E., Burgis, J., Zand, A., . . . Ahn, G. J. (2020). Sunrise to sunset: Analyzing the end-to-end life cycle and effectiveness of phishing attacks at scale. In *29th USENIX Security Symposium (USENIX Security 20)* (pp. 361-377). USENIX.

Peng, T., Harris, I., & Sawa, Y. (2018, January). Detecting phishing attacks using natural language processing and machine learning. In *2018 IEEE 12th international conference on semantic computing (ICSC)* (pp. 300-301). IEEE. DOI:10.1109/ICSC.2018.00056

Phishing Activity Trends Report. (2020). Retrieved from https://docs.apwg.org/reports/apwg_trends_report_q2_2020.pdf

Phishing Stats You Should Know In 2021 | Expert Insights. Expert Insights. (2021). Retrieved 4 November 2021, from https://expertinsights.com/insights/50-phishing-stats-you-should-know/

Prakash, P., Kumar, M., Kompella, R. R., & Gupta, M. (2010, March). Phishnet: predictive blacklisting to detect phishing attacks. In 2010 Proceedings IEEE INFOCOM (pp. 1-5). IEEE.DOI: doi:10.1109/INFCOM.2010.5462216

Ramzan, Z. (2010). Phishing attacks and countermeasures. Handbook of information and communication security, 433-448. DOI: doi:10.1007/978-3-642-04117-4_23

Rao, S., Verma, A. K., & Bhatia, T. (2021). A review on social spam detection: Challenges, open issues, and future directions. *Expert Systems with Applications, 186*, 115742. doi:10.1016/j.eswa.2021.115742

Rehman Javed, A., Jalil, Z., Atif Moqurrab, S., Abbas, S., & Liu, X. (2020). Ensemble adaboost classifier for accurate and fast detection of botnet attacks in connected vehicles. *Transactions on Emerging Telecommunications Technologies, 4088*. Advance online publication. doi:10.1002/ett.4088

Sahingoz, O. K., Buber, E., Demir, O., & Diri, B. (2019). Machine learning based phishing detection from URLs. *Expert Systems with Applications, 117*, 345–357. doi:10.1016/j.eswa.2018.09.029

Sahoo, D., Liu, C., & Hoi, S. C. (2017). *Malicious URL detection using machine learning: A survey*. DOI: doi:10.36227/techrxiv.11492622.v1

San Martino, A., & Perramon, X. (2010). Phishing Secrets: History, Effects, Countermeasures. *International Journal of Network Security, 11*(3), 163–171.

Sharma, A., Singh, A., Sharma, N., Kaushik, I., & Bhushan, B. (2019, July). Security countermeasures in web based application. In *2019 2nd International Conference on Intelligent Computing, Instrumentation and Control Technologies (ICICICT)* (Vol. 1, pp. 1236-1241). IEEE. DOI: 10.1109/ICICICT46008.2019.8993141

Singh, A., Sharma, A., Sharma, N., Kaushik, I., & Bhushan, B. (2019, July). Taxonomy of attacks on web based applications. In *2019 2nd International Conference on Intelligent Computing, Instrumentationand Control Technologies (ICICICT)* (Vol. 1, pp. 1231-1235). IEEE. DOI: 10.1109/ICICICT46008.2019.8993264

Somesha, M., Pais, A. R., Rao, R. S., & Rathour, V. S. (2020). Efficient deep learning techniques for the detection of phishing websites. *Sadhana*, *45*(1), 1–18.

Teraguchi, N. C. R. L. Y., & Mitchell, J. C. (2004). *Client-side defense against web-based identity theft*. Computer Science Department, Stanford University. Available: http://crypto. stanford. edu/SpoofGuard/webspoof. pdf

Tsalis, N., Virvilis, N., Mylonas, A., Apostolopoulos, T., & Gritzalis, D. (2014, August). Browser blacklists: the Utopia of phishing protection. In *International Conference on E-Business and Telecommunications* (pp. 278-293). Springer. DOI: 10.1007/978-3-319-25915-4_15

Tweneboah-Koduah, S., Skouby, K. E., & Tadayoni, R. (2017). Cyber security threats to IoT applications and service domains. *Wireless Personal Communications*, *95*(1), 169–185. doi:10.2139srn.3170187

Van Der Heijden, A., & Allodi, L. (2019). Cognitive triaging of phishing attacks. In *28th USENIX Security Symposium (USENIX Security 19)* (pp. 1309-1326). USENIX.

Verma, P., Goyal, A., & Gigras, Y. (2020). Email phishing: Text classification using natural language processing. *Computer Science and Information Technology*, *1*(1), 1–12. doi:10.11591/csit.v1i1.p1-12

Williams, J., King, J., Smith, B., Pouriyeh, S., Shahriar, H., & Li, L. (2021). Phishing Prevention Using Defense in Depth. In *Advances in Security, Networks, and Internet of Things* (pp. 101–116). Springer. doi:10.1007/978-3-030-71017-0_8

Yue, C., & Wang, H. (2008, December). Anti-phishing in offense and defense. In *2008 Annual Computer Security Applications Conference (ACSAC)* (pp. 345-354). IEEE. DOI:10.1109/ACSAC.2008.32

Chapter 7
Web Mining and Web Usage Mining for Various Human– Driven Applications

Avinash Kumar
School of Engineering and Technology, Sharda University, India

Bharat Bhushan
ⓘ https://orcid.org/0000-0002-9345-4786
School of Engineering and Technology, Sharda University, India.

Nandita Pokhriya
School of Engineering and Technology, Sharda University

Raj Chaganti
Department of Computer Science, University of Texas at San Antonio, USA

Parma Nand
School of Engineering and Technology, Sharda University, India

ABSTRACT

The current century has seen a huge amount of data being produced every day by various computational platforms. These data are very large in amount when compared to the past. These data have emerged in form of big data (BD), and it's vital to manage these data for processing as well as extracting. The big data are emerging from Facebook, Instagram, and various other social as well as private platforms. Web mining has the capabilities to mine or extract data from a very huge set of data. The mining of useful information is essential for optimal functioning of various systems. In this chapter, the usage of web mining and one of its sub categories, web usage mining, for various human-driven applications has been discussed. This chapter focuses on the background that leads to the emergence of web mining. The chapter also deeply explores various subdomains that are essential for tackling data extraction using web mining.

DOI: 10.4018/978-1-7998-9426-1.ch007

INTRODUCTION

The commencement of a huge amount of data due to various new technologies and social media platforms has resulted in a new term called big data. This huge data couldn't be worked on (processed and analysed) with the help of existing technologies, theories, and methodologies (Quinto, 2018). Some typical properties of big data are volume, value, velocity, and variety (Somoza Sánchez, 2020). Studies show that the total amount of big data at the global level has reached about $58.9 billion in the year 2017, with an increment of about 29.1% (Alam et al., 2020). Big data has innate to it the capability to improve the governance, promote research, and make production more efficient (Chen et al., 2019; Emrouznejad & Marra, 2016). Cloud computing as of now has emerged as one of the novel paradigms that is being used to implement a shared pool of computing resources (storage, applications, and services), it has become increasingly easy to configure cloud computing tasks (Gill & Buyya, 2019; Miyachi, 2018). The establishment of these services based on big data makes for a great performing data cloud platform. Big data often suffers from repeated changes in size and scope, making powerful techniques the need of the day in order to cope with these changes. Therefore, it is important that the components of big data processing architecture are designed keeping in mind not only its volatile nature but also factors like cost, speed, and system scalability (Arostegi et al., 2018). Big data finds its applications in almost all walks of life, from finance to education to healthcare to defense and governance. In the Internet of Things (IoT) big data can be employed to realize applications like smart vehicles, indoor localization, innovative computer architectures (Chen et al., 2021).

Data mining has emerged as a vital step in the discovery of useful patterns and information in databases (Howard & Rayward-Smith, 1999). Many different routines from other domains such as statistics, databases, machine learning, pattern recognition, algorithms, high-performance computing, visualization, information retrieval, are included in data mining (Robardet, 2013; Yie et al., 2021). The first three methods being the entities that fundamentally contribute to data mining (Shi et al., 2018). Summarization, clustering, analysis of outliers, association, classification, regression, and analysis of trends, characterization, are some of the most common application areas of data mining methodologies (Ye et al., 2019). With the advancement in technology, even small-scale businesses have come to be a part of the community that finds itself inclined to use computer-based decision systems to get a better and clearer picture. With the usage of these technologies, the organizations more often than not, find themselves making profits leading to an overall benefit to both the stakeholders and the owners (Kumar, 2020). These systems over time have been evolved so as to reduce the burdens on humans when and where it comes to making decisions based on analysis of organizational data. There have been many researches in the field giving powerful insights on big data analysis and its resulting decision-making capabilities (Bumblauskas et al., 2017). In order to overcome the errors encountered in the production systems, the key factors are experience and knowledge. Data mining techniques have found usage in a circle of domains mining time-series data, web mining, spatial data mining, temporal data mining, medical, science, educational data mining, business, and engineering.

Today's world is marked by people relying on the World Wide Web (WWW) to send, receive and retrieve information, to distribute or to gain knowledge, for conducting businesses online, to express their opinions, to have discussions with people from all around the world, for education and entertainment. Therefore, it comes as no surprise that the web has become the biggest and most varied data store for mining tasks. The information present on the web, the whole ocean of it could be useful or maze-like depending upon the preferences of people searching for that information. While data mining techniques are used for web page analysis, web mining techniques, essentially a subset of data mining techniques are used for particular websites and electronic services (Panchal, 2019). Web Mining can be summed up as the method in which data mining techniques are used to automatically recognize and extract insight from Web documents. Web mining can be further classified into three subcategories which are, web content mining, weblog mining, and web structure mining. Whenever a website is visited by any user a log file gets created automatically. The log files document the complete information about each user's use of the website. The size of these log files has as of late been seeing tremendous growth because of how the web pages have pretty much become a part and parcel of every individual's life and routine (Sathiyamoorthi, 2017). Web mining is used to find and process confidential information from these log files. Web mining helps in refining the control of web search engines by helping in classifying the web documents and recognizing web pages. Web mining also finds its application in web penetrating google, yahoo, and searching vertically. Web mining is also used to predict user performance. Prasad et al. (Shivaprasad et al., 2015) suggested that the neuro-fuzzy as a concept binds the notion of neural networks and fuzzy computing together. They used a neural net-based hybrid system to determine hidden data patterns present in the data stored in the Web Log Server. The paper employed combined methodologies and weblog pre-processing methods based on dimensionality reduction techniques. Several researchers have shown to have used a method to further refine the prediction of the next web page the user might want to visit based on the already visited web pages. The same is then recommended to the current users who are interested in visiting similar types of sites (Al-Dabooni & Wunsch, 2020). This paper tries its best to cover the vital aspects of web mining and its implementation in various domains.

In summary, the major contributions of this paper are as follows.

- This work presents the need behind employing Web Mining techniques for tackling various Web related applications
- This work outlines how web mining has emerged as a state-of-art solution for tackling the huge amounts of data processed in various organizations and companies
- The various areas where the use of web mining would provide best optimal solution for extracting data have also been discussed in this paper.
- This work, towards the end focuses on the idea of Web Usage Mining being one of the critical solutions for the processing of data using extraction of meaningful data and information

The remainder of the paper is organized as follows. Section 2 presents the background of web mining highlighting the various challenges faced in the domain of mining web data and the steps that have been taken so far to tackle those challenges. Section 3 introduces web mining and its sub-domains. Section 4 presents Web Usage Mining. Section 5 presents applications of web mining. Finally, section 6 presents the conclusion and is followed by future research directions.

BACKGROUND

Every year we witness a huge influx in the number of people using the internet, trying through it to make use of the various products and services available online. Every single possible requirement in the life of an individual can now be potentially fulfilled by the internet, be it paying the bills or booking a flight, or grocery shopping (Kumar et al., 2019). Most of these services can be implemented and made available through web-based approaches. Therefore, web applications have excessively become a one-stop destination for internet users to get their net fodder at and to exchange information (Kasemsap, 2017). However, with the increasing influx comes the problem of managing data or what has lately come to be known as big data, this includes everything from the news to the cookbooks available online. Many of these applications operate by sourcing data from the users to deliver better results. While these applications have come a long way to become an indispensable part of our day-to-day lives, they don't come without a price, most of these applications and websites especially today, with the advent of big data carry a huge computational overhead especially in terms of space and time complexity. Another issue faced by these applications is the network traffic every time they try to access, manipulate or alter a record remotely or over a network (Zhang et al., 2021). The process using which useful information is extracted from this big data, often based on some arbitrary criteria and standards, falls under the realm of data mining (Witten et al., 2011). The qualities of outcomes thus produced depend to a very large extent on the features selected, which vary depending on the application's nature and usage. For instance, in a web-mining application, the features would be things like web content, users' activities and behaviour, links, frequency of visiting web pages, blogging data (Ristoski et al., 2015).

Multiple existing researches focus on improving web mining accuracy via the application of various machine learning and rule-based algorithms. Blogging is one prevalent feature offered by web applications worldwide, characteristically by Web2.0 (Xu et al., 2019). The netizens use these blogs to get out there in the virtual world and share snapshots from their lives. Be it an item review or a diary detailing a shopping thrift, blogs have it all which brings us to the conclusion that blogs have different categories ranging from cultural, social, political to scientific, educational, and entertainment. Therefore, blogs are emerging as a huge base for researchers to engage their resources on, with a window for the development of a classifier that would help identify the reader's thoughts and ideas. This would help the bloggers to further familiarize themselves with reader opinions and create content based on popularity and reader requirements. A hybrid mechanism (combining 'KNN' and 'ANN' techniques) has been proposed by (Lumchanow & Udomsiri, 2019). The idea was to conduct experiments on Kohkiloye and Boyer Blogger's dataset (Lumchanow & Udomsiri, 2019) and the accuracy obtained in this experiment was 89.4%.

The content of a particular website or web app defines the type of information in that the topics which are chosen to deliver a certain piece of information (Ali et al., 2017). Generally speaking, content on the web could contain any, images, object files, tables, maps, text, audio, video content. This sort of web content tends to be publicly accessible. Moreover, the presence or absence of the aforementioned items can be used to get a working idea of how engaging the website would be. Counting the number of views, ratings, feedback, comments, and shares are a few of the many ways in which a website's popularity can be measured (Oleinik, 2021). An instance of the same would be the usage of probabilistic rule-based measures to rank video sharing (Broxton et al., 2011). Broxton et al. (Broxton et al., 2011) proposed a solution that tracked videos shared, including the non-social and the social ones by performing a set of experiments via content ranking on YouTube, search engine, and the URL of about 100 websites. The results thus obtained make the rise and fall trends in social video popularity as compared to the non-social ones highly apparent.

On the other side of this trend rests the increasing e-commerce activities followed closely by an increase in data volume and an uphill slope in the business bent (Yılmaz & Gönen, 2018). There exist several recommendation systems that serve these e-commerce apps. Although these traditional recommendation systems suffer from many limitations such as systems getting slowed down due to an excessive number of customers or products, recommendations based on user's clickstream- no new items getting recommended, already wish-listed or carted items getting re recommended. To deal with these issues, many new approaches have been proposed including things like recommendations for unregistered users based on products, user-based recommendations for the registered ones, and behaviour-based recommendations for either (Singh & Shaw, 2020). These dynamic systems start with data cleaning, the data itself is collected from frequently visited and long-stayed at blogs which also contain information on things like product name, category, IP addresses, and the prime feature that differentiates these dynamic systems from the traditional ones is that the data itself is dynamic. For the evaluation of these dynamic systems three different metrics have been proposed: user interest, visit frequency, and similarity measure. The most assuring accuracy so far has been gathered from the behaviour-based technique which goes up to 82% (Singh & Shaw, 2020).

News portals everywhere seem to have a great bearing on the lives of people (Lui et al., 2014). The content provided by these portals today is dynamic much like the nature of 'news' itself and hence keeps changing in a matter of seconds (Boister & Burchill, 2017). Hence, it would be only right to say that extracting the perfect tidbit of information, from millions of things that could pass as news, that would not only catch but hold onto the interest of the masses is a vital task if the patronage to the site is to be ensured. An existing solution uses a Back Propagation Neural Network (BPNN) to mine news from big portals such as the British Broadcasting Corporation (BBC) and Cable News Network (CNN) websites (Kaur & Mamoon Rashid, 2016). Kaur et al. (Kaur & Mamoon Rashid, 2016) proposed a multiple-layer network with its weights getting updated iteratively. News records act as the input for the model, when learned the model then classifies the input news records based on the classes (entertainment, health, business, education and crime) it has been trained on. This measure would reduce the overhead of the users browsing the entire website in search of riveting content because now they would get reduced and classified 'big' news records. This would result in reduced time complexity and an enhanced user experience. The surveys conducted on the widely used state-of-the-art web mining methodologies have resulted in the following conclusions (Maghdid, 2019):

- The current web mining solutions sport varying accuracies based on the type and number of features or attributes used while training the model.
- The precisions and accuracy of these models are in need of further enrichment if these are to have a real-time application with user experience enhancement
- There is a need for improvement in space and time-based performance since the data is only going to get large from here on.

These conclusions provide a working explanation on why the current web-mining solutions might not be the best for anytime, anywhere implementations on different applications. To deal with this Maghdid et al. (Maghdid, 2019) proposed an automotive mining approach, a viable fit for most web applications. The functionalities provided are stable classification for multiple purposes (application independent), various categories included with supporting data to provide accurate results (uses geolocation to map content based on location), and uses time information feature to provide recommendations in lesser time.

WEB MINING

One of the many applications of data mining is web mining, it extracts meaningful information from the data available on the web by identifying and discovering patterns innate to this data. It makes use of automated methodologies to extract both organized and unorganized data from the web. Web content mining is a sub-category of web mining that trades in the extraction of data from within a page (Lingaraju & Jagannatha, 2019). Another sub-category, web structure mining works by discovering the relations and connections between various web pages available online. While the last sub-category named web usage mining finds patterns of web usage. There is a myriad of issues encountered while dealing with either the user view (how to find relevant content) or the information provider view (what content would bring in the maximum number of patrons) of the web. While web mining is primarily concerned with retrieving useful data, a possible situation is the availability of multiple copies of the said useful data. One of the techniques used to deal with this problem of redundancy is the usage of Self-Organizing Maps (SOM) (Kamimura, 2012). The various sub-domains of web mining along with a few of its emerging application areas are discussed in the subsections below and a compact summary has been listed in Table1.

Web Content Mining

Web content mining is a subcategory of web mining, the application of which has to do with the extraction and utilization of useful information from the content of web documents. The content consists of the various facts and figures a web page is in general designed to render. The content itself has innate to it, features that help determine the patterns related to user behaviour and needs. Web content mining, sometimes also called text mining, is usually the second step in the whole process of web mining (Aggarwal, 2012). It is the combined process of scanning and mining that consists of text, video, images, tabular data. With how extensive the web is and how it makes it so that most services including information about all sorts of things are a mere click away, it shouldn't exactly come as a surprise that one of the most researched topics among the technical community is the application of text mining to web content. Text mining addresses issues like title discovery and tracking, extracting related patterns, forming web document clusters, and classifying web pages. Research in this field encompasses the process of discovering resources from the web, document clustering and categorizing, and information extraction (Kutbay, 2018).

Web Structure Mining

A standard web graph is made up of nodes denoting web pages and edges denoting hyperlinks between related pages (Bonato, 2008). While web content mining works on the inner documents (the nodes), web structure mining works on discovering and exploiting the link structure of the interlinked documents via their hyperlinks. The web structure mining-based algorithms work at the edges of the web graph and based on the topology of hyperlinks render the results related to inter-page/ inter-site relationships and similarities. Structure mining can be summed up as a very detailed procedure of identifying the underlying structure of the data on the web (Sathiyamoorthi, 2017). This provides opportunities for businesses to link their own website information to allow navigation and make clusters of information into the web graphs, which further allows the visitors of the websites to access content based on the presence or absence of selected keywords. This process can further be classified into two different categories based on the kind of information structure being used, hyperlink (a unit that connects a page on the web to another page or to a different section on the same page- intra and inter document links), document structure (the web content on any website can be visualized to have a tree format based on the XML or HTML tags used to create the page). Hyperlink hierarchy also comes in handy when creating associations based on competitor links and search engine connections and third-party links.

Web Usage Mining

Web usage mining is another subcategory of web mining that works on the exploitation and analysis of web usage data so as to figure out the existence of unique as well as useful usage patterns, this helps in the betterment of web-based browsing experience as it provides a basic understanding of users' common behaviours while browsing at any particular website (Baeza-Yates, 2008). The web usage data collected from different sources represents the patterns indigenous to the particular level of web traffic. The data could be obtained at the server level (servers explicitly record the behaviours of visitors of a particular site, this data shows the records on possibly simultaneous access of the website by the user(s)), or at the client level (this type of data collection could be carried out by using a remote assistant or by manipulating the code of an already present and used browser to further enhance its data collection capacity), or at the proxy level (proxy traces may serve as a medium to determine the browsing behaviours of a group of geographically dispersed anonymous users). The data collected from the aforementioned sources can be all used to identify different types of data abstractions such as users, episodes, click-streams, a consistency among these abstraction terms is maintained with the help of a published draft for web usage related terms (Juan & Chang, 2005).

E-Commerce

E-commerce or electronic commerce can be defined as the exercise of buying or selling of products or services or the transferring of funds or data electronically over the Internet. Transactions such as these occur either as Consumer to Consumer (C2C), as a Consumer to Business (C2B), as Business to Consumer (B2C), or as business to business (B2B). It uses in its implementation technologies like management of supplying chains, mobile-based commerce services, online marketing, electronic funds transfer, Electronic Data Interchange (EDI), processing of online transactions, and much more (Spiekermann et al., 2019). One major challenge faced by the e-commerce industry is to comprehend the users using their services, comprehending things such as their needs, demands, likes, and dislikes, and use the conclusions thus drawn to render their items and services in a manner that maximizes not only the visitors but also the business done at the end of the day. This kind of understanding would go a long way in not only providing the businesses a competitive advantage but also improving the service quality and overall user experience.

E-Politics and E-Democracy

The continuous shift from what could very well be called the real world to the virtual world (with its own set of standards and rules), has set in motion a number of challenges, one of which is the shift of e-governance from dormant to a highly dynamic state. The United States presidential elections of 2008 saw an unprecedented use of social media in the election campaigning. Social network platforms like YouTube and Facebook played a huge role in fundraising and acting as a forum for the candidates to get their messages across to the people (Vittoria & Napolitano, 2020). A work done by the researchers at the Massachusetts Institute of Technology (MIT), shows a high correlation between the amount of social media usage by candidates and the end results (I.O., 2018). The inclusion of politics into the e- world has further enforced people's right to information along with political transparency as now political information is a mere click away. Information about elections, polling results, members of parliaments, and the like is part of the services that come under e-politics. Despite how important the sector of e-politics has grown to become for democracies all around the world there still aren't many web mining methodologies available to felicitate user experience in this arena.

Security and Crime Investigation

'Redefining security' has recently come into the light as somewhat of a cottage industry lookalike. Most efforts to ensure and enforce security are concerned with redefining agendas, passing proposals, and so on. This trend of redefining security also extends to what would be called an individual's virtual security (Buzan & Hansen, 2018). Web mining techniques find usage in this area of security as well by attempting to protect the users and their sensitive information against cybercrimes such as internet fraud, hacking, illegal online gambling, distribution of child pornography, cyber terrorism, web mining uses clustering and classification methodologies to rule out identities of cybercriminals while neural network-based web mining algorithms find usage in tracing malicious patterns and website network visualization.

Table 1. The subcategories and few application areas of web mining

SI. No.	Application areas	Contribution/Summary
1	Web Content Mining (Aggarwal, 2012)	Extracting information from the patterns that are innate to the content of a web document.
2	Web Structure Mining (Bonato, 2008; Sathiyamoorthi, 2017)	Deals with the discovery and extraction of structure based knowledge from the websites.
3	Web Usage Mining (Baeza-Yates, 2008; Juan & Chang, 2005)	Extracting and analysing usage patterns at the server, client or proxy level.
4	E- Commerce (Spiekermann et al., 2019)	The use of web mining techniques has made the whole process more customer oriented thereby increasing the overall patronage of these sites.
5	E- Politics and E- Democracy (I.O., 2018; Vittoria & Napolitano, 2020)	The involvement of social media in politics is on the rise creating an upsurge in the political (campaign or otherwise) data available over the web that can use better rendering and processing methods to make it more palatable to the end users.
6	Security and Crime Investigation (Buzan & Hansen, 2018)	To ensure that the user's sensitive data is protected against crimes of cyber theft and the like.

Web Usage Mining

As must be apparent from the points discussed so far, web mining is an incredibly fast-paced research area. Web being the gigantic, unstructured, and the diversified entity that it is, the research faces a lot of challenges, a few of which are scalability issues, temporal and multimedia issues. This nature of the web is why users find themselves more often than not, immersed in what could only be rightfully called a universe of information leading to problems such as information overload during web interactions. Web usage mining is also called weblog mining. It deals with the exploration and processing of the data logs stored in the server (Nguyen et al., 2014). Vast developments in the WWW have enlarged the overall difficulty faced by users while they try to navigate it successfully. In order to increase the overall throughput of websites both the design of the websites and the services they offer need to be better aligned to the user's preferences as well as perspectives. The capability to figure out the patterns common to different users' habits and interests helps the enterprises to achieve this goal. Difficulty in finding relevant/ needed information, learning useful information (data mining oriented), personalization/ customization of information, are some of the problems that are often talked about in web-related research works as well as applications. Web usage mining helps by keeping an eye out for the user's activities and findings on the internet, by keeping track of things like whether the user is searching for text-based data or if the user wants to search for multimedia such as audio, video,

Web usage mining as a sub field of web mining mainly deals with the methods to withdraw useful information from weblogs. It employs data mining procedures to learn unique but useful patterns of usage of web data so as to comprehend, thereby serving the need of the customer base, different types of web-based applications cater to in general. Web usage data contains notes on each and every user's identity and the way they browse the web at any specific website. Usage data is then documented in the form of log files. A Weblog file is a file that is used by the server to store requisite data, every time user makes a request to a specific server for a site response. Web servers, web proxy servers, and the user's browser are the three different locations where a log file can be saved.

Log files of a web server are files that are stored in the server and note down the various activities of the clients who access the web server while using a particular website through their web browsers. Proxy servers on any network, live between the client machine and the machine running the server software and facilitate the communication between the two by performing a wide variety of functions. These proxy servers have their own cached-up log information. The web server receives a request from the client which is transferred to it by the proxy server. The entries then made on the log file are the data stored in and forwarded by the proxy servers and not that of the actual client machine. User Browsers log files are files that are meant to be stored in the browser window of the client's machine. A variety of software exists which a user can download for future uses directly into their browser. Although the log files exist in the client's system, the logs to that specific file are created by the webserver only. In the following subsections, the web usage mining phases along with the technique's most prominent advantages and disadvantages have been discussed in detail.

Web Usage Mining Phases

Utilizing techniques based on the principles of statistics is one of the most basic ways of deriving visitor pattern knowledge from a site. Session files can be analyzed via descriptive methods such as mean, median, frequency distribution, most tools that are meant for web traffic analysis work by representing information in periodic reports using statistical methods. In the present context, the use of association rules is to figure out the relationship between pages that are visited simultaneously in single sessions. These pages in order to be correlated might not actually need to be related via hyperlinks. For instance, association rules might point to a correlation between users shopping for electronics with users looking into carpentry tools. In the below subsections and Figure 1, the basic methods employed or the basic phases involved have been discussed in detail.

Collecting Data

Collecting data is the initial step of the process in which the user's log data is obtained from a variety of sources. This step is important because it is to ensure that only data that is relevant to the application (problem) at hand is collected. The aforementioned sources include but are not limited to, the server, client, proxy servers, or the database of an enterprise, which might contain in its store either business or aggregated Web data.

Data Pre-Processing

Sometimes log files obtained at the data collection phase turn out to be lacking insufficiency, consistency, or including noise. The data pre-processing is done so as to perform a unification-based transformation on such databases. This renders the database, integrate and consistent, and minable. The data pre-processing work mainly includes tasks like data cleaning, identifying users, identifying sessions, and completing paths. This step helps in removing the unnecessary and repetitive log entries and also helps correct or remove corrupted entries from the database files.

Performing user and session identification helps in the task of obtaining the session use information of different users from the original web access log. Phinyomark et al. (Phinyomark et al., 2017) has proposed various novel methods to preprocess rfMRI data (the pre-processing of which using existing tools had become difficult due to its 'big' nature), using tools with their foundations rooted in the algebraic maths. Song et al. (Song et al., 2020) proposed the implementation of Bitshuffle preprocessing algorithm on Field Programmable Gate Array (FPGA) to convert raw data into another format that would support huge sizes.

Discovering Patterns

After the log file data has been transformed into a formatted, well-defined structure, the process of pattern discovery takes place. Pattern Discovery Tools apply a wide variety of techniques ranging from data mining algorithms to machine learning algorithms to discrete and integral mathematics and pattern identification algorithms, and many more. Pattern discovery helps in finding patterns, classifying or clustering data by applying mining procedures. The process through which relationships between variables are searched for is called the association rule. Web usage mining makes use of the association rules to figure out what all pages are most commonly visited together in the duration of a single session while keeping in mind the goal of discovering what kind of websites and what kind of sectors are regularly visited together by the people accessing the web. This helps in finding collections of data that often occur successively within the sequences. Sze-To et al. (Sze-To & Wong, 2018) proposed a method known as Pattern-Directed Aligned Pattern Clustering (PD-APCn) to discover patterns in protein functional regions. Mining of sequential patterns helps extract commonly occurring subsequence from within a database, acts as the footing for a variety of applications, a few of which are stock market prediction, web user analysis, analyzing DNA sequences. Ouyang et al. (Ouyang et al., 2020) in his paper suggests that finance related planning when guided by pattern discovery might produce even more realistic and efficient results than the traditional methods.

Pattern Analyses

This serves as the final stage in the whole process of Web Usage Analysis (WUA). Pattern analysis, as the name suggests works by finding latent or hidden facts and information from the discovered pattern. The useful or interesting patterns found are kept while the irrelevant or redundant patterns are omitted. Pattern Analysis consists of interpreting and validating the mined patterns. Validation is done in an effort to remove the unnecessary or inconsequential patterns thereby facilitating the extraction of patterns that are of some consequence from the results obtained from pattern discovery. The final result thus obtained tends to be in a mathematical form which humans find difficult to interpret if not sometimes, impossible. So, visualization procedures are employed to better evaluate and understand the final results. Wang et al (Wang et al., 2021) proposed a novel Multi-Modality and Discriminant SCCA algorithm (MD-SCCA) to overcome the limitations imposed as a result of the traditional algorithm seeking linear correlation, as well as to improve learning results by inculcating important discriminant similarity data into the SCCA algorithm.

Figure 1. Phases of web usage mining

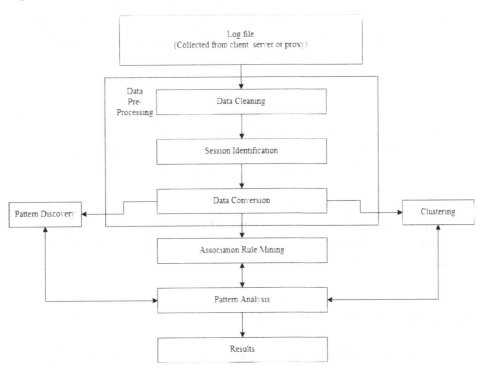

Advantages and Disadvantages

The numerous advantages of web usage mining that make it appealing to various enterprises including government agencies are as follows:

- Various e-commerce websites have employed this method to target the customer base in a more personalized manner, which ultimately results in elevated volumes of trade.

- Government agencies all around the world are making use of this technology to classify threats, interpret and intercede them thereby fighting terrorism.
- Companies are now able to establish loyal customer bases by providing them what they need, in some cases even before they themselves realize it, this they do by understanding the requirements of the customers better which in turn helps them respond to customer demands faster and in a more reliable manner. This shift has allowed companies to make even more profit by indulging in the practice of targeting prices based on the consumer profiles generated.

Like any other technology, this one also has its own set of disadvantages which are:

- Invasion of Privacy is the main issue encountered with web usage mining.
- Another major concern is that sometimes there could be cases when companies collect the data for some explicitly stated, distinct purpose but instead, they end up using the data for another purpose, these kinds of practices essentially violate the user's concerns.
- Some techniques have been found to employ highly questionable attributes such as religion, gender, racial identity, or sexual inclination for the classification of individuals. Acts of these types sometimes violate the laws against discrimination yet, there is no set way of figuring out whether or not such practice has been used.
- With how data is increasingly coming to become a commodity website owners often feel encouraged to buy and sell personal data. This trend has resulted in an increase in the amount of data being obtained and traded further aggravating the privacy concerns.

APPLICATIONS OF WEB MINING

The popularity of the web in the past few years has far outpaced the research in web-related technologies i.e., the industry has seen a much faster rate in the development of web-based applications. Many of these applications use web mining concepts as their foundation blocks, a lucky coincidence in most cases as the organizations that developed these applications might not necessarily be aiming for that particular outcome as such. Web mining itself is an application of data mining - techniques, used to discover a variety of patterns based on the web mining subcategory, so as to better understand and match pace with the evolving needs of web-based applications. Listed below are some of the most common application areas of web mining:

Education

The usage of web mining techniques in the educational domain has seen an exponential rise in the last few decades owing to the recent developments in the field of e-education. A broad range of educational applications have been introduced, these applications have become increasingly interactive, with a huge portion available as web apps. An application of web mining in this field is the Link Recommender System (LRS) (Bustos López et al., 2020). This system facilitates user navigation on websites by preventing them from getting lost during their web searches. An emerging field of research that has recently come to garner its fair share of interest is the use of mining techniques in educational content. Educational Data Mining (EDM) is primarily concerned with finding interesting patterns from the different types of educational settings. Some researches in the area of web usage mining particularly use all sorts of student information available in popular learning management systems such as WebCT, BlackBoard, Moodle, for determining browsing routes and recommending personalized links. These approaches generally consist of three steps namely preparation of data, the discovery of patterns, and recommendation. Data is converted into a workable format in the data preparation phase, followed by the usage of data mining routines such as association mining and clustering to figure out patterns in the data. Finally, personalized links are recommended.

Health Informatics

The healthcare domain is among the many fields that have greatly benefited from the advent of the digital age. Tools for tasks such as signal processing, image processing, have helped in providing accurate analysis of medical information and helping physicians gain a better understanding of the ailment thereby improving the quality of health to a great extent. Recently the usage of the internet as a potential communication tool in the field of healthcare has seen rapid growth. The behaviour associated with seeking health-related information to a great deal depend on the type of information along with the experience in searching and the domain knowledge possessed. Research shows that women are more regular patrons of these health-related information websites than men are. The health of any individual being the sensitive matter it is the credibility and trustworthiness of the sources available online are of great consequence to the users accessing these websites. It has further been found that physicians tend to present internet-sourced printed information to patients. Data mining methods such as clustering, regression, clustering, are often used to solve issues occurring in the medical referral process (Nasraoui, 2008). These mining techniques result in a more effective retrieval of information. The Internet has also come to act as a backbone in the healthcare domain, providing value to healthcare providers, their suppliers, and the patients by helping implement supply chain solutions. Research shows that the popularity of network-based health care systems came with the advent of the internet, despite the fact that information systems existed in clinics, labs, and hospitals, linked via a local area or wide area networks even prior to the invention of the internet (Scott, 2019). Internet, intranets, and extranets being the three primary networks used by health industries, not only to communicate with providers or to search for information but also to send complicated and huge medical files over the web.

Human-Computer Interaction

Machines as tools made and used for hum convenience can perform only as well as the humans operating or using them can make them. Human-Computer Interaction (HCI) is a field of research that focuses on the interaction between humans (users) and computers. The research mainly observes how the interaction between humans and computers works followed by coming up with innovations to further enhance the whole experience. The notion behind coining the term was to liken it to the analogy of human-to-human interaction. Web mining utilizes data mining methodologies to unveil important information derivable from the navigation behaviour exhibited by web users. Web mining provides a way to better comprehend the web applications' server needs and design requirements by using data mining algorithms to discover useful unique patterns in the web usage data. The web usage data consists of detailed information about the identities of users, their origins, and the behaviour they exhibit while browsing the web. Common applications of web usage mining, a subcategory of web mining include things like link prediction, reorganizing site, pre-fetching web. The traffic information- tested and evaluated, obtained by using web mining techniques is used in the formulation of guidelines for decision making, for instance, introducing new products to fulfil customer demands or needs (Knickerbocker & Rycik, 2019). One possible way to facilitate human-computer interaction is by minimizing the number of features for analysis and clustering. Among the extensive variety of visualization-based models proposed in the past decade only a few deal with feature minimization to ease human-computer interaction. All phases of web mining provide log files that are consistent and free from unneeded data (Liu et al., 2011). Another subcategory of web mining - web structure mining plays a vital role in providing a number of benefits like shorter response time to the web users, decreasing the average number of transactions taking place between the users and the servers thereby saving the server memory space and improved usage of bandwidth along with saving server's processor time.

Social Media

Social media platforms provide a way to disseminate media content created in lieu of social interaction in a highly accessible way. These platforms make use of the internet and web based technologies. Researches show that social networking products have experienced a growing peak. Web sites like Instagram and Facebook attract hundreds and thousands of visitors in a single day alone moreover, maintaining a similar type of visitor trend on a daily basis, and hence are approaching the traffic on the similar level of search sites. These social networking sites provide tools that are used by individuals to establish communities and participate in activities happening within those communities, to upload and share content generated by individual users, and interact with other users using the same site or platform. Analysing the social network patterns and trends is about finding the groups lodged into the depths of the datasets maintained by these social networking sites and analysing how these groups evolve and interrelate in a dynamic environment. The pattern thus obtained sometimes provides interesting insights into the trends along which these groups function. Social media content mining is a type of social computing. Social computing makes use of social media applications along with applications and researches for "computational social studies (Zorrilla et al., 2018)". Web 2.0 technologies along with the introduction of the present-day online social media have changed the scenario by making the move from one-way communication driven by traditional media such as newspapers, televisions, to where now almost anybody has the means to publish audio, written, or video content to the people. Web mining plays an important role in the analysis of social media data trends. It has proven to be increasingly useful in the analytical study of extracted social network data. The communication and usage data of a particular user on a social networking website can be transformed into relational data which can then be used for social network construction. Moreover, over the year web usage mining has come to be used as a tool for measuring the degree of centrality. In some recent articles, many users have been reported to have complained about how they might soon need to hire full-time employees to deal with the operations associated with their ever-expanding social network accounts. Social media has increasingly come into the limelight as a viable alternative for expensive marketing, providing a means to promote about anything and everything and hence is the ideal place to study the implications and methods best employed to further explore its marketing potential (Ghosh, 2016). However, due to how big and diverse social media has come to become, mining techniques are the only viable answer as of now to study and exploit these trends.

CONCLUSION AND FUTURE RESEARCH DIRECTIONS

The digital era has seen a large volume of data and information being produced by various platforms every day. The data has now become a driving force for various organizations and companies to carry out their business and daily routine work. The web has now become a container of a huge amount of data. Therefore, it becomes very essential to carry our processing of data in order to achieve useful outcomes. There are various strategies among which data mining and web mining are two vital ones. Web usage mining is another aspect of web mining that is more useful for tackling large amounts of data. Various applications such as educational organizations, social media platforms, and many others require web mining for resolving their processing critical issues arising due to huge amounts of data. The paper begins with the background study of web mining. The paper then tries its best to explain the processing and use of various sub-domains of web mining. The paper covers various aspects of web usage mining that discuss the various advantages as well as limitations of web usage mining. The paper also focuses on various applications of web mining and its effects.

The future guidelines have been indicated in various sections. The paper provides a platform for various research that could be carried out based upon the domains and methodological details provided by web mining as one of the solutions. The web usages could be used as a reference to future research having the need to process and extract large amounts of data like Smart healthcare, cloud system, and many others that deal with the huge amounts of data. Apart from the application areas discussed such as education, social media platforms, the paper can also serve as a reference to new applications using web mining as its backbone for data extraction and processing.

REFERENCES

Aggarwal, C. C. (2012). Mining text streams. *Mining Text Data*, 297–321. doi:10.1007/978-1-4614-3223-4_9

Al-Dabooni, S., & Wunsch, D. (2020). Convergence of recurrent neuro-fuzzy value-gradient learning with and without an actor. *IEEE Transactions on Fuzzy Systems*, 28(4), 658–672. doi:10.1109/TFUZZ.2019.2912349

Alam, A., Ullah, I., & Lee, Y.-K. (2020). Video Big Data Analytics in the cloud: A reference architecture, survey, opportunities, and open research issues. *IEEE Access: Practical Innovations, Open Solutions*, 8, 152377–152422. doi:10.1109/ACCESS.2020.3017135

Ali, F., Khan, P., Riaz, K., Kwak, D., Abuhmed, T., Park, D., & Kwak, K. S. (2017). A fuzzy ontology and SVM–based web content classification system. *IEEE Access: Practical Innovations, Open Solutions*, 5, 25781–25797. doi:10.1109/ACCESS.2017.2768564

Arostegi, M., Torre-Bastida, A., Bilbao, M. N., & Del Ser, J. (2018). A heuristic approach to the Multicriteria design of IaaS cloud infrastructures for big data applications. *Expert Systems: International Journal of Knowledge Engineering and Neural Networks*, 35(5), e12259. Advance online publication. doi:10.1111/exsy.12259

Baeza-Yates, R. (2008). Web usage mining in search engines. *Web Mining*, 307–321. doi:10.4018/978-1-59140-414-9.ch014

Boister, N., & Burchill, R. (2017). The implications of the Pinochet decisions for the extradition or prosecution of former South African heads of State for crimes committed under apartheid. *International Crimes*, 558–575. doi:10.4324/9781315092591-15

Bonato, A. (2008). The web graph. *Graduate Studies in Mathematics*, 19–32. doi:10.1090/gsm/089/02

Broxton, T., Interian, Y., Vaver, J., & Wattenhofer, M. (2011). Catching a viral video. *Journal of Intelligent Information Systems*, 40(2), 241–259. doi:10.100710844-011-0191-2

Bumblauskas, D., Gemmill, D., Igou, A., & Anzengruber, J. (2017). Smart maintenance decision support Systems (SMDSS) based on corporate big data analytics. *Expert Systems with Applications*, 90, 303–317. doi:10.1016/j.eswa.2017.08.025

Bustos López, M., Alor-Hernández, G., Sánchez-Cervantes, J. L., Paredes-Valverde, M. A., & Salas-Zárate, M. P. (2020). EduRecomSys: An Educational Resource Recommender system based on collaborative filtering and emotion detection. *Interacting with Computers*, 32(4), 407–432. doi:10.1093/iwc/iwab001

Buzan, B., & Hansen, L. (2018). *Defining–redefining security*. Oxford Research Encyclopedia of International Studies., doi:10.1093/acrefore/9780190846626.013.382

Chen, Y., Wang, J., Xia, R., Zhang, Q., Cao, Z., & Yang, K. (2021). Retraction note to: The visual object tracking algorithm research based on adaptive combination kernel. *Journal of Ambient Intelligence and Humanized Computing*. Advance online publication. doi:10.100712652-021-03500-6

Chen, Y., Zhou, M., & Zheng, Z. (2019). Learning sequence-based fingerprint for magnetic indoor positioning system. *IEEE Access: Practical Innovations, Open Solutions*, 7, 163231–163244. doi:10.1109/ACCESS.2019.2952564

Emrouznejad, A., & Marra, M. (2016). Big data: Who, what and where? Social, cognitive and journals map of big data publications with focus on optimization. *Studies in Big Data*, 1–16. doi:10.1007/978-3-319-30265-2_1

Ghosh, M. (2016). Case study: Text-mining customers view point and perceived value about brand. *International Journal of Business Analytics and Intelligence*, *4*(1). Advance online publication. doi:10.21863/ijbai/2016.4.1.016

Gill, S. S., & Buyya, R. (2019). A taxonomy and future directions for sustainable cloud computing. *ACM Computing Surveys*, *51*(5), 1–33. doi:10.1145/3241038

Howard, C., & Rayward-Smith, V. (1999, January 1). Discovering knowledge from low-quality meteorological databases. *Data Mining and Knowledge Discovery*, 180–203. doi:10.1049/PBPC001E_ch9

I.O., A. (2018). An improved model for web usage mining and web traffic analysis. *Journal of Computer Science and Information Technology*, *6*(1). Advance online publication. doi:10.15640/jcsit.v6n1a5

Juan, Y.-F., & Chang, C.-C. (2005). An analysis of search engine switching behaviour using click streams. *Lecture Notes in Computer Science*, *3828*, 806–815. doi:10.1007/11600930_82

Kamimura, R. (2012). Social interaction and self-organizing maps. *Applications of Self-Organizing Maps*. doi:10.5772/51705

Kasemsap, K. (2017). Mastering web mining and information retrieval in the Digital age. *Advances in Data Mining and Database Management*, 1–28. doi:10.4018/978-1-5225-0613-3.ch001

Kaur, S., & Mamoon Rashid, E. (2016). Web news mining using back propagation neural network and clustering using K-means algorithm in Big Data. *Indian Journal of Science and Technology*, *9*(41). Advance online publication. doi:10.17485/ijst/2016/v9i41/95598

Knickerbocker, J. L., & Rycik, J. A. (2019). Changing literature, changing readers, changing classrooms. *Literature for Young Adults*, 1–29. doi:10.4324/9781351067683-1

Kumar. (2020). Data mining based marketing decision support system using Hybrid machine learning algorithm. *Irojournals*, *2*(3), 185–193. doi:10.36548//jaicn.2020.3.006

Kumar, A., Mukherjee, A. B., & Krishna, A. P. (2019). Application of conventional data mining techniques and web mining to aid disaster management. *Environmental Information Systems*, 369–398. doi:10.4018/978-1-5225-7033-2.ch017

Kutbay, U. (2018). *Partitional clustering*. Recent Applications in Data Clustering., doi:10.5772/intechopen.75836

Lingaraju, D. G. M., & Jagannatha, D. S. (2019). Review of web page classification and web content mining. *Journal of Advanced Research in Dynamical and Control Systems*, *11*(10), 142–147. doi:10.5373/JARDCS/V11I10/20193017

Liu, B., Mobasher, B., & Nasraoui, O. (2011). Web usage mining. *Web Data Mining*, 527–603. doi:10.1007/978-3-642-19460-3_12

Lui, D., Modhafar, A., Glaister, J., Wong, A., & Haider, M. A. (2014). Monte Carlo bias field correction in endorectal diffusion imaging. *IEEE Transactions on Biomedical Engineering*, *61*(2), 368–380. doi:10.1109/TBME.2013.2279635 PMID:24448596

Lumchanow, W., & Udomsiri, S. (2019). Image classification of malaria using hybrid algorithms: Convolutional Neural Network and method to find appropriate K for K-nearest neighbor. *Indonesian Journal of Electrical Engineering and Computer Science*, *16*(1), 382. doi:10.11591/ijeecs.v16.i1.pp382-388

Maghdid, H. S. (2019). Web news mining using new features: A comparative study. *IEEE Access: Practical Innovations, Open Solutions*, *7*, 5626–5641. doi:10.1109/ACCESS.2018.2890088

Miyachi, C. (2018). What is "Cloud"? It is time to update the NIST definition? *IEEE Cloud Computing*, *5*(3), 6–11. doi:10.1109/MCC.2018.032591611

Nasraoui, O. (2008). Web data mining. *SIGKDD Explorations*, *10*(2), 23–25. doi:10.1145/1540276.1540281

Nguyen, T. T., Hai, Y. L., & Lu, J. (2014). Web-page recommendation based on web usage and domain knowledge. *IEEE Transactions on Knowledge and Data Engineering*, *26*(10), 2574–2587. doi:10.1109/TKDE.2013.78

Oleinik, A. (2021). *Relevance in web search: Between content, authority and popularity. Quality & Quantity.* doi:10.100711135-021-01125-7

Ouyang, H., Wei, X., & Wu, Q. (2020). Discovery and prediction of stock Index pattern VIA Three-Stage architecture Of ticc, TPA-LSTM and Multivariate LSTM-FCNs. *IEEE Access: Practical Innovations, Open Solutions*, *8*, 123683–123700. doi:10.1109/ACCESS.2020.3005994

Panchal, A. (2019). A survey of web mining and various web mining techniques. *International Journal for Research in Applied Science and Engineering Technology*, 7(9), 933–939. doi:10.22214/ijraset.2019.9130

Phinyomark, A., Ibanez-Marcelo, E., & Petri, G. (2017). Resting-State fMRI Functional Connectivity: Big data PREPROCESSING pipelines and topological data analysis. *IEEE Transactions on Big Data*, 3(4), 415–428. doi:10.1109/TBDATA.2017.2734883

Quinto, B. (2018). Big data visualization and data wrangling. *Next-Generation Big Data*, 407–476. doi:10.1007/978-1-4842-3147-0_9

Ristoski, P., Bizer, C., & Paulheim, H. (2015). Mining the web of Linked Data with rapidminer. SSRN *Electronic Journal*. doi:10.2139/ssrn.3198927

Robardet, C. (2013). Data mining techniques FOR Communities' detection in dynamic social networks. *Data Mining*, 719–733. doi:10.4018/978-1-4666-2455-9.ch037

Sathiyamoorthi, V. (2017). Web usage mining. *Advances in Data Mining and Database Management*, 107–130. doi:10.4018/978-1-5225-1877-8.ch007

Scott, P. (2019). Welcome to BMJ Health & Care Informatics. *BMJ Health & Care Informatics*, 26(1). Advance online publication. doi:10.1136/bmjhci-2019-000010 PMID:31039116

Shi, L., Jianping, C., & Jie, X. (2018). Prospecting information extraction by text mining based on convolutional neural networks–a case study of the Lala Copper Deposit, China. *IEEE Access: Practical Innovations, Open Solutions*, 6, 52286–52297. doi:10.1109/ACCESS.2018.2870203

Shivaprasad, G., Reddy, N. V. S., Acharya, U. D., & Aithal, P. K. (2015). Neuro-Fuzzy based hybrid model for web USAGE MINING. *Procedia Computer Science*, 54, 327–334. doi:10.1016/j.procs.2015.06.038

Singh, A., & Shaw, S. (2020). Optimizing approach of recommendation system using web usage mining and social media for e-commerce. *International Journal of Computers and Applications*, 176(40), 34–38. doi:10.5120/ijca2020920510

Somoza Sánchez, V. (2020). Why users do not accept big data: Benefits and challenges of big data implementation. *Academy of Management Proceedings*, 2020(1), 20225. doi:10.5465/AMBPP.2020.20225abstract

Song, Y., Zhu, Y., Hou, J., Du, S., & Song, S. (2020). Astronomical data preprocessing implementation based on FPGA and data Transformation strategy for the FAST telescope as a giant CPS. *IEEE Access: Practical Innovations, Open Solutions, 8,* 56837–56846. doi:10.1109/ACCESS.2020.2981816

Spiekermann, S., Korunovska, J., & Langheinrich, M. (2019). Inside the organization: Why privacy and security engineering is a challenge for Engineers. *Proceedings of the IEEE, 107*(3), 600–615. doi:10.1109/JPROC.2018.2866769

Sze-To, A., & Wong, A. K. (2018). Discovering patterns from sequences using pattern-directed aligned pattern clustering. *IEEE Transactions on Nanobioscience, 17*(3), 209–218. doi:10.1109/TNB.2018.2845741 PMID:29994222

Vittoria, M. P., & Napolitano, P. (2020). Identifying localized entrepreneurial projects through semantic social network analysis. *New Metropolitan Perspectives,* 12–21. doi:10.1007/978-3-030-52869-0_2

Wang, M., Shao, W., Hao, X., Shen, L., & Zhang, D. (2021). Identify consistent cross-modality imaging genetic patterns via discriminant sparse canonical correlation analysis. *IEEE/ACM Transactions on Computational Biology and Bioinformatics, 18*(4), 1549–1561. doi:10.1109/TCBB.2019.2944825 PMID:31581090

Witten, I. H., Frank, E., & Hall, M. A. (2011). Data transformations. *Data Mining: Practical Machine Learning Tools and Techniques,* 305–349. doi:10.1016/B978-0-12-374856-0.00007-9

Xu, G., Yu, Z., Yao, H., Li, F., Meng, Y., & Wu, X. (2019). Chinese text sentiment analysis based on extended sentiment dictionary. *IEEE Access: Practical Innovations, Open Solutions, 7,* 43749–43762. doi:10.1109/ACCESS.2019.2907772

Ye, Z., Zhao, H., Zhang, K., Wang, Z., & Zhu, Y. (2019). Network representation based on the joint learning of three feature views. *Big Data Mining and Analytics, 2*(4), 248–260. doi:10.26599/BDMA.2019.9020009

Yie, L. F., Susanto, H., & Setiana, D. (2021). Collaborating decision support and business intelligence to enable Government digital connectivity. *Research Anthology on Decision Support Systems and Decision Management in Healthcare, Business, and Engineering,* 830–847. doi:10.4018/978-1-7998-9023-2.ch040

Yilmaz, E. N., & Gönen, S. (2018). Attack detection/prevention system against Cyber Attack in Industrial Control Systems. *Computers & Security, 77,* 94–105. doi:10.1016/j.cose.2018.04.004

Zhang, P., Zhang, F., Xu, S., Yang, Z., Li, H., Li, Q., Wang, H., Shen, C., & Hu, C. (2021). Network-wide forwarding anomaly detection and localization in software defined networks. *IEEE/ACM Transactions on Networking*, *29*(1), 332–345. doi:10.1109/TNET.2020.3033588

Zorrilla, M., Florez, J., Lafuente, A., Martin, A., Montalban, J., Olaizola, I. G., & Tamayo, I. (2018). Saw: Video analysis in social media with web-based Mobile Grid Computing. *IEEE Transactions on Mobile Computing*, *17*(6), 1442–1455. doi:10.1109/TMC.2017.2766623

Chapter 8
Web User Behavior Analysis Using Pre-Processing of Web Documents to Create Effective Web Designs

Abhijit Dnyaneshwar Jadhav
Dr. D. Y. Patil Institute of Technology, Pimpri, India

Santosh V. Chobe
Dr. D. Y. Patil Institute of Technology, Pimpri, India

ABSTRACT

The interactions with web systems is huge because of COVID-19, where every system is run through online interactions. The world wide web is continuously expanding, and users' interactions with websites generate a vast quantity of data. Web usage mining is the use of data mining techniques to extract important and hidden information about users. It allows you to see the most frequently visited sites, imagine user navigation, and track the progress of your website's structure, among other things. The web mining techniques help us to analyze the user's behavior and accordingly create the required web designs, which will appear in the relevant searches of the users. In this scenario, one of the important processes is web document preprocessing, which will help us to extract the particular quality data inputs for analyzing the behaviors which helps in effective web design. Here, the authors discuss preprocessing of web documents. From the four different phases of the web mining, web document pre-processing is a very important phase.

DOI: 10.4018/978-1-7998-9426-1.ch008

WEB MINING

The World Wide Web is a collection of web sites that provides internet users with a wealth of information. For internet users, the knowledge available on the internet has evolved into a valuable resource. Because the number of websites available on the internet is growing and becoming more complicated, the total volume of web is enormous. A website serves as a link between the customer and the business. The corporations can update visitor's performance during web inquiry, and identify the trends. Web mining is defined as the search for and analysis of useful information on the World Wide Web. Web content mining, web structure mining, and web use mining are the three types of web mining. The extraction of useful information and online knowledge from web resources or web contents such as text, picture, audio, video, and structured data is referred to as web content mining (Mehra & Thakur, 2018). Web use mining may be defined as the discovery and analysis of user access patterns using log file mining. The WUM's output may be utilised for web personalisation, recovering system performance, site modification, and use description, among other things. Web log file is a server log file that contains access logs of the web server and is a vital data source in Web use mining. The Data Preprocessing segment is a crucial stage in the WUM. Data cleansing, session identification, user identification, and path completion are all included. Material preprocessing is used to remove unwanted data from log files so that the pattern discovery algorithm can detect the user pattern (Anand & Aggarwal, 2012).

Need of Web Mining

Web mining is the use of Data Mining methods to locate and extract information from Web publications and services automatically. Web mining's major goal is to extract relevant information from the World Wide Web and its usage trends. The focus on web mining in academics, the software business, and online-based organizations has resulted in a substantial amount of expertise. By recognizing online pages and categorizing web content, web mining helps to increase the power of web search engines. E-commerce websites and e-services benefit greatly from web mining (Chu et al., n.d.).

Types of Web Mining

As seen in Figure 1, web mining may be separated into three types.

- **Web Content Mining:**

The practice of obtaining meaningful information from the content of Web pages is known as web content mining. The contents of a web document relate to the notions that the page was designed to convey to users. Text, picture, video, music, and records like lists and tables can all be used to create this content. Text mining has received greater attention than other fields (Jokar et al., 2016).

Figure 1. Types of web mining

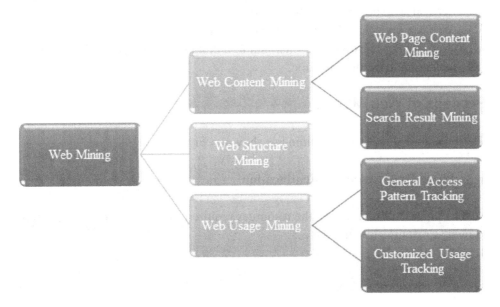

• **Web Structure Mining:**

The web may be seen as a graph, with nodes and edges representing the connections between documents. The method of obtaining structural information from the web is known as web structure mining (Jokar et al., 2016).

• **Web Usage Mining:**

Web use mining is the use of data mining techniques to uncover trends on the Internet in order to better understand and satisfy the requirements of users. This sort of web mining looks at information about how people utilise the internet. It's worth noting that there aren't any apparent distinctions between web mining groups. Web content mining algorithms, for example, can leverage user information in addition to documents. It is also possible to attain greater outcomes by combining the approaches mentioned above (Jokar et al., 2016) (Han et al., 2011).

Applications of Web Mining

1. By categorizing web documents and identifying web pages, web mining helps to boost the power of web search engines.
2. Web Mining utilized for web searches like Google and Yahoo, as well as vertical searches like FatLens and Become.
3. Web mining is a technique for forecasting user behavior.
4. Web mining is extremely beneficial to a certain website and e-service, such as landing page optimization.

Process of Web Mining

There are four stages to web mining as shown in Figure 2:

- **Phase One: Resource Identification**

The process of identifying the resources required for information extraction is known as resource identification.

Figure 2. Phases of web mining

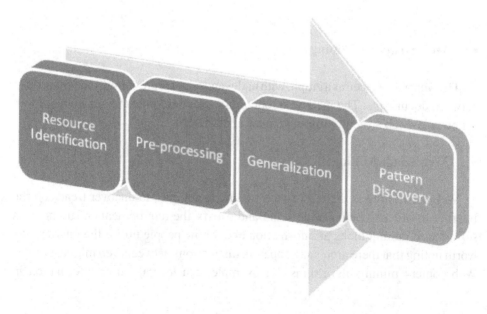

- **Phase Two: Pre-Processing**

Pre-processing is the process of selecting pertinent information from several sources. This process is inextricably linked to data extraction methods.

- **Phase Three: Generalization**

Automatic pattern finding on a large number of online documents is known as generalization. Data mining techniques, as well as clustering and classification trees, are used in this stage.

- **Phase Four: Pattern Discovery**

Pattern discovery is confirmed and interpreted throughout analysis.

These four phases are combined and implemented in various ways depending on the sort of information source they are supposed to operate on (Madhura & Padmavathamma, 2015). In the following discussion we mainly are discussing the Preprocessing phase of the Web Mining.

Pre-Processing in Web Mining

The translation of the raw dataset into a comprehensible format is known as data preparation. Data preprocessing is a critical step in data mining that improves data efficiency. Data preparation procedures have a direct impact on the results of any analytic programme; nevertheless, pretreatment methods differ depending on the application. Pre–processing data is an important part of the data mining process. Data preparation, according to an Aberdeen Group research, is any effort taken to improve the quality, usefulness, accessibility, or portability of data (Khan et al., 2019). The ultimate goal of data preparation is for analytical tools to be able to translate clean and digestible data into useful insights. Cleaning, integration, transformation, and reduction are all examples of data preparation. The preparation phase may take a long time, but the end result is a final data set that is expected to be accurate and useful for additional data mining methods.

The raw data accessible on data warehouses, data marts, and database files is usually not structured for analysis since it is incomplete, inconsistent, or scattered over several tables or represented in a different format, in short, it is unclear. Knowledge Discovery in Databases (KDD) or Data Mining is the method of discovering knowledge from huge chronological data sources (Khan et al., 2019) (Alasadi & Bhaya, 2017). It is the era of big data, and data is being generated at an unprecedented rate in every sphere of life. The most difficult job is obtaining the correct data from existing data sources.

Data preparation is the process of organizing data. It's utilized to find out what information is expected. Gülser, nci, & Murat (2011) define it as "understanding the domain-based challenge under examination followed by a gathering of focused data to fulfil expected goals." According to Forrester, data preparation consumes up to 80% of data analyst work (Goetz, 2015) (Khan et al., 2019). The preprocessed data can then be used in data mining. Pre–processing data is the most effective way to improve data quality. Data cleansing, normalization, transformation, feature extraction, and selection are all examples of data preparation.

Data Pre–Processing Stages

The most crucial step in the data mining process is data pretreatment. The goal of data preprocessing is to transform Web logs into trustworthy, full, and accurate sources for data mining algorithms to use. According to statistics, data preparation accounts for 60% of the overall burden in data mining procedures. Because real-world data is frequently incomplete and inconsistent with noise, data preparation can enhance the data quality for data mining. It can not only save a lot of time and space, but it can also help with decision-making and forecasting.

Importantly there are four stages of Data Pre-Processing:

1. Data Cleaning
2. Data Integration
3. Data Transformation
4. Data Reduction

Cleaning, integrating, transforming, and reducing data are all examples of data preparation. Through two procedures, data cleaning aims to eliminate irrelevant or unnecessary elements. Data integration is comprised of three basic issues, each of which may be addressed using a variety of approaches. Data generalisation, property creation, and standardisation are all examples of data transformation. To normalise the data, three approaches may be utilised. In the final phase, data reduction, the data is compressed to increase the quality of mining models. These four processes are inextricably linked and should not be separated. They collaborate to improve the final data mining result.

Let's learn in detail the stages of Data Pre-Processing.

Data cleaning

Data cleaning is the initial stage of data preparation, and it identifies partial, erroneous, imprecise, or unsuitable sections of datasets (Tamraparni & Theodore, 2003). Typographical mistakes may be eliminated if data is cleaned. It has the ability to disregard tuples with missing values or change values when compared to a known set of entities. The data then becomes consistent with the rest of the system's data sets (Khan et al., 2019) (Bellatreche & Chakravarthy, 2017). To be more specific, data cleaning entails the four essential procedures shown in Table 1.

Table 1. Four steps of data cleaning

Sr. No.	Procedure	Description
1	Data Analysis	Dirty data detection by reviewing dataset, quality of data, meta data.
2	Define Work Flow	Define the cleaning rules by considering heterogeneity degree among diverse data source, then make the work flow order of cleaning rules such as cleaning particular data type, condition, strategy to apply etc
3	Execute defined rules	Rendering the defined rules on source dataset process, and display resulted in clean data to the user.
4	Verification	Verify the accuracy and efficiency of the cleaning rules whether it content user requirements.

Steps 2–3 should be repeated until all data quality issues are resolved. To clean the data, repeat steps 1–4 until the user's needs are fulfilled. Missing values are challenging to manage because wrong handling might result in poor knowledge extraction (Hai & Shouhong, 2009). For missing values, the Expectation–Maximization (EM) method, Imputation, and filtering are commonly used ("Expectation maximization algorithm"). Various data cleansing technologies purify unclean data by using a certified data set. Data augmentation techniques are used by certain programmes to make deficient data sets full by adding related information (Khan et al., 2019) (Malley et al., 2016). To eliminate noisy data, binning methods might be utilized. Outliers are detected using a clustering approach (Jiawei, et al., 2012). Fitting data into a regression function can also smooth it out. To control regression function, a variety of regression processes are utilized, including linear, multiple, and logistic regression.

Data integration

Data integration is the process of combining data from several sources into a single, consistent dataset. Data on the internet is becoming increasingly large and complicated, and it is either unstructured or semi structured. Data integration is a time-consuming and iterative process. The standards of various data sources are the most important concerns throughout the integration process (Khan et al., 2019) (Xindong et al., 2014). Second, the process of integrating new data sources into an existing dataset is time–consuming, which leads to inefficient use of valuable data. ELT (Extract–Transform–Load) technologies are used to manage bigger amounts of data; they combine several sources into a single physical place, give standard conceptual schemas, and allow for querying.

The following are the primary issues with data integration:

The first issue is comparing two separate data sources' properties. For example, you should check whether the customer id attribute in one database is the same as the customer number attribute in the other database. The second issue is that of reduction. If a property can be derived from one or more characteristics, the difference in the names of the attributes may result in a reduction.

The last issue is the discovery of conflicts and the data processing of the values. In the actual world, values for the same thing from multiple data sources may differ. For example, each country's currency has distinct units, and hotel pricing in different places may include not just different currencies, but also different services. As a result, while attempting to match properties in one database to those in another, we must evaluate the data structure and confirm that the functional dependencies and referential constraints of the properties in the original system match those in the target system.

Data transformation

In most cases, raw data is translated into a format that can be analyzed. Data can be normalized by transforming a numerical variable into a common range, for example. The range normalization approach or the z–score method can be used to normalize data. Aggregation, which combines two or more qualities into a single attribute, may also be used to alter categorical data (Khan et al., 2019) (Vijayarani et al., 2015). On low–level traits that are changed to a higher level, generalization can be used. The purpose of data transformation is to convert data into formats that are acceptable for data mining. It consists of the following components:

Data generalization: You can substitute low-level or raw data with high-level concepts using the technique concept hierarchy.

Property construction and standardization: You can create a new property and add it to the attribute set using the supplied property. The data can then be proportionally narrowed or enlarged by normalizing it into a given range.

Data reduction

Multifaceted analysis of large data sets might take a long time or possibly be impossible. Mining techniques suffer from dimensionality handling issues as the number of predictor variables or instances grows big. Data reduction is the final stage of data preparation. Data reduction improves the representational effectiveness of incoming data without compromising its integrity. It's possible that data reduction isn't lossless. The final database may contain all of the original database's information in a well–organized fashion (Bellatreche & Chakravarthy, 2017). To lower the amount of the dataset, encoding methods and hierarchical distribution data cube aggregation can be utilized. The feature selection process is harmonized by data reduction. Data mining algorithms utilize two ways to minimize data size: instance selection (Vijayarani et al., 2015) and instance generation (Vijayarani et al., 2015).

Framework for Pre-Processing of Web Document

The World Wide Web is a massive library of terrible textual material, the most majority of which is generated on a regular basis and ranges from structured to semi–structured to fully unstructured (Andrew, 2015). How do we make the most of that information? What are our options for dealing with it? The answers to these two questions are entirely depending on our goal.

Figure 3. Framework for web document pre-processing

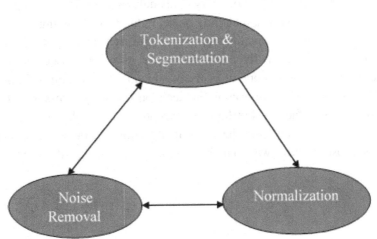

To take use of all of this data's availability, it must be preprocessed, which includes a number of procedures that may or may not apply to a particular job, but normally fall under the broad categories of tokenization, normalization, and replacement (Nguyen, 2013) (Patel & Parikh, 2017).

- Tokenization: Tokenization is used in textual data preparation to break down large strings of text into smaller chunks. For example, sentences can be tokenized into words, and so on. It's also known as lexical analysis or text segmentation.
- Normalization: It refers to a set of duties that must be completed in order to put all words on an equal footing or uniformity. For example, stemming, lemmatization, shifting case from upper to lower or lower to upper, punctuation, space or stop words removal, and replacing numerals with comparable words are all examples.
- Substitution or Noise Removal: Because text data on websites is encased in HTML or XML tags, pattern matching or regular expressions can be used to extract required content after stripping away HTML, XML, and other markup and information.

This web document preprocessing is very important step in web mining to prepare the inadequate and noisy document to correct format.

CONCLUSION

If the dataset under study is insufficient, inappropriate, or incomplete, any data analysis programme will fail to uncover hidden patterns or trends. As a result, data preparation is an important part of every data analysis procedure. Data preparation overcomes a variety of issues, including noise, redundancy, missing values, and so on. The only way to get high-quality results is to have high-quality data, which lowers the cost of data mining. The three C's of data, i.e. completeness, consistency, and correctness, are the cornerstone of every organization's decision-making system. Data quality issues have an impact on the decision-making process, which leads to lower consumer satisfaction. Furthermore, because a larger dataset has an impact on the performance of any machine learning algorithm, instance selection reduces data and is a cost-effective way to make machine learning algorithms operate well.

REFERENCES

Alasadi, S., & Bhaya, W. (2017). Review of Data Preprocessing Techniques in Data Mining. *Journal of Engineering and Applied Sciences*, *12*(16), 4102–4102. doi:10.3923/jeasci.2017.4102.4107

Anand, S., & Aggarwal, R. R. (2012). An Efficient Algorithm for Data Cleaning of Log File using File Extensions. *International Journal of Computers and Applications*.

Andrew, K. (2015). *The research of text preprocessing effect on text documents classification efficiency. International Conference Stability and Control Processes IEEE*, St. Petersburg, Russia.

Bellatreche, L., & Chakravarthy, S. (2017). Big Data Analytics and Knowledge Discovery. *Proceeding of 19th International Conference DAWak*.

Han, J., Kamber, M., & Pei, J. (2011). *Data mining: concepts and techniques*. Elsevier.

Jokar, N., Honarvar, A., Aghamirzadeh, S., & Esfandiari, K. (2016). Web mining and Web usage mining techniques. *Bulletin de la Société des Sciences de Liège, 85*.

Khan, H., Khan, M., Khurram, M., Inayatullah, S., & Athar, S. (2019). *Data Preprocessing: A preliminary step for web data mining*. doi:10.17993/3ctecno.2019. specialissue2.206-221

Madhura & Padmavathamma. (2015). A Web Mining Process for Knowledge Discovery of Web usage Patterns. *International Journal of Engineering Research & Technology, 3*(18).

Malley, B., Ramazzotti, D., & Wu, J. (2016). *Data Pre–processing; Secondary Analysis of Electronic Health Records*. Springer. Retrieved from https://link.springer.com/book/10.1007/978–3–319–43742–2

Mehra & Thakur. (2018). An Effective method for Web Log Preprocessing and Page Access Frequency using Web Usage Mining. *International Journal of Applied Engineering Research, 13*(2), 1227-1232.

Nguyen. (2013). *Web-page Recommendation based on Web Usage and Domain Knowledge*. IEEE.

Patel & Parikh. (2017). Preprocessing on Web Server Log Data for Web Usage Pattern Discovery. *International Journal of Computer Applications, 165*(10).

Srivastava, T., Desikan, P., & Kumar, V. (n.d.). Web Mining – Concepts, Applications and Research Directions. In W. Chu & T. Young Lin (Eds.), *Foundations and Advances in Data Mining. Studies in Fuzziness and Soft Computing* (Vol. 180). Springer.

Vijayarani, S., Ilamathi, M., & Nithya, M. (2015). Preprocessing Techniques for Text Mining – An Overview. *International Journal of Computer Science & Communication Networks*, 5(1), 7–16.

Xindong, W., Xingquan, Z., Gong–Qing, W., & Ding, W. (2014). Data Mining with Big Data. *IEEE Transactions on Knowledge and Data Engineering*, 26(1), 97–107. doi:10.1109/TKDE.2013.109

Chapter 9
Face Mask Classification Based on Deep Learning Framework

Safa Teboulbi
Monastir University, Tunisia

Seifeddine Messaoud
Monastir University, Tunisia

Mohamed Ali Hajjaji
Monastir University, Tunisia

Abdellatif Mtibaa
Monastir University, Tunisia

ABSTRACT

Since the infectious coronavirus disease (COVID-19) was first reported in Wuhan, it has become a public health problem around the world. This pandemic is having devastating effects on societies and economies. Due to the lack of health resources in a short period, all countries and continents are likely to face particularly severe damage that could lead to a large epidemic. Wearing a face mask that stops the transmission of droplets in the air can still be helpful in combating this pandemic. Therefore, this chapter focuses on implementing a face mask detection model as an embedded vision system. The six pre-trained models, which are MobileNet, ResNet-50, MobileNet-V2, VGG-19, VGG-16, and DenseNet, are used in this context. People wearing or not wearing masks were detected. After implementing and deploying the models, the selected models achieved a confidence score. Therefore, this study concludes that wearing face masks helps reduce the virus spread and fight this pandemic.

DOI: 10.4018/978-1-7998-9426-1.ch009

INTRODUCTION

Coronavirus disease (COVID-19) is an emerging respiratory infectious disease caused by Severe Acute Respiratory Syndrome Coronavirus 2 (SARS-CoV2) (Qin & Li, 2020). All over the world, especially in the third wave, COVID-19 has been an important health care challenge (Wang et al.,). Many shutdowns in different industries have been caused by this pandemic. Moreover, many sectors like maintenance projects and infrastructure construction have not been suspended owing to their serious effect on people's routine life (Zhang et al., 2020) (Razavi et al.,). By now, the virus has speedily spread to the majority of the countries worldwide (Qin & Li, 2020). According to the centers for Disease Control and Prevention (CDC), coronavirus infection is transmitted predominantly by respiratory droplets produced when people breathe, talk, cough or sneeze (Wang et al.,) with common droplet size 5-10 μm but aerosol emission increases when humans speak and shout loudly (Dey & Howlader, 2021). No one can deny that COVID-19 is a global pandemic and affects several domains. Nonetheless, it created a path for researchers in computer science. We have seen numerous research topics, like creating new automatic detection methods of COVID-19, detecting people with or without masks, etc. (Echtioui et al., 2020). Before coronavirus, some people put masks to protect themselves from air pollution. While other people put face masks to hide their faces and their emotions from others. Protection against coronavirus is a mandatory counter measure, according to the World Health Organization (WHO) (Loey et al., 2021). In reality, wearing a mask is an effective method of blocking 80% of all respiratory infections (Wang et al.,). All over the world, governments are struggling against this type of virus and many organizations enforce face mask rules for the personal protection. Checking manually if individuals entering an organization are wearing masks is cumbersome and possibly conflicting (Loey et al., 2021). This chapter is organized as follow: the proposed face mask detection framework based on deep learning models is firstly discussed. Then, the data collection and the evaluation metrics are presented. After that, the numerical results of six models and of the implementation in the Raspberry Pi are discussed. And finally, the chapter is ended with a conclusion.

PROPOSED FACE MASK DETECTION FRAMEWORK BASED ON DEEP LEARNING MODELS

The proposed framework consists into two principal blocks. For the first block, our labeled dataset was divided into three classes. The first class is focused on the training and represents 70% of the dataset images. However, the validation step required only 10% to validate the performance for the trained models. 20% of the dataset was devoted to the testing phase. For each epoch, each model is trained on the training dataset. The training results, as well as, the training accuracy and the training loss, are presented in the form of curves in figures of "accuracy in terms of epoch" and "loss in terms of epoch", respectively. After training, each model is validated on the validation dataset. Like the training results, the obtained validation results are the validation accuracy and the validation loss. Then, the two results are compared with the loss function. An error function value tending toward zero means a well-trained model. Otherwise, the hyper-parameters are tuned to train the model in another epoch. The process of calculating errors and updating the network's parameters is called Backward propagation, which is the second important process elaborated in the training phase of any neural network, after the Forward propagation process. The hyper-parameters, as well as, learning rate, batch size, number of epochs, optimizer, Anchor Boxes, loss function are tuned to build an optimal model. However, the learning rate is denoted as the learning step where the model updates its learned weights. It contains inputs which are fed into the algorithm and also an output to calculate the errors. The batch size defines the number of trials to work along before updating the parameters of the internal model. A training dataset could be dissected into just one or supplemental batches. Optimizers are assisted to minimize the loss function. They update the model in regard to the loss function output. The loss function, is also called error function, which is the heart of the different algorithms of the Machine Learning (ML). Thus, the weights can be restored to minimize the loss of the following evaluation. In the testing phase, our two models will be scanned. After that, the proposed framework with the best trained deep learning model will be implemented on an embedded vision system that consists of raspberry pi 4 board and webcam.

DATA COLLECTION

In this research, the experiments are ran on just one original dataset. It includes wholly 3835 images. It is a balanced dataset, that contains two categories which are faces with masks containing 1919 images and faces without masks containing 1916 images. This dataset is utilized for training, validation, and also testing (Google, n.d.).

EVALUATION METRICS

Accuracy is the all number of the correct predictions divided by the total number of predictions produced for a dataset. We can be informed by it instantly if the training of a model is done correctly or not and with which method it may accomplish in general. Nonetheless, the detailed information according its utilization to the issue are not given. Equation (1) present how to calculate the accuracy (Qin & Li, 2020).

$$\text{Accuracy} = \frac{\text{TP} + \text{TN}}{\left(\text{TP} + \text{FP}\right) + \left(\text{TN} + \text{FN}\right)} \tag{1}$$

Precision, called also Positve Pedictive Value (PPV), is a sufficient measure to the determination, while the cost of false positives is high. The way of calculating the precision (Cyril & Eric, 2005) is shown in equation (2).

$$\text{Precision} = \frac{\text{TP}}{\text{TP} + \text{FP}} \tag{2}$$

Recall is the representation of a model. It is used to choose the best model especially when there is a high cost associated with false negative. The recall helps when the cost of false negatives is high. Equation (3) determinate how to compute the recall (Qin & Li, 2020).

$$\text{Recall} = \frac{\text{TP}}{\text{TP} + \text{FN}} \tag{3}$$

F1-score is mandatory when we would like to look for a symmetry between precision and recall. It is a global measure of the model's accuracy. Having low false positives with low false negatives explains that a good F1-score is achieved (Peter & Meelis, 2015). Equation (4) present the way of calculating the F1-score.

$$\text{F1} - \text{score} = \frac{2*\text{Precision}*\text{Recall}}{\left(\text{Precision} + \text{Recall}\right)} \tag{4}$$

The four terms: TP, FP, TN, and FN, point to the test result and also the classification correctness. With TP represent the computing of the true positives samples, TN is the counting of true negatives samples, FP is the enumeration of the false positives samples, and FN is the calculation of the false negatives samples, through a confusion matrix.

The sensitivity and the specificity are two numerical measures which are largely used especially in medicine. Sensitivity, familiar as True Positive Rate (TPR), calculates the division of positives that are faithfully recognized. The specificity, well-known as True Negative Rate (TNR), measures the division of negatives that are accurately identified.

Macro-averaging is utilized for models with two and more targets. Several macro-averaged measures are expressed (Grandini et al., 2020). Firstly, macro-averaged precision calculates the average precision to each class. It is familiar as macro precision. The macro-precision score can be arithmetically determined by the mean of every precision scores of the distinct classes. It is a harmonic metric to the global accuracy. Secondly, the mean of the recall scores of all divers classes represent the macro-average recall. It is well-known as macro-recall. Thirdly, the macro-averaged F1-score, also called the macro F1-score, represented the harmonic mean of the macro-precision and the macro-recall. Weighted average or weighted avg is a counting that accounts for the diversified levels of the numbers importance in a dataset. When a weighted avg is calculated, each number in the dataset is multiplied by a predetermined weight before the last calculation. A simple average can be less correct than weighted avg. weighted avg precision, weighted avg F1-score and weighted avg recall are among weighted average scores.

NUMERICAL RESULTS

In this section, the numerical results will be introduced. For the two simulated deep learning models, as well as MobileNet, ResNet-50, MobileNet-V2, VGG-19, VGG-16 and DenseNet, the Tensorflow-GPU is used as a deep learning framework to train the deep learning models. The hyperparameters utilized in our experiments are summarized as follows: the batch size is set to 32, the training epochs is from 20 to 40, the learning rate is set to 0.0001, with the Adam optimizer used to update network weights. The training platform utilizes windows 10 OS with a CPU and a GPU, respectively, Intel®core TM i7-3770 @3.4 GHz and 16 GB RAM and an NVIDIA GeForce RTX 2070 GPU.

MOBILENET RESULTS

MobileNets are among the CNN-based networks, that are fundamentally built from the depthwise separable convolutions. Figure 1. (a) and figure 1. (c) present the analyze results of MobileNet model, respectively, of the training and validation loss and the training and validation accuracy. After the input of the algorithm's data, the graph of loss barely move towards zero. After five epochs of training, the graph of accuracy tend beside 100%, which express that the model sustained a high accuracy without overfitting.

The confusion matrix is a specific table layout that allows to predict the algorithm performances. A plenty of parameters can be computed for the trained model. These parameters are founded on TP, FP, FN, and also TN. In this work, TP indicates that a human wears mask and the system presents also that this person is wearing a mask. FN means that a human is without mask but the system presents that the person is with mask. FP indicates that the human wears a mask but the system presents a person is without mask. And TN means that a human is without mask and the system expresses that the person is without mask. Figure 1. (b) present the confusion matrix of MobileNet model throughout the testing phase.

Table 1 presents all the evaluation parameters: accuracy, F1-score, precision, support, sensitivity, recall, and specificity, for two cases: faces with masks and faces without masks, macro avg precision, macro avg F1-score, macro avg recall, macro avg support, weighted avg recall, weighted avg precision, weighted avg support and weighted avg F1-score. This table expresses that all values of the evaluation parameters except "the support" are equal or above 0.97. Thus, the MobileNet is an efficient model to distinguish between faces with masks and faces without masks.

Figure 1. MobileNet evaluation metrics

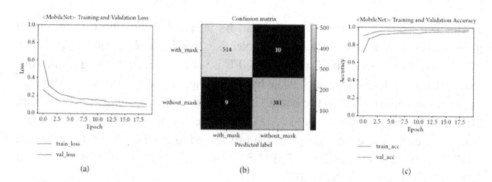

RESNET-50 RESULTS

ResNet is the abbreviation of Residual Networks. It is a network employed as a backbone for countless computer vision tasks and a winner of the Image Net challenge in 2015. It is a variant of ResNet model family. It consists of 48 convolutional layers with 1 Max Pooling and also 1 Average Pooling layer. As figure2. (a) and figure 2. (c) of the training and validation accuracy, and loss, respectively show, the loss nearly tends to zero and the accuracy is high close to 100%. The confusion matrix after testing is given in figure 1. (b). When evaluating the parameters in table. 1 of Res-Net 50 model, we note that all parameters values except "support" are over 0.97.

Therefore, the obtained results are encouraging regarding the exploitation of computer-aided models especially in the pathology field. It can be also operated in situations when the possibilities are deficient, like RT-PCR tests, radiologist and doctor.

Figure 2. ResNet-50 evaluation metrics

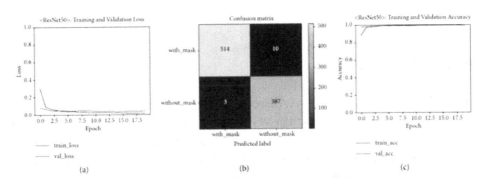

(a)   (b)   (c)

MOBILENET-V2 RESULTS

Among the deep learning models which are considered to be used in low-hardware cost tools, we find MobileNet. Object identification, segmentation and Classification can be accomplished by employing the MobileNet model. MobileNet-V2 model is progressed from the MobileNet-V1.

The training and validation loss of the MobileNetV2 are presented in figure 3. (a) . Also, the graphs of the training and validation accuracy are shown in figure 3. (c).

Afterwards, the graph presents that the model is susceptible to overfit, but it still gives a high accuracy near to 100%, after seven training epochs. The confusion matrix of MobileNetV2 in the testing phase is illustrated in figure 3. (b). In Table 1, all evaluation parameters excluding the support are greater than or equal to 0.94. Thus, the MobileNet-V2 model is trained very well and it can be considered as an efficient model to detect masked and unmasked faces. When comparing MobileNet-V2 model other ones, it is clear that this model is little bit less methodical than MobileNet.

Figure 3. MobileNet-V2 evaluation metrics

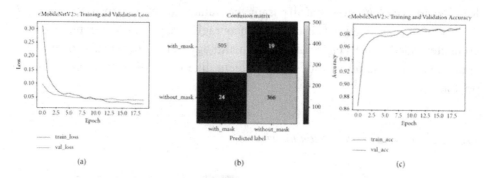

VGG-19 RESULTS

VGG-19 is a CNN, proposed by A. Zisserman and K.Simoniyan. It has 19 layers. As a result of the three more layers than VGG-16, the number of parameters in VGG19 is greater than VGG-16. Therefore, it is more costly to train. Figure 4. (a) provides evidence that both training and validation losses were minimized following each epoch for VGG-19 model. It shows that the graph nearly tends to zero. Moreover, figure 4. (c) suggests that the overall training and validation maintain a high accuracy close to 100% without overfitting, after seven training epochs. Figure 4. (b) illustrates the confusion matrix for the VGG-19 model in the testing phase. It shows that the VGG-19 performance is satisfactory on the test set. Table. 1 expresses the evaluation metrics of the VGG-19 model. All the metrics values, except "the support" are over 0.98. Therefore, the VGG-19 is a model that can be used to detect masked and unmasked faces efficiently.

Figure 4. VGG-19 evaluation metrics

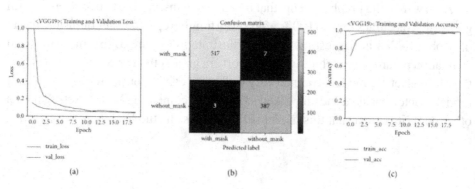

VGG-16 RESULTS

VGG-16 is a CNN proposed by A. Zisserman and K. Simoniyan. It has 16 layers.

Figure 5. (a) shows the training and validation loss of VGG-16 model. In fact, their graphs are decreased following each epoch. And after ten epochs, these graphs almost tends to zero. In addition, figure 4. (c) shows the graphs of the training and validation accuracy of VGG-16 model all over each epoch. Next, the graphs shows that the model preserves a high accuracy near to 100% at epochs 6 to 20, after six training epochs. Figure 5. (b) presents the confusion matrix of VGG-16 in the testing phase. Table 1 reveals the VGG-16 evaluation measures. It shows that all measures values except the "support" are greater or equal to 0.98. These values are representative of powerful performance of the VGG-16 model. When comparing this model with some of the previous ones, it is clear that the VGG-16 have the same efficacy as the ResNet-50, but it outperformed the MobileNet, and the MobileNet-V2 models.

Figure 5. VGG-16 evaluation metrics

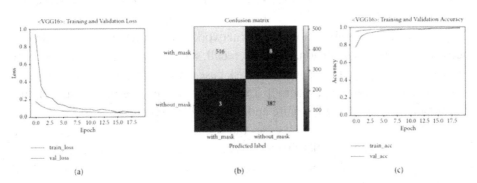

DENSENET RESULTS

DenseNet is a modern architecture of CNN. It exists distinct DenseNet models such as DenseNet-201, DenseNet-121, DenseNet-160, etc. In this study the DenseNet-201 is employed. This DenseNet was trained in 20 epochs in order to organize images into two categories: faces with mask and faces without mask. The corresponding graphs of training and validation loss of DenseNet-201 are shown in Figure 6. (a) and the ones corresponding of accuracy are presented in figure 6. (c). In figure (a), after inputting the algorithm's data, the model barely tends to keep a very high accuracy greater than 85% without overfitting. The confusion matrix of DenseNet model in the testing phase is illustrated in figure 6. (b). In table 1, for the masked faces cases, the results of accuracy and F1-score surpassed 0.92. And the accuracy, sensitivity and recall results are equal to 0.91.

Figure 6. DenseNet evaluation metrics

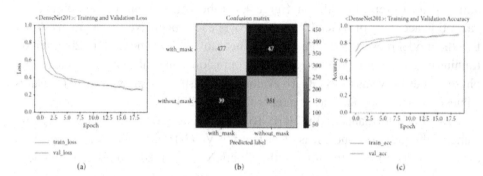

COMPARATIVE STUDY BETWEEN THE PROPOSED MODELS

The performance of the six various models network is shown in table 1. The evaluation metrics are: accuracy, precision, F1-score, recall, support, specificity and sensitivity; for faces with mask and faces without mask cases, macro avg precision, macro avg F1-score, macro avg recall, macro avg support, weighted avg precision, weighted avg support, weighted avg F1-score and weighted avg recall.

In detecting faces with mask case, the highest precision is corresponding to VGG-19, VGG-16 and ResNet-50 models. In detecting faces without mask case, the highest precision, weighted avg precision and macro avg precision are for VGG-19 and VGG-16 models.

In detecting people with mask case, the highest recall is just for VGG-19 model. In detecting people without mask case, the highest macro avg recall, recall and the weighted avg recall are for VGG- 19, VGG-16 and ResNet-50 models. In wearing mask case, the highest F1-score, macro weighted F1-score and macro avg F1-score, are for VGG-19, VGG-16 and ResNet-50 models.

Nevertheless, in not wearing mask case, the highest F1-score is corresponding to VGG-16 and VGG-19 models. In the two cases: people with and without mask, the support, the weighted avg support and the macro avg support have identical values for the distinct models. The highest specificity and accuracy are corresponding to ResNet-50, VGG-19 and VGG-16 networks.

Table 1. Performance evaluation of the proposed models

		Precision	Recall	F1-score	Support	Accuracy	Sensitivity	Specificity
MobileNet	With mask	0.98	0.98	0.98	524	0.98	0.98	0.98
	Without mask	0.97	0.98	0.98	390			
	Macro average	0.98	0.98	0.98	914	-	-	-
	Weighted average	0.98	0.98	0.98	914	-	-	-
ResNet-50	With mask	0.99	0.98	0.99	524	0.99	0.98	0.99
	Without mask	0.97	0.99	0.98	390			
	Macro average	0.98	0.99	0.99	914	-	-	-
	Weighted average	0.99	0.99	0.99	914	-	-	-
MobileNet-V2	With mask	0.95	0.96	0.96	524	0.95	0.96	0.94
	Without mask	0.95	0.94	0.94	390			
	Macro average	0.95	0.95	0.95	914	-	-	-
	Weighted average	0.95	0.95	0.95	914	-	-	-
VGG-19	With mask	0.99	0.99	0.99	524	0.99	0.99	0.99
	Without mask	0.98	0.98	0.99	390			
	Macro average	0.99	0.99	0.99	914	-	-	-
	Weighted average	0.99	0.99	0.99	914	-	-	-
VGG-16	With mask	0.99	0.98	0.99	524	0.99	0.98	0.99
	Without mask	0.98	0.99	0.99	390			
	Macro average	0.99	0.99	0.99	914	-	-	-
	Weighted average	0.99	0.99	0.99	914	-	-	-
DenseNet	With mask	0.92	0.91	0.92	524	0.91	0.91	0.99
	Without mask	0.88	0.90	0.89	390			
	Macro average	0.90	0.91	0.90	914	-		
	Weighted average	0.91	0.91	0.91	914	-		

Eventually, the VGG-19 has the highest sensitivity. As a conclusion, the VGG-19 network is the greatest trained model, when comparing it with the other studied models.

EMBEDDED FACE MASK DETECTION: RASPBERRY PI IMPLEMENTATION

After evaluating the proposed face mask detection models, in this step, the two models with their high accuracy rate will be applied to the embedded vision system, which consists of a Raspberry Pi-4 platform coupled with a Web camera and Touch

Screen, and sound a buzzer when someone is not wearing their face mask (Green or Red Led) as shown in figure 7. (a) and figure 7. (b).

Figure 7. Embedded vision system for face mask detection

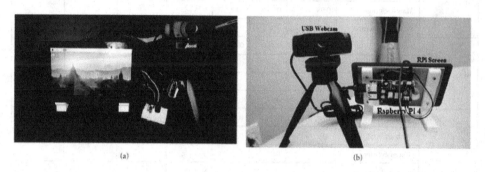

Thus, after installing Raspberry Pi OS and all libraries, such as TensorFlow, OpenCV, and imutils, the embedded vision system will be able to detect if a user is wearing a face mask or not. When someone is not wearing a face mask, it will be designated with a red box around his face with the text, "No Face Mask Detected.". The same thing when someone is wearing a face mask, it will be seen a green box around his face with the text, "Thank you. Mask On." An example of a result is depicted in figure 8. (a) and figure 8. (b).

Figure 8. Test of the proposed framework on the embedded vision system

CONCLUSION

Due to the urgency of controlling COVID-19, the application value and importance of real-time mask detection are increasing. This work reproduced the training and testing of the most used deep pretrained-based CNN models (ResNet-50 and VGG-19) on the face mask dataset. After that, evaluated the numerical results. Finally, the two models are tested on an embedded vision system consisted of Raspberry Pi board and web camera where an efficient real time deep learning-based techniques are implemented to automate the process of detecting masked faces. This embedded vision-based application can be used in any working environment like public place, station, corporate environment, streets, shopping malls, examination centers, etc., where accuracy and precision are highly desired to serve the purpose. It can be used in smart city innovation and it would boost up the development process in many developing countries. Our framework presents a chance to be more ready for the next crisis, or to evaluate the effects of huge scope social change in respecting sanitary protection rules.

REFERENCES

Cyril, G., & Eric, G. (2005). A probabilistic interpretation of precision, recall and F-score, with implication for evaluation. In *European conference on information retrieval*. Springer.

Dey, S. K., & Howlader, A. (2021). A Multi-phase Face Mask Detection Model to Prevent Person-To-Person Transmission of SARS-CoV-2. In *Proceedings of International Conference on Trends in Computational and Cognitive Engineering* (pp. 603-613). Springer. 10.1007/978-981-33-4673-4_49

Echtioui, A., Zouch, W., Ghorbel, M., Mhiri, C., & Hamam, H. (2020). Detection Methods of COVID-19. *SLAS Technology*, 25(6), 566–572. doi:10.1177/2472630320962002 PMID:32997560

Google. (n.d.). https://drive.google.com/drive/folders/1IPwsC30wNAc74_GTXuEWX_F8m2n-ZBCH

Grandini, M., Bagli, E., & Visani, G. (2020). *Metrics for multi-class classification: An overview*. https://arxiv.org/abs/2008.05756

Loey, M., Manogaran, G., Taha, M. H. N., & Khalifa, N. E. M. (2021). A hybrid deep transfer learning model with machine learning methods for face mask detection in the era of the COVID-19 pandemic. *Measurement, 167*, 108288. doi:10.1016/j.measurement.2020.108288 PMID:32834324

Peter, A. F., & Meelis, K. (2015). Precision-Recall-Gain Curves: PR Analysis Done Right. NIPS.

Qin, B., & Li, D. (2020). Identifying Facemask-Wearing Condition Using Image Super-Resolution with Classification Network to Prevent COVID-19. *Sensors (Basel), 20*(18), 5236. doi:10.339020185236 PMID:32937867

Razavi, M., Alikhani, H., Janfaza, V., Sadeghi, B., & Alikhani, E. (in press). *An Automatic System to Monitor the Physical Distance and Face Mask Wearing of Construction Workers in COVID-19 Pandemic.* Academic Press.

Wang, Z., Wang, P., Louis, P. C., Wheless, L. E., & Huo, Y. (in press). *Fast In-browser Face Mask Detection with Serverless Edge Computing for COVID-19.* Academic Press.

Zhang, X., Saleh, H., Younis, E. M., Sahal, R., & Ali, A. A. (2020). Predicting Coronavirus Pandemic in Real-Time Using Machine Learning and Big Data Streaming System. *Complexity, 2020*, 1–10. doi:10.1155/2020/6688912

Chapter 10

A Hybrid EM–Based Boosting Classification Model for Microarray Somatic Disease Prediction

Shaik Mahaboob Basha
Acharya Nagarjuna University, India

Nagaraju Devarakonda
Vellore Institute of Technology, India

ABSTRACT

As the size of the micro-array disease databases increase, finding an essential feature set for the classification problem is complex due to the large data size and sparsity problems. Traditional feature subset models are based on static clustering and classification models due to the fixed sized dimensions cluster-based disease prediction process. Sparsity, missing values, and imbalance are the major issues that affect the selection of essential feature clusters for data classification process. In this chapter, a hybrid cluster-based Bayesian probability estimation model is proposed in order to predict the disease class label on high dimensional databases. The proposed cluster-based classification model selects optimal clusters for feature ranking and classification problems to improve the true positive rate and accuracy. Experimental results are simulated on different training datasets for accuracy prediction. The results proved that the gene-disease-based patterns have better optimization than the conventional methods in terms of statistical metrics and classification models.

DOI: 10.4018/978-1-7998-9426-1.ch010

INTRODUCTION

As the size of the microarray datasets is growing day by day, finding a significant feature in the large feature space have become highly complicated because of data size and sparsity issues (Nagpal, 2018). Feature ranking of Microarray and classification is the main difficulties to technical and biomedical researchers because of its high dimensional feature space and restricted samples. Each microarray contains many identical DNA molecules that are used to identify a specific gene-related disease (X. H. Han, 2019). Microarrays are available in a wide variety of technologies. Microarrays are most commonly used to quantify mRNAs transcribed by various genes and different encoding proteins. Many cell types extract RNA and convert it into CDNA or cRNA, preferably one cell type.

RtPCR should upgrade copies. Fluorescent tags are added enzymatically within a cDNA/cRNA sequence or can be affixed to a further DNA strand, chemically or in a second. DNA's knowledge microarray processes give thousands of genes under several experimental gene expression levels. (S. Sayed, 2018) Proposed analysing the data on DNA microarray expression as a powerful tool for biological mechanisms study and developing predictive and prognostic categorisers to identify the patients who need treatment and the best treatment applicants. In (M. Sun, 2019), examining the data obtained through the microscope technology was very practical to understand how the genetic information turns into practical genetic products. Such a biclustering examination can determine a collection of genes under a set of provisional conditions. (M. Daoud, 2019) Proposed a method for classifying trajectories in road networks for discriminative patterns. By analysing the conduct of road trajectories, they found that the order of these visited locations was essential to improving classification accuracy, apart from the locations they had visited. This method challenged sequential patterns on the analysis feature as they retained order information to be good applicants.

The successful diagnosis and treatment of cancer needed to be properly identified and classified as cancer types. Certain gene expression analysis using a built-in CMOS microarray showed a successful diagnosis of time-resolved fluorescence. (Halder, 2019) Have likewise submitted OpenFlyData to the Drosophila Melanogaster exemplary web data that integrates gene expression data. Combining heterogeneous data across distributed sources is an important requirement for silicon-bioinformatics to support translational research. One of the major drawbacks in cancer data sets class discovery is that the cancer gene expression profiles contained many genes and lots of noisy genes. Reduce the effect of noisy genes on the expression profile of cancer genes. The two new consensus frameworks for gene-expression profile cancer discovery have been suggested by Zhiwen Y and others, namely triple spectral clusters (SC3) and dual spectral clusters (SC2 N cut). Although Mining Discriminatory paths increased the accuracy of the specification to define pathways on road networks, this approach was not effective and successful for a pattern-based classification scheme in the classification system. SC3 submitted spectral clustering's for gene and cancer clustering and finally split the consensus matrix from multiple solutions. However, the defects were that this method was only appropriate for cancer gene expression profiles. Critical to accurate classification is between irrelevant or redundant genes. Gene selection is a popular tool for reducing computational complexity by reducing data size and increasing classification accuracy and interpretation of learning outcomes.

The Adaptive Resonance Theory (ART) algorithms are neural networks designed to imitate how the human brain recognises patterns. The reason for Microarray data using the Adaptive Resonance Theories is to deal with the stability-plasticity dilemma. The learning model of a neural network keeps the new information found in new patterns unremoved from the previously stored information. Bioinformatics are the science of organising and analysing biological data. It is an impact of many artificial and biological neural learning systems. These data are obtained in many different fields, including deoxyribonucleic acid (DNA), ribonucleic acid (RNA), genes and proteins, and their impact on the body's function, for example, in the brain. Many signs of progress have been made in research over the past few years, and quite a few new data have been recorded. Lu and Han (2003) divided gene selection methods into two categories: ranking of genes and sub-set ranking of the genes (J. Lee, 2021). A criterion function that measures the discriminatory power of individual genes is provided by an individual gene-rating method.

The maximum probability ratios (F. Morais, 2020), BW (Kawamura,2008) and Info Gain (IG) (Kilicarslan, 2020) are examples of this method. This ranking is easy but does not consider gene correlations (Potharaju, 2019). Gene sub-set evaluation searches the best criterion for a sub-set of genes. If the classification criterion function is based, it is called the wrapper method. In feature selection studies, these methods are different from the filter methods named in the classification (Kumar, 2020). Gene subset selection is usually performed using classification devices like K Nearest Neighbors (Kumaran,2019) and Support Vector Machine (SVM) in a wrapper approach.

The aim is to identify a gene subset of genes contributing to a certain learning model's best prediction. An algorithm is available to assess the prediction quality of the candidate's gene subsets around the classification model (Sahu, 2017). The SVM-RFE (Zheng, 2019) and the genetic algorithm (GA) are examples of wrapper methods. The wrapping method is not as efficient as the filter method because it runs in the dataset algorithm and is computationally expensive. The accuracy excess can be over-used if the data is small since the goodness measure can happen (Shibata, 2020). The meta-heuristic methods have been mostly used to address gene selection problems, and its performance has proved to be one of the best methods for solving problem genetic selection. While several approaches to the problem of gene selection have been proposed, many of which are still affected by stagnation problems with local optima and high computational costs, and the acquisition of optimal sub-group genes cannot be guaranteed, the huge scope of search has caused these problems. An effective algorithm is thus needed for gene selection. Bat algorithm is a Metaheuristic of the behaviour of bats.

RELATED WORKS

In the earliest phase, the genes are filtered with minimum redundancy maximum relevance (MRMR). For evaluation purposes, the Naïve Bayes (NB) and the Support Vector Machine (SVM) classifier were used in the second phase to generate the gene subsets. An optimal feature subset is selected by the feature selection process depending on the specifications of requirement. Based on this criterion, subsets of measuring features are specified. Based on the purpose, the criterion is selected for the selection of feature. E.g., minimum subset is an optimal subset. In a subset, better predictive estimation of accuracy is provided. Specified number in the subset in few circumstances, gets together the criterion that is found based on the feature number. With a set of N functionalities in mind, choosing a subset of M functionalities means that data are cut in the hypothesis room and that a learning algorithm is easier to learn from the reduced data available. For reducing the feature, a filter-based tool known as Rough Sets Attribute Reduction (RSAR) is used for the data extraction and information maintenance in the knowledge reduction process involved. Analysis Rough Sets are carried out on the provided data basis, and the operation is performed without external parameters. The structure of data granularity is used in this method. However, it still presupposes the models for few available information having each item in the discourse Universe that which reflects the real world accurately and truly. The Rough Sets selection's ideal criterion is to discover minimum or shortest reductions to obtain elevated grades on the features selected features.

The number of rules generated by the reductions obtained can also be another criterion. Determination of feature subset's redundancy and pertinence is performed. Declaration of relevant features for the predicted decision feature. Or else, it is inappropriate. It will be considered redundant if it is highly correlated with other features. Therefore, in search of a good feature subset, it is important to find those features that are highly correlated with but not related to the decision features. A Principal Component Analysis (PCA) approach reduces dimension through the main components construction that are the original predictor's linear combinations or the variable explanation. Depending on the supposition PCA technique is used with large characteristics variance providing necessary information and very low variance is measured and it is less useful. Feature maximization along with the explicative variable's linear combination is used in Orthogonally-linear combinations (Nguyen et al., 2004).

The approach translates the original data characteristics into a system with less uncorrelated characteristics. Such additional components of the compound have been included. To study the performance of the classification models, Wilcoxon tests are combined with various feature selection methods. In (Clayman et al., 2020), the methods for feature features are discussed and indicated that different methods for selecting features could be combined using the feature selection approaches instead of choosing a feature selection method or accepting its results as the final sub-feature. An investigation is being carried out to see whether the feature of several function selection methods affects classification performance. Here, Symmetric Uncertainty, RELIEFF, Random forest and SVM performed a separate function ranking as functional selectors. The ensemble was compiled by aggregating the single rankings using linear aggregation by weighted voting. Combining multiple filtering algorithm(s) with classifiers improves the accuracy of the classification and the stability of the gene rank results (Hambali et al., 2020).

Two different feature fusion methods are proposed for microarray data classification. For classifying the kNN classification, the first method considers the equal number of features of each dimensionality reduction method. The second method consideration for each dimension reduction method is the minimum number of features needed to give maximum accuracy in classification. The concept of set-feature selection is extended. A mapping strategy is developed to fuse the information of each gene by the MF-GE system, which has enhanced sample classification accuracy. An effective gene selection algorithm (NMI), Correlation-based Selection Feature (CFS), and Particle Swarm Optimization (PSO) are proposed to be integrated into a set technique, and SVM with leave-one-out cross-validation is used as a classification. One of the simplest and most popular classifications, Fix and Hodges, was first introduced to the k-nearest neighbour method (k-NNN). As a learner, the k-NN has a simple strategy. The k-NN classification has two phases, and the first phase consists of the determination of the k-neighbours and the second phase of class definition using the neighbours. It maintains all training instances instead of generating an explicit model. This takes a test example feature in a vector form and finds the Euclidean distance from each example to the vector representation. The closest sample to the test sample is called the closest neighbour. As the trained sample is in some sense the most similar in terms of our trial samples, it makes sense to allocate its class marking to the test sample. The removal of such negligible features by selecting adequate and fewer information elements helps overcome the 'dimensionality curse' problem and helps to make learning more efficient. Feature selection techniques do not alter but select a subset, the original representation of the variables. So the original semantics of the variables are preserved. The selection methods are filters, wrappers, embedded features and hybrid methods based on the selection criteria. The filter methods are separate algorithms of categories (Rani & Ramyachitra, 2018). They select the best feature subset only based on the distinctive data characteristics, such as distance, correlation, and consistency. They are using gene ranking statistical methods. Either uniform or multivariate filters are used. For each feature, univariate methods provide a value, and multivariate measures take groups of functions or characteristic interaction into account.

PROPOSED MODEL

Improved EM Gene-Disease Clustering Approach

In the expectation maximisation model, two phases are implemented on the training data to predict the best-clustered features for the gene-disease prediction. In this algorithm, the E step predicts the model variables using probability. In the M step, missing sparse values and the feature values are estimated using the non-linear mutual information and Chebyshev formula. Finally, these E and M steps integrate the KNN classification problem for density-based clustering and classification process. In this proposed framework, microarray datasets are taken as input, and the subset of ranked features is selected using optimal feature selection measures (Yao et al., 2010) (Dabba et al., 2021; Kawamura et al., 2008; Nagpal & Singh, 2018). In this framework, a hybrid cluster-based classification model is proposed on the training data, as represented in figure 1.

Step 1: E-step: Depending on the model parameters, the model proposed calculates the each data point's probability as a cluster.

Step 2: M-step: In this step, missing label filling and the model findings improves the data similarity likelihood.

EM clusters are used to find features as SIF.

For every pair of feature in F[]

Do

$$\eta_1 = \sum_{i=1}^{|S_r|} F_i[i] . S(F_p, F_q)$$

$$\eta_2 = \sum_{i=1}^{|S_{IF}|} F_j[i].S(F_p, F_q)$$

MI = *Mutual – Information*(S_i, S_j)

$Chebyshev = d(i, j) = \max_r | x(i, r) - x(j, r) |$

S(F_p,F_q) = *Max*{MI, Min{Chebyshev(F_r(x,y)), Chebyshev(F(x,y))}}

Similar Segmented measure = *Max*{$\eta 1, \eta 2$}

Step 3: These similar segmented patterns are used in the cluster measure based knn classifier for the disease prediction.

Figure 1. Proposed clustering classification framework on large databases

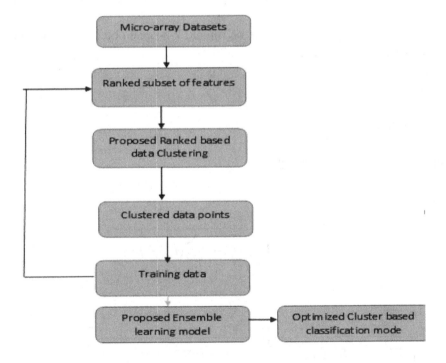

Proposed Cluster-Based Classification Model

1: Read pre-processing training datasets.

    These input patterns are partitioned 'm' clusters based on the EM approach.

2: To each clustered

3: do

4: Apply the proposed ensemble decision tree model on each cluster data.

5: In the proposed classification model, a novel gene-disease feature selection measure is implemented on each cluster.

Classifier-1

Probabilistic Kernel Density-Based KNN Classification Model

Input: D as filtered data, C is classes of Training data, K as KNN data points.

1. Read data filtered with class labels.
2. Execute the k-nearest neighbour approach to find the nearest data objects on data D.
3. Perform density estimation on the filtered k-nearest objects to find the local density objects for the E-step.

θ = Conditional Prior Prob(si$_j$;

ϕ = Joint Prob(D/si$_j$;

PropBayesScore = $\log(\theta) + \log(\phi)$

where

$$Dist(JP(D \ / \ s_i)) = \max\{\mu^K + \Pr\sqrt{\frac{1}{N-1}\sum_{i=1}^{N}(\psi_i^K - \mu^K)^2},$$

$$\prod_{i=0}^{n}\prod_{j=0}^{q_i}\frac{\Gamma(\sum_{k=1}^{r}\alpha_{ijk}\cos(\alpha_{ijk}))}{\Gamma(\sum_{k=1}^{r}\alpha_{ijk} + \sum\log(N_{ij}))}\prod^{r}\frac{\Gamma(\sum_{k=1}^{r}\exp(\alpha_{ijk})\exp(\alpha_{ijk}) + \sum N_{ijk})}{\Gamma(\sum_{k=1}^{r}\alpha_{ijk}\log(\alpha_{ijk}))}\}$$

where N is the number of k nearest neighbor points in the KNN approach, ψ_i^K is the mean distance between Kth nearest neighbor to pint i.

$$\psi_t^K = max_j \in KNN_i(d_{ij}), \text{ and}$$

μK is the average of ψ_i^K, computed as $\mu^K = \dfrac{1}{N} \displaystyle\sum_{i=1}^{N} \psi_i^K$

$$Pr = Pr(i,C_m) = Max\{Prob(i/C_m); i \in KNN\}$$

$$LDE(\rho_i) = \frac{1}{\eta} \exp\left(-\frac{d_{ij} - Dist(JP(D/s_i))^2}{2\sigma^2}\right) \sum_{j \in KNN_i} Pr(d_{ij},C_m) \exp\left(-\frac{d_{ij}^2}{Dist(JP(D/s_i))}\right)$$

4. Combine nearest local density objects using the conditional probability estimation measure on the filtered objects.

Classifier-2

Random tree feature selection measure:

Math.cbrt(entropy(data)*total*GHDSplitCriterion.computeHellinger(data))*Pr/(chiVal(data))

The boosting mechanism employs a collection of weak classifiers to increase the rate of classification in the boosting algorithm proposed. The method used by Decision Tree is a poor classification for the creation of samples on the Adaboost algorithm in this approach. A novel decision-making and conditional entropy are optimised using the updated decision tree ranking steps. For example, the low classification error rate classifier is chosen in this algorithm.

EXPERIMENTAL RESULTS

Experimental results are performed on real-time micro-array high dimensional somatic cancer datasets. Proposed feature selection-based ensemble approaches improves the F-measure, recall and accuracy efficiency on the datasets with high dimension. The proposed model utilizes the whole training data set for the decision pattern construction; thus, the accuracy of prediction for every cross-validation results with high accuracy than the conventional ensemble classification approaches. Simulation results represent the proposed ensemble classification enhances the entire rate of true positive and rate of false-negative. In addition, the major advantages of utilizing this proposed model is the error rate reduction on the features of high dimension. The input to the proposed model is taken from the source https://github. com/ikalatskaya/ISOWN/tree/master/training_data.

Somatic Patterns

```
dbSNP = true
|   inExAct = true
|   |   isFlanking < 0.8
|   |   |   VAF < 30.73
|   |   |   |   CNT < 0.5
|   |   |   |   |   Feat_mutAss = neutral
|   |   |   |   |   |   Feat_SeqContent = ATT: false (0.98/0)
|   |   |   |   |   |   Feat_SeqContent = CTT: false (1.98/0)
|   |   |   |   |   |   Feat_SeqContent = GTT: true (1.97/0.98)
|   |   |   |   |   |   Feat_SeqContent = TAT: false (1/0)
|   |   |   |   |   |   Feat_SeqContent = AAA: true (0/0)
|   |   |   |   |   |   Feat_SeqContent = CAA: false (0.98/0)
|   |   |   |   |   |   Feat_SeqContent = AAC: true (0/0)
|   |   |   |   |   |   Feat_SeqContent = CAC: false (3.97/0)
|   |   |   |   |   |   Feat_SeqContent = GAA: false (0.98/0)
|   |   |   |   |   |   Feat_SeqContent = AAG: false (2.97/0)
|   |   |   |   inExAct = false: true (0/0)
|   |   |   Feat_mutAss = high: true (0/0)
|   |   |   Feat_mutAss = stopgain: true (0/0)
|   |   |   Feat_mutAss = stoploss: true (0/0)
|   |   Feat_SeqContent = CTT: false (3/0)
|   |   Feat_SeqContent = GTT
|   |   |   polyphen = benign
|   |   |   |   Feat_mutAss = neutral: true (1/0.5)
|   |   |   |   Feat_mutAss = low: false (0.5/0)
|   |   |   |   Feat_mutAss = medium: false (1.5/0)
|   |   |   |   Feat_mutAss = high: true (0/0)
|   |   |   |   Feat_mutAss = stopgain: true (0/0)
|   |   |   |   Feat_mutAss = stoploss: true (0/0)
|   |   |   polyphen = probably
|   |   |   |   inExAct = true
```

```
|   |   |   |   |   inExAct = true
|   |   |   |   |   |   Feat_mutAss = neutral: true (1/0.5)
|   |   |   |   |   |   Feat_mutAss = low: false (0.5/0)
|   |   |   |   |   |   Feat_mutAss = medium: false (0.5/0)
|   |   |   |   |   |   Feat_mutAss = high: false (1/0)
|   |   |   |   |   |   Feat_mutAss = stopgain: true (0/0)
|   |   |   |   |   |   Feat_mutAss = stoploss: true (0/0)
|   |   |   |   |   inExAct = false: true (0/0)
|   |   |   |   inExAct = false: true (0/0)
|   |   |   polyphen = possibly: true (0/0)
|   |   Feat_SeqContent = TAT
|   |   |   pattern = CG: true (0/0)
|   |   |   pattern = CA: true (0/0)
|   |   |   pattern = CT: true (0/0)
|   |   |   pattern = TA
|   |   |   |   polyphen = benign: true (1/0)
|   |   |   |   polyphen = probably: false (1/0)
|   |   |   |   polyphen = possibly: false (1/0)
|   |   |   pattern = TC
|   |   |   |   CNT < 0.5: false (12/0)
|   |   |   |   CNT >= 0.5: true (3/0)
|   |   |   pattern = TG: false (3/0)
|   |   Feat_SeqContent = AAA: false (3/0)
|   |   Feat_SeqContent = CAA
|   |   |   isFlanking < 0.5: false (8.56/0)
|   |   |   isFlanking >= 0.5
|   |   |   |   CNT < 0.5: false (0.44/0)
|   |   |   |   CNT >= 0.5: true (2/0)
|   |   Feat_SeqContent = AAC
|   |   |   CNT < 0.5: false (10/0)
|   |   |   CNT >= 0.5
|   |   |   |   inExAct = true
|   |   |   |   |   VAF < 33.88: true (1/0)
|   |   |   |   |   VAF >= 33.88: false (1/0)
|   |   |   |   inExAct = false: true (0/0)
|   |   Feat_SeqContent = CAC
|   |   |   Feat_mutAss = neutral
|   |   |   |   VAF < 42.66: false (2.27/0)
|   |   |   |   VAF >= 42.66: true (1/-0)
|   |   |   Feat_mutAss = low: false (1.09/0)
```

199

```
|   |   |   Feat_mutAss = medium
|   |   |   |   VAF < 25.8: false (4.64/0)
|   |   |   |   VAF >= 25.8
|   |   |   |   |   CNT < 0.5: false (2/0)
|   |   |   |   |   CNT >= 0.5: true (1/0)
|   |   |   Feat_mutAss = high: true (0/0)
|   |   |   Feat_mutAss = stopgain: true (0/0)
|   |   |   Feat_mutAss = stoploss: true (0/0)
|   |   Feat_SeqContent = GAA: false (11/0)
|   |   Feat_SeqContent = AAG
|   |   |   VAF < 37.25: true (2/0)
|   |   |   VAF >= 37.25
|   |   |   |   VAF < 70.18: false (12/0)
|   |   |   |   VAF >= 70.18
|   |   |   |   |   inExAct = true
|   |   |   |   |   |   CNT < 0.5: false (1/0)
|   |   |   |   |   |   CNT >= 0.5: true (1/0)
|   |   |   |   |   inExAct = false: true (0/0)
|   |   Feat_SeqContent = CAG
|   |   |   VAF < 40.83: true (3/0)
|   |   |   VAF >= 40.83: false (11/0)
|   |   Feat_SeqContent = GAC: false (8/0)
|   |   Feat_SeqContent = GAG
|   |   |   VAF < 43.06
|   |   |   |   VAF < 41.77
|   |   |   |   |   polyphen = benign
|   |   |   |   |   |   pattern = CG: true (0/0)
|   |   |   |   |   |   pattern = CA: true (0/0)
|   |   |   |   |   |   pattern = CT: true (0/0)
|   |   |   |   |   |   pattern = TA: true (0/0)
|   |   |   |   |   |   pattern = TC: false (1.86/0.43)
|   |   |   |   |   |   pattern = TG: false (2.86/0)
|   |   |   |   |   polyphen = probably
|   |   |   |   |   |   VAF < 17.2: false (0.86/0)
|   |   |   |   |   |   VAF >= 17.2
|   |   |   |   |   |   |   CNT < 0.5: true (1.86/0.43)
|   |   |   |   |   |   |   CNT >= 0.5
|   |   |   |   |   |   |   |   fre < 0.03: true (1/0)
|   |   |   |   |   |   |   |   fre >= 0.03: false (1/0)
|   |   |   |   |   polyphen = possibly: true (1.57/0.43)
```

```
|   |   |   |   VAF >= 41.77: true (1/0)
|   |   |   VAF >= 43.06: false (4/0)
|   |   Feat_SeqContent = TGA
|   |   |   Feat_mutAss = neutral: true (2/0)
|   |   |   Feat_mutAss = low
|   |   |   |   inExAct = true
|   |   |   |   |   CNT < 0.5: false (2/0)
|   |   |   |   |   CNT >= 0.5: true (2/0)
|   |   |   |   inExAct = false: true (0/0)
|   |   |   Feat_mutAss = medium: false (3/0)
|   |   |   Feat_mutAss = high: true (0/0)
|   |   |   Feat_mutAss = stopgain: true (0/0)
|   |   |   Feat_mutAss = stoploss: true (0/0)
|   |   Feat_SeqContent = TGC: false (10/0)
|   |   Feat_SeqContent = TCA: true (0/0)
|   |   Feat_SeqContent = AAT
|   |   |   polyphen = benign: false (12.6/0)
|   |   |   polyphen = probably: true (1.8/0.8)
|   |   |   polyphen = possibly: false (3.6/0)
|   |   Feat_SeqContent = TCC: true (0/0)
|   |   Feat_SeqContent = TGG
|   |   |   CNT < 0.5: false (1/0)
|   |   |   CNT >= 0.5: true (1/0)
|   |   Feat_SeqContent = CAT
|   |   |   VAF < 50.5
|   |   |   |   VAF < 49.06
|   |   |   |   |   CNT < 0.5
|   |   |   |   |   |   VAF < 22.32
|   |   |   |   |   |   |   CNT < NaN: true (0/0)
|   |   |   |   |   |   |   CNT >= NaN
|   |   |   |   |   |   |   |   VAF < 21.41: false (2/0)
|   |   |   |   |   |   |   |   VAF >= 21.41: true (1/0)
|   |   |   |   |   |   VAF >= 22.32: false (7/0)
|   |   |   |   |   CNT >= 0.5: true (3/0)
|   |   |   |   VAF >= 49.06: true (1/0)
|   |   |   VAF >= 50.5: false (12/0)
|   |   Feat_SeqContent = TCG: true (0/0)
|   |   Feat_SeqContent = GAT
|   |   |   CNT < 39.5: false (10/0)
|   |   |   CNT >= 39.5: true (1/0)
```

```
|    |    Feat_SeqContent = TGT
|    |    |    pattern = CG: false (2/0)
|    |    |    pattern = CA
|    |    |    |    inExAct = true
|    |    |    |    |    CNT < 1: false (3/0)
|    |    |    |    |    CNT >= 1: true (1/0)
|    |    |    |    inExAct = false: true (0/0)
|    |    |    pattern = CT: true (0/0)
|    |    |    pattern = TA: true (0/0)
|    |    |    pattern = TC: true (0/0)
|    |    |    pattern = TG: true (0/0)
|    |    Feat_SeqContent = TTA: false (1/0)
|    |    Feat_SeqContent = TTC
|    |    |    Feat_mutAss = neutral: false (3/0)
|    |    |    Feat_mutAss = low: true (1/0)
|    |    |    Feat_mutAss = medium: false (1/0)
|    |    |    Feat_mutAss = high: true (0/0)
|    |    |    Feat_mutAss = stopgain: true (0/0)
|    |    |    Feat_mutAss = stoploss: true (0/0)
|    |    Feat_SeqContent = TCT: true (0/0)
|    |    Feat_SeqContent = TTG: false (4/0)
|    |    Feat_SeqContent = TTT: false (5/0)
|    |    Feat_SeqContent = AGA
|    |    |    CNT < 0.5: false (11/0)
|    |    |    CNT >= 0.5
|    |    |    |    polyphen = benign
```

Figure 2 explains the proposed model performance on the somatic dataset. The cancer datasets are predicted utilizing the model proposed to discover the average rate of true positive on the datasets of high dimension. The figure shows that this approach has a best rate of true positive than the existing approaches.

Figure 3 explain the proposed model's performance on the somatic dataset. The cancer datasets are predicted utilizing the model proposed to discover the average rate of true positive on the datasets of high dimension. From the figure, it is visualised that the present technique has best recall over the existing models.

Table 1 explains the proposed model performance on all training datasets. At this time, all the datasets are estimated utilizing the proposed model for finding the regular accuracy of the training datasets. The table visualises that the present approach has better average accuracy than the existing models.

Figure 2. Comparative analysis of the proposed model to the conventional models on somatic cancer datasets

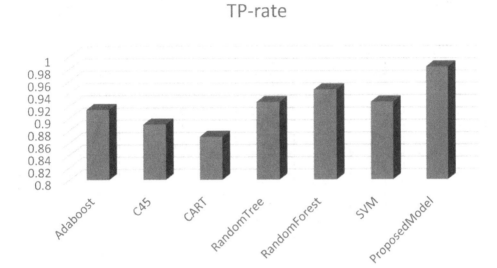

Figure 3. The proposed model to the conventional model's comparative analysis on somatic cancer datasets using recall measure

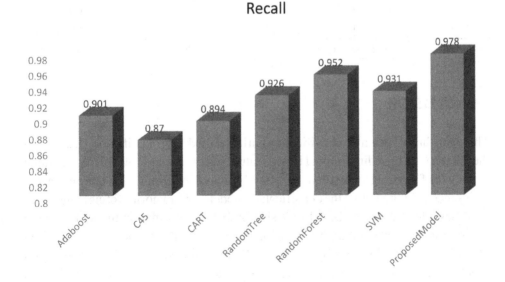

Table 1. Comparative analysis of the present technique to the conventional techniques utilizing accuracy on various real-time average accuracy of somatic datasets

Test Samples	PCA+RF	IG+SVM	PCA+NN	T-test+ Naïve Bayes	Proposed Model
5	0.93	0.94	0.86	0.95	0.98
10	0.93	0.93	0.85	0.93	0.98
15	0.94	0.93	0.86	0.93	0.98
20	0.94	0.92	0.88	0.94	0.97
25	0.95	0.94	0.86	0.94	0.97
30	0.94	0.94	0.87	0.95	0.97
35	0.94	0.92	0.87	0.92	0.98
40	0.94	0.92	0.87	0.93	0.98
45	0.94	0.92	0.86	0.93	0.98
50	0.95	0.95	0.88	0.94	0.98
55	0.93	0.92	0.88	0.94	0.97
60	0.93	0.95	0.88	0.93	0.98
65	0.94	0.93	0.87	0.94	0.98
70	0.94	0.94	0.86	0.92	0.98
75	0.93	0.93	0.86	0.93	0.98
80	0.95	0.95	0.86	0.92	0.98
85	0.93	0.93	0.86	0.93	0.98
90	0.94	0.95	0.87	0.94	0.98
95	0.92	0.93	0.87	0.95	0.99
100	0.92	0.94	0.87	0.93	0.98

CONCLUSION

The algorithm of ensemble classification is a better model for classification learning in the dataset with high dimension. Hybrid feature selection measures are implemented in this work for testing the test data accuracy. Various feature ranking sets are extracted in this model for predicting the classification model's best majority voting. This paper proposes a hybrid cluster-based Bayesian probability estimation model to predict the disease class label on high dimensional databases. The proposed cluster-based classification model selects optimal clusters for feature ranking and classification problems for improving the rate of true positive and accuracy. Experimental results are simulated on different training datasets for accurate prediction. Proposed results proved that the gene-disease based patterns have better optimisation than the conventional methods of statistical metrics and classification models.

Figure 4. Comparative runtime analysis of present technique to the conventional techniques by using accuracy on different real-time average accuracy of all the training datasets

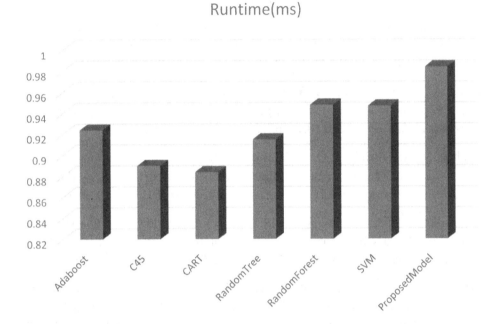

REFERENCES

Alzubi, O. A., Alzubi, J. A., Dorgham, O., & Alsayyed, M. (2020). Cryptosystem design based on Hermitian curves for IoT security. *The Journal of Supercomputing*, *76*(11), 8566–8589. doi:10.100711227-020-03144-x

Clayman, C. L., Srinivasan, S. M., & Sangwan, R. S. (2020, January). K-means Clustering and Principal Components Analysis of Microarray Data of L1000 Landmark Genes. *Procedia Computer Science*, *168*, 97–104. doi:10.1016/j.procs.2020.02.265

Dabba, A., Tari, A., Meftali, S., & Mokhtari, R. (2021, March). Gene selection and classification of microarray data method based on mutual information and moth flame algorithm. *Expert Systems with Applications*, *166*, 114012. doi:10.1016/j.eswa.2020.114012

Daoud, M., & Mayo, M. (2019, June). A survey of neural network-based cancer prediction models from microarray data. *Artificial Intelligence in Medicine*, *97*, 204–214. doi:10.1016/j.artmed.2019.01.006 PMID:30797633

Giannakeas, N., Karvelis, P. S., Exarchos, T. P., Kalatzis, F. G., & Fotiadis, D. I. (2013, July). Segmentation of microarray images using pixel classification—Comparison with clustering-based methods. *Computers in Biology and Medicine*, *43*(6), 705–716. doi:10.1016/j.compbiomed.2013.03.003 PMID:23668346

Grisci, B. I., Feltes, B. C., & Dorn, M. (2019, January). Neuroevolution as a tool for microarray gene expression pattern identification in cancer research. *Journal of Biomedical Informatics*, *89*, 122–133. doi:10.1016/j.jbi.2018.11.013 PMID:30521855

Halder, A., & Kumar, A. (2019, April). Active learning using rough fuzzy classifier for cancer prediction from microarray gene expression data. *Journal of Biomedical Informatics*, *92*, 103136. doi:10.1016/j.jbi.2019.103136 PMID:30802546

Hambali, M. A., Oladele, T. O., & Adewole, K. S. (2020, June). Microarray cancer feature selection: Review, challenges and research directions. *International Journal of Cognitive Computing in Engineering*, *1*, 78–97. doi:10.1016/j.ijcce.2020.11.001

Han, X. H., Li, D. A., & Wang, L. (2019, January). A Hybrid Cancer Classification Model Based Recursive Binary Gravitational Search Algorithm in Microarray Data. *Procedia Computer Science*, *154*, 274–282. doi:10.1016/j.procs.2019.06.041

Kawamura, T., Mutoh, H., Tomita, Y., Kato, R., & Honda, H. (2008, November). Cancer DNA Microarray Analysis Considering Multi-subclass with Graph-based Clustering Method. *Journal of Bioscience and Bioengineering*, *106*(5), 442–448. doi:10.1263/jbb.106.442 PMID:19111639

Kilicarslan, S., Adem, K., & Celik, M. (2020, April). Diagnosis and classification of cancer using hybrid model based on ReliefF and convolutional neural network. *Medical Hypotheses*, *137*, 109577. doi:10.1016/j.mehy.2020.109577 PMID:31991364

Kumar, A., & Halder, A. (2020, May). Ensemble-based active learning using fuzzy-rough approach for cancer sample classification. *Engineering Applications of Artificial Intelligence*, *91*, 103591. doi:10.1016/j.engappai.2020.103591

Kumaran, S. R., Othman, M. S., Yusuf, L. M., & Yunianta, A. (2019, January). Estimation of Missing Values Using Hybrid Fuzzy Clustering Mean and Majority Vote for Microarray Data. *Procedia Computer Science*, *163*, 145–153. doi:10.1016/j.procs.2019.12.096

Lee, J., Choi, I. Y., & Jun, C.-H. (2021, March). An efficient multivariate feature ranking method for gene selection in high-dimensional microarray data. *Expert Systems with Applications*, *166*, 113971. doi:10.1016/j.eswa.2020.113971

Morais-Rodrigues, F., Silv́erio-Machado, R., Kato, R. B., Rodrigues, D. L. N., Valdez-Baez, J., Fonseca, V., San, E. J., Gomes, L. G. R., dos Santos, R. G., Vinicius Canário Viana, M., da Cruz Ferraz Dutra, J., Teixeira Dornelles Parise, M., Parise, D., Campos, F. F., de Souza, S. J., Ortega, J. M., Barh, D., Ghosh, P., Azevedo, V. A. C., & dos Santos, M. A. (2020, February). Analysis of the microarray gene expression for breast cancer progression after the application modified logistic regression. *Gene, 726*, 144168. doi:10.1016/j.gene.2019.144168 PMID:31759986

Nagpal, A., & Singh, V. (2018, January). A Feature Selection Algorithm Based on Qualitative Mutual Information for Cancer Microarray Data. *Procedia Computer Science, 132*, 244–252. doi:10.1016/j.procs.2018.05.195

Potharaju, S. P., & Sreedevi, M. (2019, June). Distributed feature selection (DFS) strategy for microarray gene expression data to improve the classification performance. *Clinical Epidemiology and Global Health, 7*(2), 171–176. doi:10.1016/j.cegh.2018.04.001

Rahim, Murugan, Mostafa, Dubey, Regin, Kulkarni, & Dhanalakshmi. (2020). Detecting the Phishing Attack Using Collaborative Approach and Secure Login through Dynamic Virtual Passwords. *Webology, 17*(2).

Rani, R. R., & Ramyachitra, D. (2018, January). Microarray Cancer Gene Feature Selection Using Spider Monkey Optimization Algorithm and Cancer Classification using SVM. *Procedia Computer Science, 143*, 108–116. doi:10.1016/j.procs.2018.10.358

Sahu, B., Dehuri, S., & Jagadev, A. K. (2017, January). Feature selection model based on clustering and ranking in pipeline for microarray data. *Informatics in Medicine Unlocked, 9*, 107–122. doi:10.1016/j.imu.2017.07.004

Sayed, S., Nassef, M., Badr, A., & Farag, I. (2019, May). A Nested Genetic Algorithm for feature selection in high-dimensional cancer Microarray datasets. *Expert Systems with Applications, 121*, 233–243. doi:10.1016/j.eswa.2018.12.022

Shibata, M., Okamura, K., Yura, K., & Umezawa, A. (2020, December). High-precision multiclass cell classification by supervised machine learning on lectin microarray data. *Regenerative Therapy, 15*, 195–201. doi:10.1016/j.reth.2020.09.005 PMID:33426219

Sun, M., Liu, K., Wu, Q., Hong, Q., Wang, B., & Zhang, H. (2019, June). A novel ECOC algorithm for multiclass microarray data classification based on data complexity analysis. *Pattern Recognition, 90*, 346–362. doi:10.1016/j.patcog.2019.01.047

Yao, Y., Chen, Y. H., Wang, Y., Li, X. P., Wang, J. L., Shen, D. H., & Wei, L. H. (2010, August). Molecular classification of human endometrial cancer based on gene expression profiles from specialised microarrays. *International Journal of Gynaecology and Obstetrics*, *110*(2), 125–129. doi:10.1016/j.ijgo.2010.03.020 PMID:20471643

Zainuddin, Z., & Ong, P. (2011, October). Reliable multiclass cancer classification of microarray gene expression profiles using an improved wavelet neural network. *Expert Systems with Applications*, *38*(11), 13711–13722. doi:10.1016/j.eswa.2011.04.164

Zheng, X., Zhu, W., Tang, C., & Wang, M. (2019, July). Gene selection for microarray data classification via adaptive hypergraph embedded dictionary learning. *Gene*, *706*, 188–200. doi:10.1016/j.gene.2019.04.060 PMID:31085273

Chapter 11

Progressive Bearing Fault Detection in a Three-Phase Induction Motor Using S-Transform via Pre-Fault Frequency Cancellation

Deekshit K. K. C.
Sreenidhi Institute of Science and Technology, India

G. Venu Madhav
Anurag University, India

ABSTRACT

Detection of bearing faults have become crucial in electrical machines, particularly in induction motors. Conventional monitoring procedures using vibration sensors, temperature sensors, etc. are costly and need more tests to estimate the nature of fault. Hence, the current monitoring attracts the concentration of many industries for continuous monitoring. Spectral analysis of stator current to estimate motor faults, FFT analysis, is commonly preferred. But the problems associated with normal FFT analysis will mislead the fault diagnosis. Therefore, advanced spectral methods like wavelet transforms, matrix pencil method, MUSIC algorithm, s-transforms have been proposed. But each technique requires special attention to get good results. On the other hand, faults experienced by the induction motor can be categorized into bearing-related, rotor- and stator-related, and eccentricity. Among these faults, bearing damage accounts for 40-90% and requires additional concentration to estimate.

DOI: 10.4018/978-1-7998-9426-1.ch011

INTRODUCTION

Induction motors are extensively used electrical machines in industries for various applications. These motors frequently suffer from faults due to electrical, mechanical, and thermal stresses and cause calamitous damage to industries' production and financial aspects. To prevent unnecessary maintenance costs and burdens, continuous assessment for these faults at the nascent stage is essential. In induction motors, most common bearing faults, broken rotor faults, stator inter turn faults, and eccentricity faults (PEOCO,2014). Several reports like IEEE and PES have mentioned the percentage involvement of these faults like 42, 37, 10 and 12 for 200HP and above (Zhang,2011). Hence, the contribution of bearing faults is more for high rating machines and further increases to 90% in small and medium ratings (El Houssin,2013). These faults can be primarily classified into localized faults and distributed faults. Localized faults are categorized into the inner race, outer race, cage, ball defects (Nath,2020) and distributed faults into corrosion, misalignment, and generalized roughness (Zhou,2008). Localized faults (Single point defect) will produce a perceivable impact on the machine parameters and take place due to the usage of the motor for a long duration without any maintenance (Frosini,2010). On the other hand, distributed faults of bearing like generalized roughness are difficult to trace through the indicators as they are obscure. These faults are progressive and become calamitous if non detected at a premature stage. Fault detection using popular methods using vibration sensors, temperature sensors, chemical procedures etc., are costly and needs more tests to estimate the nature of the fault.

For instance, vibration monitoring is most popularly used but needs a lot of manpower, costly equipment, and difficult to direct motor access in hazardous situations (Zhou,2008). Because of this, there is a requirement of cost-effective, suitable for all environments and non-intrusive methods to detect faults in an induction motor. Motor current spectral analysis will meet all these requirements and require less manpower (Dalvand,2017). This attracts the attention of many recent researchers for fault diagnosis in 3 phase induction motor. Many recent works provide (Sun, 2019) motor current signature analysis based fault detection and suffer from major complications like not being suitable for nonstationary nature, resolution problems. Fast Fourier transform (FFT) based spectral analysis has issues like inaccurate resolution, computational time, and inefficacious to provide time-frequency resolution (Kim, 2007).

The resolution issues under stationary condition are overcome using MUSIC and ESPRIT algorithms in (Garcia,2011) (Kia, 2005) (Bracale, 2007) and have computational issues (Liu,2017), whereas for nonstationary condition time-frequency spectral analysis using short-time Fourier transform (STFT) (Henao,2011). This gives inappropriate magnitudes for the signals due to fixed window size. As the fault frequencies will exist in the wide band width range, the higher and lower frequency components are captured using a fixed window, leading to spectral leakage. To avoid this problem, variable size window, i.e., large window for lower frequency component and smaller window higher frequency components using wavelet transforms. Discrete wavelets transform-based fault detection is proposed in (Deekshit Kompella,2017) and is suitable for nonstationary conditions. But for the stationary condition of the machine, stationary wavelet transform (Kompella,2017) have shown good results.

Wavelet packet decomposition-based fault detection is proposed (Liling,2019). But for higher-level decomposition, large numbers of coefficients are required to analyze the fault, which takes more detecting time. To overcome this problem, advanced spectral tools like the matrix pencil method (MPM) (Deekshit Kompella,2020) and s-transform (ST) (Singh, 2016) (Deekshit Kompella, 2020) have been implemented for fault detection. Moreover, removing regular components in the current spectrum is another important issue in fault detection using MCSA. These components are treated as pre-fault frequencies (PFF). Conventional Notch filter will remove all these frequencies (Amirat,2019) but have bandwidth issues due to sideband effects. To overcome this issue, current spectral subtraction (Bouchikhi, 2013) (Kompella, 2018), park's vector transformation (Saeidi,2014), Teager-Kaiser approach (Liu,2015), Kalman filter (Zarei, 2019), Taylor-Kalman series (Trujillo-Guajardo, 2018) and Wiener filter, (Kompella,2020) (Kompella, 2021) are proposed in the literature. But they have major issues like computational difficulties, linearity, proper spectral technique, and selection of features after cancellation. This paper identifies progressive type bearing faults, namely misalignment, generalized roughness and combination of outer race and generalized roughness faults, and motor current signature analysis. The PFF is cancelled using an extended Wiener filter with the window technique. After PFF cancellation, S-transform is used for spectral analysis and the fault magnitude is estimated using feature parameter, i.e., RMS value of residual stator current. The rest of the paper is arranged by discussing wiener filter design using extended window technique in Section-II, S-transform in Section-III, Experimental work in Section-IV and the results are presented in section-V.

PRE-FAULT FREQUENCY CANCELLATION (PFFC)

The proposed fault detection scheme is shown in Fig.1 and has 5 stages of current signal processing. In the beginning, the stator current is captured from the machine under different states and is processed for wavelet-based de-noising, as mentioned in (Kompella 2021). In this stage, the signal is decomposed into 4 levels to remove the noise acquired during data capturing due to various sources. This noise is estimated and removed using the proper threshold value in real-time. Once the noise is removed, the second stage is initiated to remove estimated frequency components to get fault indication by PFFC. In the PFFC, the regular motor stator current components are estimated and subtracted from the test signal using the Wiener filter.

Figure 1. The flow of the proposed fault detection scheme

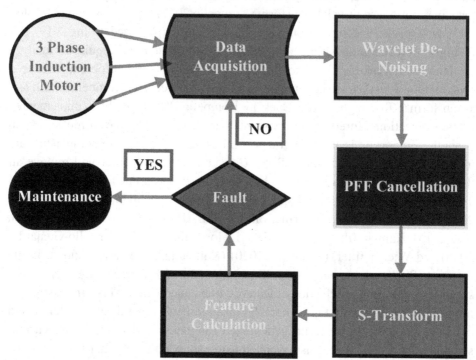

Stator current under a healthy state of the machines will consist of fundamental supply frequency, its multiple odd frequencies as harmonics and noise frequencies. The extended Wiener filter is designed using a window function, and the corresponding filter coefficients are used to estimate regular components. These components are treated as predicted components in (Dalvand 2018) and are mentioned here onwards as pre-fault frequencies (PFF) in this paper. Mathematical modelling of these components is given in the following equation (1).

$$I_e(n) = I_0(n) + \sum_{p=1,5,7,11} I_p(n) \tag{1}$$

Where $I_0(n)$ is the DC component, $I_e(n)$ is the estimated current components $I_p(n)$ is the supply fundamental and their harmonics. When fault appears, the fault component will join in equation (1) and is mentioned in the following.

$$I_a(n) = I_0(n) + \sum_{p=1,5,7,11} I_p(n) + \delta(n) + I_f(n) \tag{2}$$

Where $I_a(n)$ is the total fault current under abnormal conditions, $\delta(n)$ is the noise due to different sources and $I_f(n)$ is the fault component due to various faults. After the first processing stage, equation (2) becomes noise-free and is expressed in the following way.

$$I_d(n) = I_0(n) + \sum_{p=1,5,7,11} I_p(n) + I_f(n) \tag{3}$$

The DC component will inject even harmonics into the current spectrum with its intensity and cause the frequency spectrum to be the most complex. Moreover, the regular frequencies with high magnitude may cause the fault frequencies to be invisible. These components will be cancelled using a wiener filter. The design of the Wiener filter is explained in the following Fig.2. Due to the practical problems associated with the design of the Wiener filter, the estimated frequencies do not match the original value and result in an error in cancellation. Depending on the magnitude of this error, the accuracy of fault identification is estimated. Hence, minimization of this error becomes crucial in the design of the filter and is done using minimum mean square error in this work. This is given by

Figure 2. Block diagram of PFF cancellation

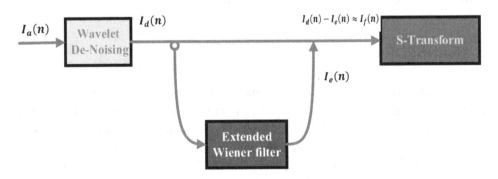

$$\vartheta = E\left\{\left|\beta\left(n\right)\right|^2\right\} = E\left\{\left|I_d\left(n\right) - \sum_{k=0}^{L-1} W_e\left(k\right)I_e\left(n - n_0 - k\right)\right|^2\right. \tag{4}$$

Where υ is an error, $E\{\}$ is the expectation, $I_d(n)$ is denoised stator current, and I_e is estimated current. The error minimization involves equating the derivative of υ to zero. After simplification, the filter coefficients are as follows.

$$W = R_d^{-1}r_{cd} \tag{5}$$

The extended wiener filter coefficients are obtained by multiplying with a suitable window function. Blackman Harris window has shown good performance in fault detection and Wiener filter (Kompella & Madhav, n.d.). Therefore, equation (5) is multiplied with the blackman harris window function and the modified coefficients are obtained as

$$W_m\left(n\right) = \sum_{k=-\infty}^{\infty} W\left(n\right)B\left(n - k\right) \tag{6}$$

Where B(n) is the blackman harris window and is given by

$$B\left(n\right) = 0.358 - 0.488\cos\left(\frac{2\pi n}{L-1}\right) + 0.141\cos\left(\frac{4\pi n}{L-1}\right) - 0.011\cos\left(\frac{6\pi n}{L-1}\right) \tag{7}$$

After the PFF cancellation, the residual components of stator current is processed for stage 3 using S-Transform. The detailed mathematical description of the S-transform is discussed in the following section.

S-TRANSFORM

S-Transform is a multi resolution spectral analysis tool that provides the best frequency resolution of a signal. It is also known as a hybrid of short-time Fourier transform and wavelet transform containing elements of both and made effective use of them in an advanced manner. As obtained from continuous wavelet analysis, s-transform is defined as multiplication of CWT of g(t) using Gaussian mother wavelet with phase correction given by (Alzubi et al., 2020; Rahim et al., 2020; Singh & Shaik, 2016b).

$$S(\tau, f) = e^{e^{-j2\,f\pi}} U(\tau, n) \tag{8}$$

$U(\tau,n)$ is the CWT of the signal I(t)is given as

$$U(\tau, n) = \int_{-\infty}^{\infty} I(t) U(t - \tau, n) dt \tag{9}$$

And the Gaussian window $U(t,f)$ is given by

$$U(t, f) = \frac{|f|}{\sqrt{2\pi}} e^{-\frac{t^2 f^2}{2}} e^{i 2\pi ft} \tag{10}$$

The generalized S-Transform is given by

$$S(\tau,f,m) = \int_{-\infty}^{\infty} g(t) w(-t, f, m) e^{-j2\,\text{Å}ft} dt \tag{11}$$

Where m represents a set of parameters that determine the shape and properties of w, and w denotes the S transform window shown as

$$\omega(t, f, m) = \frac{|f|}{\sqrt{2\pi m}} e^{\frac{-t^2 f^2}{2m^2}} \tag{12}$$

After spectral analysis of residual stator current using S-transform, the feature parameter is calculated to estimate the fault magnitude. RMS values of the remaining components are treated as feature parameters. The complete experimental procedure is discussed in the following section.

FRAMEWORK OF EXPERIMENTAL SYSTEM

In the experimental verification of the proposed testing scheme, a 2HP, 3-Phase 415V autotransformer fed induction motor has been taken. It is operated with a balanced spring load at 4 different conditions. This is for testing of proposed topology under nonstationary nature. A current transducer made by LEM is chosen for current sensing, and the captured current is stored in the LabVIEW environment and processed for proposed spectral analysis in MATLAB. The complete experimental framework is shown in Fig.3. The progressive nature of bearing fault is tested using misalignment fault, generalized roughness fault (Corrosion) and combined outer race and GR Fault are tested one by one. Various faulty bearings with proposed categories are shown in Fig.4. The current acquisition using the national instrument NI MyRio is shown in Fig.5. As mentioned in Fig.5, the stator current at various motor conditions is acquired with a 10KHz sampling frequency to get better resolution in the frequency domain. Stator current magnitude is normalized to get a relatively good indication for faulty parts. There are two analogue input ports for NI MyRio and are named ai0 and ai1. The current transducer is connected to aio, and the voltage values across a resistor are stored in .csv format. The following results section discusses the complete picture of stator current in both the time and frequency domain.

Figure 3. The exhibit of testing equipment

EXPERIMENTAL RESULTS

The stator current under various conditions of the induction motor at different load conditions is presented in Fig.6 and 7. In Fig.6, stator current under normal and misalignment fault conditions at 4 different loads are presented, whereas, in Fig.7, stator current with GR and GR with outer race faults are presented at the same loads. From these pictures, it can be observed that the fault does not indicate the instantaneous value of stator current. But in GR with outer race fault at load 4, the magnitude of instantaneous current in the time domain has a little high magnitude. Even though the magnitude is a little high, it is difficult to estimate the fault. Therefore, frequency domain analysis is proposed, and the corresponding fault frequencies are to be estimated. The periodogram using conventional FFT of each signal is performed and plotted in Fig.8 to 9. The conventional FFT spectrum has shown the pre-fault frequencies clearly but cannot distinguish fault frequencies. It is noticed that the signals have a lot of noise in every machine's condition. Especially, bearing misalignment and GR fault have noise in all load conditions. Therefore, wavelet de-noising is applied, and the corresponding data is processed for the next stage. The stator current under various machine states after de-noising is shown in Fig.10. The noise after 500Hz is removed completely to avoid misinterpretation.

Figure 4. Faulty bearings used for the experiment

Figure 5. Stator current acquisition in the LabVIEW environment

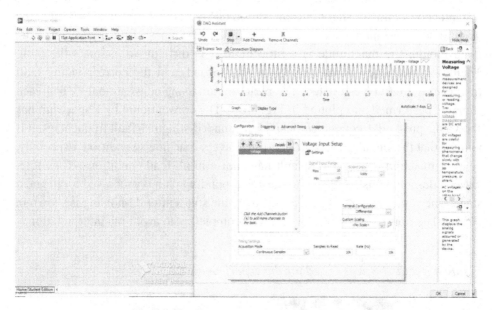

PFF cancellation is processed in the next stage to remove the paramount components in the stator current spectrum. Fig.11 shows the frequency spectrum of stator current at all bearing conditions after PFFC. All the components of paramount frequencies are eliminated using the Wiener filter, and the fault frequencies are difficult to distinguish using FFT. Therefore, S-transform based spectrum analysis is carried out to estimate the fault frequencies.

The s-transform of the stator signal is computed and plotted in Fig.12, and it is observed that the frequency spectrum is obtained at each instant of the current sample in the time domain. This leads to a lot of confusion in the frequency variations. Therefore, under the stationary nature of the stator current, it is sufficient with one sample of the frequency spectrum, as shown in Fig.13-14.

From Fig.13 & 14, it is noticed that the s-transform does not affect by de-noising due to its perfectness. Therefore, the S-transform of current after PFFC has a good indication of the remaining fault frequencies. But fault severity estimation is difficult due to invisible magnitudes of fault frequencies. This leads to misinterpretation about fault existence and causes unnecessary maintenance. Therefore, it is essential to use proper fault indexing parameters to identify the exact fault magnitude and severity. RMS value of stator current is treated as FIP in this paper and computed at every stage of current signal processing. The bar graphs for each fault at every load condition are computed and shown in Fig.15-18. From bar graphs, it is concluded that fault indications are very good after PFFC based s-transform at each load except load-3.

Whereas for load-3, the direct s-transform has shown better indication than PFFC and may be due to cancellation of fault frequencies that are very nearer to healthy components. This will recover by a suitable window function that gives good fault information at every load condition.

Figure 6. Stator current with normal and misalignment fault

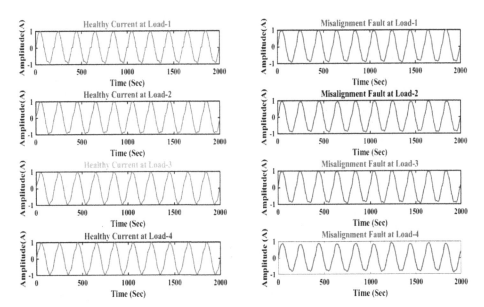

CONCLUSION

This paper presents the detection of progressive bearing faults in 3 phase induction motor like generalized roughness faults. These faults do not have characteristic fault frequencies and are difficult to estimate at an incipient state. Therefore, in this paper, s-transform based spectral analysis is carried out to get good resolution, especially after PFF cancellation using the Wiener filter. The results are greatly improved after wavelet de-noising and PFF cancellation due to the proper cancellation of sensor noise and regular components in the current spectrum. The proposed fault detection topology is tested using progressive faults like misalignment, generalized roughness using corrosion and a combination of outer race and GR faults. As the load varies, different faults are identified due to good resolution using S-transform. The proposed fault detection topology is examined using a 2HP induction motor, and the results have shown good signs for fault. Further, the PFF cancellation can be made using better window functions to get a constant indication for fault.

Figure 7. Stator current with GR and GR with outer race fault

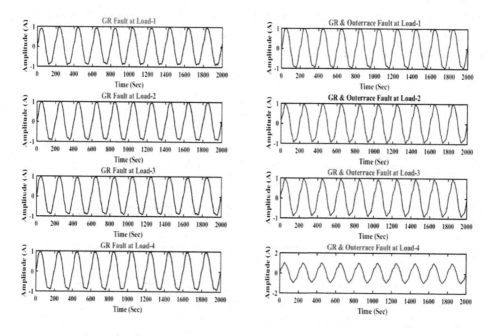

Figure 8. The frequency spectrum of stator current under normal and misalignment fault conditions

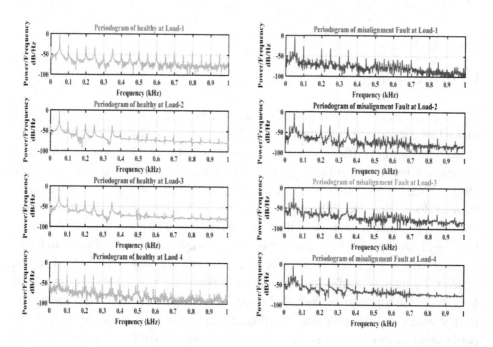

Figure 9. The frequency spectrum of stator current under GR and GR with outer race fault conditions

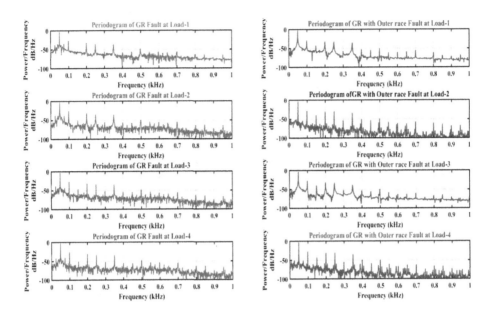

Figure 10. The frequency spectrum of current under both normal & abnormal conditions at load-1

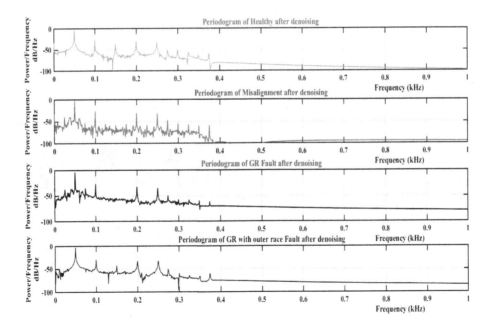

Figure 11. Frequency spectrum after PFFC at load-1

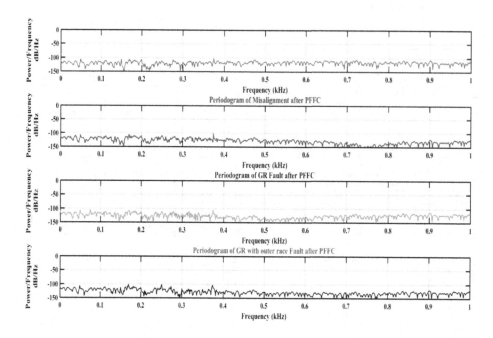

Figure 12. S-Transform of stator current under the healthy condition at normal and after PFFC

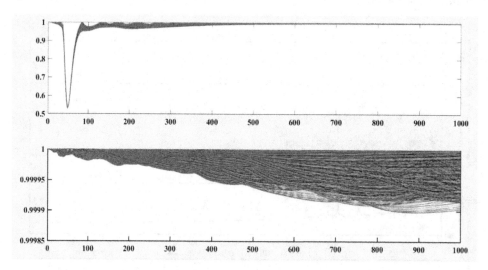

Figure 13. S-Transform of stator current under the health condition with one sample

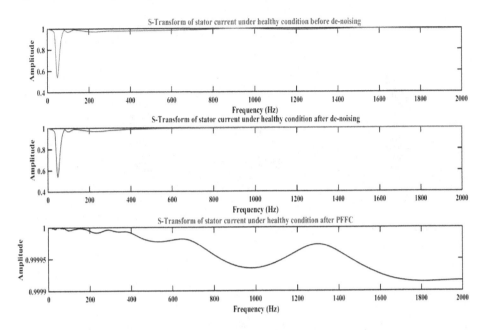

Figure 14. S-Transform of stator current under combined fault conditions with one sample

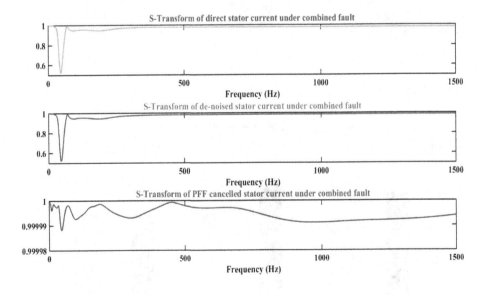

Figure 15. Bar graph of various faults at load-1

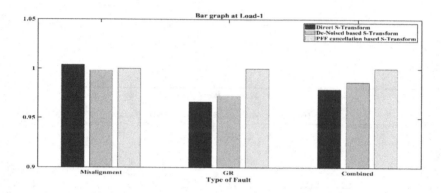

Figure 16. Bar graph of various faults at load-2

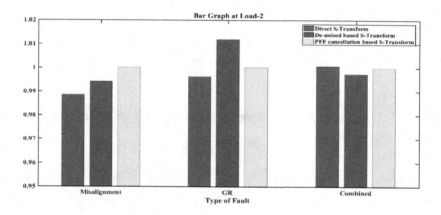

Figure 17. Bar graph of various faults at load-3

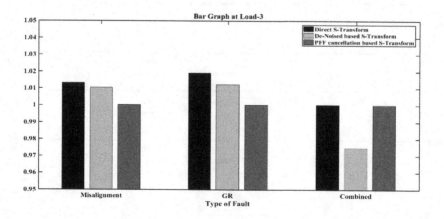

Figure 18. Bar graph of various faults at load-4

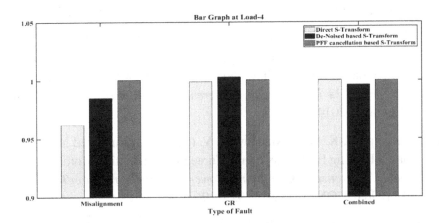

REFERENCES

Alzubi, O. A., Alzubi, J. A., Dorgham, O., & Alsayyed, M. (2020). Cryptosystem design based on Hermitian curves for IoT security. *The Journal of Supercomputing*, *76*(11), 8566–8589. doi:10.100711227-020-03144-x

Amirat, Y., Elbouchikhi, E., Zhou, Z., Benbouzid, M., & Feld, G. (2019). Variational Mode Decomposition-based Notch Filter for Bearing Fault Detection. *IECON 2019 - 45th Annual Conference of the IEEE Industrial Electronics Society*, 6028-6033. 10.1109/IECON.2019.8926891

Bouchikhi, E. H. E., Choqueuse, V., & Benbouzid, M. E. H. (2013, March). Current Frequency Spectral Subtraction and Its Contribution to Induction Machines Bearings. *Condition Monitoring. IEEE Transactions on Energy Conversion*, *28*(1), 135–144. doi:10.1109/TEC.2012.2227746

Bracale, A., Carpinelli, G., Piegari, L., & Tricoli, P. (2007). A high resolution method for online diagnosis of induction motors faults. *Proceedings of the 2007 IEEE PowerTech*, 994-998. 10.1109/PCT.2007.4538451

Dalvand, Dalvand, Sharafi, & Pecht. (2017). Current noise cancellation for bearing fault diagnosis using time-shifting. *IEEE Trans. Ind. Electron.*, *64*. doi:10.1109/TIE.2017.2694397

Dalvand, F., Kang, M., Dalvand, S., & Pecht, M. (2018, December). Detection of Generalized-Roughness and Single-Point Bearing Faults Using Linear Prediction-Based Current Noise Cancellation. *IEEE Transactions on Industrial Electronics*, *65*(12), 9728–9738. doi:10.1109/TIE.2018.2821645

Deekshit Kompella, K. C. (2020). Estimation of Premature Bearing Faults in a Three Phase Induction Motor Using S-Transform. *Journal of Green Engineering, 10*(4), 1878–1896.

Deekshit Kompella, K. C., Gopala Rao, M. V., Rao, R. S., & Sreenivasu, R. N. (2014). Estimation of bearing faults in induction motor by MCSA using Daubechies wavelet analysis. *2014 International Conference on Smart Electric Grid (ISEG),* 1-6. 10.1109/ISEG.2014.7005577

Deekshit Kompella, K. C., & Madhav, G. V. (2020). An Improved Matrix Pencil Method based Bearing Fault detection in Three Phase Induction Motor. *2020 IEEE International Conference on Computing, Power and Communication Technologies,* 51-56. 10.1109/GUCON48875.2020.9231196

Detection and classification of induction motor faults using Motor Current Signature Analysis and Multilayer Perceptron. (2014). *IEEE 8th International Power Engineering and Optimization Conference (PEOCO2014),* 35-40.

Frosini, L., & Bassi, E. (2010, January). Stator current and motor efficiency as indicators for different types of bearing faults in induction motors. *IEEE Transactions on Industrial Electronics, 57*(1), 244–251. doi:10.1109/TIE.2009.2026770

Garcia-Perez, A., de Jesus Romero-Troncoso, R., Cabal-Yepez, E., & Osornio-Rios, R. (2011, May). The application of high-resolution spectral analysis for identifying multiple combined faults in induction motors. *IEEE Transactions on Industrial Electronics, 58*(5), 2002–2010. doi:10.1109/TIE.2010.2051398

Henao, Rastegar, Capolino, & Sieg-Zieba. (2011). Wire rope fault detection in a hoisting winch system by motor torque and current signature analysis. *IEEE Trans. on Ind. Electr., 58*(5), 1727–1736.

Hmida, M. A., & Braham, A. (2020, October). Fault Detection of VFD-Fed Induction Motor Under Transient Conditions Using Harmonic Wavelet Transform. *IEEE Transactions on Instrumentation and Measurement, 69*(10), 8207–8215. doi:10.1109/TIM.2020.2993107

Kia, Henao, & Capolino. (2005). Zoom-MUSIC frequency estimation method for three-phase induction machine fault detection. *31st Annual Conference of IEEE Industrial Electronics Society.* . doi:10.1109/IECON.2005.1569317

Kim, Lee, Lee, Ni, Song, & Lee. (2007). A comparative study on damage detection in speed-up and coast-down process of grinding spindle-typed rotor-bearing system. *J. Materials Technology, 187,* 30–36.

Kompella & Madhav. (n.d.). Performance Analysis of Wiener Filter with different window functions in detecting Broken Rotor fault in 3 Phase Induction Motor *International Journal of Engineering Trends and Technology, 68*(12), 153-159.

Kompella, Rao, & Rao. (2017). SWT based bearing fault detection using frequency spectral subtraction of stator current with and without an adaptive filter. *TENCON 2017 - 2017 IEEE Region 10 Conference,* 2472-2477. . doi:10.1109/TENCON.2017.8228277

Kompella, Rayapudi, & Rongala. (2020). Investigation of Bearing faults in three phase Induction motor using Wavelet De-Noising with improved Wiener Filtering. *International Journal of Power and Energy Conversion.*

Kompella, K. C. (2021). Robustification of Fault Detection Algorithm in a 3 Phase Induction Motor using MCSA for various Single and Multiple Faults. *IET Electric Power Applications.* Advance online publication. doi:10.1049/elp2.12049

Kompella, K. D., Rao, M. V. G., & Rao, R. S. (2018). Bearing fault detection in a 3 phase induction motor using stator current frequency spectral subtraction with various wavelet decomposition techniques. *Ain Shams Engineering Journal, 9*(4), 2427–2439. doi:10.1016/j.asej.2017.06.002

Liling, S., Kuankuo, Z., & Xiangdong, L. (2019). Stator inter-turn fault diagnosis of induction motor based on wavelet packet decomposition and random forest. *8th Renewable Power Generation Conference (RPG 2019),* 1-6. 10.1049/cp.2019.0667

Liu, H., Sun, Y., Huang, J., Hou, Z., & Wang, T. (2015). Inter-turn fault detection for the inverter-fed induction motor based on the Teager-Kaiser energy operation of switching voltage harmonics. *2015 18th International Conference on Electrical Machines and Systems (ICEMS),* 1214-1219. 10.1109/ICEMS.2015.7385224

Liu, Y., & Bazzi, A. M. (2017). A review and comparison of fault detection and diagnosis methods for squirrel-cage induction motors: State of the art. *ISA Transactions, 70*(June), 400–409. Advance online publication. doi:10.1016/j.isatra.2017.06.001

Nath, S., Wu, J., Zhao, Y., & Qiao, W. (2020). Low Latency Bearing Fault Detection of Direct-Drive Wind Turbines Using Stator Current. *IEEE Access: Practical Innovations, Open Solutions, 8,* 44163–44174. doi:10.1109/ACCESS.2020.2977632

Rahim, Murugan, Mostafa, Dubey, Regin, Kulkarni, & Dhanalakshmi. (2020). Detecting the Phishing Attack Using Collaborative Approach and Secure Login through Dynamic Virtual Passwords. *Webology, 17*(2).

Saeidi, M., Zarei, J., Hassani, H., & Zamani, A. (2014). Bearing fault detection via Park's vector approach based on ANFIS. *2014 International Conference on Mechatronics and Control (ICMC)*, 2436-2441. 10.1109/ICMC.2014.7232006

Sangeetha, P., & S, H. (2019, June). Rational-Dilation Wavelet Transform Based Torque Estimation from Acoustic Signals for Fault Diagnosis in a Three-Phase Induction Motor. *IEEE Transactions on Industrial Informatics*, *15*(6), 3492–3501. doi:10.1109/TII.2018.2874463

Singh, M., & Shaik, A. G. (2016a). Bearing fault diagnosis of a three phase induction motor using stockwell transform. *2016 IEEE Annual India Conference*, 1-6. 10.1109/INDICON.2016.7838972

Singh, M., & Shaik, A. G. (2016b). Application of stockwell transform in bearing fault diagnosis of induction motor. In *2016 IEEE 7th Power India International Conference (PIICON)*. IEEE. 10.1109/POWERI.2016.8077436

Sun, Yin, Liu, & Chai. (n.d.). A novel rolling bearing vibration impulsive signals detection approach based on dictionary learning. *IEEE/CAA Journal of AutomaticaSinica.* . doi:10.1109/JAS.2020.1003438

Trujillo-Guajardo, L. A., Rodriguez-Maldonado, J., Moonem, M. A., & Platas-Garza, M. A. (2018, June). A Multiresolution Taylor–Kalman Approach for Broken Rotor Bar Detection in Cage Induction Motors. *IEEE Transactions on Instrumentation and Measurement*, *67*(6), 1317–1328. doi:10.1109/TIM.2018.2795895

Zarei, J., Kowsari, E., & Razavi-Far, R. (2019, June). Induction Motors Fault Detection Using Square-Root Transformed Cubature Quadrature Kalman Filter. *IEEE Transactions on Energy Conversion*, *34*(2), 870–877. doi:10.1109/TEC.2018.2877781

Zhang, P., Du, Y., Habetler, T. G., & Lu, B. (2011). A survey of condition monitoring and protection methods for medium-voltage induction motors. *IEEE Transactions on Industry Applications*, *47*(1), 34–46. doi:10.1109/TIA.2010.2090839

Zhou, W., Habetler, T. G., & Harley, R. G. (2008, December). Bearing Fault Detection Via Stator Current Noise Cancellation and Statistical Control. *IEEE Transactions on Industrial Electronics*, *55*(12), 4260–4269. doi:10.1109/TIE.2008.2005018

Chapter 12
Design of Wireless IoT Sensor Node and Platform for Fire Detection

P. V. D. S. Eswar
Koneru Lakshmaiah Education Foundation, India

N. Siva
Koneru Lakshmaiah Education Foundation, India

A. V. Harish
Koneru Lakshmaiah Education Foundation, India

Arunmetha Sundaramoorthy
KL University, India

K. Praghash
Koneru Lakshmaiah Education Foundation, India

ABSTRACT

We observe fire hazards causing life loss and property loss frequently in domestic and industrial scenarios. In industries we usually have many blocks or buildings, and it is impossible to check every building every second of the day. So, the authors' model continuously checks for fire and gives a signal: either buzzer or light depending on the requirement. This is an embedded way of hardware application and software. They also used different machine learning models and algorithms to predict the future time of the fire, using regression. For prototype applications, they use linear regression, and for real-time applications, they use k-means clustering or any other model for better accuracy.

DOI: 10.4018/978-1-7998-9426-1.ch012

INTRODUCTION

Today the industrial sector is facing many issues regarding fire hazards situations so this project may help my many cases where we predict future hazards activities may happen and we can stop them. Not only the industrial sector, but we can also use this application where hazardous situations may happen due to fire. Here we use requirements like ESP8266, Humidity and Temperature Sensor. Here the significance of NodeMCU is that it makes doing the work easier, it will upload the values into Google Sheets. NodeMCU is Wi-Fi, a module where inbuilt Wi-Fi is present in it and all the required libraries are imported into it. NodeMCU has an inbuilt microcontroller with a specified pin configuration. Here google sheets are used as a replica of a miniature and static database to collect the temperature and humidity values. Later the sheet in which the data is stored is used to link different automated services making the developers work easy. The functionality performed by the sheet is programmed by using google script through API. And we use machine learning algorithms to train and test the given form of data using regression and detect when the fire hazardous situation comes in future. In a real application, we can implement it in many sectors of industry.

LITERATURE REVIEW

The authors in the paper (Shi & Songlin, 2020) demonstrated the conventional smoke sensing structures have a few drawbacks as they are consisting of excessive implementation costs, problems in perceiving operating states, low precision, accuracy and many issues in management. To cope with those problems, a brand-new form of smart wi-fi heat or temperature tracking machine primarily based totally on NB-IoT generation is innovatively designed, which realizes real-time remote monitor.

The planned system (Benzekri et al., 2020) relies on grouping environmental wireless sensing element network knowledge from the forest and predicting the prevalence of a fire victimization artificial intelligence, a lot of significantly Deep Learning (DL) models. the mix of such a system supported the construct of the net of Things (IoT) is formed of an LPWAN network.

The implemented prototype (Putra & Nazaruddin, 2019) gives us the basic understanding and implementation of interaction Between the Virtual facet mistreating the Virtual automaton experimentation platform. It is often employed in hearth rescue operations to flee from blocked conditions and to possess a quicker response within the case of a U-turn.

We can say from the work of (Kshirsagar et al., 2020) that the Internet of Things is a platform where sensors can connect and exchange information over the Internet. This review paper presents the idea of solving health-related issues such as body temperature, blood pressure, heart rate using the latest technology, the Internet of Things. The health of a person is predicted using Mongo DB the data is stored from node MCU and given to the machine learning algorithm like ARMA algorithm where the health of the patient is plotted in a linear way. The usage of this health monitoring system in Android App for better development of health.

IoT has been an important and popular technological aspect for many years. We can see its rapid growth (Aziz, 2018) in every field like medical etc now it also entered into lifestyle controllability. Communication approaches between intelligent devices. This also gives us the privilege to access and control the devices anywhere and anytime, the trend of this aspect is communication between different devices regarding the ESP8266 Node MCU module.

The practical style and implementation of a system (Shinde & Patil, 2021), (Asvany et al., 2017; Bajrami & Murturi, 2018; Mannepalli et al., 2017; Rajakumar, 2017; Rajeswari et al., 2017) for watching environmental conditions through employing a WSN and Node MCU. The system is developed for web applications. The user will monitor measurement data from any place via the web with the aid of web and mobile applications. If the information measured by a device node exceeds the organized price range, an alert will be sent to improve the conditions.

Implementation of the concept for the good home appliance, (Kodali & Mahesh, 2016) (Ansari et al., 2018; Kadiravan, 2017; Mallikarjuna Rao et al., 2018; Uthayakumar et al., 2017) street light system meant for SCs, hearth care techniques, climate reporting system etc. The local area network facilitated ESP8266 panel integrates with DHT11 device & LDR module to observe close conditions and in step with the light intensity of 8*8 modern picture element pattern is regulated. The clients on smartphones and portable computers subscribe to the parameters such as temperature, moisture and lux level gets the real-time update.

Micro python artificial language (Bajrami & Murturi, 2018), (Eswar, n.d.) and (Rao & Manikonda, 2019) that enables the quick response which can be adjusted for shared input to operate over an embedded system (Ashok Kumar, 2022; Manoharan, 2022; Peter, 2022a; Peter, 2022b; Sripada & Mohammed Ismail, 2019; Teekaraman et al., 2022; Veena & Meena, 2022). The DHT11 device is employed to ascertain Temperature and wetness where the values are shown in ESP8266 and victimization OLED show the values are represented (Andrabi & Wahid, 2022; Andrabi & Wahid, 2019; Suma et al., 2021; Bandla et al., 2022; Basit & Kumar, 2015; Bharathidasan et al., 2022; Kamaleshwar & Lakshminarayanan, 2021; Manoharan et al., 2021; Syed & Kumar, 2020).

DESIGN AND EXPERIMENTAL SETUP

Nowadays we are observing many fire accidents occurring in our daily life. We tend to see them more often, particularly in the industrial areas (Gupta, Jain, Vaisla et al, 2021; Gupta, Vaisla, Jain et al, 2021; Jain et al., n.d.; Kumar & Jain, 2021; Misra et al., 2021). With the rapidly increasing consumption, industries also must keep up with the requirements (Kumar, Jain, Kumar Agarwal et al, 2021). In that race, fire safety is an enormously large issue. Because one unattended fire accident can cause severe damage to all the adjacent sectors (Agrawal et al., 2019; Ghai et al., 2020; Jain & Kumar, 2021; Kumar, Jain, Shukla et al, 2021; Sharma et al., 2019). Previously the fire was detected manually, then sand, water, and extinguishers were used to put off the fire. Later, in the beginning, days of automation technology smoke sensors were placed to find if there was any smoke that indirectly suggests the presence of fire. But a huge amount of time is required for the fire to burn any object and cause the smoke (Agarwal & Jain, 2019; Almahirah et al., 2021; Jain et al., 2017; Jain et al., 2018; Jain et al., 2015; Nayak et al., 2022). Here, the fire is being detected after a particular object is partial if not destroyed (Kumar, 2021).

Now the technology is developed to a greater extent to put off the fire in a very less amount of time by automating the sprinklers which are perfectly placed in such a way they cover the whole area (Kakti et al., 2021; Kumar & Baag, 2021a; Kumar & Baag, 2021b; Kumar et al., 2021a; Kumar et al., 2021b; Roland et al., 2021). Now different machine learning models are being developed using libraries like Open-CV to continuously capture the pictures of a location and continuously analyze the pixels of the picture and check if there is any fire detected and report it to the automated sprinklers or the fire controlling system installed. This takes a lot of time and more importantly computation power.

So, in this paper, we are proposing a model in such a way it does not take as much computation power as analyzing pixels and does not respond as slow as the model using the smoke sensor.

The design of the node is remarkably simple (as shown in Figure 1) just an ESP8266 is connected to a DHT11 sensor, and the power supply is given to the microcontroller as displayed in figure 2.

Here in this setup, we used the DHT11 sensor as the main component. This helps us to sense both the relative humidity and the temperature of its surroundings and transmits the data every two seconds in the programmed format. Unlike the earlier discussed model one we are not depending on only one physical quantity (in smoke sensor case), we are observing both humidity and the temperature. Even if either one reads an error the other parameter can be used to detect the fire. As we know fire causes an abrupt rise in temperature and relative humidity is inversely proportional to temperature.

Figure 1. Design of the node

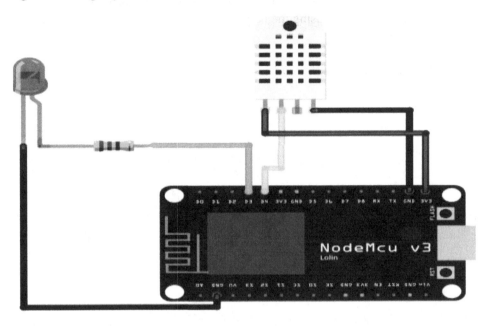

Firstly, the room is divided into four parts, and greater than four nodes and less than eight nodes are placed in the room by following the equidistant rule (maintaining a constant distance between every two nodes).

As mentioned in the block diagram (Figure 2) there are mainly three phases in the design and the working of the model. We can divide them into physical setup, connecting to the internet, and finally applying machine learning algorithms. Initially, in the zeroth phase, all we have is a bunch of microcontrollers and sensors. The complete flow chart describes the flow of work in Figure 3.

The first step of the design is to establish communication between the microcontroller and the sensor (i.e creating a node). Later depending on the dimensions of the room, the required number of nodes must be installed equidistantly. The next step is to connect the node to the local network by programming the esp8266 microcontroller by giving the network name (BSSID) and password.

After that, we can notice that the values of the relative humidity and the temperature can be logged or recorded on the serial monitor of the Arduino IDE, the same software which we used to program the ESP8266 board. Now we can record data of one-eighth part of the room (considering we made the space into eight parts). Next, we should repeat the same process for all the other nodes. They need not be connected to the same network. Now we can observe the data of each node but only at that node's serial monitor. Now to make the logged data accessible we must publish it on the internet. As the collected data is structured data it is best stored in table format. So, we are using the help of google sheets to complete this task.

Figure 2. Block diagram of the model

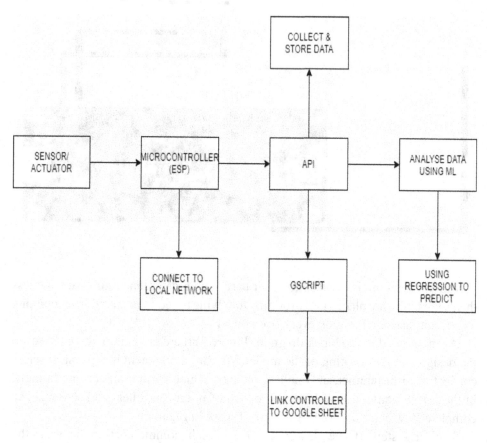

Now we browse the google sheets web page and create blank google Sheets. Every created sheet has a static sheet id and a dynamic sheet name. These should be stored for later usage to access the sheet. Now an API (Application Programming Interface) should be created as we are trying to automate the data logging into the google sheets by using JavaScript. Then we should establish the connection between the created API and the created blank google sheet by providing the previously saved sheet id and the sheet name. Finally, the API connected to google Sheets is published onto the internet (which can be done free of cost by using google sheets).

Now each node is to be reprogrammed to send the logged data to the API created thus redirected to the google sheet. This can be done by interconnecting them on the network layer by providing parameters like handshake, googlescriptid, HTTPs port. Now we have successfully established the connection between all the nodes to the internet. Now, depending on the user permissions which were allotted by us during the time of publishing the API the accessibility of the logged data varies. If left default the stored data can be observed by anyone across the internet. This is the end of the second phase.

Figure 3. Flow chart of the model

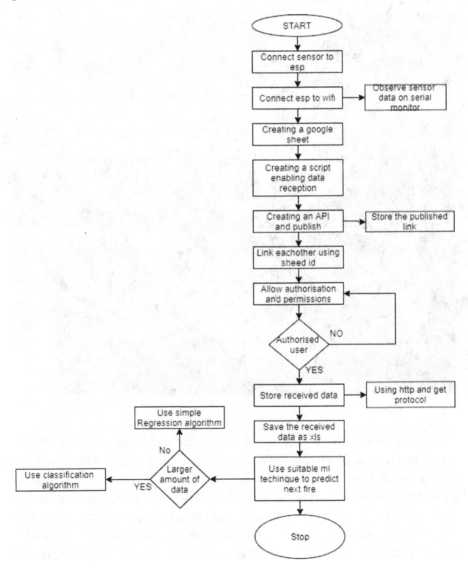

At this stage, we can observe the temperature and relative humidity at all nodes of the room at a single place and extract the data at two-second intervals. To perform a normal fire detection, we can just add a comparison algorithm where the recorded readings are greater than a threshold value, we can enable the fire alarm or stopping system (figure 4).

Figure 4. Hardware setup of the project

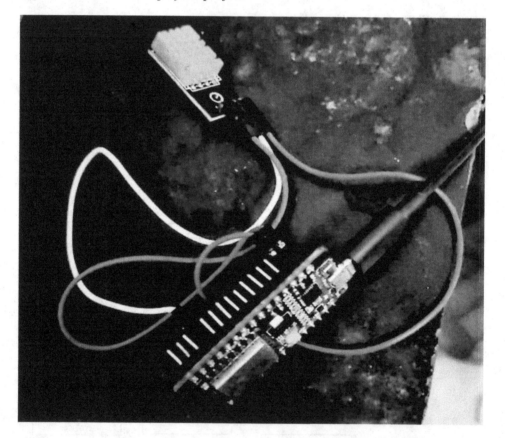

In the last phase of the design, we plot the data received and observe if there is any pattern involved like if any node is regularly detecting fire or if all nodes are detecting fire at a particular time in a day etc. Then depending on the amount of data we have and the situation we divided the machine learning models into two categories for this problem. If we have a large amount of data and many nodes, it's better to use classification algorithms like decision trees or support vector machines. But in this case, we only had a limited amount of data (less than 1000 entries) we decided to choose a regression algorithm (logistic or linear is fine). We applied linear regression and predicted the next fire's (i.e., next rise in temperature) time with higher accuracy.

RESULTS

First, we connect the Pin1 of the DHT11 to +3v of Node MCU. Now connect the Pin 2 of the DHT11 to Digital pin D4 of Node MCU at last Pin 3 of the DHT11 should be connected to the ground pin of Node MCU. With the help of a Micro USB Cable, You have to connect your Node MCU system.

After the demonstration of the hard ware model the serial monitor displays as shown in figure 5.

Figure 5. Display of serial monitor

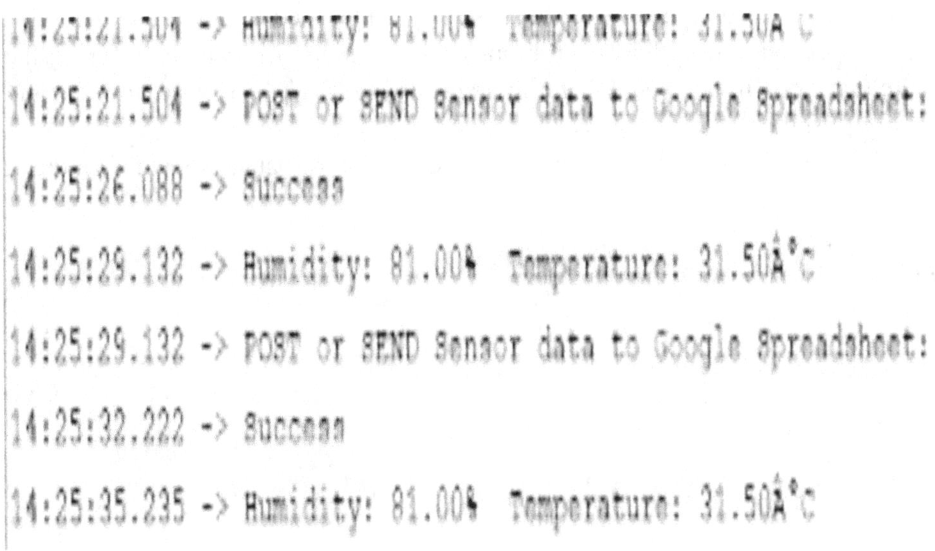

```
14:25:21.504 -> Humidity: 81.00%   Temperature: 31.50Â C

14:25:21.504 -> POST or SEND Sensor data to Google Spreadsheet:

14:25:26.088 -> Success

14:25:29.132 -> Humidity: 81.00%   Temperature: 31.50Â°c

14:25:29.132 -> POST or SEND Sensor data to Google Spreadsheet:

14:25:32.222 -> Success

14:25:35.235 -> Humidity: 81.00%   Temperature: 31.50Â°c
```

We can see that the serial monitor connected to Arduino IDE is displaying the respective temperature and humidity values at that particular node for every two seconds. In the same way, the data is shown at every node indicating the individual temperature and humidity values in their proximity. This is the first phase of implementation.

The values displayed by the serial monitor will be stored in a google sheet as shown in figure 6.

Figure 6. Google sheet data

We can see that the temperature and humidity data which is recorded by the sensor are now Stored in google sheets which can be used for data analytics. This type of data set is used for data training and validation. In Machine learning the more data you provide you will get more accurate the model is faster to learn and improve itself.

With the help of the data in google sheets, we plot the data as shown in figure 7.

Figure 7. Plotting temperature values

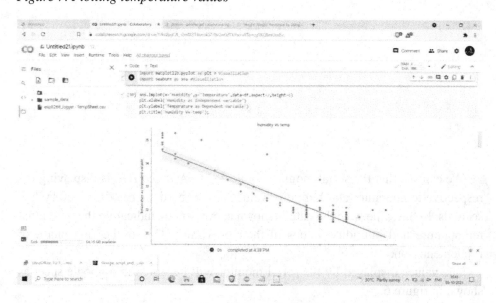

For visualization of data stored in google sheet here, we use the Mathplotlib library. The data is going to plot at a low level from higher values to lower values. Here the data is easily understood after this process. We can also use

Matplotlib APIs for the plotting purpose. To import this library first you install python and pip in our system. The accuracy of the plotted data will be obtained now. Different types of Machine learning algorithms are used for finding the Accuracy of data. Mostly the Linear Regression is used for getting the good accuracy of data. For clustering we use K means algorithm. Linear Regression is very easy to understand and it is used for statistics and the machine learning process. This algorithm will minimize the errors and give or predictive more Accuracy. Based on the accuracy levels it will detect the rise in temperature in future.

CONCLUDING REMARKS

Machine learning processes play a crucial part in constructing a self-reliant fire prediction system. Real-time circumstances require the model to have higher accuracy. This is an embedded way of hardware application and software. We also used different machine learning models and algorithms to predict the future time of the fire, using regression. For prototype applications, we use linear regression and for real-time applications, we may use k-means clustering or any other model for better accuracy. Using 3 to 4 modules through the internet we have created data sheets where we find fire detection values where scripting language is used for built API's.

REFERENCES

Agarwal, A. K., & Jain, A. (2019). Synthesis of 2D and 3D NoC mesh router architecture in HDL environment. *Journal of Advanced Research in Dynamical and Control Systems, 11*(4), 2573–2581.

Agrawal, N., Jain, A., & Agarwal, A. (2019). Simulation of Network on Chip for 3D Router Architecture. *International Journal of Recent Technology and Engineering, 8,* 58–62.

Almahirah, Jahan, Sharma, & Kumar. (2021). Role of Market Microstructure in Maintaining Economic Development. *Empirical Economics Letters, 20*(2).

Andrabi & Wahid. (2022). Machine Translation System Using Deep Learning for English to Urdu. *Computational Intelligence and Neuroscience.* Advance online publication. doi:10.1155/2022/7873012

Andrabi, S. A. B., & Wahid, A. (2019). Sentence Alignment for English Urdu Language Pair. *International Journal of Recent Technology and Engineering, 8.*

Andrabi, S. A. B., & Wahid, A. (2021). A Comprehensive Study of Machine Translation Tools and Evaluation Metrics. In V. Suma, J. I. Z. Chen, Z. Baig, & H. Wang (Eds.), *Inventive Systems and Control. Lecture Notes in Networks and Systems* (Vol. 204). Springer. doi:10.1007/978-981-16-1395-1_62

Ansari, K., Panda, S. K., & Corumluoglu, O. (2018). Mathematical modelling of ionospheric TEC from Turkish permanent GNSS Network (TPGN) observables during 2009–2017 and predictability of NeQuick and Kriging models. *Astrophysics and Space Science, 363*(3), 1–13. doi:10.100710509-018-3261-x

Ashok Kumar, L. (2022). *Design and Implementation of Automatic Water Spraying System for Solar Photovoltaic Module* (Vol. 2022). Mathematical Problems In Engineering.

Asvany, T., Amudhavel, J., & Sujatha, P. (2017). Lightning search algorithm for solving coverage problem in wireless sensor network. *Advances and Applications in Mathematical Sciences, 17*(1), 113–127.

Aziz, D. (2018). Webserver Based Smart Monitoring System Using ESP8266 Node MCU Module. *International Journal of Scientific and Engineering Research, 9*, 801.

Bajrami, X., & Murturi, I. (2018). An efficient approach to monitoring environmental conditions using a wireless sensor network and NodeMCU. *Elektrotech. Inftech., 135*(3), 294–301. doi:10.100700502-018-0612-9

Bandla, P. B., Vairavasundaram, I., Teekaraman, Y., & Nikolovski, S. (2022). Real Time Sustainable Power Quality Analysis of Non-Linear Load under Symmetrical Conditions. *Energies, 15*(01), 57. doi:10.3390/en15010057

Basit, S. A., & Kumar, M. (2015). A review of routing protocols for underwater wireless sensor networks. *International Journal of Advanced Research in Computer and Communication Engineering, 4*(12), 373–378.

Benzekri, W., El Moussati, A., Moussaoui, O., & Berrajaa, M. (2020). Early Forest Fire Detection System using Wireless Sensor Network and Deep Learning. *International Journal of Advanced Computer Science and Applications, 11*(5), 496. doi:10.14569/IJACSA.2020.0110564

Bharathidasan, Indragandhi, Kuppusamy, Teekaraman, Urooj, & Alwadi. (2022). Intelligent Fuzzy Based High Gain Non-Isolated Converter for DC Micro-Grids. *CMC-Computers, Materials & Continua, 71*(2).

Eswar. (n.d.). *Microcontroller Manipulated As Human Interface Device Performing Keystroke Injection Attack.* Academic Press.

Ghai, D., Gianey, H. K., Jain, A., & Uppal, R. S. (2020). Quantum and dual-tree complex wavelet transform-based image watermarking. *International Journal of Modern Physics B, 34*(04), 2050009. doi:10.1142/S0217979220500095

Gupta, N., Jain, A., Vaisla, K. S., Kumar, A., & Kumar, R. (2021). Performance analysis of DSDV and OLSR wireless sensor network routing protocols using FPGA hardware and machine learning. *Multimedia Tools and Applications, 80*(14), 22301–22319. doi:10.100711042-021-10820-4

Gupta, N., Vaisla, K. S., Jain, A., Kumar, A., & Kumar, R. (2021). Performance Analysis of AODV Routing for Wireless Sensor Network in FPGA Hardware. *Computer Systems Science and Engineering, 39*(2), 1–12.

Jain, A., Dwivedi, R., Kumar, A., & Sharma, S. (2017). Scalable design and synthesis of 3D mesh network on chip. In *Proceeding of International Conference on Intelligent Communication, Control and Devices* (pp. 661-666). Springer. 10.1007/978-981-10-1708-7_75

Jain, A., Dwivedi, R. K., Alshazly, H., Kumar, A., Bourouis, S., & Kaur, M. (n.d.). *Design and Simulation of Ring Network-on-Chip for Different Configured Nodes.* Academic Press.

Jain, A., Gahlot, A. K., Dwivedi, R., Kumar, A., & Sharma, S. K. (2018). Fat Tree NoC Design and Synthesis. In *Intelligent Communication, Control and Devices* (pp. 1749–1756). Springer. doi:10.1007/978-981-10-5903-2_180

Jain, A., & Kumar, A. (2021). Desmogging of still smoggy images using a novel channel prior. *Journal of Ambient Intelligence and Humanized Computing, 12*(1), 1161–1177. doi:10.100712652-020-02161-1

Jain, A., Kumar, A., & Sharma, S. (2015). Comparative Design and Analysis of Mesh, Torus and Ring NoC. *Procedia Computer Science, 48,* 330–337. doi:10.1016/j.procs.2015.04.190

Kadiravan, G. (2017). A state of art approaches on energy efficient routing protocols in mobile wireless sensor networks. *The IIOAB Journal, 8*(2), 234–238.

Kakti, A., Kumar, S., John, N. K., Ratna, V. V., Afzal, S., & Gupta, A. D. (2021). Impact of Patients Approach towards Healthcare Costs on their perception towards Health: An Empirical Study. Tobacco Regulatory Science, 7(6), 7380-7390.

Kamaleshwar, T., & Lakshminarayanan, R. (2021). A Self-Adaptive framework for Rectification and Detection of Blackhole and Wormhole attacks in 6LoWPAN. *Wireless Communications and Mobile Computing, 2021*, 1–8. doi:10.1155/2021/5143124

Kodali, R. K., & Mahesh, K. S. (2016). A low cost implementation of MQTT using ESP8266. *2016 2nd International Conference on Contemporary Computing and Informatics (IC3I)*, 404-408. 10.1109/IC3I.2016.7917998

Kshirsagar, P., Pote, A., Paliwal, K., Hendre, V., Chippalkatti, P., & Dhabekar, N. (2020). *A Review on IOT Based Health Care Monitoring System.* . doi:10.1007/978-981-13-8715-9_12

Kumar & Baag. (2021a). Ethics Erosion in Capital Market: Lehman Brothers' Case Study of Repo 105. *AIMS-18*.

Kumar & Baag. (2021b). Erosion of Ethics in Credit Derivatives: A Case Study. *AIMS-18*.

Kumar, Baag, & V. (2021a). Impact of ESG Integration on Equity Performance between Developed and Developing Economy: Evidence from S and P 500 and NIFTY 50. *Empirical Economics Letters, 20*(4).

Kumar, Baag, & V. (2021b). Financial Engineering and Quantitative Risk Analytics. *SYBGEN Learning, 1*(1).

Kumar, A., & Jain, A. (2021). Image smog restoration using oblique gradient profile prior and energy minimization. *Frontiers of Computer Science, 15*(6), 1–7. doi:10.100711704-020-9305-8 PMID:34221535

Kumar, S. (2021). Relevance of Buddhist Philosophy in Modern Management Theory. *Psychology and Education, 58*(3), 2104–2111.

Kumar, S., Jain, A., Kumar Agarwal, A., Rani, S., & Ghimire, A. (2021). Object-Based Image Retrieval Using the U-Net-Based Neural Network. *Computational Intelligence and Neuroscience, 2021*, 2021. doi:10.1155/2021/4395646 PMID:34804141

Kumar, S., Jain, A., Shukla, A. P., Singh, S., Raja, R., Rani, S., & Masud, M. (2021). A Comparative Analysis of Machine Learning Algorithms for Detection of Organic and Nonorganic Cotton Diseases. *Mathematical Problems in Engineering, 2021*, 2021. doi:10.1155/2021/1790171

Mallikarjuna Rao, Subramanyam, & Satya Prasad. (2018). Cluster-based mobility management algorithms for wireless mesh networks. *International Journal of Communication Systems, 31*(11).

Mannepalli, K., Sastry, P. N., & Suman, M. (2017). A novel Adaptive Fractional Deep Belief Networks for speaker emotion recognition. *Alexandria Engineering Journal, 56*(4), 485–497. doi:10.1016/j.aej.2016.09.002

Manoharan, H. (2022). Acclimatization Of Nano Robots. In *Medical Applications Using Artificial Intelligence System With Data Transfer Approach* (Vol. 2022). Wireless Communications And Mobile Computing.

Manoharan, H., Teekaraman, Y., Kuppusamy, R., & Radhakrishnan, A. (2021). A Novel Optimal Robotized Parking System Using Advanced Wireless Sensor Network. *Journal of Sensors, 2021*, 1–8. doi:10.1155/2021/2889504

Misra, N. R., Kumar, S., & Jain, A. (2021, February). A Review on E-waste: Fostering the Need for Green Electronics. In *2021 International Conference on Computing, Communication, and Intelligent Systems (ICCCIS)* (pp. 1032-1036). IEEE. 10.1109/ICCCIS51004.2021.9397191

Nayak, Kumar, Gupta, Suri, Naved, & Soni. (2022). Network mining techniques to analyze the risk of the occupational accident via bayesian network. *International Journal of System Assurance Engineering and Management.*

Peter, G. (2022a). *Histogram Shifting based Quick Response Steganography method for Secure Communication* (Vol. 2022). Wireless Communications and Mobile Computing.

Peter, G. (2022b). *Design of Automated Deep Learning-based Fusion Model for Copy-Move Image Forgery Detection* (Vol. 2022). Computational Intelligence and Neuroscience.

Putra, M., & Nazaruddin, Y. (2019). *Development of Virtual Firefighting Robots Using Breitenberg and Fuzzy Logic Methods*. Academic Press.

Rajakumar, R. (2017). GWO-LPWSN: Grey wolf optimization algorithm for node localization problem in wireless sensor networks. *Journal of Computer Networks and Communications.*

Rajeswari, M., Amudhavel, J., & Dhavachelvan, P. (2017). Vortex search algorithm for solving set covering problem in wireless sensor network. *Adv. Appl. Math. Sci, 17*, 95–111.

Rao & Manikonda. (2019). CSRR-loaded T-shaped MIMO antenna for 5G cellular networks and vehicular communications. *International Journal of RF and Microwave Computer-Aided Engineering, 29*(8).

Roland, G., Kumaraperumal, S., Kumar, S., Gupta, A. D., Afzal, S., & Suryakumar, M. (2021). PCA (Principal Component Analysis) Approach towards Identifying the Factors Determining the Medication Behavior of Indian Patients: An Empirical Study. Tobacco Regulatory Science, 7(6), 7391-7401.

Sharma, S. K., Jain, A., Gupta, K., Prasad, D., & Singh, V. (2019). An internal schematic view and simulation of major diagonal mesh network-on-chip. *Journal of Computational and Theoretical Nanoscience, 16*(10), 4412–4417. doi:10.1166/jctn.2019.8534

Shi, X., & Songlin, L. (2020). Design and Implementation of a Smart Wireless Fire-Fighting System Based on NB-IoT Technology. *Journal of Physics: Conference Series, 1606*(1), 012015. doi:10.1088/1742-6596/1606/1/012015

Shinde & Patil. (2021). *A Review of IoT based Health Monitoring and Future Health Prediction System*. Academic Press.

Sripada, N. K., & Mohammed Ismail, B. (2019). Challenges In Generative Modeling And Functioning Nature Of Generative Adversarial Networks. *Journal Of Mechanics Of Continua And Mathematical Sciences, 14*, 83.

Syed, A. B. A., & Kumar, M. (2020). Energy Efficient Routing Technique for Underwater Wireless Sensor Networks. *International Journal of Advanced Science and Technology, 29*(11s), 859–868.

Teekaraman, Kumar, Kuppusamy, & Thelkar. (2022). SSNN Based Energy Management Strategy in Grid-Connected System for Load Scheduling and Load Sharing. Mathematical Problems in Engineering.

Uthayakumar, J., Vengattaraman, T., & Amudhavel, J. (2017). A simple lossless compression algorithm in wireless sensor networks: An application of seismic data. *The IIOAB Journal, 8*(2), 274–280.

Veena, K., & Meena, K. (2022). *Cybercrime Detection using C SVM and KNN Techniques* (Vol. 2022). Wireless Communications and Mobile Computing.

Chapter 13
An Experiment to Find Disease Detection for Rice Plants Using ResNet

Sekar R.
Koneru Lakshimaiah Education Foundation, India

Satya Deepika Bandi
Koneru Lakshmaiah Education Foundation, India

Hema Likhitha Godavarthi
Koneru Lakshmaiah Education Foundation, India

Sri Vandhana Dadi
Koneru Lakshmaiah Education Foundation, India

K. Praghash
Koneru Lakshmaiah Education Foundation, India

ABSTRACT

In India, around 70% of the populace depends on agribusiness. The identification of plant infections is significant to forestall misfortunes inside the yield. It's problematic to notice plant illnesses physically. It needs a colossal amount of work, skill inside the plant infections, and conjointly needs an unreasonable time stretch. Subsequently, picture handling models can be utilized for the location of plant illnesses. In this venture, the authors have depicted the procedure for the discovery of imperfections of plant illnesses with the assistance of their leaves pictures. Here they are utilizing the rice plant for recognizing the deformities. Picture handling is a part of sign handling, which can separate the picture properties or valuable data from the picture. The shade of leaves, measure of harm to leaves, space of the leaf, surface boundaries are utilized for arrangement. In this task, the authors have examined diverse picture boundaries or highlights to recognize distinctive plant passes on infections to accomplish the best accuracy.

DOI: 10.4018/978-1-7998-9426-1.ch013

INTRODUCTION

Since forever ago, humanity has been subject to our forefathers' use to work in the fields to make a living. extended lengths tracking down food, the same old thing in that the principal human race started after the disclosure of horticulture (Kumar, Arora, & Harsh, 2020). Yields are a fundamental piece of humans. People will find it impossible to live absent crops. The horticulture production is ruined by harvest sickness. It poses a significant threat to the food supply (Gavhale & Gawande, 2014). As a result, recognizing, managing harvest illnesses is critical to guaranteeing a good return, good performance, and more utility of appealing crops. Customary procedures in analysis for sicknesses request a lot of field contribution and capability. Plant pathologies can be distinguished utilizing different schedules (Guo et al., 2020; Kumar, Chaudhary, & Chandra, 2020; Sabrol & Satish, 2016; Singh & Misra, 2016; Zeiler & Fergus, 2014). Few illnesses don't show any distinguishable manifestations, or they take too long to even consider displaying any recognizable side effects, and henceforth in these conditions, a high-level assessment is required (Jiang et al., n.d.). Notwithstanding, practically all sicknesses show a type of appearance in the apparent stretch of range, along these lines' investigation through eyes by experienced experts, is the normal methodology embraced progressively (Durmus et al., 2017; Fouda et al., 2013; Hasaballah, 2015; Hassan et al., 2013). However, giving a definite report of yield illness necessitates that pathologists should be outfitted with a better perception range of abilities altogether than analyze trademark characteristics varieties shown by unhealthy yield plants. It is frequently troublesome since awkward ranchers When compared to a skilled scientist, horticulturists have difficulty detecting it and frequently make incorrect decisions (Singh & Saini, 2018a; Singh & Saini, 2019; Singh & Saini, 2021a; Singh & Saini, 2021b; Singh & Saini, 2021c). Yet, these days, because of headways in the web and advanced innovations, ranchers can use crop pictures scientists will assist in assessing harvests. illnesses from a distance. However, for this situation, the assessment is inclined to less proficiency and wrong decisions (Hasaballah, 2018; Sajja, Rane, Phasinam et al, 2021; Singh & Saini, 2018b; Singh & Saini, 2018c).

In addition, research shows that environmental varieties can meddle in stages and paces of microbe development and this moreover changes have, which could prepare for physiological changes (Pallathadka et al., 2021). The way that these days, illnesses are passed on overall all the more effectively further confounds the circumstance (Arcinas et al., 2021; Hasaballah, 2021; Kubiczek & Hadasik, 2021; Sajja, Mustafa, Ponnusamy et al, 2021). Well planned and definite conclusion of harvest illnesses, the establishment of precision agronomics, which includes early shield measures. Robotized systems of illness ID possibly deal with these problems and the modern investigation (Panjwani et al., 2019). New advancements in PC vision made computerized pictures helpful innovation to distinguish, group illnesses. It notices side effects will end up being of incredible help, not exclusively to non-proficient horticulturists yet in addition to experienced experts as a technique for affirmation of illness distinguished and ordered (Manta, Nagraik, Sharma et al, 2020; Mohan et al., 2019; Panjwani, Singh, Rani, & Mohan, 2021; Panjwani, Singh, Rani, & Mohan, 2021). Various forward leaps in picture grouping space have been raised by profound convolutional neural organizations. The organization profundity has its significance and practically all famous picture grouping strategies use profoundly models that are significant. In this article, execution of ResNet. (ResNet50) for leaf sicknesses distinguishing proof, an arrangement is talked about (Chhabra et al., 2016; Manta, Chandra Singh, Deep et al, 2021; Mohan et al., 2018; Mohan et al., 2017). The instinct of utilizing ResNet is inspired by massive accomplishment in the circle of PC vision, for instance, picture order and well-known assignment of article location as shown by later examine (Chhabra et al., 2020). Giving elective associations with the customary associations and producing leftover associations is the primary inspiration of working with Res-Net (Chhabra et al., 2019; Manta, Chauhan, Gandhi et al, 2021; Rawat et al., 2020). The application of Res-Net to the issue viable isn't new as has been investigated in some past examinations (Govindaraj et al., 2013). To see if ResNet may get improved plant disease classifying outcomes, ResNet50. For the tests, ResNet50 is effectively applied to the dataset containing 240 pictures. Resnet accomplishes best plant infection arrangement results, Res-Net, For the trials, ResNet50 is effectively applied to the dataset containing 240 pictures.

BLOCK DIAGRAM

Firstly (figure 1), we have to take the sample rice leaf image of a diseased leaf and we did the image transformation we need to augment the image of the rice plant which we are taking and we need to do the normalization process, the normalization is about the process of reducing the redundancy. And here we are taking the residual network to do the process and next need to create a model of RESNET (Rathinam et al., 2016). The data should be trained and then tested. so now we need to train the model on the given dataset which consists of 3 defects that are blast, blight, tungro by the trained classifier need to interpret the model to observe the features of the rice leaf and next unfreeze the model to the initial stage so that we can know the error rate and find the optimal learning rate (Manta, 2020). In the above block diagram, the decision making symbol is present it represents models with a minimum loss if the model is not min loss then it will go back to the before step it is finding the optimal learning rate, and if yes then the data will be trained and next test the rice plant images. so that it will display the accuracy of the disease of the rice plant (Rathinam et al., 2015).

Figure 1. Block diagram

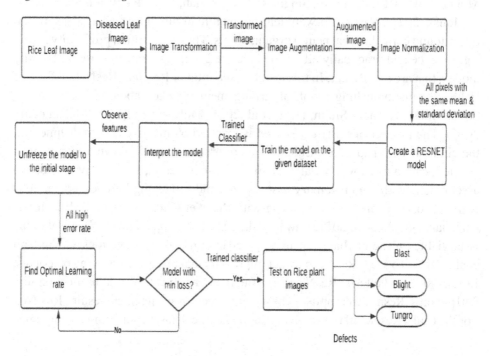

INTERACTION OF PLANT DISEASE DETECTION

It includes the following steps (figure 2 and 3):

A)   Data Acquisition
B)   Data Pre-processing
C)   Feature Extraction
D)   Detection

Figure 2. Flowchart

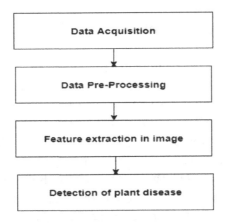

Figure 3. Dataset images

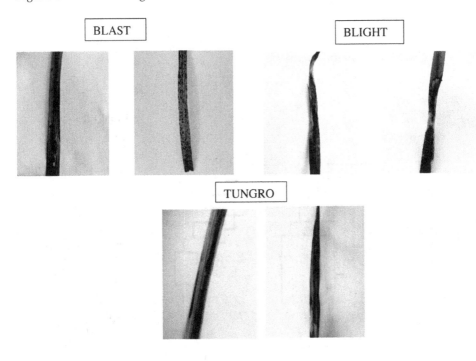

ALGORITHMS

Convolution Neural Network

The discovery of a class of calculations that fits within the circle of profound learning was driven by inspiration from how the human cerebrum functions. It entails ANN preparation to set expectations. An ANN is a multi-facet structure of neurons (Jayanthi et al., 2018; Manta, Wahi, Bharadwaj et al, 2021). As information, the yield of one layer passes to the next layer. Because profound learning models naturally separate elements during preparation, no extra methodology is needed for the component extraction step of the fundamental interaction previously noted. Low-level highlights (like edges) become acquainted with the underlying layers of ANN, and higher-level highlights (like total articles) become more profound (Rathinam & Pattabhi, 2019). CNN is a sort of ANN that is unique has been modified to handle images. CNN's ability to provide excellent accuracy in picture handling tasks has been proven in studies (figure 4) (Manta, Kapoor, Kour et al, 2020).

Figure 4. Convolution neural network

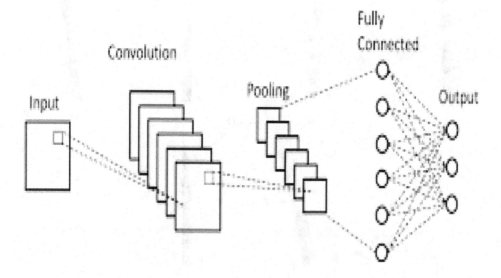

Convolutional Layer

CNN was supplied to the convolutional layer. A sequence of convolutional procedures is used to minimize the resolution of the image (Brindha et al., 2021; Rathinam &

Govindaraj, 2021; Umadevi et al., 2021). The channel/bit is initially inserted in the image's top-left corner, thereafter dragged along the image's width by a step amount towards the center. The channel jumps to a comparable stride value after reaching the whole width and repeats the operation from the left to reach the complete width. That conversation continues until the entire picture has been crossed. The quantity of results of related values in the covered part of the picture and channel is assessed in a single phase. This results in the creation of a unique framework (or volume) from the existing information framework (or volume) (figure 5).

Figure 5. Convolutional layer

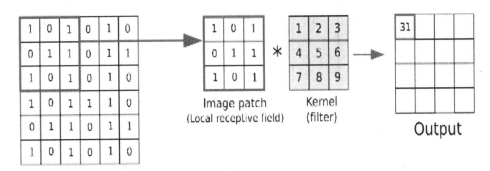

Pooling Layer

This layer's functions include decreasing the image and erasing the most visible elements. A channel works in the same way as a convolutional layer in terms of position and motion. A capacity is applied in a single advance in this layer. This capacity can be either a maximum capacity (called Max- pooling) that records the limit of all qualities in the covered portion of the information picture and the channel or a typical capacity (called avg-pooling). For the most part, the channel size and step used is 2. The avg-pooling method is preferred over the max-pooling scheme (figure 6).

Fully Connected Layer

A network is the result of the development of convolutional and pooling layers (or volume). This is smoothed, and then a grouping of entirely related layers, such as ANN, is used. In a layer, a solitary neuron receives results from the past layer's neurons. FC Layers are only employed after a set of convolutional and pooling layers have reduced the size of the image to the level that the related layers do not have a large number of boundaries to learn.

Figure 6. Pooling Layer

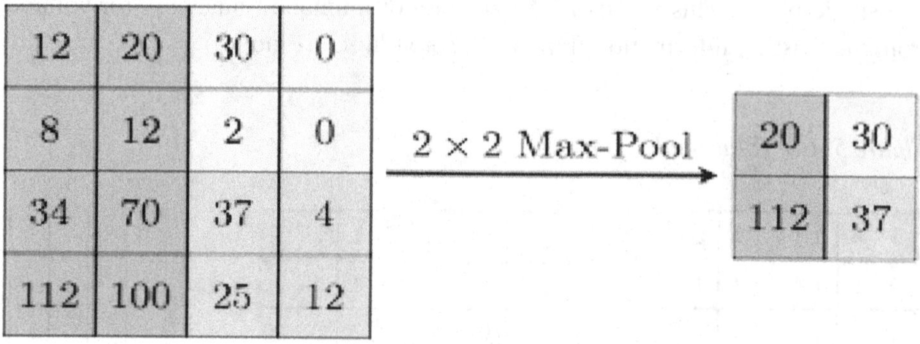

Activation Layer

Every component of the input matrix receives an initiating work (or volume). As a result, the information and yield components for this layer are similar. Direct initiation abilities can only aid in the approximate approximation of straight theory abilities. Because complicated challenges frequently involve a non-straight relationship between input and outcome, nonlinear enactment capacity is frequently used. The majority of the time, ReLU work is used since it speeds up learning.

PROPOSED MODEL

Residual Neural Network (RES-NET)

Past investigations unveiled the greatest amount of significance of network profundity. Hypothetically, the exactness should increment by stacking an ever-increasing number of layers in a neural organization. Truly, it ends up being a misguided judgment. By expanding the profundity of the organization, the exactness will in general get immersed and afterwards corrupts rapidly. This is known as the corruption issue. Shockingly, overfitting isn't the reason. The peculiarity of disappearing/detonating inclinations in profound neural networks prompts this infamous corruption issue. In the disappearing inclination issue, the slopes become vastly little because of rehashed augmentation during the backpropagation step, bringing about unimportant updates to the boundaries. Detonating inclinations is an issue wherein slopes collect and lead to extremely enormous updates to the boundaries during preparing, forestalling the model to gain from the information. It is related to the use of standardized statements, middle-of-the-road standardization layers prior to the disclosure of remaining organizations (figure 7).

Figure 7. Residual neural network (RES-NET)

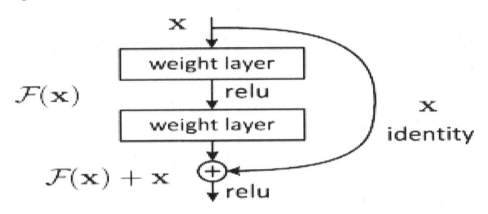

A leftover square utilizes skip associations to address the debasement issue. Associations that avoid at least one layer are Shortcut associations (otherwise called skip associations). In the preparation cycle, the remaining alternate way ensures the organization's uprightness if the normal association's coefficient combines with nothing. The elective associations work on the organization by giving the choice of picking these easy routes when a route is required. Speculation work H(x) = F(x) + x, the leftover capacity F(x) is learned by the layers. This is expected to be the way lingering capacity is enhanced without any problem. To demonstrate that a more profound organization doesn't have higher preparing mistakes low partner, the creators utilized profound connection that produced using the low organization connecting remaining square toward the end and afterwards showed that the leftover square goes about as a personality planning. ResNet50 design produced using 50 helix CNN organization simply presenting delay associations. ResNet50 is a model that is pre-prepared on ImageNet Database. A prepared system aids in getting more exactnesses simply utilizing the limited quantity of information so it reduces time. In our area of work, a pre-trained ResNet50 system for leaf illness discovery. The debasement issue tended to utilize few appropriate procedures. ResNet50 utilizes skip associations to settle this issue. The strength of ResNet50 to tackle the debasement the issue to provide more exactnesses, the benefits. The pre-prepared model is the inspiration utilizing the arrangement strategy in the work we did (figure 8).

Figure 8. ResNet50 utilizes skip associations

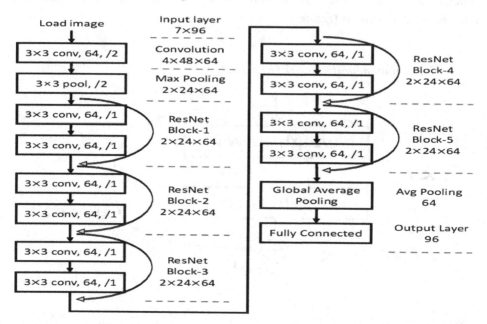

Confusion Matrix

The disarray grid is a method for summing up the exhibition of an order calculation. Order precision alone can be deluded if you have an inconsistent number of perceptions in each class or then again if you have multiple classes in your dataset. Working out a disarray grid can provide you with a superior thought of what your characterization model is getting right and what sorts of blunders it is making (figure 9).

EXPERIMENTAL RESULTS AND DISCUSSION

Dataset

Using photos from the 'Rice leaf Diseases' database, the suggested ResNet50 is trained and tested, containing a total of 240 images labeled with 3 distinct defects

Figure 9. Confusion Matrix

Training

Using the train group photos, the system is initially trained. After that, the trained model is used to conduct classification on the test set photos.

Performance Evaluation

Accuracy: The degree of similarity between measurement and its true value is known as accuracy.

Accuracy = Number of correct predictions

Total number of predictions

Precision: Precision is the amount of information sent by a number in terms of its digits; it shows how close two or more measurements can be to each other. It is untouched to precision.

Prediction = TruePositive

TruePositive + FalsePositive

Classification Report

It's one of the metrics used to assess the performance of a classification-based machine learning model. It shows precision, recall, F1 score, and support of your model. It provides a better understanding of the overall performance of our trained model (figures 10,11 and12).

Figure 10. Classification report

```
print(classification_report(test_test,test_pred))

                precision      recall  f1-score    supↄ

            0        0.91        1.00      0.95
            1        1.00        0.90      0.95
            2        0.90        0.90      0.90

    accuracy                              0.93
   macro avg         0.94        0.93      0.93
weighted avg         0.94        0.93      0.93
```

Figure 11. Loss versus validation loss plot

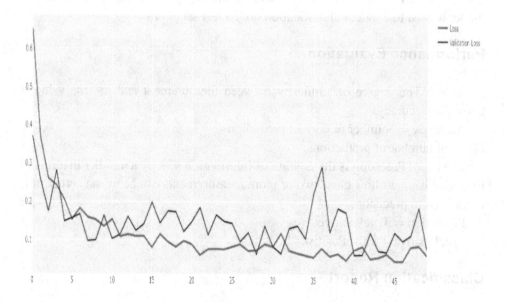

Figure 12. Accuracy versus validation accuracy plot

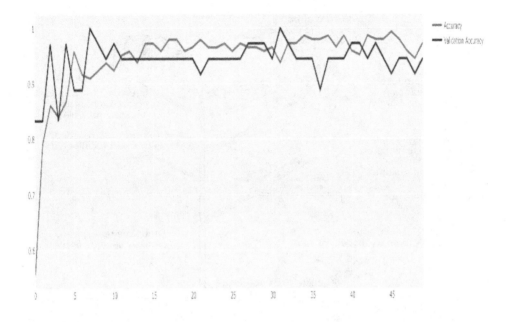

DISEASES OF RICE PLANT BLAST DISEASE

The parasite assaults the yield at all phases of harvest development. Side effects show up on leaves, hubs, rachis, and glumes. On the leaves, the sores show up as little pale blue- green bits, which amplify under soggy climate to frame the trademark shaft molded spots with dim focus and dull earthy colored edge (Leaf impact). The spots blend as the sickness advances and huge spaces of the leaves evaporate and shrink. Spots additionally show up on sheath. Seriously tainted nursery and field show up as consumed. Dark injuries show up on hubs supporting them. The impacted hubs might separate and all the plant parts over the contaminated hubs might kick the bucket (nodal impact). During blossom development, the parasite assaults the peduncle and the injury goes to tarnish dark which is alluded to as bad neck/neck decay/panicle impact (neck impact). In early neck disease, grain filling doesn't happen while in late contamination, incomplete grain filling happens. Little brown to dark spots may likewise be seen on glumes of the vigorously contaminated panicles. The microorganism causes yield misfortunes going from 30-61 percent relying on the phases of contamination (figure 13).

Figure 13. Diseases of rice plant blast disease

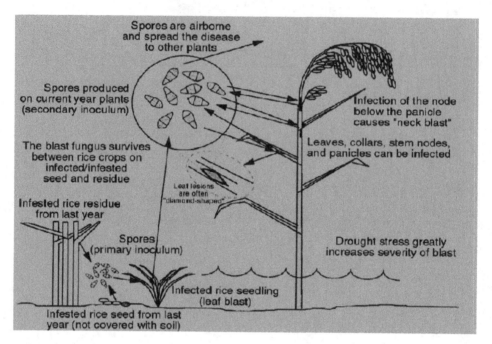

Blight Disease

The organism influences the yield from tillering to the leading stage. Beginning indications are taken note of leaf sheaths close to water level. On the leaf sheath, oval or circular or unpredictable greenish dim spots are framed. As the spots augment, the middle becomes grayish-white with a sporadic blackish brown or purple earthy colored boundary. Sores on the upper pieces of plants broaden quickly coalescing with one another to cover whole turners from the water line to the banner leaf. The presence of a few huge injuries on a leaf sheath for the most part causes the passing of the entire leaf, and in serious cases, every one of the leaves of a plant might be scourged. The contamination reaches out to the inward sheaths bringing about the death of the whole plant. More established plants are profoundly powerless. Plants intensely contaminated in the early heading and grain filling development stages produce inadequately filled grain, particularly in the lower part of the panicle (figure 14).

Figure 14. Blight disease

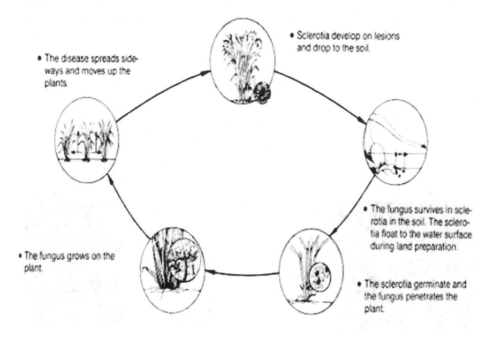

Tungro Disease

Both the nursery and the main field are infected. The plants are severely stunted. Yellow to orange discolouration and interveinal chlorosis can be seen on the leaves. Young leaves may be speckled, while elder leaves may have rusty patches. With a deficient root system, tillering is decreased. Panicles that do not form in the early stages of infection, if they do form, are tiny and contain few, malformed, and chaffy grains (figure 15).

CONCLUSION

The model is prepared to utilize the pictures from 'Rice Plant Diseases Dataset', which contains pictures having a place with 3 various classes. Average weighted accuracy of 94% and a precision of 94% were accomplished by our model. These two execution measurements for the Res-Net model. The undertaking is about rice plant illness recognition so we utilized some order strategies and a calculation for Res-Net strategy that can be utilized for programmed discovery just as characterization of plant leaf infections later. Here we are utilizing rice plant abandons by utilizing a portion of the calculations. Consequently, related imperfections for these plants were taken for ID. It demonstrates the usefulness of the suggested calculation in recognizing and identifying leaf diseases, as well as providing the highest level of precision.

Figure 15. Tungro disease

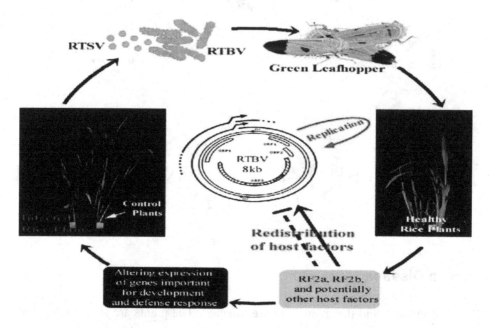

Future Work

In the future, modeling techniques can be developed with a huge sample of illnesses and yields. Data can be expanded by contributing an ever-increasing number of pictures as information focuses so that the organization can recognize and characterize a more extensive scope of sicknesses and plant species. By expanding the utilization of cameras also, improve their quality, it turns out to be to an ever-increasing extent logical that exact judgments utilizing cell phones are just a matter of time. Additionally, models can be prepared with information, for example, scene perspective ashore regions, ethereal photographs, and pictures of various phases of various sicknesses. Besides, the impact of picture pivot on the organization could be investigated.

REFERENCES

Arcinas, M., Sajja, G., Asif, S., Gour, S., Okoronkwo, E., & Naved, M. (2021). Role Of Data Mining In Education For Improving Students Performance For Social Change. *Türk Fizyoterapi ve Rehabilitasyon Dergisi/Turkish Journal of Physiotherapy and Rehabilitation, 32*, 6519.

Brindha, T. R., Rathinam, R., & Dheenadhayalan, S. (2021). Antibacterial, Antifungal and Anticorrosion Properties of Green Tea Polyphenols Extracted Using Different Solvents. *Asian Journal of Biological and Life Sciences, 10*(1), 62–66. doi:10.5530/ajbls.2021.10.10

Chhabra, H., Mohan, V., Rani, A., & Singh, V. (2016). *Multi objective PSO tuned fractional order PID control of robotic manipulator. In The international symposium on intelligent systems technologies and applications.* Springer.

Chhabra, H., Mohan, V., Rani, A., & Singh, V. (2019). Trajectory tracking of Maryland manipulator using linguistic Lyapunov fuzzy controller. *Journal of Intelligent & Fuzzy Systems, 36*(3), 2195–2205. doi:10.3233/JIFS-169931

Chhabra, H., Mohan, V., Rani, A., & Singh, V. (2020). Robust nonlinear fractional order fuzzy PD plus fuzzy I controller applied to robotic manipulator. Neural Computing and Applications, 32(7), 2055-2079. doi:10.100700521-019-04074-3

Durmus, Gunes, & Kırcı. (2017). Disease detection on the leaves of the tomato plants by using deep learning. *Agro-Geoinformatics, IEEE 6th International Conference on*, 1-5.

Fouda, M. A., Hassan, M. I., Hammad, K. M., & Hasaballah, A. I. (2013). Effects of midgut bacteria and two protease inhibitors on the reproductive potential and midgut enzymes of Culex pipiens infected with Wuchereria bancrofti. *Journal of the Egyptian Society of Parasitology, 43*(2), 537–546. doi:10.21608/jesp.2013.94836 PMID:24260832

Gavhale, K. R., & Gawande, U. (2014). An Overview of the Research on Plant Leaves Disease detection using Image Processing Techniques. *IOSR Journal of Computer Engineering, 16*(1), 10–16. doi:10.9790/0661-16151016

Govindaraj, M., Rathinam, R., Sukumar, C., Uthayasankar, M., & Pattabhi, S. (2013). Electrochemical oxidation of bisphenol-A from aqueous solution using graphite electrodes. *Environmental Technology, 34*(4), 503–511. doi:10.1080/09593330.2012.701333 PMID:23530365

Guo, Zhang, Yin, Hu, Zou, Xue, & Wang. (2020). *Plant Disease Identification Based on Deep Learning Algorithm.* Academic Press.

Hasaballah, A. I. (2015). Toxicity of some plant extracts against vector of lymphatic filariasis, Culex pipiens. *Journal of the Egyptian Society of Parasitology, 45*(1), 183–192. PMID:26012233

Hasaballah, A. I. (2018). Impact of gamma irradiation on the development and reproduction of Culex pipiens (Diptera; Culicidae). *International Journal of Radiation Biology, 94*(9), 844–849. doi:10.1080/09553002.2018.1490040 PMID:29913104

Hasaballah, A. I. (2021). Impact of paternal transmission of gamma radiation on reproduction, oogenesis, and spermatogenesis of the housefly, Musca domestica L. (Diptera: Muscidae). *International Journal of Radiation Biology, 97*(3), 376–385. doi:10.1080/09553002.2021.1864046 PMID:33320767

Hassan, M. I., Fouda, M. A., Hammad, K. M., & Hasaballah, A. I. (2013). Effects of midgut bacteria and two protease inhibitors on the transmission of Wuchereria bancrofti by the mosquito vector, Culex pipiens. *Journal of the Egyptian Society of Parasitology, 43*(2), 547–553. PMID:24260833

Jayanthi, K., Rathinam, R., & Pattabhi, S. (2018). Electrocoagulation treatment for removal of Reactive Blue 19 from aqueous solution using Iron electrode. *Research Journal of Life Sciences, Bioinformatics, Pharmaceutical and Chemical Sciences, 4*(2), 101–113.

Jiang, Xue, & Guo. (n.d.). *Research on Plant Leaf Disease Identification Based on Transfer Learning Algorithm.* doi:10.1088/1742-6596/1576/1/012023

Kubiczek, J., & Hadasik, B. (2021, December). Challenges in Reporting the COVID-19 Spread and its Presentation to the Society. *J. Data and Information Quality, 13*(4), 1–7. doi:10.1145/3470851

Kumar, Arora, & Harsh. (2020). *Res-Net-based approach for Detection and Classification of Plant Leaf Diseases.* IEEE Xplore Part Number: CFP20V66-ART.

Kumar, Chaudhary, & Chandra. (2020). *Plant Disease Detection Using CNN.* Academic Press.

Manta, Chandra Singh, Deep, & Kapoor. (2021). Temperature-regulated gold nanoparticle sensors for immune chromatographic rapid test kits with reproducible sensitivity: a study. *IET Nanobiotechnol.* doi:10.1049/nbt2.12024

Manta, P. (2020). Analytical approach for the optimization of desiccant weight in rapid test kit packaging: Accelerated predictive stability (APS). *Systematic Reviews in Pharmacy, 11*(8), 102–113. doi:10.31838rp.2020.8.15

Manta, P., Chauhan, R., Gandhi, H., Mahant, S., & Kapoor, D. N. (2021). Formulation rationale for the development of SARS-COV-2 immunochromatography rapid test kits in India. *Journal of Applied Pharmaceutical Science*. Advance online publication. doi:10.7324/JAPS.2021.1101017

Manta, P., Kapoor, D. N., Kour, G., Kour, M., & Sharma, A. K. (2020). critical quality attributes of rapid test kits - a practical overview. *Journal of Critical Reviews, 7*(19), 377–384. doi:10.31838/jcr.07.19.48

Manta, P., Nagraik, R., Sharma, A., Kumar, A., Verma, P., Paswan, S. K., Bokov, D. O., Shaikh, J. D., Kaur, R., Leite, A. F. V., Filho, S. J. B., Shiwalkar, N., Persaud, P., & Kapoor, D. N. (2020). Optical density optimization of malaria pan rapid diagnostic test strips for improved test zone band intensity. *Diagnostics (Basel), 10*(11), 880. doi:10.3390/diagnostics10110880 PMID:33137871

Manta, P., Wahi, N., Bharadwaj, A., Kour, G., & Kapoor, D. N. (2021). A statistical quality control (SQC) methodology for gold nanoparticles based immune-chromatographic rapid test kits validation. *Nanoscience & Nanotechnology-Asia, 11*(6), 1–5. doi:10.2174/2210681210666210108111055

Mohan, V., Chhabra, H., Rani, A., & Singh, V. (2018). Robust self-tuning fractional order PID controller dedicated to non-linear dynamic system. *Journal of Intelligent & Fuzzy Systems, 34*(3), 1467–1478. doi:10.3233/JIFS-169442

Mohan, V., Chhabra, H., Rani, A., & Singh, V. (2019). An expert 2DOF fractional order fuzzy PID controller for nonlinear systems. *Neural Computing & Applications, 31*(8), 4253–4270. doi:10.100700521-017-3330-z

Mohan, V., Rani, A., & Singh, V. (2017). Robust adaptive fuzzy controller applied to double inverted pendulum. *Journal of Intelligent & Fuzzy Systems, 32*(5), 3669–3687. doi:10.3233/JIFS-169301

Pallathadka, H., Mustafa, M., Sanchez, D. T., Sekhar Sajja, G., Gour, S., & Naved, M. (2021). Impact of machine learning on management, healthcare and agriculture. *Materials Today: Proceedings*. Advance online publication. doi:10.1016/j.matpr.2021.07.042

Panjwani, Singh, Rani, & Mohan. (2021). Optimum multi-drug regime for compartment model of tumour: cell-cycle-specific dynamics in the presence of resistance. *Journal of Pharmacokinetics and Pharmacodynamics, 48*(4), 543-562.

Panjwani, B., Mohan, V., Rani, A., & Singh, V. (2019). Optimal drug scheduling for cancer chemotherapy using two degree of freedom fractional order PID scheme. *Journal of Intelligent & Fuzzy Systems, 36*(3), 2273–2284. doi:10.3233/JIFS-169938

Panjwani, B., Singh, V., Rani, A., & Mohan, V. (2021). Optimizing Drug Schedule for Cell-Cycle Specific Cancer Chemotherapy. Singapore. doi:10.1007/978-981-16-1696-9_7

Rathinam, R., & Govindaraj, M. (2021). Photo electro catalytic Oxidation of Textile Industry Wastewater by RuO2/IrO2/TaO2 Coated Titanium Electrodes. *Nature Environment and Pollution Technology, 20*(3), 1069–1076. doi:10.46488/NEPT.2021.v20i03.014

Rathinam, R., Govindaraj, M., Vijayakumar, K., & Pattabhi, S. (2015). Removal of Colour from Aqueous Rhodamine B Dye Solution by Photo electrocoagulation Treatment Techniques. *Journal of Engineering, Scientific Research and Application, 1*(2), 80-89. http://www.dsecjesra.com/

Rathinam, R., Govindaraj, M., Vijayakumar, K., & Pattabhi, S. (2016). Decolourization of Rhodamine B from aqueous by electrochemical oxidation using graphite electrodes. *Desalination and Water Treatment, 57*(36), 16995–17001.

Rathinam, R., & Pattabhi, S. (2019). Removal of Rhodamine B Dye from Aqueous Solution by Advanced Oxidation Process using ZnO Nanoparticles. *Indian Journal of Ecology, 46*(1), 167–174. http://indianecologicalsociety.com/

Rawat, A., Jha, S., Kumar, B., & Mohan, V. (2020). Nonlinear fractional order PID controller for tracking maximum power in photo-voltaic system. *Journal of Intelligent & Fuzzy Systems, 38*(5), 6703–6713. doi:10.3233/JIFS-179748

Sabrol, H., & Satish, K. (2016). Tomato plant disease classification in digital images using classification tree. *2016 International Conference on Communication and Signal Processing (ICCSP)*, 1242-1246. 10.1109/ICCSP.2016.7754351

Sajja, Mustafa, Ponnusamy, Abdufattokhov, Murugesan, & Prabhu. (2021). Machine Learning Algorithms in Intrusion Detection and Classification. *Annals of the Romanian Society for Cell Biology, 25*(6), 12211–12219.

Sajja, G. S., Rane, K. P., Phasinam, K., Kassanuk, T., Okoronkwo, E., & Prabhu, P. (2021). Towards applicability of blockchain in agriculture sector. *Materials Today: Proceedings*. Advance online publication. doi:10.1016/j.matpr.2021.07.366

Singh & Misra. (2016). *Detection of plant leaf diseases using image segmentation and soft computing techniques*. Academic Press.

Singh & Saini. (2018a). Security for Internet of Thing (IoT) based Wireless Sensor Networks. *Journal of Advanced Research in Dynamical and Control Systems, 6,* 1591-1596.

Singh & Saini. (2018b). Security Techniques for Wormhole Attack in Wireless Sensor Network. *International Journal of Engineering & Technology, 7*(2), 59-62.

Singh & Saini. (2019). Detection Techniques for Selective Forwarding Attack in Wireless Sensor Networks. *International Journal of Recent Technology and Engineering, 7*(6S), 380-383.

Singh, S., & Saini, H. S. (2018c). Security approaches for data aggregation in Wireless Sensor Networks against Sybil Attack. *2018 Second International Conference on Inventive Communication and Computational Technologies*, 190-193. 10.1109/ICICCT.2018.8473091

Singh, S., & Saini, H. S. (2021a). Learning-Based Security Technique for Selective Forwarding Attack in Clustered WSN. *Wireless Personal Communications, 118*(1), 789–814. doi:10.100711277-020-08044-0

Singh, S., & Saini, H. S. (2021b). PCTBC: Power Control Tree-Based Cluster Approach for Sybil Attack in Wireless Sensor Networks. *Journal of Circuits, Systems, and Computers, 30*(07), 2150129. doi:10.1142/S0218126621501292

Singh, S., & Saini, H. S. (2021c). Intelligent Ad-Hoc-On Demand Multipath Distance Vector for Wormhole Attack in Clustered WSN. *Wireless Personal Communications*. Advance online publication. doi:10.100711277-021-08950-x

Umadevi, M., Rathinam, R. S., Poornima, S., Santhi, T., & Pattabhi, S. (2021). Electrochemical Degradation of Reactive Red 195 from its Aqueous Solution using RuO2/IrO2/TaO2 Coated Titanium Electrodes. *Asian Journal of Chemistry, 33*(8), 1919–1922. doi:10.14233/ajchem.2021.23330

Zeiler, M. D., & Fergus, R. (2014). Visualizing and understanding convolutional networks. In *European Conference on Computer Vision*. Springer.

Chapter 14
Analysis of Encryption and Compression Techniques for Hiding Secured Data Transmission

M. Ravi Kumar
Department of Electronics and Communication Engineering, Koneru Lakshmaiah Education Foundation, India

K. Mariya Priyadarshini
Department of Electronics and Communication Engineering, Koneru Lakshmaiah Education Foundation, India

Chella Santhosh
Department of Electronics and Communication Engineering, Koneru Lakshmaiah Education Foundation, India

J Lakshmi Prasanna
Department of Electronics and Communication Engineering, Koneru Lakshmaiah Education Foundation, India

G. U. S. Aiswarya Likitha
Department of Electronics and Communication Engineering, Koneru Lakshmaiah Education Foundation, India

ABSTRACT

Galois finite field arithmetic multipliers are supported by two-element multiplication of the finite body thereby reducing the result by a polynomial $p(x)$ which is irreducible with degree m. Galois field (GF) multipliers have a variety of uses in communications, signal processing, and other fields. The verification methods of GF circuits are

DOI: 10.4018/978-1-7998-9426-1.ch014

uncommon and confined to circuits of critical information sources and yields with realized piece locations. They also require data from the final polynomial P(x), which affects the execution of the final equipment. Here the authors introduce a math method that is based on a PC variable that easily verifies and figures out GF (2m) multipliers from the use of the initial level and compares with Vedic multiplier and Wallace tree multiplier. The technique relies on the parallel elimination of extraordinary final polynomial and proceeds in three phases: 1) decision of the yield bit – the situation is made; 2) decision of the info bit – the situation is made; and 3) the invariable polynomial used in the structure is segregated.

INTRODUCTION

Galois Finite Fields GF (2) is defined by the primary element (p) and the positive integer (m) whose possible values are two of a bit and Boolean are a branch of mathematics that was developed by Évariste Galois (Ravi et al., 2011). Encryption, Reed-Solomon encoding, and cryptography applications all make use of the properties of the fields. The polynomial method, in which a field-generating polynomial, known as an irreducible polynomial p(x), is defined in such a way that it can work with the results of operations to bring a typical presentation is the product to the field-defined fixed length. The Galois field is a number framework with definite constituents and two fundamental number-crunching activities, augmentation, and expansion, from which various jobs can be derived (Paar & Pelzl, 2009; Ravi et al., 2011; Soniya, 2013). In cryptography, coding theory and their innumerable applications, GF number-crunching plays an important role where the explicit rules for the use of equipment in GF number manipulation/shuffling circuits, particularly for the finite field augmentation are critical and their optimal execution is a usually unchanging polynomial with a base number of components (Priyadarshini et al., 2021), although this isn't always the case. Breaking down restricted field circuits becomes increasingly important as the number of threats to equipment security grows.

The multiplier in finite fields is usually more complex than the regular multiplier (Soniya, 2013) due to which the importance of deciphering the circuit support logic, for these modules and developing an efficient model for their design on FPGA hardware has been studied. The arithmetic multipliers of Galois' finite fields are based on multiplying two finite body elements that cut down the result with a degree m polynomial p(x) that is not reducible further. Depending on the need for these arithmetic modules to operate at high frequencies, an algorithmic model that reproduces the multiplier's actions sequentially (Paar & Pelzl, 2009) or parallel models can be used to take up the least amount of space possible, necessitating a delicate balance between these variables. As research in this field has shown (Priyadarshini et al., 2021), this commitment has led to a quest for efficient algorithms and architectures.

The GF was primarily used in error correction algorithms and cryptography. Encryption is the method of preventing information from being read by someone other than humans (Ramesh et al., 2012). When encrypting data, run it through a cypher, that requires a key for encrypting and decrypting. The operations viz., addition, subtraction, multiplication can be performed using the standard integer operations, followed by reduction modulo p which is fundamental to comprehending any cryptography (Halbutogullari & Koç, 2000). Here we will be using these Galois field polynomial techniques in the Verilog code (of normal multipliers) to reduce the factors of simulation, with which we can effectively differentiate the used technique from the normal multipliers.

A primitive polynomial is a binary polynomial P(X) with degree m which divides $X^{(n+1)}$ for n = $P^{(m-1)}$ (P=2) and does not divide $X^{(i+1)}$ for $i<n$ and is irreducible. Once a primitive p(X) polynomial is found, then it is possible to generate the Galois field components. The two polynomials g(x) and f(x) multiplication are a little more complicated and are defined as follows in Eq. (1).

$$M(x) = Mod(p(x)) \, (g(x) * f(x)) \tag{1}$$

Using the AND operator, bitwise multiplication is done. The result for f(x)*g(x) is separated by the primitive polynomial of GF and is considered as the result.

MATERIALS AND METHODS

Vedic Multiplier

Vedic arithmetic decreases the commonplace counts and simplifies. This is true since the Vedic formulas are said to be laid by the conventional standards of human personality functions. Trigonometry, simple and round geometry, analytics, conics, and applied arithmetic of various forms may be honestly applied to these techniques and thoughts. In Vedic mathematics, multiplication techniques are thoroughly discussed. To optimize the process, VM suggests several shortcuts and tricks and the architecture of 4*4 (Priyadarshini & Ravindran, 2019).

Wallace Tree Multiplier

The need for a low-power VLSI device gives rise to two major forces. Following that, massive currents must be transmitted with a gradual increase in operating frequency and processing energy per chip, and heat must be collected using appropriate cooling techniques due to the high-power consumption. The second element is the battery life of portable electronic devices. In these portable units, the low power architecture specifically contributes to a longer running time (Bieleń & Kubiczek, 2020; Gupta, Jain, Vaisla et al, 2021; Gupta, Vaisla, Jain et al, 2021; Kumar & Jain, 2021; Misra et al., 2021). The multiplication of the Wallace tree requires algorithms by sorting the partial products into 3 groups (Manta, Wahi, Bharadwaj et al, 2021).

To add the columns, connect three rows at a time (Singh & Saini, 2018c). A set of two rows is created from each set of three rows. There is a row for the number and a row for the execution in the resulting set of two rows. There are some strange rows that have been left behind. Rep the procedure. There are two three-row sets (Kitsos et al., 2003). Therefore, there are two sets of two rows. Summation pieces have been shifted down to the carry-out row, as shown by grey boxes. This time, there is just one set of three rows, with an additional row to carry down. They have already measured the five LSBs (Srikanth & Arunmetha, 2021). Final Supplement, the result is determined as the final two rows are inserted. Wallace tree multiplier is the final product (Hassan, 2018; Hassan, 2020; Mohammed et al., 2020; Paradhasaradhi et al., 2016; Parnaik & Chaturvedi, 2015; Zhao et al., 2020).

Proposed Finite Multiplier

Galois field is the regular operation on integers that can be used to perform operations followed by reduction modulo p (Ghayvat et al., n.d.; Gupta et al., 2020; Hassan, Eesa, Mohammed et al, 2021; Hassan, Hussein, Eesa et al, 2021; Mulla et al., 2021; Sehgal & Chaturvedi, 2022; Singh & Saini, 2019; Singh & Saini, 2021). On Vedic, Wallace tree multiplier, the above-mentioned GF (2) Multiplier is applied, and Verilog HDL extracts the notion of irreducible polynomials and compares the parameters such as power, LUT slices, efficiency etc (Sharnil, 2021).

Furthermore, the in-field product sets (s_0, s_1, s_{m-1}) appear exactly in one part of GF(2^m) each, given a GF(2^m) duplication, and the out-field object sets (s_m, s_{m+1}, s_{2m-1}) shows two components of GF(2m) in any case, due to the decrease mod $P(x)$. The number of yields in which the out-field set s_k occurs is equal to the number of monomials in the above object $x_{(k-m)} P_0(x)$, given that each monomial x_j with $m<j$ is repeatedly decreased mod $P_0(x)$, by using the relation $x_m = P_0(x)$. We depict this fact in the left half of Figure 1 by using the final polynomial $P_1(x) = x_4 + x_3 + 1$ to

reflect a rise in GF (24) (4). s_0, s_1, s_2, s_3 are the in-field sets associated that yields z_0, z_1, z_2, z_3. Since:

$$P_1(x) = x_4 + x_3 + 1 = 0, \tag{2}$$

we obtain

$$x_4 = x_3 + 1 \tag{3}$$

Figure 1. Polynomial P1(x) and P2(x) used to create two GF (24) multiplications

			a3	a2	a1	a0
			b3	b2	b1	b0
			a3b0	a2b0	a1b0	a0b0
		a3b1	a2b1	a1b1	a0b1	
	a3b2	a2b2	a1b2	a0b2		
a3b3	a2b3	a1b3	a0b3			
S6	S5	S4	S3	S2	S1	S0

$P1(x)=x^4 + x^3 + 1$				$P2(x)=x^4 + x + 1$			
S3	S2	S1	S0	S3	S2	S1	S0
S4	0	0	S4	0	0	S4	S4
S5	0	S5	S5	0	S5	S5	0
S6	S6	S6	S6	S6	S6	0	0
Z3	Z2	Z1	Z0	Z3	Z2	Z1	Z0

Therefore, set s_4 exists in 2 yield parts, z3 and z0.

$$x_5 = x_4 * x \tag{4}$$

$$x_5 = x * (x_3 + 1) \tag{5}$$

$$x_5 = x_3 + x + 1 \tag{6}$$

from eq (4-6) it is evident that s_5 occurs in three yields: z3, z1, and z0.

Finally,

$$x_6 = x_5 * x \tag{7}$$

$$x_6 = x*(x_3 + x + 1) \tag{8}$$

$$x_6 = x_4 + x_2 + x \tag{9}$$

$$x_6 = x_3 + x_2 + x + 1 \tag{10}$$

from Eq (7-10) That is, in four yields, s6 will turn up: z3, z2, z1, z0. Algebraic expressions are derived and shown in Figure 2.

Figure 2. Algebraic expressions derived

Output	Polynomial Expression
Z3	(a0b0)+a1b3+a2b2+a3b1
Z2	(a0b1+a1b0)+a1b3+a2b2+a2b3+a3b1+a3b2
Z1	(a0b2+a1b1+a2b0)+a2b3+a3b2+a3b3
Z0	(a0b3+a1b2+a2b1+a3b0)+a3b3

RESULTS AND DISCUSSION

On Vedic, Wallace tree multiplier, the foresaid GF(2) Multiplier is applied, and Verilog HDL extracts the notion of irreducible polynomials. For conducting behavioural simulation and producing synthesis reports, XILINX VIVADO software is used (Abolfazl Mehbodniya, 2021; Ghayvat, Awais, Gope et al, 2021; Gupta, 2021; Gupta et al., 2018a; Gupta, Pachauri, Maity et al, 2021; Mehta & Pandya, 2020; Pandya & Ghayvat, 2021). Figure 3 display the 4-bit Galois multiplier schematic of performance simulated waveforms and technologies using the Vedic multiplier (Ghayvat et al., 2019; Manta et al., 2020; Mehta et al., 2021; Mishra & Pandya, 2021). The behavioural waveforms and technological schematics of using the Wallace tree multiplier are also shown. Figures 4 and 5 show the implementation of simulations other than behavioural (Manta, Chandra Singh, Deep et al, 2021). We had also taken a detailed report (i.e., Power report, Utilization report, Synthesis report) of simulations for both Wallace tree multiplier and Vedic multiplier for a clear view by differing the simulation of multipliers using Galois field (polynomial techniques) and simulation of multipliers without using Galois field (Ghayvat, Pandya, Bhattacharya et al, 2021; Gupta et al., 2018b; Gupta, Maity, Anandakumar et al, 2021; Singh & Saini, 2018a; Singh & Saini, 2018b). As the Finite fields (Galois fields) are the cornerstones for Cryptography, it's important to understand them in "Science of Encryption and Decryption to prevent unauthorized access" (Jain et al., n.d.; Kubiczek & Hadasik, 2021; Kumar & Jain, 2021).

Figure 3. (a) Waveform of encrypted data generated using Vedic multiplier and (b) RTL schematic of Vedic Finite field multiplier

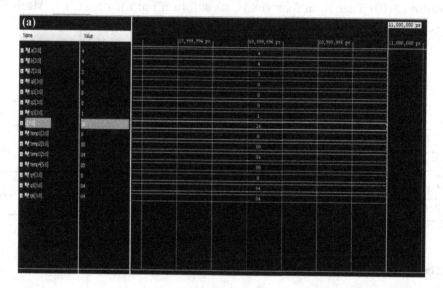

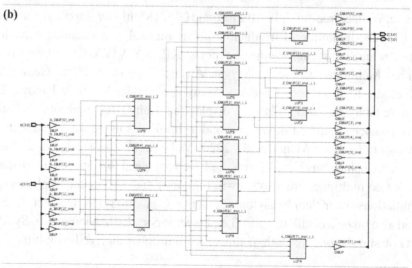

Figure 4. Implementation of (a) Functional, (b) Timing, (c) Synthesis of Functional and (d) Synthesis of Timing

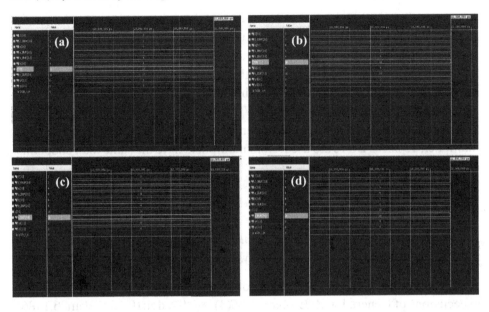

Figure 5. Waveforms of encrypted data produced using Wallace tree multiplier

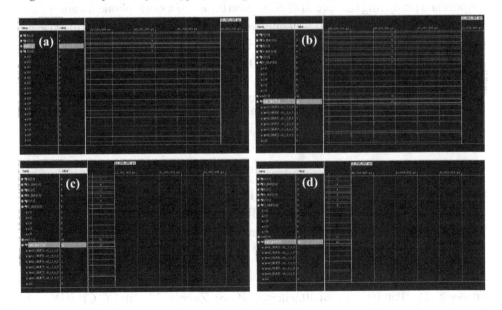

CONCLUDING REMARKS

The proposed GF (2) multiplier architecture greatly improves the performance. By using shift registers and simple adder circuits, the encoded multiplier decreases the complexity, delay, cost and power dissipation. The Point - Addition with various multipliers is compared, and it discovered that the Galois field Wallace tree multiplier has 6.695W on-chip power and is better than the traditional Wallace tree multiplier and that the Vedic multiplier has 5.562W with Galois field when compared to the normal one. For the Wallace tree multiplier, 30 slice LUTs are used, and for the Vedic multiplier, 15 slices LUTs are used. Both multipliers have the same total endpoints.

REFERENCES

Abolfazl Mehbodniya, L. (2021). *Fetal Health Classification from Cardiotocographic Data Using Machine Learning, Expert Systems*. Wiley.

Bieleń, M., & Kubiczek, J. (2020). Response of the labor market to the needs and expectations of Generation Z. E-Mentor, 86(4), 87–94. doi:10.15219/em86.1486

Ghayvat, H., Awais, M., Gope, P., Pandya, S., & Majumdar, S. (2021). Recognizing suspect and predicting the spread of contagion based on mobile phone location data: A system of identifying COVID-19 infectious and hazardous sites, detecting disease outbreaks based on the internet of things, edge computing, and artificial intelligence. *Sustainable Cities and Society, 69*, 102798. doi:10.1016/j.scs.2021.102798

Ghayvat, H., Awais, M., Pandya, S., Ren, H., Akbarzadeh, S., Chandra Mukhopadhyay, S., Chen, C., Gope, P., Chouhan, A., & Chen, W. (2019, February 13). Smart Aging System: Uncovering the Hidden Wellness Parameter for Well-Being Monitoring and Anomaly Detection. *Sensors (Basel), 19*(4), 766. doi:10.339019040766 PMID:30781852

Ghayvat, H., Pandya, S., Bhattacharya, P., Mohammad, Z., Mamoon, R., Saqib, H., & Kapal, D. (2021). CP-BDHCA: Blockchain-based Confidentiality-Privacy preserving Big Data scheme for healthcare clouds and applications. *IEEE Journal of Biomedical and Health Informatics, 25*, 1–22. doi:10.1109/JBHI.2021.3097237 PMID:34260362

Ghayvat, H., Pandya, S., Bhattacharya, P., & Zuhair, M. (n.d.). CP-BDHCA: Blockchain-based Confidentiality-Privacy preserving Big Data scheme for healthcare clouds and applications. *IEEE Journal of Biomedical and Health Informatics*. . doi:10.1109/JBHI.2021.3097237

Gupta, A. K. (2021). Sun Irradiance Trappers for Solar PV Module to Operate on Maximum Power: An Experimental Study. *Turkish Journal of Computer and Mathematics Education, 12*(5), 1112–1121.

Gupta, A. K., Chauhan, Y. K., & Maity, T. (2018a). A new gamma scaling maximum power point tracking method for solar photovoltaic panel Feeding energy storage system. *Journal of the Institution of Electronics and Telecommunication Engineers, 67*(1), 1–21.

Gupta, A. K., Chauhan, Y. K., & Maity, T. (2018b). Experimental investigations and comparison of various MPPT techniques for photovoltaic system. *Sadhana, 43*(8), 1–15. doi:10.100712046-018-0815-0

Gupta, A. K., Chauhan, Y. K., Maity, T., & Nanda, R. (2020). Study of Solar PV Panel Under Partial Vacuum Conditions: A Step Towards Performance Improvement. *Journal of the Institution of Electronics and Telecommunication Engineers*, 1–8. doi:10.1080/03772063.2020.1749145

Gupta, A. K., Maity, T., Anandakumar, H., & Chauhan, Y. K. (2021). An electromagnetic strategy to improve the performance of PV panel under partial shading. *Computers & Electrical Engineering, 90*, 106896. doi:10.1016/j.compeleceng.2020.106896

Gupta, A. K., Pachauri, R. K., Maity, T., Chauhan, Y. K., Mahela, O. P., Khan, B., & Gupta, P. K. (2021). Effect of Various Incremental Conductance MPPT Methods on the Charging of Battery Load Feed by Solar Panel. *IEEE Access: Practical Innovations, Open Solutions, 9*, 90977–90988. doi:10.1109/ACCESS.2021.3091502

Gupta, N., Jain, A., Vaisla, K. S., Kumar, A., & Kumar, R. (2021). Performance analysis of DSDV and OLSR wireless sensor network routing protocols using FPGA hardware and machine learning. *Multimedia Tools and Applications, 80*(14), 22301–22319. doi:10.100711042-021-10820-4

Gupta, N., Vaisla, K. S., Jain, A., Kumar, A., & Kumar, R. (2021). Performance Analysis of AODV Routing for Wireless Sensor Network in FPGA Hardware. *Computer Systems Science and Engineering, 39*(2), 1–12.

Halbutogullari, A., & Koç, C. K. (2000). Mastrovito multiplier for general irreducible polynomials. *IEEE Transactions on Computers, 49*(5), 503–518. doi:10.1109/12.859542

Hassan, M. M. (2018). Bayesian Sensitivity Analysis to Quantifying Uncertainty in a Dendroclimatology Model. *ICOASE 2018 -International Conference on Advanced Science and Engineering*, 363–368. 10.1109/ICOASE.2018.8548877

Hassan, M. M. (2020). A Fully Bayesian Logistic Regression Model for Classification of ZADA Diabetes Dataset. *Science Journal of University of Zakho, 8*(3), 105–111. doi:10.25271juoz.2020.8.3.707

Hassan, M. M., Eesa, A. S., Mohammed, A. J., & Arabo, W. K. (2021). Oversampling Method Based on Gaussian Distribution and K-Means Clustering. Computers. *Materials and Continua, 69*(1), 451–469. doi:10.32604/cmc.2021.018280

Hassan, M. M., Hussein, H. I., Eesa, A. S., & Mstafa, R. J. (2021). Face Recognition Based on Gabor Feature Extraction Followed by FastICA and LDA. Computers. *Materials and Continua, 68*(2), 1637–1659. doi:10.32604/cmc.2021.016467

Jain, A., Dwivedi, R. K., Alshazly, H., Kumar, A., Bourouis, S., & Kaur, M. (n.d.). *Design and Simulation of Ring Network-on-Chip for Different Configured Nodes.* Academic Press.

Kitsos, P., Theodoridis, G., & Koufopavlou, O. (2003). An efficient reconfigurable multiplier architecture for Galois field GF (2m). *Microelectronics Journal, 34*(10), 975–980. doi:10.1016/S0026-2692(03)00172-1

Kubiczek, J., & Hadasik, B. (2021, December). Challenges in Reporting the COVID-19 Spread and its Presentation to the Society. *J. Data and Information Quality, 13*(4), 1–7. doi:10.1145/3470851

Kumar, A., & Jain, A. (2021). Image smog restoration using oblique gradient profile prior and energy minimization. *Frontiers of Computer Science, 15*(6), 1–7. doi:10.100711704-020-9305-8 PMID:34221535

Manta, Chandra Singh, Deep, & Kapoor. (2021). Temperature-regulated gold nanoparticle sensors for immune chromatographic rapid test kits with reproducible sensitivity: A study. *IET Nanobiotechnol.*

Manta, P., Nagraik, R., Sharma, A., Kumar, A., Verma, P., Paswan, S. K., Bokov, D. O., Shaikh, J. D., Kaur, R., Leite, A. F. V., Filho, S. J. B., Shiwalkar, N., Persaud, P., & Kapoor, D. N. (2020). Optical density optimization of malaria pan rapid diagnostic test strips for improved test zone band intensity. *Diagnostics (Basel), 10*(11), 880. doi:10.3390/diagnostics10110880 PMID:33137871

Manta, P., Wahi, N., Bharadwaj, A., Kour, G., & Kapoor, D. N. (2021). A statistical quality control (SQC) methodology for gold nanoparticles based immune-chromatographic rapid test kits validation. *Nanoscience & Nanotechnology-Asia, 11*(6), 1–5. doi:10.2174/2210681210666210108111055

Mehta, P., & Pandya, S. (2020). A review on sentiment analysis methodologies, practices and applications. *International Journal of Scientific & Technology Research*, *9*(2), 601–609.

Mehta, P., Pandya, S., & Kotecha, K. (2021). Harvesting social media sentiment analysis to enhance stock market prediction using deep learning. *Peer J. Computer Science*, *7*, e476. Advance online publication. doi:10.7717/peerj-cs.476 PMID:33954250

Mishra, N., & Pandya, S. (2021, April). Internet of Things Applications, Security Challenges, Attacks, Intrusion Detection, and Future Visions: A Systematic Review. *IEEE Access: Practical Innovations, Open Solutions*, *9*, 59353–59377. doi:10.1109/ACCESS.2021.3073408

Misra, N. R., Kumar, S., & Jain, A. (2021, February). A Review on E-waste: Fostering the Need for Green Electronics. In *2021 International Conference on Computing, Communication, and Intelligent Systems*. IEEE. 10.1109/ICCCIS51004.2021.9397191

Mohammed, A. J., Hassan, M. M., & Kadir, D. H. (2020). Improving Classification Performance for a Novel Imbalanced Medical Dataset Using SMOTE Method. *International Journal of Advanced Trends in Computer Science and Engineering*, *9*(3), 3161–3172. doi:10.30534/ijatcse/2020/104932020

Mulla, G. A. A., Demir, Y., & Hassan, M. M. (2021). Combination of PCA with SMOTE Oversampling for Classification of High-Dimensional Imbalanced Data. In BEU. *Journal of Science*, *10*(3).

Paar, C., & Pelzl, J. (2009). *Understanding cryptography: a textbook for students and practitioners*. Springer Science & Business Media.

Pandya, S., & Ghayvat, H. (2021). Ambient acoustic event assistive framework for identification, detection, and recognition of unknown acoustic events of a residence. *Advanced Engineering Informatics*, *47*, 1012. doi:10.1016/j.aei.2020.101238

Paradhasaradhi, D., Priya, K. S., Sabarish, K., Harish, P., & Narasimharao, G. V. (2016). Study and analysis of CMOS carry look ahead adder with leakage power reduction approaches. *Indian Journal of Science and Technology*, *9*(17), 1–8. doi:10.17485/ijst/2016/v9i17/93111

Parnaik, V. K., & Chaturvedi, P. (2015). Fluorescence recovery after photobleaching studies reveal complexity of nuclear architecture. *International Journal of Chemistry*, *4*(4), 297–302.

Priyadarshini, K. M., & Ravindran, D. R. E. (2019). Novel Two Fold Edge Activated Memory Cell with Low Power Dissipation and High Speed. *International Journal of Recent Technology and Engineering, 8*(1), 1491–1495.

Priyadarshini, K. M., Ravindran, R. E., Krishna, S. V., & Bhavani, K. D. (2021, February). Design of Compact and Smart Full Adders for High-Speed Nanometer Technology IC's. []. IOP Publishing.]. *Journal of Physics: Conference Series, 1804*(1), 012152. doi:10.1088/1742-6596/1804/1/012152

Ramesh, Tilak, & Prasad. (2012). Efficient Implementation of 16-bit Multiplie Accumulator Using Radix-2 Modified Booth Algorithm and SPST Adder Using Verilog. *International Journal of VLSI Design & Communication Systems, 3*(3).

Ravi, N., Subbaiah, Y., Prasad, T. J., & Rao, T. S. (2011). A novel low power, low area array multiplier design for DSP applications. In *2011 International Conference on Signal Processing, Communication, Computing and Networking Technologies* (pp. 254-257). IEEE. 10.1109/ICSCCN.2011.6024554

Sehgal, P., & Chaturvedi, P. (2022). *Survival Strategies in Cold-adapted Microorganisms* (1st ed.). Springer Singapore. doi:10.1007/978-981-16-2625-8

Sharnil, P. (2021). Covidsaviour: A Novel Sensor-Fusion and Deep Learning-Based Framework for Virus Outbreaks. *Frontiers in Public Health, 9*, 797808. Advance online publication. doi:10.3389/fpubh.2021.797808

Singh & Saini. (2018a). Security for the Internet of Thing (IoT) based Wireless Sensor Networks. *Journal of Advanced Research in Dynamical and Control Systems, 6*, 1591-1596.

Singh & Saini. (2018b). Security approaches for data aggregation in Wireless Sensor Networks against Sybil Attack. *2018 Second International Conference on Inventive Communication and Computational Technologies*, 190-193.

Singh & Saini. (2018c). Security Techniques for Wormhole Attack in Wireless Sensor Network. *International Journal of Engineering & Technology, 7*(2), 59-62.

Singh & Saini. (2019). Detection Techniques for Selective Forwarding Attack in Wireless Sensor Networks. *International Journal of Recent Technology and Engineering, 7*(6S), 380-383.

Singh, S., & Saini, H. S. (2021). Intelligent Ad-Hoc-On Demand Multipath Distance Vector for Wormhole Attack in Clustered WSN. *Wireless Personal Communications*.

Soniya, S. K. (2013). A review of different type of multipliers and multiplier-accumulator unit. *International Journal of Emerging Trends & Technology in Computer Science, 2*(4), 364–368.

Srikanth, I., & Arunmetha, S. (2021, February). High Level Synchronization and Computations of Feed Forward Cut-Set based Multiply Accumulate Unit. *Journal of Physics: Conference Series, 1804*(1), 012201. doi:10.1088/1742-6596/1804/1/012201

Zhao, B., Chaturvedi, P., Zimmerman, D. L., & Belmont, A. S. (2020). Efficient and reproducible multigene expression after single-step transfection using improved bac transgenesis and engineering toolkit. *ACS Synthetic Biology, 9*(5), 1100–1116. doi:10.1021/acssynbio.9b00457 PMID:32216371

Chapter 15
A New Insight on the Morphology of Web Mining

Joshua Ojo Nehinbe

https://orcid.org/0000-0002-0098-7437

Federal University, Oye, Nigeria

ABSTRACT

Recent surveys have revealed that about 199 million of active and over 1.2 Billion of inactive websites exist across the globe. The categories of websites have also increased beyond espionage networks of spies, computer networks for corporate organizations, networks for governments' agencies, networks for social interactions, search engines and networks for religious bodies, etc. These diversities have generated complex issues regarding the morphology and classification of webs and web mining. Thus, the validity of the generic web classification, web mining taxonomy, and contemporary studies on the regularities of web usage, web content, web semantic, web structures, and the process of extracting useful information and interesting patterns from the intricate of the Internet are frequently questionable. The existing web mining taxonomy can also lead to misinformation, misclassification, and crisscrossed issues such that numerous webs' patterns could be marked with crossing and inexplicable lines. By using qualitative virtual interviews of 26 skilled web-designers and a focus group-conference of 7 experts in web-usage to brainstorm on the above issues, this chapter comprehensively discusses the above concepts and how they relate to web classification and web mining taxonomy. The themes obtained elucidate the techniques that commonly underpin basic web mining taxonomy. New concepts like existence of esoteric web data, exoteric web data; mysterious, inexplicable, and mystifying patterns; and cryptic vocabularies are discussed to assist web analytics. Finally, the author suggests eight classification attributes for web mining patterns (illustrative, expositive, educative, advisory, interpretative, demonstrative, revealing, and informatory) and proposes a new web mining taxonomy to minimize the impacts of the above concerns on global settings.

DOI: 10.4018/978-1-7998-9426-1.ch015

INTRODUCTION

The Art and science of websites' designs require web designers to possess creative and imaginative skills and capability to combine some standard technologies such as Hypertext Markup Language (HTML), Cascading Style Sheets (CSS); Extensible Markup Language (XML), Scalable Vector Graphics (SVG) to build and synthesize images and Application Programming Interfaces (APIs) or the intermediary software that enable two web applications to link and communicate with each other (W3C, 2021). Visual studies suggest that the morphology of web classification hints that modern websites now combine various branches of creative activities like music, painting and literary composition to typically produce visual works on websites that are primarily appreciated for their beauty, innovativeness and quality. In other words, the ontology and structure of the words that are frequently published on different websites and parts of such words could be classified on the basis of root, stem, prefix and suffix. For these reasons, websites regularly publish and keep the records of countless web data in diverse morphological components and formats.

Web data is a combination of piece of information and semantic of facts on websites. Fundamentally, web data subsumes diversity of web users, variety of web structure and array of web content regarding websites that are hosted on the Internet (Busetto et al., 2020; Singh et al., 2014). Web users are computer services and end-users such as the consumers, customers and clients that access websites. Web structure includes the arrangement, organization, composition, configuration, framework and makeup of websites. Similarly, web content is the variety of information that is published on the websites for the audience or web users (end-users). Information retrieval is the central part of the concept of web mining. Logically, the information that is retrieved from the web is indirectly extracted from web servers. The web servers usually log rich on the above web data. Such information may include remote hosts, successful and unsuccessful responses; parameters required to identify web users, authentications, status codes such as resource requested and the HTTP protocol, etc in standard formats. Nonetheless, web data or information that is retrieved from the webs might require high level of pre-processing due to their uniqueness and diversities in their sources, kinds, purposes and meanings. The pre-processing of web data required and the changeable meaning of the linguistics together with the logical combinations of the above groups of web data begin to pose serious challenges to web data analytics in two different ways on a daily basis (Chawan & Pamnani, 2010). Modern web data is perceived in terms of the logical semantics and lexical semantics in the above context. The logical semantics of web data are concerned with the common sense, reference, preconception and the conclusion that can be implicitly drawn from web data while the lexical semantics of web data are concerned with the analysis of the meanings and the relationship between particular words or the entire texts (words) on the websites.

Recent survey has shown the complexity of extracting and classifying information from over 199 millions of active and over 1.2 billion of inactive websites that exist across the globe (Siteefy, 2021; WebsiteSetup, 2021). Lack of statistics on the exact numbers of the available websites that are mobile-friendly and the numbers of websites that are not mobile-friendly can limit the accuracy of web mining taxonomy in categorizing websites on the basis of mobile-friendliness and responsiveness (Siteefy, 2021). Consequently, web mining then becomes a complex issue in recent time. Web mining is a branch of data mining that deals with the extraction of hidden but interesting and predictive information from the interactive information on the web (Griazev & Ramanauskaitè, 2018). The fact is that categories of the existing websites on the Internet have drastically increased from the traditional websites designed for attracting customers, boosting profitability and gaining wider publicity to the categories of the websites that are hosted purposely to advance malicious and avenging socio-political ideologies in recent time. The above trend has also progressed over the years through the evolutions of the espionage networks of spies, and networks of researchers and academicians, networks of corporate organizations, networks of governments' agencies, networks of social partners and networks of religious bodies to cite a few.

Comparative analysis of websites is often required to understand how web users, web data and web structure correlate to each other and how they vary from one website to another website. Comparative analysis in this context refers to the comparison of all websites or certain websites on the basis of the patterns in their data processes, data sets, documents or other items. The premise is that patterns can be derived from the intelligence extraction of the regularities in the words, designs, shapes, colours, phrases, abstract and figurative ideas and their usage on the webs. In essence, some patterns might indicate elements of the predictable and unpredictable manners of the above three categories of web data. Thus, one of the main problems with the above discoveries is that the residual impacts of the challenges inherent in the various categories of websites have affected the extraction of the predictive information from web category, the security, integrity, social policies and privacy issues of web-based systems internationally. Thus, it is often difficult for most web mining algorithms to accurately extract useful information from the collections of the existing websites without incurring overheads (Tavares et al., 2022). The inability of web mining tools to discriminate descriptive or narrative property of web data from highly prescriptive quality of web data could trigger serious issues like misinformation and mismatches of the web patterns whenever several web data share common attributes with each other and whenever they exhibit unusual conceptual schemes.

The intricacy could arise whenever the information and facts extracted from the various categories of the existing websites are matched badly. The resulting patterns are likely to be unsuitable for supporting lateral thinking and procedures required for the development of innovative strategies and business decision making in industrial environment. Similarly, once the top management is prone to make unrealistic projections if they unintentionally make the mistakes of matching webs information that conforms together. Overreliance of the top management teams on extracts from web servers that are founded on unrealistic projections in corporate settings may suddenly lead the entire organizations to systemic failure; redundancy or peripheral closure of certain segments of their business operations (Tavares et al., 2022). Consequently, a new insight into the concepts of the web classification and web mining taxonomy is urgently required to cognitively arrange the existing websites into suitable categories and distinctive classes of the same type.

Furthermore, newly discovered challenges and social issues have begin to confront some end-users of the generic web mining taxonomy and contemporary studies on the regularities of the categories of web usage, web content, web semantic and web structures (Singh et al., 2014). The process of extracting useful information and interesting patterns from the intricate and interconnected networks of search engines and websites that are not designed to perform web searches have shown that most web mining algorithms and web mining tools are restricted to the identification of patterns from the generic taxonomy on web mining. Some well-known indices such as minor patterns, secondary patterns and equivalent patterns can be specific or occasionally fluctuate across different websites' groups. Pattern analysis and web filtering analytics have shown that main patterns are very important in comparison with other patterns. Studies have also made it known that most web mining algorithms can suddenly exhibit low performance evaluation in the course of substituting and switching seemingly of the equivalent patterns with regular patterns during the exclusion of the uninteresting patterns from the retrievals of useful information and interesting patterns across the number of numerous websites on the Internet. With experience, these core issues constantly challenge the validity of the generic web mining taxonomy and contemporary studies on the regularities of web usage, web content, web semantic; web structures and the process of pattern discovery from the intricate and interconnected systems of many computer resources and networks in the Internet

This chapter argues that the techniques for archiving and indexing online records, correlations and aggregation of the massive online records must be efficient to eliminate irregular content among the billions of WebPages in the Internet. These techniques must also be able to accurately retrieve the needed information without exposing any researcher, web data analytics and web developers to any practical challenge. Accordingly, we discovered that the categories of websites embrace the espionage networks of spies, networks for corporate organizations, networks for governments' agencies, networks for social interactions, networks for religious bodies, etc. Nonetheless, most web mining algorithms and tools are restricted to the identification of patterns, on the basis of web logs, textual data, multimedia (text, graphic and sound) data, hypermedia systems and hyper structure of websites. Besides, the above indices generally fluctuate across different websites' groups. Consequently, contextual information extracted from websites is limited to the association analysis and clustering techniques for web data analytics. Moreover, with the inevitable inclusion of websites of the webby and espionage networks on the web, the existing web mining taxonomy can lead to misinformation and crisscrossed issues such that numerous patterns could be marked with crossing lines. These issues are indirectly clamoring for a suitable taxonomy for web mining. Thus, the objective of this chapter is to thoroughly discuss all the above concepts with respect to web mining taxonomy, the challenges confronting researchers in formulating universally accepted taxonomy for web mining and then proffer potential solutions on how they can be completely checkmated. We qualitatively interviewed 26 experienced web designers and incorporated their perceptions with a focus group conference on Skype involving 7 experts in web usage to brainstorm and elucidate the strengths and weaknesses of the above data mining techniques that commonly underpin basic web mining taxonomy. Two main contributions of this chapter is that it clarifies the morphology of web data and patterns extracted from the webs and the discussion of the usage of entropy index in the statistical classification and determination of the informative content of web patterns. The chapter also identifies some hard problems and non-obvious mistakes that web mining forensics can observe during web mining analytics and offers solutions so that they can promptly lessen them. The paper finally evolves and adopts eight criteria to categorize web mining and web mining taxonomy to minimize the impacts of the above concerns on web-users.

BACKGROUND

There are numerous issues that surround web mining taxonomy in recent years. Contemporary studies on the regularities of web usage have shown that the validity of the generic web classification and web mining taxonomy on the basis of web content, web semantic and web structures are flawed (Tavares et al., 2022; Singh et al., 2014). This implies that the process of using the above variables to extract useful information and interesting patterns from the intricate of the Internet are most likely to be questionable. Most web mining algorithms and web mining tools that are restricted to the variables are equally prone to misclassification problems. Some indices for mining websites can be specific while some of them can occasionally fluctuate across different websites' groups. Consequently, the contextual information extracted from websites is limited to association analysis and clustering techniques during web data analytics. These care issues have raised series of contentions over the years.

Two or more websites may have closely identical attributes in an acceptable certain proportion. For instance, there are some corporate websites that possess closely related attributes with some marketing websites. Besides, the inevitable inclusion of some websites hosted by crime syndicates, terrorist's consortium, webby and espionage networks have also suggest the fact that the existing web mining taxonomy can lead to misinformation, misclassification and crisscrossed issues. In essence, it is plausible that numerous web's patterns may be marked with crossing and inexplicable lines with the above diversities.

DEFINITIONS OF TERMS

Web is an intricate networks or an interconnected system of computers, things and people. The web usually comprises of computer networks, hypertext transfer protocol and a collection of internet or websites to offer text, graphics, sound and animation to the global community.

Websites is a set of computers connected to the cyberspace that keep successive web pages on the World Wide Web (www).

Morphology of web data describes the various structures and categories of the words in each website so that analysts can understand how they are formed and how they relate to each other.

Web portal is a website that the owners have designed as an entrance to other or main websites on the Internet.

Web mining is the act of extracting hidden facts and informative patterns from the web with the intention to increase human knowledge.

Taxonomy is the classification of something into groups on the basis of the similarities of their features, appearance, structures or general principles. It is a practice of classifying websites according to their assumed internal or external relationships.

Web classification is the cognitive process of distributing or arranging websites into categories or classes of the same type.

Association analysis is the assessment, interaction; the dependence of the organization and casual relationships within the structures, features, etc in a set of events or data.

Clustering is defined as the grouping of a number of similar events together to form a group, cluster or conceptual scheme.

Web category is defined as a collection of webs that share a common attribute with the aim to categorize webs on a general concept that symbolizes the divisions into a definite class or conceptual scheme.

Equivalent pattern is defined as a web pattern that is equal to another pattern in effect, value or significance. Equivalent pattern can seemingly substitute another pattern.

Secondary pattern is a kind of web patterns that is ranked second in terms of importance or value to the other patterns. Secondary patterns are patterns that do not of major importance to the web analytics and decision makers.

Minor pattern is a kind of web patterns that is of lesser importance in ranking. Minor patterns usually depict less severe threats or dangers from the webs.

Multimedia patterns are sequences of transmission that combine text, graphics and sound together.

Hypermedia pattern describes a sequence of multimedia system in the web such that excessively related and active pieces of web information are connected and accessible together.

A NEW WEB MINING TAXONOMY

The main thrust of the chapter is the new web mining taxonomy discussed below. Websites have been classified into different types or categories on the basis of several criteria including but not limited to the technical nature, topic and theme on the websites, but there is hardly an exhaustive list of the types or categories of website till date (Siteefy, 2021). Webs are basically classified into two groups such as the publicly accessible websites and privately (internally) accessible websites. The former are websites that are accessible to the general public while the latter are groups of websites that are accessed to certain users of private networks. Web mining is a significant topic in web data analytics especially whenever there is need for analysts to practically fetch, understand and discover facts or knowledge from the different groups of web data (Tavares et al., 2022).

The precise goal of the search engines is to furnish the users with the information that closely matches their search objectives. The results usually include individual pages being publicized on the Search Engine Results Pages (SERPs) as an alternative to the websites (Siteefy, 2021). We discovered that many websites generally use graphical pictures, textual data, animation and sound to communicate their missions and services to the global community. This chapter premises that useful patterns are hidden in textual, sound, graphical and animation data that can be extracted by suitable clustering techniques.

Figure 1 illustrates that web mining can result into the extraction of hidden or secret and predictive information from web textual data, sound data, graphical data and animation data.

Figure 1. A new web mining taxonomy

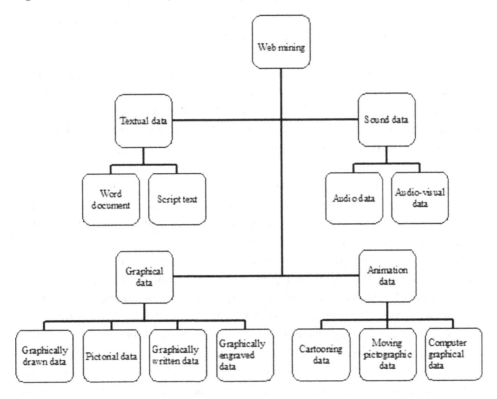

Graphical pictures in this context consist of some historic films and statistical records like charts, diagrams, grids and tables. Websites also analyze, interpret and describe a number of the relations that exist in their stored data and remarkable concepts in the forms of visual diagrams such as bar charts, histogram, pie charts, scatter or linear graphs. These kinds of digital data can also appear in the forms of graven images, written and drawn data. The outward appearance of graphically written data is a major issue over the years. Such data can appear in many fonts, different sizes and single or multiple colours. Graphically engraved data may involve the cutting, inscribing or carving a collection of short text messages or certain designs on the surface of a hard object such as rings or stones. Examples of graphically engraved data in some private and public websites include monument, tribute, slogan, motto and tombstone. However, adages, jingles and watchword that some websites used as catchphrases create different impressions to different visitors to the websites. There are some visitors that would not be pleased with some graphically engraved data especially if they connote discrimination, unfairness and abuse. Pictorial data signify web data and feelings that are expressed or illustrated in the form of pictures to the viewers. They can be photographs of past activities, symbolic or memorable events in the organizations. Nonetheless, the problem with web pictorial data is how to achieve the representational and figurative benchmarks that would make and create the same impression to all the viewers of the pictures in the websites in the same way. The general problem with graphical data is that it is inappropriate to perfectly analyze series of datasets that are not in the formats of categorical and qualitative data. Inconsistency is a major problem whenever technical updates are required for the web data that are presented in written or drawn or engraved formats.

The textual data can subsume scripts like numbers, alphabets, special symbols and their combinations in writing or lettering formats. Web textual data also consist of script text (such as book, manuscripts and textbooks), word documents and glossary (such as speech, vocabulary and lexicon). Web textual data consists of semantics, lexis; morphology and syntactically connected in written and printed formats. The morphology of web textual data is meant to analyze the various structures and categories of the words in the web to understand how they are formed and how they are related together. Additionally, animation data may consist of automation of successive photographed films, photographs, images of painted objects, decorated figures and figures or mages drawn by hands that appear to be moving images or moving objects. Web designers adopt animation to create an illusion to the viewers and visitors to the websites that the objects or images are moving in a sequential or successive order. Animation data can also be expressed in the form of a set of moving picture, cartoon and computer graphical data. The hard problem with animation is the recreation of the entire process of the simulations in different environment despite of getting the copyright approvals from the rightful owners.

Furthermore, sound data may encompass pleasant vibrations of metallic objects such as bells with the motive of producing continuous, lovely and regular vibrations to attract visitors to the websites. Digital sound data can occur in the form of audio data and audio-visual data. Audio-visual data is a collection of recorded videotapes and other digital information on the websites that are presented to the viewers both in audible and visible formats. They data could signify customers' services voice, musicians or a group of people that have been recorded to advance the promotion of certain products and services in an organization. On the other hand, sound data can signify spectrograms or visual representations of the spectrum of frequencies of waves, signals and time series that illustrate variations of certain variables with time. Segmentation and classification analysis are common methods that are often used to analyze visual and audio datasets. Nevertheless, different rhythms of sound may convey diverse impressions to the listeners when compared to the specified impressions web designers have envisage they would produce whenever they are heard. Some rhythms may sound worried whenever they go off or whenever they reverberate. The pattern or interval of the resonance of the sound and moving data to resound, repeat the pattern of movement in the sound (or rejuvenate the sound) may please web-users in different ways.

Issues, Controversies, Problems on Web Mining Taxonomy

By using qualitative interview of 26 skilled web-designers and a focus group-conference of 7 experts in web-usage over Skype to brainstorm on the above issues, this chapter comprehensively discusses the above concepts and how they relate to web classification and web mining taxonomy. The results obtained elucidate the strengths and weaknesses of data mining techniques that commonly underpin basic web mining taxonomy. New concepts like existence of esoteric web data, exoteric web data; mysterious, inexplicable and mystifying patterns and cryptic vocabularies are discussed to assist web analytics. Finally, we suggest and adopt eight criteria such as the degree of illustrative, expositive, educative, advisory, interpretative, demonstrative; revealing and informatory of providing and conveying information to categorize and propose a new web mining taxonomy in other to minimize the impacts of the above concerns on global settings.

Figure 2. Classification of web mining patterns

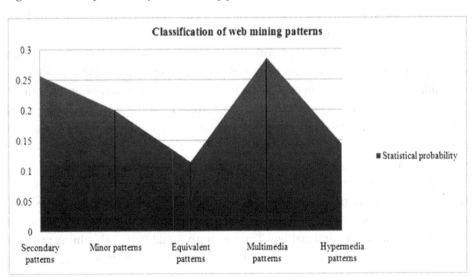

This section further presents new perspectives regarding critical issues, controversies and hard problems on web mining in recent time. Figure 2 provides a new classification of web mining patterns. The results suggest what new knowledge is reported about web patterns and what makes it non-obvious to most visitors to some websites is that there are secondary patterns, minor patterns; equivalent patterns, multimedia patterns and hypermedia patterns hidden in some classical websites.

Therefore, it is imperative that the web data analytics must endeavour to identify the implications and connotations of the above groups of patterns, the improvements and impacts they suggest to decision makers and end-users. For instance, minor patterns depict less dreadful dangers or less serious information to the web users. The respondents agree that secondary patterns are not of major importance to most end-users. The equivalent patterns are sequential patterns that are often equal to other sequential patterns in meaning, value, effect and significance.

The results further give a picture of web multimedia and web hypermedia patterns. The observations reveal that some sequences of web transmission can combine text, graphics and sound data together to form less active data and occasionally more active web data than normal is generated. The respondents argue that overheads and new challenges (such as cost of download, space, sentiment, sensation and feeling) are associated with web multimedia and web hypermedia patterns in recent years especially with the explosive growth of web data on a daily basis. Misinterpretations and numbness on the part of the people that host the websites are major issues that can affect the impacts of web multimedia and web hypermedia patterns in web mining. People often construe, read, analyze and interpret multimedia data in diverse ways. Web multimedia and web hypermedia patterns are meant to convey certain ideas about salient facts on the web. Thus, getting the wrong ideas about the inherent meanings of such patterns could deprive online FOREX traders from achieving high profitability. The reason is that web owners might be unconscious of the severity of the negative effects associated with the kinds of the web multimedia and web hypermedia data they display on their websites. The severity of these challenges may endanger online investments, trust, customer's loyalty, power of online-public relations and patronage. On the whole, grave impacts of the web multimedia and web hypermedia patterns can surge if the web owners continue to be misconstrued and if they continue to lack the total feelings of the web users on the kinds of the multimedia and web hypermedia data they present on their websites.

Figure 3 provides a new classification of attributes for web mining patterns. Accordingly, web mining patterns must be illustrative, educative, advisory expositive, interpretative, demonstrative, revealing and informatory for them to be useful for strategic and lateral decision making. The illustrative quality of web mining patterns implies that the patterns must serve to demonstrate clarity of web information by citing useful examples that can support lateral thinking. The concept of expositive nature of web mining patterns is that the extracted patterns should serve to develop web analytics and set to enlighten users on various categories of the hidden patterns in the webs.

Figure 3. Classification of attributes of the web mining patterns

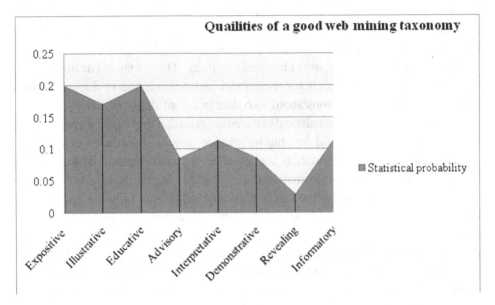

With the existence of minor patterns, web mining patterns must be educative. In other words, the resulting web patterns must contain educative sequences of patterns that can enable web owners and help them to perform regulatory check on their customers. In terms of advisory, web mining patterns should connote "advice-giving" and counseling information. They must be embodiment of useful informative advice that is extracted to furnish vital recommendations on the winning strategies to the lateral thinkers. The advisory patterns must be helpful but they usually encompass optional and suggested patterns.

Web mining patterns must be interpretative, unambiguous and instantly recognizable to web data analyzers. The interpretations of the web mining patterns must be clearly meant to identify and assess risks, detect and prevent online misdemenour. Web mining patterns should be demonstrative with the growth of secondary patterns on the Internet. The extracted patterns must markedly express the attitudes and emotions of web users. The extracted information must serve to demonstrate innovative strategies required to create values to online visitors to websites.

Web mining patterns must be revealing. The extracted patterns must be able to unintentionally disclose insightful information from digitalized data to the strategic decision makers in corporate settings. Web mining should make flawed business initiatives explicit to the Chief Executives., Making unknown web information known to the community of the web users on the need-to-know and need-to-use basis is a core security issue concerning system audit of web mining patterns. Web patterns may previously be known to few web users. It is also plausible that some of the components of such patterns are meant to be kept as secret entities. The challenge with the disclosure of the above web patterns directly through web mining may involve incurring huge expenses and complex tasks. These may occur in terms of how to design suitable models for refinement and construction of digital journey and how to make big decisions about web data in a confidence manner.

The performance of web analytical patterns suggests that they must be informatory. Web mining patterns should be able to provide details and convey distinctions between exoteric web information and esoteric web information. The extracted patterns must isolate web information that is suitable for the general public from web information that is confined to and understandable by only the enlightened web users. There are some web patterns that are interesting and uninteresting. Web mining patterns must be instructive for them to serve to enlighten decision makers. We also found out that web patterns must be informative. The extracted patterns must tend to increase knowledge and dissipate ignorance of web users to certain extent. Web mining patterns that do not serve to instruct, inform and enlighten web users are likely to provide inconclusive evidence or communicate disjointed information to the web users.

RECOMMENDATIONS TO LESSEN THE CHALLENGES WITH WEB MINING TAXONOMY

The standards for building web sites require immediate review and extension. Information extracted from inactive websites might be flawed in making well-informed decisions. Thus, web audits and routine regulation of websites are recommended so that the quantity of inactive websites across the globe can drastically reduce. In addition, websites publish and update web data that can occur in the form of text, graphic, sound and animation. The taxonomic relationships between the longest and least average time spent on each website usually varies. Therefore, it is imperative for web designers to critically reexamine some of the most frequently visited websites such as google.com, Facebook, YouTube.com and 360.cn to attract traffics and enhance entrants into their websites (Siteefy, 2021).

Web analysis of the content of web textual data should be able to furnish analysts with knowledge or informative facts concerning web books and other written or printed work on the web. One of the methods for achieving this objective is to ensure that web standardization should establish standard ontology and morphology for designing websites. These would enable web mining algorithms to be able to extract web patterns that would reflect how words are formed on the web and matching their relationship to other words both in the same language and in other languages.

Additionally, the morphology of the web contents should be designed to avoid crisscrossed issues. This would help web mining algorithms to avoid patterns that are marked with crossing of lines and patterns that consist of crossed lines. Similarly, the output of web mining algorithm should be constructed to avoid webbing outputs to enhance interpretability. Attributes of web data have made some information extracted from the web servers to conform to the formats of categorical datasets. The degree of similarity in clustering patterns extracted from web data can be determined with Entropy. The logarithm function of the probability of each cluster that web attributes generate can be expressed as $(\log_{10}(p(c_i)))$. This variable can subsequently be divided by the logarithmic function of $\log_{10}(2)$. Mathematically, the entropy of each attribute of web data can be calculated as follows:

$$Entropy_{attribute} = -\sum_{i=1}^{n} p(c_i) \log_2 p(c_i) \tag{1}$$

Suppose $P(c_i)$ is the probability that an event extracted from the web would belong to c_i. Then, $-logP(c_i)$ is how web data analyst may be overwhelmingly surprised if he/she desires to select an event from the outcomes in the cluster c_i. Usually, $P(c_i)$ ranges from 0 (impossible events) to 1 (certain events). The surprise can range from the infinity (impossible events) to 0 (certain events). Furthermore, the above studies suggest that web analytics can result into cryptic details that have obscure nature and secret or hidden meanings. We therefore suggest that web taxonomy should be illustrative, expositive, educative, advisory, interpretative, demonstrative and revealing. These would help web data analysts to isolate secondary patterns that are not of major importance from minor patterns that are of lesser importance and of lesser root causes in terms of consequences and inherent threats they can pose to the web users.

The paper qualitatively interviewed 26 experienced web designers and incorporated their perceptions with a focus group conference on Skype. The participants also involve 7 experts with wide experience in web usage. Qualitative research entails the examination of different manifestations, the nature of phenomena and the perspectives from which they can be perceived (Busetto et al., 2020). Thus, the interviews are semi-structured and all the respondents were engaged in open-ended questions to brainstorm and elucidate the strengths and weaknesses of data mining techniques that commonly underpin basic web mining taxonomy (Busetto et al., 2020). The perceptions of the participants were transcribed immediately. Thematic analysis of their perceptions was carried out with the aim to extract salient points in them. Similarly, all related themes from the analysis were aggregated to form well-informative themes. The themes obtained are discussed in the subsequent section.

New Challenges on Web Mining Taxonomy

New challenges often confront many researchers in formulating universally accepted taxonomy for web mining and potential solutions to checkmate them. Most websites publish web data in different formats [5]. The purpose of publicly available information, font size, word counts within a web page also vary from website to website. The most popular websites also vary from one country to another (Siteefy, 2021). Suitable taxonomy for web mining then becomes a major challenge with the prevalence of several online syndicates and consortium of online interest groups that operate like webby on the web. Matching two webs that do not often correlate or go together would lead to a bad or unsuitable match. The existence of portals with different structures is posing a new challenge to attempts to establish suitable web mining taxonomy. The owners of most web portals often positioned that as entrances to other websites on the Internet. For this reason, less intelligent mining algorithms have the tendency to mismatch some portals with websites that share related attributes on the Internet. The problem with the mismatches of web classifications can worsen the situations whereby two or more webs would match badly.

Meanwhile, some feelers and proffers conceptualize that a good web mining taxonomy should classify websites into the same type, class, category or group and on the basis of the similarities of their structures, contents, data and natural relationships [6]. Accordingly, there could be different web mining algorithms to determine the session length of users for agro-business care services, social media, healthcare services, animal healthcares, regulatory healthcares such as World Health Organization (WHO), financial services, etc (Siteefy, 2021). Notwithstanding, studies have now shown that some web documents are sensitive and classified information with restricted access. Conversely, some web documents are nonsensitive, unrestricted and unclassified information. The existence of esoteric web data that are confined to and understandable by selected and inner caucus of elites in some developed society and the exoteric web data that are broadly accessible to the general public are impediments to the researchers and taxonomists. In addition, some new websites are dynamic and cryptic with secret and hidden languages while significant numbers of websites that are dynamic could have some static data that are designed without mysterious and cryptic vocabularies.

This paper believes that the appearance of words on websites may vary in terms of the structure of the words and words' components. Words in some websites can also vary in terms of their roots, stems, prefixes and suffixes. The dynamic website frequently and automatically changes itself. In static websites, the desired outward appearance of the websites is usually hardcoded and non-interactive but the owner can update the websites occasionally through manual process (Tavares et al., 2022). Consequently, the above data mining techniques for joining attributes of webs and together and for grouping similar web data, web semantic, web structure, etc into their respective clusters begin to attain the limit of their efficacies given rise to many undesirable patterns and mismatches. Besides, aggregation of websites by joining several web attributes and grouping them together to form complete and informative patterns begin to generate inexplicable and incomprehensible patterns. Numerous inexplicable and mystifying patterns from several websites can obscure the nature and knowledge general inherent in the web mining concepts, and these could degenerate to direct ruining of small internal relationships, divisions and conceptual schemes in the web analytics.

Figure 4. Classification of web mining patterns

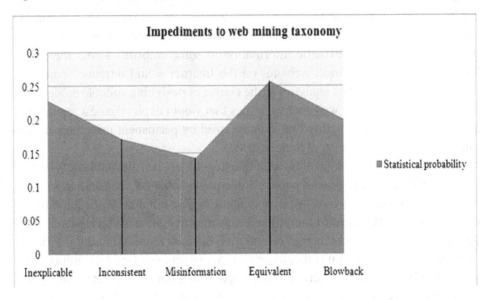

Figure 4 depicts that impediments to web mining taxonomy include inexplicable web patterns, inconsistent web patterns, equivalent web patterns, web patterns that can misinform web data analyzers and web patterns that indicate blow back. Inconsistent patterns are indicative of irregular and infrequent sequence of web information. They are mostly difficult to discern and read. Inexplicable web patterns are indication of information extracted from the web that is incapable of being explained. They may contain inexplicable and incomprehensible web errors due to lack of proper web authoring and web audit. Web patterns that are indicative of misinformation are kinds of incorrect information that is web mining algorithms extract from the web during data analytics. The above results suggest that web patterns that indicate blowback are indications of misinformation. Such misinformation may result from the recirculation of disinformation previously planted online by foreign intelligence service. The unintended negative consequences of these kinds of web patterns usually impact severely on foreign social policies and interventions.

FUTURE TRENDS

There will be viability of the above paradigms coupled with new ways of modeling and new challenges of implementations of web mining taxonomy in the nearest future. Sudden surge in the demands for the universally acceptable benchmark that can be used for web mining taxonomy is about to happen. The future of web mining taxonomy is most likely to be influenced with the existence of exoteric textual data, exoteric data and exoteric information in some websites across the globe. The dynamic nature of most websites on the Internet would introduce emerging challenges to the web data analytics in the course of designing suitable models that will identify appropriate web characteristics that would depict the best regularities and the most excellent quality that characterized by permanent principles in web mining taxonomy (Feldman & Sanger, 2007).

The exoteric data is a kind of information on the websites that publishers believe they are suitable for the general public. Some publishers may change their motives in the future time. Therefore, we expect them to also emphasize the adoption of esoteric data with the intention to confine certain information to and understandable of handful enlightened inner caucus. Presently, it is difficult for most mining algorithms to perform the compilation and comprehensive extractions of esoteric information across the Internet without erroneously suppressing some vital information that strategic management would need for knowledge discovery and decision making in their organizations. Sometimes, the performance evaluation of the mining algorithms tends to dwindle due to inability of the evaluators to evaluate them with cryptic data from the webs. We expect that significant numbers of exoteric data in the future time to exhibit obscure, secret and hidden meanings that are difficult to understand by inexperienced web data analytics.

We submit that web mining taxonomy should enlighten general public in the nearest future. New classifications should convey no puzzling vocabulary. Classifiers should ware that mining taxonomy that cannot recognize cryptic data or differentiate cryptic data from other kinds of web data discussed above may mismatch mysterious terms on the webs with words with unclear intentions. The more such events occur, the more they can worsen the problems of confusing the succinctness and incomprehensible of cryptic web writings with dependability of the end-users on the web mining.

CONCLUSION

With over 1 billion of websites across the globe, contemporary studies on the ontology, morphology and regularities of web usage, web content and web structures of the existing websites have shown that web mining has the capability to extract useful information and interesting patterns from the intricate and interconnected systems of many computer resources and networks in this setting. This chapter has exhaustively shown that the generic web mining taxonomy is often defective and we have explicated several concepts that have been over-sighted over the years. Most web mining algorithms and tools are restricted to the identification of patterns, on the basis of web logs, textual data, multimedia data and hyper structure of websites. These indicators are often specific and fluctuate across different websites' groups. Consequently, contextual organization of websites is limited to association analysis and clustering techniques for web data analytics.

The morphology of websites reveals that there are many intricacies associated with the process of mining computer networks of websites given the fact that modern websites now offer different categories of graphical images, textual data, animation, sound and resources through the hypertext transfer protocol. Besides, we observed variations in the categories of websites and most popular websites. Websites have also spanned espionage networks of spies, networks of corporate organizations, networks of governments' agencies, networks of social interactions, networks of religious bodies, etc. As a matter of fact, web mining can easily lead to crisscrossed patterns such that the resulting patterns are marked with series of crossing lines. This problem is usually difficult to counteract due to the prevalence of the webby and espionage networks on the web.

The chapter also buttresses the fact that suitable taxonomy for web mining is a major challenge especially with the insurgent cases of several syndicates and consortium of online interest groups that operate like webby. We opine that a good web mining taxonomy should classify websites into the same type, class, category or group based on the similarities of their structure, content, data and natural relationships. However, significant numbers of web documents that are sensitive and classified with restricted access and some documents are nonsensitive, unrestricted and unclassified are geometrically increasing on a daily basis. These dilemmas have brought new challenges to web miners in recent years.

Esoteric web data are usually confined to and understandable by selected and inner caucus of elites in some society. Users would usually require authorization such as sign on details before they can access them in most cases. Conversely, exoteric web data are accessible to the general public. The explorations we made on numerous websites reveal that some new websites are cryptic with secret and hidden language while there are evolutions of new websites that are structurally designed without mysterious and cryptic vocabularies. Thus, the association analysis for joining attributes of website together, how they are connected together and various clustering techniques designed for grouping similar web data, web semantic and web structure into their succinct groups begin to attain their limitations. Most often, their outputs are crippled with incurrent of mismatches. Another trouble with these issues is that the aggregation of websites by joining several web attributes and grouping them together to form a whole pattern begin to generate inexplicable and incomprehensible patterns. But then, whenever inexplicable and mystifying web patterns are numerous, they can compound and obscure the nature and general perceptions of web mining concepts. These problems can directly ruin the simple divisions and conceptual schemes in the web analytics. Therefore, future research should evolve models to ensure that contextual information extracted from the existing active and inactive websites are not limited to the morphological associative analysis and logical clustering during web data analytics. One method to achieve this goal is to ensure that web mining taxonomy should recognize the existence of the websites hosted by crime syndicates, terrorist's consortium, webby and espionage networks. Otherwise, the resulting web mining taxonomy may lead to misinformation, misclassification and crisscrossed issues such that numerous webs' patterns could be marked with crossing and inexplicable facts.

REFERENCES

Babu, D. S., Nabi, S. K. A., Ali, M., & Raju, Y. (2011). Web Usage Mining: A Research Concept of Web Mining. *International Journal of Computer Science and Information Technologies*, 2(5), 2390–2393.

Busetto, L., Wick, W., & Gumbinger, C. (2020). How to use and assess qualitative research methods. Neurological Research and Practice, 2.

Chawan, P., & Pamnani, R. (2010). *Web usage mining: A research area in Web mining. Department of computer technology.* VJTI University.

Feldman, R., & Sanger, J. (2007). The text mining handbook. Cambridge University Press.

Griazev, K., & Ramanauskaitè, S. (2018). Web mining taxonomy. *2018 Open Conference of Electrical, Electronic and Information Sciences (eStream),* 1-4. 10.1109/eStream.2018.8394124

Kosala, R., & Blockeel, H. (2000). Web mining research: A survey. *SIGKDD Explorations, 2*(1), 1–15. doi:10.1145/360402.360406

Samanta, D., Dutta, S., Galety, M. G., & Pramanik, S. (2022). A Novel Approach for Web Mining Taxonomy for High-Performance Computing. In J. M. R. S. Tavares, P. Dutta, S. Dutta, & D. Samanta (Eds.), *Cyber Intelligence and Information Retrieval. Lecture Notes in Networks and Systems* (Vol. 291). Springer. doi:10.1007/978-981-16-4284-5_37

Singh, S., Gupta, D., & Chandhoke, A. (2014). Web Mining: Taxonomy and Survey. *Advances in Computer Science and Information Technology, 1*(2), 56–60.

Siteefy. (2021). *How Many Websites Are There in the World?* Retrieved November 13, 2021, from: https://siteefy.com/how-many-websites-are-there/

W3C. (2021). *W3C standards.* Retrieved November 11, 2021, from: https://www.w3.org/standards/

WebsiteSetup. (2021). *How Many Websites Are There?* Retrieved November 11, 2021, from https://websitesetup.org/news/how-many-websites-are-there/#number-of-active-websites

Compilation of References

Phishing Stats You Should Know In 2021 | Expert Insights. Expert Insights. (2021). Retrieved 4 November 2021, from https://expertinsights.com/insights/50-phishing-stats-you-should-know/

Abolfazl Mehbodniya, L. (2021). *Fetal Health Classification from Cardiotocographic Data Using Machine Learning, Expert Systems*. Wiley.

Afroz, S., & Greenstadt, R. (2011, September). Phishzoo: Detecting phishing websites by looking at them. In *2011 IEEE fifth international conference on semantic computing* (pp. 368-375). IEEE. DOI: 10.1109/ICSC.2011.52

Agarwal, A. K., & Jain, A. (2019). Synthesis of 2D and 3D NoC mesh router architecture in HDL environment. *Journal of Advanced Research in Dynamical and Control Systems, 11*(4), 2573–2581.

Aggarwal, C. C. (2012). Mining text streams. *Mining Text Data*, 297–321. doi:10.1007/978-1-4614-3223-4_9

Aggarwal, J. K., & Cucchiara, R. (2006). Special issue on multimedia surveillance SYSTEMS: Guest editorial. *Multimedia Systems, 12*(3), 165–167. doi:10.100700530-006-0072-7

Agrawal, N., Jain, A., & Agarwal, A. (2019). Simulation of Network on Chip for 3D Router Architecture. *International Journal of Recent Technology and Engineering, 8*, 58–62.

Ajzen, I. (1991). The theory of planned behavior. *Organizational Behavior and Human Decision Processes, 50*(2), 179–211. doi:10.1016/0749-5978(91)90020-T

Akaishi, S., & Uda, R. (2019). Classification of XSS attacks by machine learning with frequency of appearance and co-occurrence. In *2019 53rd Annual Conference on Information Sciences and Systems (CISS)* (pp. 1-6). IEEE.

Al Hadwer, A., Tavana, M., Gillis, D., & Rezania, D. (2021). A Systematic Review of Organizational Factors Impacting Cloud-based Technology Adoption Using Technology-Organization-Environment Framework. *Internet of Things, 15*(1), 100407. doi:10.1016/j.iot.2021.100407

Al-Abdallah, R. Z., & Al-Taani, A. T. (2017). *Arabic single-document text summarization using particle swarm optimization algorithm. Procedia Computer Science*.

Alabdan, R. (2020). Phishing attacks survey: Types, vectors, and technical approaches. *Future Internet, 12*(10), 168. doi:10.3390/fi12100168

Alam, T. (2020). IoT-Fog a communication framework using blockchain in the Internet of things. doi:10.36227/techrxiv.12657200.v1

Alam, T., & Rababah, B. (2020). Convergence of MANET in communication among smart devices in IoT. doi:10.22541/au.159164757.78780485/v2

Alam, A., Ullah, I., & Lee, Y.-K. (2020). Video Big Data Analytics in the cloud: A reference architecture, survey, opportunities, and open research issues. *IEEE Access: Practical Innovations, Open Solutions, 8*, 152377–152422. doi:10.1109/ACCESS.2020.3017135

Alam, T., & Benaida, M. (2018). The role of cloud-manet framework in the internet of things (iot). *International Journal of Online and Biomedical Engineering, 14*(12), 97. doi:10.3991/ijoe.v14i12.8338

Alasadi, S., & Bhaya, W. (2017). Review of Data Preprocessing Techniques in Data Mining. *Journal of Engineering and Applied Sciences, 12*(16), 4102–4102. doi:10.3923/jeasci.2017.4102.4107

Al-Dabooni, S., & Wunsch, D. (2020). Convergence of recurrent neuro-fuzzy value-gradient learning with and without an actor. *IEEE Transactions on Fuzzy Systems, 28*(4), 658–672. doi:10.1109/TFUZZ.2019.2912349

Alenezi, M., Nadeem, M., & Asif, R. (2021). SQL injection attacks countermeasures assessments. *Indonesian Journal of Electrical Engineering and Computer Science, 21*(2), 1121–1131.

AlEroud, A., & Karabatis, G. (2020, March). Bypassing detection of URL-based phishing attacks using generative adversarial deep neural networks. In *Proceedings of the Sixth International Workshop on Security and Privacy Analytics* (pp. 53-60) DOI: 10.1145/3375708.3380315

Aleroud, A., & Zhou, L. (2017). Phishing environments, techniques, and countermeasures: A survey. *Computers & Security, 68*, 160–196. doi:10.1016/j.cose.2017.04.006

Alghoul, A., Al Ajrami, S., Al Jarousha, G., Harb, G., & Abu-Naser, S.S. (2018). Email Classification Using Artificial Neural Network. *Int. J. Acad. Eng. Res.*

Ali, F., Khan, P., Riaz, K., Kwak, D., Abuhmed, T., Park, D., & Kwak, K. S. (2017). A fuzzy ontology and SVM–based web content classification system. *IEEE Access: Practical Innovations, Open Solutions, 5*, 25781–25797. doi:10.1109/ACCESS.2017.2768564

Alimi, A. I., Tavares, A., & Pinho, C. (2019). Enabling Optical Wired and wireless technologies for 5G and beyond networks. Telecommunication Systems - Principles and Applications of Wireless-. *Optics Technology*. Advance online publication. doi:10.5772/intechopen.85858

Ali, W. (2017). Phishing website detection based on supervised machine learning with wrapper features selection. *International Journal of Advanced Computer Science and Applications, 8*(9), 72–78. doi:10.14569/IJACSA.2017.080910

Alkamil, A., & Perera, D. G. (2020). Towards dynamic and partial reconfigurable hardware architectures for cryptographic algorithms on embedded devices. *IEEE Access: Practical Innovations, Open Solutions, 8*, 221720–221742. doi:10.1109/ACCESS.2020.3043750

Alkhalil, Z., Hewage, C., Nawaf, L., & Khan, I. (2021). Phishing Attacks: Recent Comprehensive Study and a New Anatomy. *Frontiers of Computer Science, 3,* 6. doi:10.3389/fcomp.2021.563060

Al-Khurafi, O. B., & Al-Ahmad, M. A. (2015). Survey of web application vulnerability attacks. In *2015 4th International Conference on Advanced Computer Science Applications and Technologies (ACSAT)* (pp. 154-158). IEEE. 10.1109/ACSAT.2015.46

Allman, E., Callas, J., Delaney, M., Libbey, M., Fenton, J., & Thomas, M. (2005). *Domain keys identified mail.* IETF Internet Draft.

Alloghani, M., Al-Jumeily, D., Mustafina, J., Hussain, A., & Aljaaf, A. (2020). A Systematic Review on Supervised and Unsupervised Machine Learning Algorithms for Data Science. In In M. Berry, A. Mohamed, & B. Yap (Eds.), Supervised and Unsupervised Learning for Data Science. Unsupervised and Semi-Supervised Learning. Springer. doi:10.1007/978-3-030-22475-2_1

Almahirah, Jahan, Sharma, & Kumar. (2021). Role of Market Microstructure in Maintaining Economic Development. *Empirical Economics Letters, 20*(2).

Almomani, A., Gupta, B. B., Atawneh, S., Meulenberg, A., & Almomani, E. (2013). A survey of phishing email filtering techniques. *IEEE Communications Surveys and Tutorials, 15*(4), 2070–2090. doi:10.1109/SURV.2013.030713.00020

Al-Ramahi, M., Elnoshokaty, A., El-Gayar, O., Nasralah, T., & Wahbeh, A. (2021). Public Discourse Against Masks in the COVID-19 Era: Infodemiology Study of Twitter Data. *JMIR Public Health and Surveillance, 7*(4), e26780. doi:10.2196/26780 PMID:33720841

Alsobhi, H., & Alshareef, R. (2020). SQL Injection Countermeasures Methods. In *2020 International Conference on Computing and Information Technology (ICCIT-1441)* (pp. 1-4). IEEE.

Alzubi, O. A., Alzubi, J. A., Dorgham, O., & Alsayyed, M. (2020). Cryptosystem design based on Hermitian curves for IoT security. *The Journal of Supercomputing, 76*(11), 8566–8589. doi:10.100711227-020-03144-x

Amazon 'thwarts largest ever DDoS cyber-attack'. (2020). *BBC News.* Retrieved 3 November 2021, from https://www.bbc.com/news/technology-53093611

Ambedkar, M. D., Ambedkar, N. S., & Raw, R. S. (2016). *A comprehensive inspection of cross site scripting attack. In 2016 international conference on computing, communication and automation (ICCCA).* IEEE.

Amirat, Y., Elbouchikhi, E., Zhou, Z., Benbouzid, M., & Feld, G. (2019). Variational Mode Decomposition-based Notch Filter for Bearing Fault Detection. *IECON 2019 - 45th Annual Conference of the IEEE Industrial Electronics Society,* 6028-6033. 10.1109/IECON.2019.8926891

Anand, S., & Aggarwal, R. R. (2012). An Efficient Algorithm for Data Cleaning of Log File using File Extensions. *International Journal of Computers and Applications*.

Anderson, R. (2020). *Security engineering: a guide to building dependable distributed systems.* John Wiley & Sons. doi:10.1002/9781119644682

Andrabi & Wahid. (2022). Machine Translation System Using Deep Learning for English to Urdu. *Computational Intelligence and Neuroscience*. Advance online publication. doi:10.1155/2022/7873012

Andrabi, S. A. B., & Wahid, A. (2019). Sentence Alignment for English Urdu Language Pair. *International Journal of Recent Technology and Engineering, 8*.

Andrabi, S. A. B., & Wahid, A. (2021). A Comprehensive Study of Machine Translation Tools and Evaluation Metrics. In V. Suma, J. I. Z. Chen, Z. Baig, & H. Wang (Eds.), *Inventive Systems and Control. Lecture Notes in Networks and Systems* (Vol. 204). Springer. doi:10.1007/978-981-16-1395-1_62

Andrew, K. (2015). *The research of text preprocessing effect on text documents classification efficiency. International Conference Stability and Control Processes IEEE*, St. Petersburg, Russia.

Andryukhin, A. A. (2019, March). Phishing attacks and preventions in blockchain based projects. In *2019 International Conference on Engineering Technologies and Computer Science (EnT)* (pp. 15-19). IEEE. DOI: 10.1109/EnT.2019.00008

Anitha, T., & Uppalaiah, T. (2016). Android Based Home Automation using Raspberry Pi. *International Journal of Innovative Technologies., 4*(1), 2351–8665.

Anonymous. (2016). Retrieved 6 November 2021, from https://insights.cynergistek.com/infographics/symantec-s-2016-internet-security-threat-report

Ansari, K., Panda, S. K., & Corumluoglu, O. (2018). Mathematical modelling of ionospheric TEC from Turkish permanent GNSS Network (TPGN) observables during 2009–2017 and predictability of NeQuick and Kriging models. *Astrophysics and Space Science, 363*(3), 1–13. doi:10.100710509-018-3261-x

Aonzo, S., Merlo, A., Tavella, G., & Fratantonio, Y. (2018, October). Phishing attacks on modernandroid. In *Proceedings of the 2018 ACM SIGSAC Conference on Computer and Communications Security* (pp. 1788-1801). DOI:10.1145/3243734.3243778

Arasaratnam, O. (2011). Introduction to cloud computing. *Auditing Cloud Computing*, 1–13. doi:10.1002/9781118269091.ch1

Arcinas, M., Sajja, G., Asif, S., Gour, S., Okoronkwo, E., & Naved, M. (2021). Role Of Data Mining In Education For Improving Students Performance For Social Change. *Türk Fizyoterapi ve Rehabilitasyon Dergisi/Turkish Journal of Physiotherapy and Rehabilitation, 32*, 6519.

Arostegi, M., Torre-Bastida, A., Bilbao, M. N., & Del Ser, J. (2018). A heuristic approach to the Multicriteria design of IaaS cloud infrastructures for big data applications. *Expert Systems: International Journal of Knowledge Engineering and Neural Networks*, *35*(5), e12259. Advance online publication. doi:10.1111/exsy.12259

Arsan, T. (2016). Smart systems: From design to implementation of embedded Smart Systems. *2016 HONET-ICT*. . doi:10.1109/HONET.2016.7753420

Ashok Kumar, L. (2022). *Design and Implementation of Automatic Water Spraying System for Solar Photovoltaic Module* (Vol. 2022). Mathematical Problems In Engineering.

Asvany, T., Amudhavel, J., & Sujatha, P. (2017). Lightning search algorithm for solving coverage problem in wireless sensor network. *Advances and Applications in Mathematical Sciences*, *17*(1), 113–127.

Ates, C., Özdel, S., & Anarim, E. (2020). Graph-based fuzzy approach against DDoS attacks. *Journal of Intelligent & Fuzzy Systems*, 1–10.

Awa, H., Ojiabo, O., & Orokor, L. (2017). Integrated technology-organization-environment (T-O-E) taxonomies for technology adoption. *Journal of Enterprise Information Management*, *30*(6), 893–921. doi:10.1108/JEIM-03-2016-0079

Awa, H., Ukoha, O., & Emecheta, B. (2016). Using T-O-E theoretical framework to study the adoption of ERP solution. *Cogent Business & Management*, *3*(1), 1196571. doi:10.1080/2331 1975.2016.1196571

Azeez, N., Misra, S., Margaret, I. A., & Fernandez-Sanz, L. (2021). Adopting Automated Whitelist Approach for Detecting Phishing Attacks. *Computers & Security*.

Aziz, D. (2018). Webserver Based Smart Monitoring System Using ESP8266 Node MCU Module. *International Journal of Scientific and Engineering Research*, *9*, 801.

Babu, D. S., Nabi, S. K. A., Ali, M., & Raju, Y. (2011). Web Usage Mining: A Research Concept of Web Mining. *International Journal of Computer Science and Information Technologies*, *2*(5), 2390–2393.

Baeza-Yates, R. (2008). Web usage mining in search engines. *Web Mining*, 307–321. doi:10.4018/978-1-59140-414-9.ch014

Baitha, A. K., & Vinod, S. (2018). Session Hijacking and Prevention Technique. *International Journal of Engineering & Technology, 7*(2.6), 193-198.

Bajrami, X., & Murturi, I. (2018). An efficient approach to monitoring environmental conditions using a wireless sensor network and NodeMCU. *Elektrotech. Inftech.*, *135*(3), 294–301. doi:10.100700502-018-0612-9

Balaban, D. (2016). *The History and Evolution of DDoS Attacks - Embedded Computing Design.* Embedded Computing Design. Retrieved 3 November 2021, from https://www.embeddedcomputing.com/technology/security/network-security/the-history-and-evolution-of-ddos-attacks

Bandini, S., & Sartori, F. (2005). Improving the effectiveness of monitoring and control systems exploiting knowledge-based approaches. *Personal and Ubiquitous Computing, 9*(5), 301–311. doi:10.100700779-004-0334-3

Bandla, P. B., Vairavasundaram, I., Teekaraman, Y., & Nikolovski, S. (2022). Real Time Sustainable Power Quality Analysis of Non-Linear Load under Symmetrical Conditions. *Energies, 15*(01), 57. doi:10.3390/en15010057

Bansal, C., Deligiannis, P., Maddila, C., & Rao, N. (2020). Studying ransomware attacks using web search logs. In *Proceedings of the 43rd International ACM SIGIR Conference on Research and Development in Information Retrieval* (pp. 1517-1520). ACM.

Barnes, S. J., & Huff, S. L. (2003). Rising sun. *Communications of the ACM, 46*(11), 78–84. doi:10.1145/948383.948384

Basilio, M., Brum, G., & Pereira, V. (2020). A model of policing strategy choice. *Journal of Modelling in Management, 15*(3), 849–891. doi:10.1108/JM2-10-2018-0166

Basit, A., Zafar, M., Liu, X., Javed, A. R., Jalil, Z., & Kifayat, K. (2021). A comprehensive survey of AI-enabled phishing attacks detection techniques. *Telecommunication Systems, 76*(1), 139-154. DOI: / doi:10.1007/s11235-020-00733-2

Basit, S. A., & Kumar, M. (2015). A review of routing protocols for underwater wireless sensor networks. *International Journal of Advanced Research in Computer and Communication Engineering, 4*(12), 373–378.

Basole, R., Seuss, C., & Rouse, W. (2013). IT innovation adoption by enterprises: Knowledge discovery through text analytics. *Decision Support Systems, 54*(2), 1044–1054. doi:10.1016/j.dss.2012.10.029

Bautista, J. F., & Dahi Taleghani, A. (2016). The state of the art and challenges in geomechanical modeling of Injector Wells: A review paper. *Polar and Arctic Sciences and Technology, 8.* doi:10.1115/OMAE2016-54383

Baykara, M., & Gürel, Z. Z. (2018, March). Detection of phishing attacks. In *2018 6th International Symposium on Digital Forensic and Security (ISDFS)* (pp. 1-5). IEEE. DOI:10.1109/ISDFS.2018.8355389

Begum, A., Hassan, M. M., Bhuiyan, T., & Sharif, M. H. (2016). RFI and SQLi based local file inclusion vulnerabilities in web applications of Bangladesh. In *2016 International Workshop on Computational Intelligence (IWCI)* (pp. 21-25). IEEE.

Behal, S., Kumar, K., & Sachdeva, M. (2021). D-FAC: A novel φ-Divergence based distributed DDoS defense system. *Journal of King Saud University-Computer and Information Sciences, 33*(3), 291–303.

Belkebir. (2018). TALAA-ATSF: A global operation-based Arabic text summarization framework. In K. Shaalan, A. E. Hassanien, & F. Tolba (Eds.), *Intelligent natural language processing: Trends and applications*. Springer International Publishing.

Bellatreche, L., & Chakravarthy, S. (2017). Big Data Analytics and Knowledge Discovery. *Proceeding of 19th International Conference DAWak.*

Benzekri, W., El Moussati, A., Moussaoui, O., & Berrajaa, M. (2020). Early Forest Fire Detection System using Wireless Sensor Network and Deep Learning. *International Journal of Advanced Computer Science and Applications, 11*(5), 496. doi:10.14569/IJACSA.2020.0110564

Bergholz, A., Chang, J. H., Paass, G., Reichartz, F., & Strobel, S. (2008, August). Improved Phishing Detection using Model-Based Features. CEAS. DOI: 10.1.1.216.4317

Bermudez, I., Traverso, S., Munafo, M., & Mellia, M. (2014). A distributed architecture for the monitoring of clouds and CDNs: Applications to Amazon AWS. *IEEE eTransactions on Network and Service Management, 11*(4), 516–529. doi:10.1109/TNSM.2014.2362357

Bharathidasan, Indragandhi, Kuppusamy, Teekaraman, Urooj, & Alwadi. (2022). Intelligent Fuzzy Based High Gain Non-Isolated Converter for DC Micro-Grids. *CMC-Computers, Materials & Continua, 71*(2).

Bharati, K. F. (2017). Effective task scheduling and dynamic resource optimization based on heuristic algorithms in cloud computing environment. *Transactions on Internet and Information Systems (Seoul), 11*(12). Advance online publication. doi:10.3837/tiis.2017.12.006

Bhavsar, V., Kadlak, A., & Sharma, S. (2018). Study on phishing attacks. *International Journal of Computers and Applications, 182*, 27–29. doi:10.5120/ijca2018918286

Bieleń, M., & Kubiczek, J. (2020). Response of the labor market to the needs and expectations of Generation Z. E-Mentor, 86(4), 87–94. doi:10.15219/em86.1486

Bi, J., Liu, Y., Fan, Z., & Cambria, E. (2019). Modelling customer satisfaction from online reviews using ensemble neural network and effect-based Kano model. *International Journal of Production Research, 57*(22), 7068–7088. doi:10.1080/00207543.2019.1574989

Bird, S., Klein, E., & Loper, E. (2009). *Natural Language Processing with Python*. O'Reilly Media.

Biswas, S., Sajal, M. M. H. K., Afrin, T., Bhuiyan, T., & Hassan, M. M. (2018). A study on remote code execution vulnerability in web applications. *International Conference on Cyber Security and Computer Science (ICONCS 2018).*

Blei, D. (2012). Probabilistic topic models. *Communications of the ACM, 55*(4), 77–84. doi:10.1145/2133806.2133826

Blei, D., Ng, A., & Jordan, M. (2003). Latent dirichlet allocation. *Journal of Machine Learning Research, 3*(1), 993–1022.

Boister, N., & Burchill, R. (2017). The implications of the Pinochet decisions for the extradition or prosecution of former South African heads of State for crimes committed under apartheid. *International Crimes*, 558–575. doi:10.4324/9781315092591-15

Bonato, A. (2008). The web graph. *Graduate Studies in Mathematics*, 19–32. doi:10.1090/gsm/089/02

Bošnjak, L., Sreš, J., & Brumen, B. (2018). Brute-force and dictionary attack on hashed real-world passwords. In *2018 41st international convention on information and communication technology, electronics and microelectronics (mipro)* (pp. 1161-1166). IEEE.

Bouchet-Valat, M. (2020). *SnowballC: Snowball Stemmers Based on the C 'libstemmer' UTF-8 Library*. R package version 0.7.0. https://CRAN.R-project.org/package=SnowballC

Bouchikhi, E. H. E., Choqueuse, V., & Benbouzid, M. E. H. (2013, March). Current Frequency Spectral Subtraction and Its Contribution to Induction Machines Bearings. *Condition Monitoring. IEEE Transactions on Energy Conversion, 28*(1), 135–144. doi:10.1109/TEC.2012.2227746

Bozkir, A. S., & Sezer, E. A. (2016, April). Use of HOG descriptors in phishing detection. In *2016 4th International Symposium on Digital Forensic and Security (ISDFS)* (pp. 148-153). IEEE. 10.1109/isdfs.2016.7473534

Bracale, A., Carpinelli, G., Piegari, L., & Tricoli, P. (2007). A high resolution method for online diagnosis of induction motors faults. *Proceedings of the 2007 IEEE PowerTech*, 994-998. 10.1109/PCT.2007.4538451

Bracewell, P. J., Hilder, T. A., & Birch, F. (2019). Player ratings and online reputation in super rugby. *Journal of Sport and Human Performance, 7*(2).

Bracewell, P. J., McNamara, T. S., & Moore, W. E. (2017). How Rugby Moved the Mood of New Zealand. *Journal of Sport and Human Performance, 4*(4).

Brindha, T. R., Rathinam, R., & Dheenadhayalan, S. (2021). Antibacterial, Antifungal and Anticorrosion Properties of Green Tea Polyphenols Extracted Using Different Solvents. *Asian Journal of Biological and Life Sciences, 10*(1), 62–66. doi:10.5530/ajbls.2021.10.10

British Airways fined £20m over data breach. (2018). Retrieved 7 January 2022, from https://www.bbc.com/news/technology-54568784

Broadhurst, R., Skinner, K., Sifniotis, N., Matamoros-Macias, B., & Ipsen, Y. (2018). *Phishing and cybercrime risks in a university student community*. Advance online publication. doi:10.2139srn.3176319

Brous, P., & Janssen, M. (2020). Trusted Decision-Making: Data Governance for Creating Trust in Data Science Decision Outcomes. *Administrative Sciences, 10*(4), 81–99. doi:10.3390/admsci10040081

Broxton, T., Interian, Y., Vaver, J., & Wattenhofer, M. (2011). Catching a viral video. *Journal of Intelligent Information Systems*, *40*(2), 241–259. doi:10.100710844-011-0191-2

Bulakh, V., & Gupta, M. (2016, March). Countering phishing from brands' vantage point. In *Proceedings of the 2016 ACM on International Workshop on Security And Privacy Analytics* (pp. 17-24). DOI:10.1145/2875475.2875478

Bumblauskas, D., Gemmill, D., Igou, A., & Anzengruber, J. (2017). Smart maintenance decision support Systems (SMDSS) based on corporate big data analytics. *Expert Systems with Applications*, *90*, 303–317. doi:10.1016/j.eswa.2017.08.025

Busetto, L., Wick, W., & Gumbinger, C. (2020). How to use and assess qualitative research methods. Neurological Research and Practice, 2.

Bustos López, M., Alor-Hernández, G., Sánchez-Cervantes, J. L., Paredes-Valverde, M. A., & Salas-Zárate, M. P. (2020). EduRecomSys: An Educational Resource Recommender system based on collaborative filtering and emotion detection. *Interacting with Computers*, *32*(4), 407–432. doi:10.1093/iwc/iwab001

Buzan, B., & Hansen, L. (2018). *Defining–redefining security*. Oxford Research Encyclopedia of International Studies. doi:10.1093/acrefore/9780190846626.013.382

Calzavara, S., Conti, M., Focardi, R., Rabitti, A., & Tolomei, G. (2019). Mitch: A machine learning approach to the black-box detection of CSRF vulnerabilities. In *2019 IEEE European Symposium on Security and Privacy (EuroS&P)* (pp. 528-543). IEEE.

Chatterjee, S., Chaudhuri, R., & Vrontis, D. (2021). Does data-driven culture impact innovation and performance of a firm? An empirical examination. *Annals of Operations Research*, *302*(1). Advance online publication. doi:10.100710479-020-03887-z

Chaudhry, J. A., Chaudhry, S. A., & Rittenhouse, R. G. (2016). Phishing attacks and defenses. *International Journal of Security and Its Applications*, *10*(1), 247–256. doi:10.14257/ijsia.2016.10.1.23

Chawan, P., & Pamnani, R. (2010). *Web usage mining: A research area in Web mining. Department of computer technology*. VJTI University.

Chen, K. T., Chen, J. Y., Huang, C. R., & Chen, C. S. (2009). Fighting phishing with discriminative keypoint features. *IEEE Internet Computing*, *13*(3), 56–63. doi:10.1109/MIC.2009.59

Chen, Y., Wang, J., Xia, R., Zhang, Q., Cao, Z., & Yang, K. (2021). Retraction note to: The visual object tracking algorithm research based on adaptive combination kernel. *Journal of Ambient Intelligence and Humanized Computing*. Advance online publication. doi:10.100712652-021-03500-6

Chen, Y., Zhou, M., & Zheng, Z. (2019). Learning sequence-based fingerprint for magnetic indoor positioning system. *IEEE Access: Practical Innovations, Open Solutions*, *7*, 163231–163244. doi:10.1109/ACCESS.2019.2952564

Chhabra, H., Mohan, V., Rani, A., & Singh, V. (2020). Robust nonlinear fractional order fuzzy PD plus fuzzy I controller applied to robotic manipulator. Neural Computing and Applications, 32(7), 2055-2079. doi:10.100700521-019-04074-3

Chhabra, H., Mohan, V., Rani, A., & Singh, V. (2016). *Multi objective PSO tuned fractional order PID control of robotic manipulator. In The international symposium on intelligent systems technologies and applications.* Springer.

Chhabra, H., Mohan, V., Rani, A., & Singh, V. (2019). Trajectory tracking of Maryland manipulator using linguistic Lyapunov fuzzy controller. *Journal of Intelligent & Fuzzy Systems, 36*(3), 2195–2205. doi:10.3233/JIFS-169931

Chiew, K. L., Tan, C. L., Wong, K., Yong, K. S., & Tiong, W. K. (2019). A new hybrid ensemble feature selection framework for machine learning-based phishing detection system. *Information Sciences, 484,* 153–166. doi:10.1016/j.ins.2019.01.064

Chiew, K. L., Yong, K. S. C., & Tan, C. L. (2018). A survey of phishing attacks: Their types, vectors and technical approaches. *Expert Systems with Applications, 106,* 1–20. doi:10.1016/J.ESWA.2018.03.050

Chitrakala, S., Moratanch, B., & Ramya, C. G. (2018). Concept-based extractive text summarization using graph modelling and weighted iterative ranking. *Emerging research in computing, information, communication and applications, 2016,* 149–160.

Choi, H. S., Carpenter, D., & Ko, M. S. (2021). Risk Taking Behaviors Using Public Wi-Fi™. *Information Systems Frontiers,* 1–18. doi:10.100710796-021-10119-7

Chouhan, V., & Peddoju, S. K. (2013). Packet monitoring approach to prevent DDoS attack in cloud computing. *Int. J. Comput. Sci. Electr. Eng., 1*(2), 2315–4209.

Clayman, C. L., Srinivasan, S. M., & Sangwan, R. S. (2020, January). K-means Clustering and Principal Components Analysis of Microarray Data of L1000 Landmark Genes. *Procedia Computer Science, 168,* 97–104. doi:10.1016/j.procs.2020.02.265

Collins, R. T., Lipton, A. J., Fujiyoshi, H., & Kanade, T. (2001). Algorithms for cooperative multisensor surveillance. *Proceedings of the IEEE, 89*(10), 1456–1477. doi:10.1109/5.959341

Constantin, L. (2016). *Thousands of hacked CCTV devices used in DDoS attacks.* Computerworld. Retrieved 3 November 2021, from https://www.computerworld.com/article/3089365/thousands-of-hacked-cctv-devices-used-in-ddos-attacks.html

Cowan, C., Barringer, M., Beattie, S., Kroah-Hartman, G., Frantzen, M., & Lokier, J. (2001). FormatGuard: Automatic Protection From printf Format String Vulnerabilities. In *USENIX Security Symposium (Vol. 91).* Academic Press.

Cui, Y., Cui, J., & Hu, J. (2020). A survey on xss attack detection and prevention in web applications. In *Proceedings of the 2020 12th International Conference on Machine Learning and Computing* (pp. 443-449). Academic Press.

Cybulski, J., & Scheepers, R. (2021). Data science in organizations: Conceptualizing its breakthroughs and blind spots. *Journal of Information Technology*, *36*(2), 154–175. doi:10.1177/0268396220988539

Cyril, G., & Eric, G. (2005). A probabilistic interpretation of precision, recall and F-score, with implication for evaluation. In *European conference on information retrieval*. Springer.

Dabba, A., Tari, A., Meftali, S., & Mokhtari, R. (2021, March). Gene selection and classification of microarray data method based on mutual information and moth flame algorithm. *Expert Systems with Applications*, *166*, 114012. doi:10.1016/j.eswa.2020.114012

Dacosta, I., Chakradeo, S., Ahamad, M., & Traynor, P. (2012). One-time cookies: Preventing session hijacking attacks with stateless authentication tokens. *ACM Transactions on Internet Technology*, *12*(1), 1–24.

Dalvand, Dalvand, Sharafi, & Pecht. (2017). Current noise cancellation for bearing fault diagnosis using time-shifting. *IEEE Trans. Ind. Electron.*, *64*. doi:10.1109/TIE.2017.2694397

Dalvand, F., Kang, M., Dalvand, S., & Pecht, M. (2018, December). Detection of Generalized-Roughness and Single-Point Bearing Faults Using Linear Prediction-Based Current Noise Cancellation. *IEEE Transactions on Industrial Electronics*, *65*(12), 9728–9738. doi:10.1109/TIE.2018.2821645

Daoud, M., & Mayo, M. (2019, June). A survey of neural network-based cancer prediction models from microarray data. *Artificial Intelligence in Medicine*, *97*, 204–214. doi:10.1016/j.artmed.2019.01.006 PMID:30797633

Dar, M. U. J., Shah, J. L., & Khanday, G. I. A. (2019). Web abuse using cross site scripting (XSS) attacks. *Journal of Artificial Intelligence Research & Advances*, *6*(1), 69–75.

Daradkeh, M. (2019a). Critical Success Factors of Enterprise Data Analytics and Visualization Ecosystem: An Interview Study. *International Journal of Information Technology Project Management*, *10*(3), 34–55. doi:10.4018/IJITPM.2019070103

Daradkeh, M. (2019b). Determinants of Self-Service Analytics Adoption Intention: The Effect of Task-Technology Fit, Compatibility, and User Empowerment. *Journal of Organizational and End User Computing*, *31*(4), 19–45. doi:10.4018/JOEUC.2019100102

Daradkeh, M. (2019c). Determinants of visual analytics adoption in organizations: Knowledge discovery through content analysis of online evaluation reviews. *Information Technology & People*, *32*(3), 668–695. doi:10.1108/ITP-10-2017-0359

Daradkeh, M. (2019d). Understanding the Factors Affecting the Adoption of Project Portfolio Management Software Through Topic Modeling of Online Software Reviews. *International Journal of Information Technology Project Management*, *10*(3), 91–114. doi:10.4018/IJITPM.2019070106

Daradkeh, M. (2021a). Exploring the Usefulness of User-Generated Content for Business Intelligence in Innovation: Empirical Evidence From an Online Open Innovation Community. *International Journal of Enterprise Information Systems*, *17*(2), 44–70. doi:10.4018/IJEIS.2021040103

Daradkeh, M. (2021b). The Influence of Sentiment Orientation in Open Innovation Communities: Empirical Evidence from a Business Analytics Community. *Journal of Information & Knowledge Management, 20*(3), 2150029. doi:10.1142/S0219649221500313

Daradkeh, M. (2022). Organizational Adoption of Sentiment Analytics in Social Media Networks: Insights from a Systematic Literature Review. *International Journal of Information Technologies and Systems Approach, 15*(1), 15–45.

Daradkeh, M., & Sabbahein, H. (2019). Factors Influencing the Adoption of Mobile Application Development Platforms: A Qualitative Content Analysis of Developers' Online Reviews. *International Journal of Enterprise Information Systems, 15*(4), 43–59. doi:10.4018/IJEIS.2019100103

Davande, V. M., Dhanawade, P. C., & Sutar, V. B. (2016). Real Time Temperature Monitoring Using LABVIEW and Arduino. *International Journal of Innovative Research in Computer and Communication Engineering, 4*(3), 3409–3415.

Davies, S. R., Macfarlane, R., & Buchanan, W. J. (2020). Evaluation of live forensic techniques in ransomware attack mitigation. *Forensic Science International: Digital Investigation, 33*, 300979.

de Carvalho, J. A., Veiga, H., Pacheco, C. F., & Reis, A. D. (2020). Extended Performance Research on IEEE 802.11 a WPA multi-node laboratory links. *Transactions on Engineering Technologies*, 175–186. . doi:10.1007/978-981-15-8273-8_14

Dede, D. (2011). *MySQL.com compromised*. Sucuri Blog. Retrieved 3 November 2021, from https://blog.sucuri.net/2011/03/mysql-com-compromised.html

Deekshit Kompella, K. C. (2020). Estimation of Premature Bearing Faults in a Three Phase Induction Motor Using S-Transform. *Journal of Green Engineering, 10*(4), 1878–1896.

Deekshit Kompella, K. C., Gopala Rao, M. V., Rao, R. S., & Sreenivasu, R. N. (2014). Estimation of bearing faults in induction motor by MCSA using Daubechies wavelet analysis. *2014 International Conference on Smart Electric Grid (ISEG)*, 1-6. 10.1109/ISEG.2014.7005577

Deekshit Kompella, K. C., & Madhav, G. V. (2020). An Improved Matrix Pencil Method based Bearing Fault detection in Three Phase Induction Motor. *2020 IEEE International Conference on Computing, Power and Communication Technologies*, 51-56. 10.1109/GUCON48875.2020.9231196

Delone, W., & McLean, E. (2003). The DeLone and McLean Model of Information Systems Success: A Ten-Year Update. *Journal of Management Information Systems, 19*(4), 9–30. doi:10.1080/07421222.2003.11045748

Detection and classification of induction motor faults using Motor Current Signature Analysis and Multilayer Perceptron. (2014). *IEEE 8th International Power Engineering and Optimization Conference (PEOCO2014)*, 35-40.

Devdas, G., Dhanaji, B., Vaibhav, M., Saurabh, H., & Pravin, P. (2017). Home Automation System using Android Application. *Trends in Electrical Engineering, 7*(1), 19–24.

Dey, S. K., & Howlader, A. (2021). A Multi-phase Face Mask Detection Model to Prevent Person-To-Person Transmission of SARS-CoV-2. In *Proceedings of International Conference on Trends in Computational and Cognitive Engineering* (pp. 603-613). Springer. 10.1007/978-981-33-4673-4_49

Dhar, V. (2013). Data science and prediction. *Communications of the ACM, 56*(12), 64–73. doi:10.1145/2500499

Dolnák & Ivan. (2017). Content security policy (csp) as countermeasure to cross site scripting (xss) attacks. In *2017 15th International Conference on Emerging eLearning Technologies and Applications (ICETA)* (pp. 1-4). IEEE.

Domb, M. (2019). *Smart Home Systems based on Internet of Things*. IoT and Smart Home Automation. doi:10.5772/intechopen.84894

Donoho, D. (2017). 50 Years of Data Science. *Journal of Computational and Graphical Statistics, 26*(4), 745–766. doi:10.1080/10618600.2017.1384734

Dupuis, M., Geiger, T., Slayton, M., & Dewing, F. (2019, September). The Use and Non-Use of Cybersecurity Tools Among Consumers: Do They Want Help? In *Proceedings of the 20th Annual SIG Conference on Information Technology Education* (pp. 81-86). DOI: 10.1145/3349266.3351419

Durmus, Gunes, & Kırcı. (2017). Disease detection on the leaves of the tomato plants by using deep learning. *Agro-Geoinformatics, IEEE 6th International Conference on*, 1-5.

Dutta, S., Chandra, V., Mehra, K., Ghatak, S., Das, S., & Ghosh, S. (2019). *Summarizing microblogs during emergency events: A comparison of extractive summarization algorithms*. Paper presented at the International Conference on Emerging Technologies.

Dwyer, P., & Duan, Z. (2010, July). MDMap: Assisting users in identifying phishing emails. In *Proceedings of 7th Annual Collaboration, Electronic Messaging, Anti-Abuse and Spam Conference (CEAS)* (pp. 1-4). 10.1.1.1/67.3988

Echtioui, A., Zouch, W., Ghorbel, M., Mhiri, C., & Hamam, H. (2020). Detection Methods of COVID-19. *SLAS Technology, 25*(6), 566–572. doi:10.1177/2472630320962002 PMID:32997560

Eian, I. C., Yong, L. K., Li, M. Y. X., Qi, Y. H., & Fatima, Z. (2020). *Cyber attacks in the era of covid-19 and possible solution domains*. Academic Press.

Eidenmuller, M. E. (2001-2021). Rhetorical Literacy: 49 Important Speeches in 21st Century America. *American Rhetoric*. https://www.americanrhetoric.com/21stcenturyspeeches.html

Eisenhower Presidential Library. (2021). *Speeches*. Dwight D. Eisenhower Presidential Library, Museum & Boyhood Home. https://www.eisenhowerlibrary.gov/eisenhowers/speeches

Emrouznejad, A., & Marra, M. (2016). Big data: Who, what and where? Social, cognitive and journals map of big data publications with focus on optimization. *Studies in Big Data*, 1–16. doi:10.1007/978-3-319-30265-2_1

Ergado, A., Desta, A., & Mehta, H. (2021). Determining the barriers contributing to ICT implementation by using technology-organization-environment framework in Ethiopian higher educational institutions. *Education and Information Technologies*, *26*(3), 3115–3133. doi:10.100710639-020-10397-9

Eswar. (n.d.). *Microcontroller Manipulated As Human Interface Device Performing Keystroke Injection Attack*. Academic Press.

Fang, Y., Tang, K., Li, C., & Wu, C. (2018). On electronic word-of-mouth diffusion in social networks: Curiosity and influence. *International Journal of Advertising*, *37*(3), 360–384. doi:10.1080/02650487.2016.1256014

Feinerer, I., & Hornik, K. (2020). *tm: Text Mining Package*. R package version 0.7-8. https://CRAN.R-project.org/package=tm

Feinerer, I., Hornik, K., & Meyer, D. (2008). Text Mining Infrastructure in R. *Journal of Statistical Software*, *25*(5), 1–54. doi:10.18637/jss.v025.i05

Feldman, R., & Sanger, J. (2007). The text mining handbook. Cambridge University Press.

Fouda, M. A., Hassan, M. I., Hammad, K. M., & Hasaballah, A. I. (2013). Effects of midgut bacteria and two protease inhibitors on the reproductive potential and midgut enzymes of Culex pipiens infected with Wuchereria bancrofti. *Journal of the Egyptian Society of Parasitology*, *43*(2), 537–546. doi:10.21608/jesp.2013.94836 PMID:24260832

Fredj, O. B., Cheikhrouhou, O., Krichen, M., Hamam, H., & Derhab, A. (2020). An OWASP top ten driven survey on web application protection methods. In *International Conference on Risks and Security of Internet and Systems* (pp. 235-252). Springer.

Frosini, L., & Bassi, E. (2010, January). Stator current and motor efficiency as indicators for different types of bearing faults in induction motors. *IEEE Transactions on Industrial Electronics*, *57*(1), 244–251. doi:10.1109/TIE.2009.2026770

Fu, A. Y., Deng, X., & Wenyin, L. (2006). REGAP: A tool for unicode-based web identity fraud detection. *Journal of Digital Forensic Practice*, *1*(2), 83–97. doi:10.1080/15567280600995501

Fu, A. Y., Wenyin, L., & Deng, X. (2006). Detecting phishing web pages with visual similarity assessment based on earth mover's distance (EMD). *IEEE Transactions on Dependable and Secure Computing*, *3*(4), 301–311. doi:10.1109/TDSC.2006.50

Gambhir, M., & Gupta, V. (2017). "Recent automatic text summarization techniques," *A survey*. *Artificial Intelligence Review*, 1–66.

Garcia-Perez, A., de Jesus Romero-Troncoso, R., Cabal-Yepez, E., & Osornio-Rios, R. (2011, May). The application of high-resolution spectral analysis for identifying multiple combined faults in induction motors. *IEEE Transactions on Industrial Electronics*, *58*(5), 2002–2010. doi:10.1109/TIE.2010.2051398

Gartner. (2021). *2021 Magic Quadrant for Data Science and Machine Learning Platforms.* Retrieved from https://www.gartner.com/reviews/market/data-science-machine-learning-platforms

Gatlan, S. (2020). *Freepik data breach: Hackers stole 8.3M records via SQL injection.* BleepingComputer. Retrieved 3 November 2021, from https://www.bleepingcomputer.com/news/security/freepik-data-breach-hackers-stole-83m-records-via-sql-injection

Gautam, T., & Jain, A. (2015). Analysis of brute force attack using TG—Dataset. In *2015 SAI Intelligent Systems Conference (IntelliSys)* (pp. 984-988). IEEE.

Gavhale, K. R., & Gawande, U. (2014). An Overview of the Research on Plant Leaves Disease detection using Image Processing Techniques. *IOSR Journal of Computer Engineering, 16*(1), 10–16. doi:10.9790/0661-16151016

Gelbord, B., & Roelofsen, G. (2002). New surveillance techniques raise privacy concerns. *Communications of the ACM, 45*(11), 23–24. doi:10.1145/581571.581586

Georis, B. (2003). Ip-distributed computer-aided video-surveillance system. *IEE Symposium Intelligent Distributed Surveillance Systems.* 10.1049/ic:20030044

Ghai, D., Gianey, H. K., Jain, A., & Uppal, R. S. (2020). Quantum and dual-tree complex wavelet transform-based image watermarking. *International Journal of Modern Physics B, 34*(04), 2050009. doi:10.1142/S0217979220500095

Ghaleb, E., Dominic, P., Fati, S., Muneer, A., & Ali, R. (2021). The Assessment of Big Data Adoption Readiness with a Technology–Organization–Environment Framework: A Perspective towards Healthcare Employees. *Sustainability, 13*(15), 8379.

Ghayvat, H., Awais, M., Gope, P., Pandya, S., & Majumdar, S. (2021). Recognizing suspect and predicting the spread of contagion based on mobile phone location data: A system of identifying COVID-19 infectious and hazardous sites, detecting disease outbreaks based on the internet of things, edge computing, and artificial intelligence. *Sustainable Cities and Society, 69*, 102798. doi:10.1016/j.scs.2021.102798

Ghayvat, H., Awais, M., Pandya, S., Ren, H., Akbarzadeh, S., Chandra Mukhopadhyay, S., Chen, C., Gope, P., Chouhan, A., & Chen, W. (2019, February 13). Smart Aging System: Uncovering the Hidden Wellness Parameter for Well-Being Monitoring and Anomaly Detection. *Sensors (Basel), 19*(4), 766. doi:10.339019040766 PMID:30781852

Ghayvat, H., Pandya, S., Bhattacharya, P., Mohammad, Z., Mamoon, R., Saqib, H., & Kapal, D. (2021). CP-BDHCA: Blockchain-based Confidentiality-Privacy preserving Big Data scheme for healthcare clouds and applications. *IEEE Journal of Biomedical and Health Informatics, 25*, 1–22. doi:10.1109/JBHI.2021.3097237 PMID:34260362

Ghosh, M. (2016). Case study: Text-mining customers view point and perceived value about brand. *International Journal of Business Analytics and Intelligence, 4*(1). Advance online publication. doi:10.21863/ijbai/2016.4.1.016

Giannakeas, N., Karvelis, P. S., Exarchos, T. P., Kalatzis, F. G., & Fotiadis, D. I. (2013, July). Segmentation of microarray images using pixel classification—Comparison with clustering-based methods. *Computers in Biology and Medicine*, *43*(6), 705–716. doi:10.1016/j.compbiomed.2013.03.003 PMID:23668346

Gill, S. S., & Buyya, R. (2019). A taxonomy and future directions for sustainable cloud computing. *ACM Computing Surveys*, *51*(5), 1–33. doi:10.1145/3241038

Goel, D., & Jain, A. K. (2018). Mobile phishing attacks and defence mechanisms: State of art and open research challenges. *Computers & Security*, *73*, 519–544. doi:10.1016/j.cose.2017.12.006

Gonzalez, E., Stephen, B., Infield, D., & Melero, J. J. (2019). Using high-frequency SCADA data for wind turbine performance monitoring: A sensitivity study. *Renewable Energy*, *131*, 841–853. doi:10.1016/j.renene.2018.07.068

Gonzalez, M., Seren, H. R., Ham, G., Buzi, E., Bernero, G., & Deffenbaugh, M. (2018). Viscosity and density measurements using mechanical oscillators in oil and gas applications. *IEEE Transactions on Instrumentation and Measurement*, *67*(4), 804–810. doi:10.1109/TIM.2017.2761218

Google. (n.d.). https://drive.google.com/drive/folders/1IPwsC30wNAc74_GTXuEWX_F8m2n-ZBCH

Goralski, W. (2017). TCP/IP protocols and devices. *The Illustrated Network*, 47–69.. doi:10.1016/B978-0-12-811027-0.00002-3

Goswami, S., Hoque, N., Bhattacharyya, D. K., & Kalita, J. (2017). An Unsupervised Method for Detection of XSS Attack. *International Journal of Network Security*, *19*(5), 761–775.

Govindaraj, M., Rathinam, R., Sukumar, C., Uthayasankar, M., & Pattabhi, S. (2013). Electrochemical oxidation of bisphenol-A from aqueous solution using graphite electrodes. *Environmental Technology*, *34*(4), 503–511. doi:10.1080/09593330.2012.701333 PMID:23530365

Grandini, M., Bagli, E., & Visani, G. (2020). *Metrics for multi-class classification: An overview.* https://arxiv.org/abs/2008.05756

Griazev, K., & Ramanauskaitè, S. (2018). Web mining taxonomy. *2018 Open Conference of Electrical, Electronic and Information Sciences (eStream)*, 1-4. 10.1109/eStream.2018.8394124

Grisci, B. I., Feltes, B. C., & Dorn, M. (2019, January). Neuroevolution as a tool for microarray gene expression pattern identification in cancer research. *Journal of Biomedical Informatics*, *89*, 122–133. doi:10.1016/j.jbi.2018.11.013 PMID:30521855

Guo, Zhang, Yin, Hu, Zou, Xue, & Wang. (2020). *Plant Disease Identification Based on Deep Learning Algorithm*. Academic Press.

Guo, Y., Mohamed, I., Abou-Sayed, O., & Abou-Sayed, A. (2018). Cloud computing and web application-based remote real-time monitoring and data analysis: Slurry injection case study, onshore USA. *Journal of Petroleum Exploration and Production Technology*, *9*(2), 1225–1235. doi:10.100713202-018-0536-2

Gupta, C., Singh, R. K., & Mohapatra, A. K. (2020). A survey and classification of XML based attacks on web applications. *Information Security Journal: A Global Perspective, 29*(4), 183-198.

Gupta, V., Bansal, N., & Sharma, A. (2019). *Text summarization for big data: A comprehensive survey.* Paper presented at the International Conference on Innovative Computing and Communications, Singapore.

Gupta, A. K. (2021). Sun Irradiance Trappers for Solar PV Module to Operate on Maximum Power: An Experimental Study. *Turkish Journal of Computer and Mathematics Education, 12*(5), 1112–1121.

Gupta, A. K., Chauhan, Y. K., & Maity, T. (2018a). A new gamma scaling maximum power point tracking method for solar photovoltaic panel Feeding energy storage system. *Journal of the Institution of Electronics and Telecommunication Engineers, 67*(1), 1–21.

Gupta, A. K., Chauhan, Y. K., & Maity, T. (2018b). Experimental investigations and comparison of various MPPT techniques for photovoltaic system. *Sadhana, 43*(8), 1–15. doi:10.100712046-018-0815-0

Gupta, A. K., Chauhan, Y. K., Maity, T., & Nanda, R. (2020). Study of Solar PV Panel Under Partial Vacuum Conditions: A Step Towards Performance Improvement. *Journal of the Institution of Electronics and Telecommunication Engineers*, 1–8. doi:10.1080/03772063.2020.1749145

Gupta, A. K., Maity, T., Anandakumar, H., & Chauhan, Y. K. (2021). An electromagnetic strategy to improve the performance of PV panel under partial shading. *Computers & Electrical Engineering, 90*, 106896. doi:10.1016/j.compeleceng.2020.106896

Gupta, A. K., Pachauri, R. K., Maity, T., Chauhan, Y. K., Mahela, O. P., Khan, B., & Gupta, P. K. (2021). Effect of Various Incremental Conductance MPPT Methods on the Charging of Battery Load Feed by Solar Panel. *IEEE Access: Practical Innovations, Open Solutions, 9*, 90977–90988. doi:10.1109/ACCESS.2021.3091502

Gupta, B. B., Arachchilage, N. A., & Psannis, K. E. (2018). Defending against phishing attacks: Taxonomy of methods, current issues and future directions. *Telecommunication Systems, 67*(2), 247–267. doi:10.100711235-017-0334-z

Gupta, B. B., Tewari, A., Jain, A. K., & Agrawal, D. P. (2017). Fighting against phishing attacks: State of the art and future challenges. *Neural Computing & Applications, 28*(12), 3629–3654. doi:10.100700521-016-2275-y

Gupta, N., Jain, A., Vaisla, K. S., Kumar, A., & Kumar, R. (2021). Performance analysis of DSDV and OLSR wireless sensor network routing protocols using FPGA hardware and machine learning. *Multimedia Tools and Applications, 80*(14), 22301–22319. doi:10.100711042-021-10820-4

Gupta, N., Vaisla, K. S., Jain, A., Kumar, A., & Kumar, R. (2021). Performance Analysis of AODV Routing for Wireless Sensor Network in FPGA Hardware. *Computer Systems Science and Engineering, 39*(2), 1–12.

Gupta, S., & Gupta, S. K. (2019). Abstractive summarization: An overview of the state of the art. *Expert Systems with Applications*, 49–65.

Gupta, S., & Mathew, L. (2017). LabVIEW implementation of WSN for real time monitoring in Precision Agriculture. *International Journal of Computers and Applications*, *171*(4), 36–40. doi:10.5120/ijca2017915023

Gupta, V., & Lehal, G. S. (2010). A survey of text summarization extractive techniques. *Journal of Emerging Technologies in Web Intelligence*, 258–268.

Gutierrez, C. N., Kim, T., Della Corte, R., Avery, J., Goldwasser, D., Cinque, M., & Bagchi, S. (2018). Learning from the ones that got away: Detecting new forms of phishing attacks. *IEEE Transactions on Dependable and Secure Computing*, *15*(6), 988–1001.

Haider, S., Akhunzada, A., Mustafa, I., Patel, T. B., Fernandez, A., Choo, K. K. R., & Iqbal, J. (2020). A deep CNN ensemble framework for efficient DDoS attack detection in software defined networks. *IEEE Access: Practical Innovations, Open Solutions*, *8*, 53972–53983. doi:10.1109/ACCESS.2020.2976908

Hakim, Z. M., Ebner, N. C., Oliveira, D. S., Getz, S. J., Levin, B. E., Lin, T., ... Wilson, R. C. (2021). The Phishing Email Suspicion Test (PEST) a lab-based task for evaluating the cognitive mechanisms of phishing detection. *Behavior Research Methods*, *53*(3), 1342–1352.

Halbutogullari, A., & Koç, C. K. (2000). Mastrovito multiplier for general irreducible polynomials. *IEEE Transactions on Computers*, *49*(5), 503–518. doi:10.1109/12.859542

Halder, A., & Kumar, A. (2019, April). Active learning using rough fuzzy classifier for cancer prediction from microarray gene expression data. *Journal of Biomedical Informatics*, *92*, 103136. doi:10.1016/j.jbi.2019.103136 PMID:30802546

Halevi, T., Memon, N., & Nov, O. (2015). Spear-phishing in the wild: A real-world study of personality, phishing self-efficacy and vulnerability to spear-phishing attacks. *Phishing Self-Efficacy and Vulnerability to Spear-Phishing Attacks*.

Hambali, M. A., Oladele, T. O., & Adewole, K. S. (2020, June). Microarray cancer feature selection: Review, challenges and research directions. *International Journal of Cognitive Computing in Engineering*, *1*, 78–97. doi:10.1016/j.ijcce.2020.11.001

Hamilton, W. L., Leskovec, J., & Jurafsky, D. (2016). Diachronic Word Embeddings Reveal Statistical Laws of Semantic Change. *ACL 2016*. https://arxiv.org/pdf/1605.09096.pdf

Han, J., Kamber, M., & Pei, J. (2011). *Data mining: concepts and techniques*. Elsevier.

Han, X. H., Li, D. A., & Wang, L. (2019, January). A Hybrid Cancer Classification Model Based Recursive Binary Gravitational Search Algorithm in Microarray Data. *Procedia Computer Science*, *154*, 274–282. doi:10.1016/j.procs.2019.06.041

Haq, A., Gondal, I., & Murshed, M. (2010). Automated multi-sensor color video fusion for nighttime video surveillance. *The IEEE Symposium on Computers and Communications*. 10.1109/ISCC.2010.5546791

Haque, A. K. M., & Rahman, M. (2020). *Blockchain Technology: Methodology, Application and Security Issues*. arXiv preprint arXiv:2012.13366.

Haque, A. B., Bhushan, B., & Dhiman, G. (2021a). Conceptualizing smart city applications: Requirements, architecture, security issues, and emerging trends. *Expert Systems: International Journal of Knowledge Engineering and Neural Networks*. doi:10.1111/exsy.12753

Haque, A. B., Islam, A. N., Hyrynsalmi, S., Naqvi, B., & Smolander, K. (2021b). GDPR compliant Blockchains–A systematic literature review. *IEEE Access: Practical Innovations, Open Solutions*.

Haque, A. K. M. (2019). *Need for Critical Cyber Defence, Security Strategy and Privacy Policy in Bangladesh–Hype or Reality? International Journal of Managing Information Technology*, 11.

Harrell, F. E. (2021). *Hmisc: Harrell Miscellaneous. R package version 4.5-0*. https://CRAN.R-project.org/package=Hmisc

Hasaballah, A. I. (2015). Toxicity of some plant extracts against vector of lymphatic filariasis, Culex pipiens. *Journal of the Egyptian Society of Parasitology, 45*(1), 183–192. PMID:26012233

Hasaballah, A. I. (2018). Impact of gamma irradiation on the development and reproduction of Culex pipiens (Diptera; Culicidae). *International Journal of Radiation Biology, 94*(9), 844–849. doi:10.1080/09553002.2018.1490040 PMID:29913104

Hasaballah, A. I. (2021). Impact of paternal transmission of gamma radiation on reproduction, oogenesis, and spermatogenesis of the housefly, Musca domestica L. (Diptera: Muscidae). *International Journal of Radiation Biology, 97*(3), 376–385. doi:10.1080/09553002.2021.186 4046 PMID:33320767

Hassan, M. M. (2018). Bayesian Sensitivity Analysis to Quantifying Uncertainty in a Dendroclimatology Model. *ICOASE 2018 -International Conference on Advanced Science and Engineering*, 363–368. 10.1109/ICOASE.2018.8548877

Hassan, M. I., Fouda, M. A., Hammad, K. M., & Hasaballah, A. I. (2013). Effects of midgut bacteria and two protease inhibitors on the transmission of Wuchereria bancrofti by the mosquito vector, Culex pipiens. *Journal of the Egyptian Society of Parasitology, 43*(2), 547–553. PMID:24260833

Hassan, M. M. (2020). A Fully Bayesian Logistic Regression Model for Classification of ZADA Diabetes Dataset. *Science Journal of University of Zakho, 8*(3), 105–111. doi:10.25271juoz.2020.8.3.707

Hassan, M. M., Bhuyian, T., Sohel, M. K., Sharif, M. H., & Biswas, S. (2018). SAISAN: An automated Local File Inclusion vulnerability detection model. *IACSIT International Journal of Engineering and Technology, 7*(2-3), 4.

Hassan, M. M., Eesa, A. S., Mohammed, A. J., & Arabo, W. K. (2021). Oversampling Method Based on Gaussian Distribution and K-Means Clustering. Computers. *Materials and Continua*, *69*(1), 451–469. doi:10.32604/cmc.2021.018280

Hassan, M. M., Hussein, H. I., Eesa, A. S., & Mstafa, R. J. (2021). Face Recognition Based on Gabor Feature Extraction Followed by FastICA and LDA. Computers. *Materials and Continua*, *68*(2), 1637–1659. doi:10.32604/cmc.2021.016467

Hassan, M. M., Mustain, U., Khatun, S., Karim, M. S. A., Nishat, N., & Rahman, M. (2020). Quantitative Assessment of Remote Code Execution Vulnerability in Web Apps. In *InECCE2019* (pp. 633–642). Springer.

Hausken, K. (2018). A cost–benefit analysis of terrorist attacks. *Defence and Peace Economics*, *29*(2), 111–129. doi:10.1080/10242694.2016.1158440

Heartfield, R., & Loukas, G. (2015). A Taxonomy of Attacks and a Survey of Defense Mechanisms for Semantic Social Engineering Attacks. *ACM Computing Surveys*. Advance online publication. doi:10.1145/2835375

Henao, Rastegar, Capolino, & Sieg-Zieba. (2011). Wire rope fault detection in a hoisting winch system by motor torque and current signature analysis. *IEEE Trans. on Ind. Electr., 58*(5), 1727–1736.

Hmida, M. A., & Braham, A. (2020, October). Fault Detection of VFD-Fed Induction Motor Under Transient Conditions Using Harmonic Wavelet Transform. *IEEE Transactions on Instrumentation and Measurement*, *69*(10), 8207–8215. doi:10.1109/TIM.2020.2993107

Hong, J. (2012). The state of phishing attacks. *Communications of the ACM, 55*(1), 74–81. doi:10.1145/2063176.2063197

Hong, Y. (2018). *Spelling Normalization of English Student Writings* [Unpublished Master's Thesis]. Uppsala University. http://uu.divaportal.org/smash/get/diva2:1251763/FULLTEXT01.pdf

Hoque, N., Bhuyan, M. H., Baishya, R. C., Bhattacharyya, D. K., & Kalita, J. K. (2014). Network attacks: Taxonomy, tools and systems. *Journal of Network and Computer Applications, 40*, 307–324.

Hou, L., Hou, P., & Bei, C. (2017). *Abstractive document summarization via neural model with joint attention*. Paper presented at the Natural Language Processing and Chinese Computing, Dalian, China.

Howard, C., & Rayward-Smith, V. (1999, January 1). Discovering knowledge from low-quality meteorological databases. *Data Mining and Knowledge Discovery*, 180–203. doi:10.1049/PBPC001E_ch9

Hsieh, W.-B., & Leu, J.-S. (2017). Implementing secure VoIP communication over SIP-based networks. *Wireless Networks*, *24*(8), 2915–2926. doi:10.100711276-017-1512-3

Hsu, C. H., Wang, P., & Pu, S. (2011, September). Identify fixed-path phishing attack by STC. In *Proceedings of the 8th Annual Collaboration, Electronic Messaging, Anti-Abuse and Spam Conference* (pp. 172-175). DOI: 10.1145/2030376.2030396

Hubczyk, M., Domanski, A., & Domanska, J. (2012). Local and remote file inclusion. In *Internet-Technical Developments and Applications 2* (pp. 189–200). Springer.

Huluka, D., & Popov, O. (2012). Root cause analysis of session management and broken authentication vulnerabilities. In *World Congress on Internet Security (WorldCIS-2012)* (pp. 82-86). IEEE.

I.O., A. (2018). An improved model for web usage mining and web traffic analysis. *Journal of Computer Science and Information Technology*, *6*(1). Advance online publication. doi:10.15640/jcsit.v6n1a5

Imai, Y., Hori, Y., & Masuda, S. (2008). Development and a brief evaluation of a web-based surveillance system for cellular phones and other mobile computing clients. *2008 Conference on Human System Interactions*. 10.1109/HSI.2008.4581494

Isravel, D. P., Silas, S., & Rajsingh, E. B. (2020). Reliable surveillance tracking system based on software defined internet of things. *The Cognitive Approach in Cloud Computing and Internet of Things Technologies for Surveillance Tracking Systems*, 1–16. . doi:10.1016/B978-0-12-816385-6.00001-5

Iwendi, C., Jalil, Z., Javed, A. R., Reddy, T., Kaluri, R., Srivastava, G., & Jo, O. (2020). Keysplitwatermark: Zero watermarking algorithm for software protection against cyber-attacks. *IEEE Access : Practical Innovations, Open Solutions*, *8*, 72650–72660. doi:10.1109/ACCESS.2020.2988160

Jain, A., Dwivedi, R. K., Alshazly, H., Kumar, A., Bourouis, S., & Kaur, M. (n.d.). *Design and Simulation of Ring Network-on-Chip for Different Configured Nodes*. Academic Press.

Jain, A. K., & Gupta, B. B. (2017). Phishing detection: Analysis of visual similarity based approaches. *Security and Communication Networks*, *2017*. Advance online publication. doi:10.1155/2017/5421046

Jain, A. K., & Gupta, B. B. (2019). A machine learning based approach for phishing detection using hyperlinks information. *Journal of Ambient Intelligence and Humanized Computing*, *10*(5), 2015–2028. doi:10.100712652-018-0798-z

Jain, A., Dwivedi, R., Kumar, A., & Sharma, S. (2017). Scalable design and synthesis of 3D mesh network on chip. In *Proceeding of International Conference on Intelligent Communication, Control and Devices* (pp. 661-666). Springer. 10.1007/978-981-10-1708-7_75

Jain, A., Gahlot, A. K., Dwivedi, R., Kumar, A., & Sharma, S. K. (2018). Fat Tree NoC Design and Synthesis. In *Intelligent Communication, Control and Devices* (pp. 1749–1756). Springer. doi:10.1007/978-981-10-5903-2_180

Jain, A., & Kumar, A. (2021). Desmogging of still smoggy images using a novel channel prior. *Journal of Ambient Intelligence and Humanized Computing*, *12*(1), 1161–1177. doi:10.100712652-020-02161-1

Jain, A., Kumar, A., & Sharma, S. (2015). Comparative Design and Analysis of Mesh, Torus and Ring NoC. *Procedia Computer Science*, *48*, 330–337. doi:10.1016/j.procs.2015.04.190

Jakobsson, M. (2018). Two-factor authentication–the rise in SMS phishing attacks. *Computer Fraud & Security*, *2018*(6), 6–8. doi:10.1016/S1361-3723(18)30052-6

James, L. (2005). *Phishing exposed*. Elsevier.

Jampen, D., Gür, G., Sutter, T., & Tellenbach, B. (2020). Don't click: Towards an effective anti-phishing training. A comparative literature review. *Human-centric Computing and Information Sciences*, *10*(1), 1–41. doi:10.118613673-020-00237-7

Jatowt, A., & Duh, K. (2014). A framework for analyzing semantic change of words across time. In *Proceedings of ACM/IEEE-CS Conference on Digital Libraries* (pp 229–238). IEEE Press. 10.1109/JCDL.2014.6970173

Javed, A. R., Usman, M., Rehman, S. U., Khan, M. U., & Haghighi, M. S. (2020). Anomaly detection in automated vehicles using multistage attention-based convolutional neural network. *IEEE Transactions on Intelligent Transportation Systems*. Advance online publication. doi:10.1109/tits.2020.3025875

Javier, A. (2017). *A History of WordPress Security Exploits and What They Mean*. WPMU DEV Blog. Retrieved 3 November 2021, from https://wpmudev.com/blog/wordpress-security-exploits/

Jayanthi, K., Rathinam, R., & Pattabhi, S. (2018). Electrocoagulation treatment for removal of Reactive Blue 19 from aqueous solution using Iron electrode. *Research Journal of Life Sciences, Bioinformatics, Pharmaceutical and Chemical Sciences*, *4*(2), 101–113.

Jeffers, R., & Lehiste, I. (1979). *Principles and Methods for Historical Linguistics*. MIT Press.

Jemal, I., Haddar, M. A., Cheikhrouhou, O., & Mahfoudhi, A. (2020). ASCII embedding: an efficient deep learning method for web attacks detection. In *Mediterranean Conference on Pattern Recognition and Artificial Intelligence* (pp. 286-297). Springer.

Jensen, M. L., Dinger, M., Wright, R. T., & Thatcher, J. B. (2017). Training to mitigate phishing attacks using mindfulness techniques. *Journal of Management Information Systems*, *34*(2), 597–626. doi:10.1080/07421222.2017.1334499

Jeong, H.-J., Shin, C. H., Shin, K. Y., & Lee, H.-J. (2019). Seamless offloading of web app computations from mobile device to edge clouds via HTML5 web worker migration. *Proceedings of the ACM Symposium on Cloud Computing*. 10.1145/3357223.3362735

Jesudoss, A., & Subramaniam, N. (2014). A survey on authentication attacks and countermeasures in a distributed environment. *Indian Journal of Computer Science and Engineering*, *5*(2), 71–77.

Jeurissen, L., Mennink, B. J. M., & Daemen, J. J. C. (2021). *E-mail phishing prevention proposal*. CEPP.

Jiang, Xue, & Guo. (n.d.). *Research on Plant Leaf Disease Identification Based on Transfer Learning Algorithm.* doi:10.1088/1742-6596/1576/1/012023

Jokar, N., Honarvar, A., Aghamirzadeh, S., & Esfandiari, K. (2016). Web mining and Web usage mining techniques. *Bulletin de la Société des Sciences de Liège, 85.*

Jouini, M., & Rabai, L. B. (2019). A security framework for secure cloud computing environments. *Cloud Security*, 249–263. doi:10.4018/978-1-5225-8176-5.ch011

Jovanovic, N., Kirda, E., & Kruegel, C. (2006). *Preventing cross site request forgery attacks. In 2006 Securecomm and Workshops.* IEEE.

Juan, Y.-F., & Chang, C.-C. (2005). An analysis of search engine switching behaviour using click streams. *Lecture Notes in Computer Science, 3828*, 806–815. doi:10.1007/11600930_82

Kadiravan, G. (2017). A state of art approaches on energy efficient routing protocols in mobile wireless sensor networks. *The IIOAB Journal, 8*(2), 234–238.

Kakti, A., Kumar, S., John, N. K., Ratna, V. V., Afzal, S., & Gupta, A. D. (2021). Impact of Patients Approach towards Healthcare Costs on their perception towards Health: An Empirical Study. Tobacco Regulatory Science, 7(6), 7380-7390.

Kamaleshwar, T., & Lakshminarayanan, R. (2021). A Self-Adaptive framework for Rectification and Detection of Blackhole and Wormhole attacks in 6LoWPAN. *Wireless Communications and Mobile Computing, 2021*, 1–8. doi:10.1155/2021/5143124

Kamimura, R. (2012). Social interaction and self-organizing maps. *Applications of Self-Organizing Maps.* doi:10.5772/51705

Kasemsap, K. (2017). Mastering web mining and information retrieval in the Digital age. *Advances in Data Mining and Database Management*, 1–28. doi:10.4018/978-1-5225-0613-3.ch001

Kaur, S., & Mamoon Rashid, E. (2016). Web news mining using back propagation neural network and clustering using K-means algorithm in Big Data. *Indian Journal of Science and Technology, 9*(41). Advance online publication. doi:10.17485/ijst/2016/v9i41/95598

Kawamura, T., Mutoh, H., Tomita, Y., Kato, R., & Honda, H. (2008, November). Cancer DNA Microarray Analysis Considering Multi-subclass with Graph-based Clustering Method. *Journal of Bioscience and Bioengineering, 106*(5), 442–448. doi:10.1263/jbb.106.442 PMID:19111639

Khan, H., Khan, M., Khurram, M., Inayatullah, S., & Athar, S. (2019). *Data Preprocessing: A preliminary step for web data mining.* doi:10.17993/3ctecno.2019.specialissue2.206-221

Khari, M., & Sangwan, P. (2016). Web-application attacks: A survey. In *2016 3rd International Conference on Computing for Sustainable Global Development (INDIACom)* (pp. 2187-2191). IEEE.

Khonji, M., Iraqi, Y., & Jones, A. (2013). Phishing detection: A literature survey. *IEEE Communications Surveys and Tutorials, 15*(4), 2091–2121. doi:10.1109/SURV.2013.032213.00009

Kia, Henao, & Capolino. (2005). Zoom-MUSIC frequency estimation method for three-phase induction machine fault detection. *31st Annual Conference of IEEE Industrial Electronics Society*. . doi:10.1109/IECON.2005.1569317

Kilicarslan, S., Adem, K., & Celik, M. (2020, April). Diagnosis and classification of cancer using hybrid model based on ReliefF and convolutional neural network. *Medical Hypotheses*, *137*, 109577. doi:10.1016/j.mehy.2020.109577 PMID:31991364

Kilic, F., Kittel, T., & Eckert, C. (2014). Blind format string attacks. In *International Conference on Security and Privacy in Communication Networks* (pp. 301-314). Springer.

Kim, J. H., Go, J. Y., & Lee, K. H. (2015). A Scheme of Social Engineering Attacks and Countermeasures Using Big Data-based Conversion Voice Phishing. *Journal of the Korea Convergence Society*, *6*(1), 85–91. doi:10.15207/JKCS.2015.6.1.085

Kim, Lee, Lee, Ni, Song, & Lee. (2007). A comparative study on damage detection in speed-up and coast-down process of grinding spindle-typed rotor-bearing system. *J. Materials Technology*, *187*, 30–36.

Kirda, E., Kruegel, C., Vigna, G., & Jovanovic, N. (2006). Noxes: a client-side solution for mitigating cross-site scripting attacks. In *Proceedings of the 2006 ACM symposium on Applied computing* (pp. 330-337). ACM.

Kirmani, M., Manzoo, H., & Mohd, M. (2019). *Hybrid text summarization: A survey.* Paper presented at the Soft Computing: Theories and Applications, Singapore.

Kitsos, P., Theodoridis, G., & Koufopavlou, O. (2003). An efficient reconfigurable multiplier architecture for Galois field GF (2m). *Microelectronics Journal*, *34*(10), 975–980. doi:10.1016/S0026-2692(03)00172-1

Knickerbocker, J. L., & Rycik, J. A. (2019). Changing literature, changing readers, changing classrooms. *Literature for Young Adults*, 1–29. doi:10.4324/9781351067683-1

Kodali, R. K., & Mahesh, K. S. (2016). A low cost implementation of MQTT using ESP8266. *2016 2nd International Conference on Contemporary Computing and Informatics (IC3I)*, 404-408. 10.1109/IC3I.2016.7917998

Kolley, S. (2021). *Phishing attacks: Detection and prevention* (Doctoral dissertation). University of Bradford.

Kompella & Madhav. (n.d.). Performance Analysis of Wiener Filter with different window functions in detecting Broken Rotor fault in 3 Phase Induction Motor *International Journal of Engineering Trends and Technology*, *68*(12), 153-159.

Kompella, Rao, & Rao. (2017). SWT based bearing fault detection using frequency spectral subtraction of stator current with and without an adaptive filter. *TENCON 2017 - 2017 IEEE Region 10 Conference*, 2472-2477. . doi:10.1109/TENCON.2017.8228277

Kompella, K. C. (2021). Robustification of Fault Detection Algorithm in a 3 Phase Induction Motor using MCSA for various Single and Multiple Faults. *IET Electric Power Applications.* Advance online publication. doi:10.1049/elp2.12049

Kompella, K. D., Rao, M. V. G., & Rao, R. S. (2018). Bearing fault detection in a 3 phase induction motor using stator current frequency spectral subtraction with various wavelet decomposition techniques. *Ain Shams Engineering Journal, 9*(4), 2427–2439. doi:10.1016/j.asej.2017.06.002

Kompella, Rayapudi, & Rongala. (2020). Investigation of Bearing faults in three phase Induction motor using Wavelet De-Noising with improved Wiener Filtering. *International Journal of Power and Energy Conversion.*

Kosala, R., & Blockeel, H. (2000). Web mining research: A survey. *SIGKDD Explorations, 2*(1), 1–15. doi:10.1145/360402.360406

Krippendorff, K. (2012). *Content analysis: An introduction to its methodology.* Sage.

Krishnakumari, K., & Sivasankar, E. (2018). Scalable aspect-based summarization in the hadoop environment. In V. B. Aggarwal, V. Bhatnagar & D. K. Mishra (Eds.), *Big data analytics: Proceedings of CSI 2015.* Academic Press.

Kshirsagar, P., Pote, A., Paliwal, K., Hendre, V., Chippalkatti, P., & Dhabekar, N. (2020). *A Review on IOT Based Health Care Monitoring System.* . doi:10.1007/978-981-13-8715-9_12

Kubiczek, J., & Hadasik, B. (2021, December). Challenges in Reporting the COVID-19 Spread and its Presentation to the Society. *J. Data and Information Quality, 13*(4), 1–7. doi:10.1145/3470851

Kulkarni, V., Al-Rfou, R., Perozzi, B., & Skiena, S. (2014). Statistically significant detection of linguistic change. *Proceedings of International World Wide Web Conference Committee (IW3C2)*, 625–635.

Kumar & Baag. (2021a). Ethics Erosion in Capital Market: Lehman Brothers' Case Study of Repo 105. *AIMS-18.*

Kumar & Baag. (2021b). Erosion of Ethics in Credit Derivatives: A Case Study. *AIMS-18.*

Kumar, A., Mukherjee, A. B., & Krishna, A. P. (2019). Application of conventional data mining techniques and web mining to aid disaster management. *Environmental Information Systems,* 369–398. doi:10.4018/978-1-5225-7033-2.ch017

Kumar, Arora, & Harsh. (2020). *Res-Net-based approach for Detection and Classification of Plant Leaf Diseases.* IEEE Xplore Part Number: CFP20V66-ART.

Kumar, Baag, & V. (2021a). Impact of ESG Integration on Equity Performance between Developed and Developing Economy: Evidence from S and P 500 and NIFTY 50. *Empirical Economics Letters, 20*(4).

Kumar, Baag, & V. (2021b). Financial Engineering and Quantitative Risk Analytics. *SYBGEN Learning, 1*(1).

Kumar, Chaudhary, & Chandra. (2020). *Plant Disease Detection Using CNN*. Academic Press.

Kumar, H., Prasad, A., Rane, N., Tamane, N., & Yeole, A. (2021). Dr. Phish: Phishing Website Detector. In E3S Web of Conferences (Vol. 297). EDP Sciences. Doi:10.17148/IARJSET.2021.8831

Kumar. (2020). Data mining based marketing decision support system using Hybrid machine learning algorithm. *Irojournals, 2*(3), 185–193. doi:10.36548//jaicn.2020.3.006

Kumar, A., Chatterjee, J. M., & Díaz, V. G. (2020). A novel hybrid approach of SVM combined with NLP and probabilistic neural network for email phishing. *Iranian Journal of Electrical and Computer Engineering, 10*(1), 486. doi:0.11591/ijece.v10i1

Kumar, A., & Halder, A. (2020, May). Ensemble-based active learning using fuzzy-rough approach for cancer sample classification. *Engineering Applications of Artificial Intelligence, 91*, 103591. doi:10.1016/j.engappai.2020.103591

Kumar, A., & Jain, A. (2021). Image smog restoration using oblique gradient profile prior and energy minimization. *Frontiers of Computer Science, 15*(6), 1–7. doi:10.100711704-020-9305-8 PMID:34221535

Kumaran, S. R., Othman, M. S., Yusuf, L. M., & Yunianta, A. (2019, January). Estimation of Missing Values Using Hybrid Fuzzy Clustering Mean and Majority Vote for Microarray Data. *Procedia Computer Science, 163*, 145–153. doi:10.1016/j.procs.2019.12.096

Kumar, S. (2021). Relevance of Buddhist Philosophy in Modern Management Theory. *Psychology and Education, 58*(3), 2104–2111.

Kumar, S., Jain, A., Kumar Agarwal, A., Rani, S., & Ghimire, A. (2021). Object-Based Image Retrieval Using the U-Net-Based Neural Network. *Computational Intelligence and Neuroscience, 2021*, 2021. doi:10.1155/2021/4395646 PMID:34804141

Kumar, S., Jain, A., Shukla, A. P., Singh, S., Raja, R., Rani, S., & Masud, M. (2021). A Comparative Analysis of Machine Learning Algorithms for Detection of Organic and Nonorganic Cotton Diseases. *Mathematical Problems in Engineering, 2021*, 2021. doi:10.1155/2021/1790171

Kuperman, B. A., Brodley, C. E., Ozdoganoglu, H., Vijaykumar, T. N., & Jalote, A. (2005). Detection and prevention of stack buffer overflow attacks. *Communications of the ACM, 48*(11), 50–56.

Kutbay, U. (2018). *Partitional clustering*. Recent Applications in Data Clustering., doi:10.5772/intechopen.75836

L'Huillier, G., Weber, R., & Figueroa, N. (2009, June). Online phishing classification using adversarial data mining and signaling games. In *Proceedings of the ACM SIGKDD Workshop on CyberSecurity and Intelligence Informatics* (pp. 33-42). DOI: 10.1145/1599272.1599279

Latif, S., Usman, M., Manzoor, S., Iqbal, W., Qadir, J., Tyson, G., ... Crowcroft, J. (2020). Leveraging Data Science to Combat COVID-19: A Comprehensive Review. *IEEE Transactions on Artificial Intelligence, 1*(1), 85–103. doi:10.1109/TAI.2020.3020521

Lee, J., Choi, I. Y., & Jun, C.-H. (2021, March). An efficient multivariate feature ranking method for gene selection in high-dimensional microarray data. *Expert Systems with Applications*, *166*, 113971. doi:10.1016/j.eswa.2020.113971

Lee, J., Kang, J., Jun, M., & Han, J. (2019). Design of a symmetry protocol for the efficient operation of IP cameras in the IOT environment. *Symmetry*, *11*(3), 361. doi:10.3390ym11030361

Lhee, K. S., & Chapin, S. J. (2003). Buffer overflow and format string overflow vulnerabilities. *Software, Practice & Experience*, *33*(5), 423–460.

Li, B., Lu, R., Xiao, G., Bao, H., & Ghorbani, A. A. (2019). Towards insider threats detection in Smart Grid Communication Systems. *IET Communications*, *13*(12), 1728–1736. doi:10.1049/iet-com.2018.5736

Liling, S., Kuankuo, Z., & Xiangdong, L. (2019). Stator inter-turn fault diagnosis of induction motor based on wavelet packet decomposition and random forest. *8th Renewable Power Generation Conference (RPG 2019)*, 1-6. 10.1049/cp.2019.0667

Lin, H., & Ng, V. (2019). *Abstractive summarization: A survey of the state of the art.* Paper presented at the Thirty-Third AAAI Conference on Artificial Intelligence (AAAI-19).

Lingaraju, D. G. M., & Jagannatha, D. S. (2019). Review of web page classification and web content mining. *Journal of Advanced Research in Dynamical and Control Systems*, *11*(10), 142–147. doi:10.5373/JARDCS/V11I10/20193017

Liu, B., Mobasher, B., & Nasraoui, O. (2011). Web usage mining. *Web Data Mining*, 527–603. doi:10.1007/978-3-642-19460-3_12

Liu, H., Sun, Y., Huang, J., Hou, Z., & Wang, T. (2015). Inter-turn fault detection for the inverter-fed induction motor based on the Teager-Kaiser energy operation of switching voltage harmonics. *2015 18th International Conference on Electrical Machines and Systems (ICEMS)*, 1214-1219. 10.1109/ICEMS.2015.7385224

Liu, X., Yao, L., & Zeng, X. (2019). *Fusion of multi-time section measurements for state estimation of power system. In 2019 IEEE Innovative Smart Grid Technologies - Asia.* ISGT Asia. doi:10.1109/ISGT-Asia.2019.8881481

Liu, Y., & Bazzi, A. M. (2017). A review and comparison of fault detection and diagnosis methods for squirrel-cage induction motors: State of the art. *ISA Transactions*, *70*(June), 400–409. Advance online publication. doi:10.1016/j.isatra.2017.06.001

Li, W., & Chiueh, T. C. (2007). Automated format string attack prevention for win32/x86 binaries. In *Twenty-Third Annual Computer Security Applications Conference (ACSAC 2007)* (pp. 398-409). IEEE.

Liyanage, M., Ahmad, I., & Okwuibe, J. (2018). Software defined security monitoring in 5G Networks. *A Comprehensive Guide to 5G Security*, 231–243.. doi:10.1002/9781119293071.ch10

Lloret, E., Romá-Ferri, M. T., & Palomar, M. (2013). Compendium: A text summarization system for generating abstracts of research papers. *Data & Knowledge Engineering*, 164–175.

Loey, M., Manogaran, G., Taha, M. H. N., & Khalifa, N. E. M. (2021). A hybrid deep transfer learning model with machine learning methods for face mask detection in the era of the COVID-19 pandemic. *Measurement*, *167*, 108288. doi:10.1016/j.measurement.2020.108288 PMID:32834324

Louro, A., Brandão, M., & Sincorá, L. (2020). Understanding the Self-Efficacy of Data Scientists. *International Journal of Human Capital and Information Technology Professionals*, *11*(2), 50–63. doi:10.4018/IJHCITP.2020040104

Luhn, H. P. (1958). The automatic creation of literature abstracts. *IBM Journal of Research and Development*, 159–165.

Lui, D., Modhafar, A., Glaister, J., Wong, A., & Haider, M. A. (2014). Monte Carlo bias field correction in endorectal diffusion imaging. *IEEE Transactions on Biomedical Engineering*, *61*(2), 368–380. doi:10.1109/TBME.2013.2279635 PMID:24448596

Lumchanow, W., & Udomsiri, S. (2019). Image classification of malaria using hybrid algorithms: Convolutional Neural Network and method to find appropriate K for K-nearest neighbor. *Indonesian Journal of Electrical Engineering and Computer Science*, *16*(1), 382. doi:10.11591/ijeecs.v16.i1.pp382-388

Lynch, C. (2017). Welcome to smart materials and structures 2017. *Smart Materials and Structures*, *26*(2), 020401. doi:10.1088/1361-665X/aa572d

Madhura & Padmavathamma. (2015). A Web Mining Process for Knowledge Discovery of Web usage Patterns. *International Journal of Engineering Research & Technology*, *3*(18).

Maghdid, H. S. (2019). Web news mining using new features: A comparative study. *IEEE Access: Practical Innovations, Open Solutions*, *7*, 5626–5641. doi:10.1109/ACCESS.2018.2890088

Mahajan, D., & Sachdeva, M. (2013). DDoS attack prevention and mitigation techniques-a review. *International Journal of Computers and Applications*, *67*(19).

Mahajani, A., Pandya, V., Maria, I., & Sharma, D. (2019). *A comprehensive survey on extractive and abstractive techniques for text summarization*. Paper presented at the ambient communications and computer systems, Singapore.

Mahjabin, T., Xiao, Y., Sun, G., & Jiang, W. (2017). A survey of distributed denial-of-service attack, prevention, and mitigation techniques. *International Journal of Distributed Sensor Networks*, *13*(12).

Maksutov, A. A., Cherepanov, I. A., & Alekseev, M. S. (2017, April). Detection and prevention of DNS spoofing attacks. In *2017 Siberian Symposium on Data Science and Engineering (SSDSE)* (pp. 84-87). IEEE. DOI: 10.13052/jcsm2245-1439.7114

Malley, B., Ramazzotti, D., & Wu, J. (2016). *Data Pre–processing; Secondary Analysis of Electronic Health Records.* Springer. Retrieved from https://link.springer.com/book/10.1007/978–3–319–43742–2

Mallikarjuna Rao, Subramanyam, & Satya Prasad. (2018). Cluster-based mobility management algorithms for wireless mesh networks. *International Journal of Communication Systems, 31*(11).

Mannepalli, K., Sastry, P. N., & Suman, M. (2017). A novel Adaptive Fractional Deep Belief Networks for speaker emotion recognition. *Alexandria Engineering Journal, 56*(4), 485–497. doi:10.1016/j.aej.2016.09.002

Manoharan, H. (2022). Acclimatization Of Nano Robots. In *Medical Applications Using Artificial Intelligence System With Data Transfer Approach* (Vol. 2022). Wireless Communications And Mobile Computing.

Manoharan, H., Teekaraman, Y., Kuppusamy, R., & Radhakrishnan, A. (2021). A Novel Optimal Robotized Parking System Using Advanced Wireless Sensor Network. *Journal of Sensors, 2021,* 1–8. doi:10.1155/2021/2889504

Manta, Chandra Singh, Deep, & Kapoor. (2021). Temperature-regulated gold nanoparticle sensors for immune chromatographic rapid test kits with reproducible sensitivity: A study. *IET Nanobiotechnol.*

Manta, Chandra Singh, Deep, & Kapoor. (2021). Temperature-regulated gold nanoparticle sensors for immune chromatographic rapid test kits with reproducible sensitivity: a study. *IET Nanobiotechnol.* doi:10.1049/nbt2.12024

Manta, P. (2020). Analytical approach for the optimization of desiccant weight in rapid test kit packaging: Accelerated predictive stability (APS). *Systematic Reviews in Pharmacy, 11*(8), 102–113. doi:10.31838rp.2020.8.15

Manta, P., Chauhan, R., Gandhi, H., Mahant, S., & Kapoor, D. N. (2021). Formulation rationale for the development of SARS-COV-2 immunochromatography rapid test kits in India. *Journal of Applied Pharmaceutical Science.* Advance online publication. doi:10.7324/JAPS.2021.1101017

Manta, P., Kapoor, D. N., Kour, G., Kour, M., & Sharma, A. K. (2020). critical quality attributes of rapid test kits - a practical overview. *Journal of Critical Reviews, 7*(19), 377–384. doi:10.31838/jcr.07.19.48

Manta, P., Nagraik, R., Sharma, A., Kumar, A., Verma, P., Paswan, S. K., Bokov, D. O., Shaikh, J. D., Kaur, R., Leite, A. F. V., Filho, S. J. B., Shiwalkar, N., Persaud, P., & Kapoor, D. N. (2020). Optical density optimization of malaria pan rapid diagnostic test strips for improved test zone band intensity. *Diagnostics (Basel), 10*(11), 880. doi:10.3390/diagnostics10110880 PMID:33137871

Manta, P., Wahi, N., Bharadwaj, A., Kour, G., & Kapoor, D. N. (2021). A statistical quality control (SQC) methodology for gold nanoparticles based immune-chromatographic rapid test kits validation. *Nanoscience & Nanotechnology-Asia, 11*(6), 1–5. doi:10.2174/221068121066 6210108111055

Marchal, S., Armano, G., Gröndahl, T., Saari, K., Singh, N., & Asokan, N. (2017). Off-the-hook: An efficient and usable client-side phishing prevention application. *IEEE Transactions on Computers*, *66*(10), 1717–1733. doi:10.1109/TC.2017.2703808

Martínek, J., Lenc, L., & Král, P. (2020). Building an efficient OCR system for historical documents with little training data. *Neural Computing & Applications*, *32*(23), 17209–17227. doi:10.100700521-020-04910-x

Maybury, M. T. (1995). Generating summaries from event data. *Information Processing & Management*, 735–751.

McIvor, J. T., Patel, A. K., Hilder, T., & Bracewell, P. J. (2018) Commentary sentiment as a predictor of in-game events in T20 cricket. *Proceedings of the 14th Australian Conference on Mathematics and Computers in Sports*, 44-49.

McKelvey, F., & Driscoll, K. (2018). ARPANET and its boundary devices: Modems, Imps, and the inter-structuralism of infrastructures. *Internet Histories*, *3*(1), 31–50. doi:10.1080/2470147 5.2018.1548138

Medeiros, M., & Maçada, A. (2021). Competitive advantage of data-driven analytical capabilities: the role of big data visualization and of organizational agility. *Management Decision*. doi:10.1108/MD-12-2020-1681

Medeiros, M., Hoppen, N., & Maçada, A. (2020). Data science for business: Benefits, challenges and opportunities. *The Bottom Line (New York, N.Y.)*, *33*(2), 149–163. doi:10.1108/BL-12-2019-0132

Mehra & Thakur. (2018). An Effective method for Web Log Preprocessing and Page Access Frequency using Web Usage Mining. *International Journal of Applied Engineering Research*, *13*(2), 1227-1232.

Mehta, P., & Majumder, P. (2018). Effective aggregation of various summarization techniques. *Information Processing & Management*, 145–158.

Mehta, P., & Pandya, S. (2020). A review on sentiment analysis methodologies, practices and applications. *International Journal of Scientific & Technology Research*, *9*(2), 601–609.

Mehta, P., Pandya, S., & Kotecha, K. (2021). Harvesting social media sentiment analysis to enhance stock market prediction using deep learning. *PeerJ. Computer Science*, *7*, e476. Advance online publication. doi:10.7717/peerj-cs.476 PMID:33954250

Mendiboure, L., Chalouf, M. A., & Krief, F. (2021). Toward new intelligent architectures for the internet of vehicles. *Intelligent Network Management and Control*, 193–215. . doi:10.1002/9781119817840.ch8

Mhalla, A., Chateau, T., Gazzah, S., & Amara, N. E. (2019). An embedded computer-vision system for multi-object detection in traffic surveillance. *IEEE Transactions on Intelligent Transportation Systems*, *20*(11), 4006–4018. doi:10.1109/TITS.2018.2876614

Miller Center. (1993). *January 5, 1993: Address at West Point.* UVA | Miller Center, Rector and Visitors of the University of Virginia, https://millercenter.org/the-presidency/presidential-speeches/january-5-1993-address-west-point

Miller Center. (1998). *March 25, 1998: Remarks to the People of Rwanda.* UVA | Miller Center, Rector and Visitors of the University of Virginia, https://millercenter.org/the-presidency/presidential-speeches/march-25-1998-remarks-people-rwanda

Mishra, N., & Pandya, S. (2021, April). Internet of Things Applications, Security Challenges, Attacks, Intrusion Detection, and Future Visions: A Systematic Review. *IEEE Access: Practical Innovations, Open Solutions, 9*, 59353–59377. doi:10.1109/ACCESS.2021.3073408

Misra, N. R., Kumar, S., & Jain, A. (2021, February). A Review on E-waste: Fostering the Need for Green Electronics. In *2021 International Conference on Computing, Communication, and Intelligent Systems (ICCCIS)* (pp. 1032-1036). IEEE. 10.1109/ICCCIS51004.2021.9397191

Mittal, M., Iwendi, C., Khan, S., & Rehman Javed, A. (2021). Analysis of security and energy efficiency for shortest route discovery in low-energy adaptive clustering hierarchy protocol using Levenberg- Marquardt neural network and gated recurrent unit for intrusion detection system. *Transactions on Emerging Telecommunications Technologies, 32*(6), e3997. doi:10.1002/ett.3997

Miyachi, C. (2018). What is "Cloud"? It is time to update the NIST definition? *IEEE Cloud Computing, 5*(3), 6–11. doi:10.1109/MCC.2018.032591611

Mohamed, M., & Oussalah, M. (2019). SRL-ESA-TextSum: A text summarization approach based on semantic role labeling and explicit semantic analysis. *Information Processing & Management*, 1356–1372.

Mohammed, A. J., Hassan, M. M., & Kadir, D. H. (2020). Improving Classification Performance for a Novel Imbalanced Medical Dataset Using SMOTE Method. *International Journal of Advanced Trends in Computer Science and Engineering, 9*(3), 3161–3172. doi:10.30534/ijatcse/2020/104932020

Mohan, V., Chhabra, H., Rani, A., & Singh, V. (2018). Robust self-tuning fractional order PID controller dedicated to non-linear dynamic system. *Journal of Intelligent & Fuzzy Systems, 34*(3), 1467–1478. doi:10.3233/JIFS-169442

Mohan, V., Chhabra, H., Rani, A., & Singh, V. (2019). An expert 2DOF fractional order fuzzy PID controller for nonlinear systems. *Neural Computing & Applications, 31*(8), 4253–4270. doi:10.100700521-017-3330-z

Mohan, V., Rani, A., & Singh, V. (2017). Robust adaptive fuzzy controller applied to double inverted pendulum. *Journal of Intelligent & Fuzzy Systems, 32*(5), 3669–3687. doi:10.3233/JIFS-169301

Morais-Rodrigues, F., Silv́erio-Machado, R., Kato, R. B., Rodrigues, D. L. N., Valdez-Baez, J., Fonseca, V., San, E. J., Gomes, L. G. R., dos Santos, R. G., Vinicius Canário Viana, M., da Cruz Ferraz Dutra, J., Teixeira Dornelles Parise, M., Parise, D., Campos, F. F., de Souza, S. J., Ortega, J. M., Barh, D., Ghosh, P., Azevedo, V. A. C., & dos Santos, M. A. (2020, February). Analysis of the microarray gene expression for breast cancer progression after the application modified logistic regression. *Gene*, *726*, 144168. doi:10.1016/j.gene.2019.144168 PMID:31759986

Moratanch, N., & Chitrakala, S. (2017). *A Survey on Extractive Text Summarization.* Paper presented at the 2017 International Conference on Computer, Communication and Signal Processing (ICCCSP), Chennai, India.

Mulla, G. A. A., Demir, Y., & Hassan, M. M. (2021). Combination of PCA with SMOTE Oversampling for Classification of High-Dimensional Imbalanced Data. In BEU. *Journal of Science*, *10*(3).

Murphey & Luke. (2005). Secure Session Management: Preventing Security Voids in Web Applications. The SANS Institute, 29.

Nagpal, A., & Singh, V. (2018, January). A Feature Selection Algorithm Based on Qualitative Mutual Information for Cancer Microarray Data. *Procedia Computer Science*, *132*, 244–252. doi:10.1016/j.procs.2018.05.195

Nagpal, B., Chauhan, N., & Singh, N. (2017). SECSIX: Security engine for CSRF, SQL injection and XSS attacks. *International Journal of System Assurance Engineering and Management*, *8*(2), 631–644.

Nagpal, N. B., & Nagpal, B. (2014). Preventive measures for securing web applications using broken authentication and session management attacks: A study. *International Conference on Advances in Computer Engineering and Applications (ICACEA).*

Naik, N., Jenkins, P., Cooke, R., Ball, D., Foster, A., & Jin, Y. (2017). Augmented windows fuzzy firewall for preventing denial of service attack. In *2017 IEEE International Conference on fuzzy systems (FUZZ-IEEE)* (pp. 1-6). IEEE.

Namasudra, S., Chakraborty, R., Kadry, S., Manogaran, G., & Rawal, B. S. (2020). Fast: Fast accessing scheme for data transmission in cloud computing. *Peer-to-Peer Networking and Applications*, *14*(4), 2430–2442. doi:10.100712083-020-00959-6

Nasraoui, O. (2008). Web data mining. *SIGKDD Explorations*, *10*(2), 23–25. doi:10.1145/1540276.1540281

Nath, S., Wu, J., Zhao, Y., & Qiao, W. (2020). Low Latency Bearing Fault Detection of Direct-Drive Wind Turbines Using Stator Current. *IEEE Access: Practical Innovations, Open Solutions*, *8*, 44163–44174. doi:10.1109/ACCESS.2020.2977632

Nayak, Kumar, Gupta, Suri, Naved, & Soni. (2022). Network mining techniques to analyze the risk of the occupational accident via bayesian network. *International Journal of System Assurance Engineering and Management.*

Nazari, N., & Mahdavi, M. A. (2019). A survey on automatic text summarization. *Journal of Artificial Intelligence and Data Mining*, 121–135.

Nenkova, A., & McKeown, K. (2012). A survey of text summarization techniques. In C. C. Aggarwal & C. Zhai (Eds.), *Mining text data, Boston, MA*.

Ngak, C. (2012). *Yahoo reportedly hacked: Is your account safe?* Cbsnews.com. Retrieved 4 November 2021, from https://www.cbsnews.com/news/yahoo-reportedly-hacked-is-your-account-safe/

Nguyen. (2013). *Web-page Recommendation based on Web Usage and Domain Knowledge*. IEEE.

Nguyen, L. D., Le, D. N., & Vinh, L. T. (2014, December). Detecting phishing web pages based on DOM-tree structure and graph matching algorithm. In *Proceedings of the Fifth Symposium on Information and Communication Technology* (pp. 280-285). DOI:10.1145/2676585.2676596

Nguyen, T. T., Hai, Y. L., & Lu, J. (2014). Web-page recommendation based on web usage and domain knowledge. *IEEE Transactions on Knowledge and Data Engineering*, *26*(10), 2574–2587. doi:10.1109/TKDE.2013.78

Nieuwenhuis, L. J. M., Ehrenhard, M. L., & Prause, L. (2018). The shift to cloud computing: The impact of disruptive technology on the enterprise software business ecosystem. *Technological Forecasting and Social Change*, *129*, 308–313. doi:10.1016/j.techfore.2017.09.037

Nkenyereye, L., Hwang, J. Y., Pham, Q.-V., & Song, J. S. (2021). Meix: Evolving Multi-Access Edge Computing for Industrial Internet-of-things services. *IEEE Network*, *35*(3), 147–153. doi:10.1109/MNET.011.2000674

Nofal, D. E., & Amer, A. A. (2020). SQL Injection Attacks Detection and Prevention Based on Neuro—Fuzzy. *Machine Learning and Big Data Analytics Paradigms: Analysis, Applications and Challenges*, *77*, 93.

Odeh, A., Keshta, I., & Abdelfattah, E. (2020). *Efficient Detection of Phishing Websites Using Multilayer Perceptron*. Doi:10.3991/ijim.v14i11.13903

Oest, A., Safei, Y., Doupé, A., Ahn, G. J., Wardman, B., & Warner, G. (2018, May). Inside a phisher's mind: Understanding the anti-phishing ecosystem through phishing kit analysis. In *2018 APWG Symposium on Electronic Crime Research (eCrime)* (pp. 1-12). IEEE. DOI:10.1109/ECRIME.2018.8376206

Oest, A., Zhang, P., Wardman, B., Nunes, E., Burgis, J., Zand, A., . . . Ahn, G. J. (2020). Sunrise to sunset: Analyzing the end-to-end life cycle and effectiveness of phishing attacks at scale. In *29th USENIX Security Symposium (USENIX Security 20)* (pp. 361-377). USENIX.

Oleinik, A. (2021). *Relevance in web search: Between content, authority and popularity. Quality & Quantity*. doi:10.100711135-021-01125-7

Orji, I., Kusi-Sarpong, S., Huang, S., & Vazquez-Brust, D. (2020). Evaluating the factors that influence blockchain adoption in the freight logistics industry. *Transportation Research Part E, Logistics and Transportation Review, 141*(1), 102025.

Oussous, A., Benjelloun, F., Ait Lahcen, A., & Belfkih, S. (2018). Big Data technologies: A survey. *Journal of King Saud University - Computer and Information Sciences, 30*(4), 431-448. doi:10.1016/j.jksuci.2017.06.001

Ouyang, H., Wei, X., & Wu, Q. (2020). Discovery and prediction of stock Index pattern VIA Three-Stage architecture Of ticc, TPA-LSTM and Multivariate LSTM-FCNs. *IEEE Access: Practical Innovations, Open Solutions, 8,* 123683–123700. doi:10.1109/ACCESS.2020.3005994

Paar, C., & Pelzl, J. (2009). *Understanding cryptography: a textbook for students and practitioners.* Springer Science & Business Media.

Pallathadka, H., Mustafa, M., Sanchez, D. T., Sekhar Sajja, G., Gour, S., & Naved, M. (2021). Impact of machine learning on management, healthcare and agriculture. *Materials Today: Proceedings*. Advance online publication. doi:10.1016/j.matpr.2021.07.042

Panchal, A. (2019). A survey of web mining and various web mining techniques. *International Journal for Research in Applied Science and Engineering Technology, 7*(9), 933–939. doi:10.22214/ijraset.2019.9130

Pandya, S., & Ghayvat, H. (2021). Ambient acoustic event assistive framework for identification, detection, and recognition of unknown acoustic events of a residence. *Advanced Engineering Informatics, 47,* 1012. doi:10.1016/j.aei.2020.101238

Panjwani, B., Singh, V., Rani, A., & Mohan, V. (2021). Optimizing Drug Schedule for Cell-Cycle Specific Cancer Chemotherapy. Singapore. doi:10.1007/978-981-16-1696-9_7

Panjwani, Singh, Rani, & Mohan. (2021). Optimum multi-drug regime for compartment model of tumour: cell-cycle-specific dynamics in the presence of resistance. *Journal of Pharmacokinetics and Pharmacodynamics, 48*(4), 543-562.

Panjwani, B., Mohan, V., Rani, A., & Singh, V. (2019). Optimal drug scheduling for cancer chemotherapy using two degree of freedom fractional order PID scheme. *Journal of Intelligent & Fuzzy Systems, 36*(3), 2273–2284. doi:10.3233/JIFS-169938

Pannu & Kaur. (2014). A Survey on Web Application Attacks. *International Journal of Computational Science.*

Paradhasaradhi, D., Priya, K. S., Sabarish, K., Harish, P., & Narasimharao, G. V. (2016). Study and analysis of CMOS carry look ahead adder with leakage power reduction approaches. *Indian Journal of Science and Technology, 9*(17), 1–8. doi:10.17485/ijst/2016/v9i17/93111

Park, Y. M. (2021). A GPS-enabled portable air pollution sensor and web-mapping technologies for field-based learning in Health Geography. *Journal of Geography in Higher Education*, 1–21. doi:10.1080/03098265.2021.1900083

Parnaik, V. K., & Chaturvedi, P. (2015). Fluorescence recovery after photobleaching studies reveal complexity of nuclear architecture. *International Journal of Chemistry, 4*(4), 297–302.

Patel & Parikh. (2017). Preprocessing on Web Server Log Data for Web Usage Pattern Discovery. *International Journal of Computer Applications, 165*(10).

Pateli, A., Mylonas, N., & Spyrou, A. (2020). Organizational Adoption of Social Media in the Hospitality Industry: An Integrated Approach Based on DIT and TOE Frameworks. *Sustainability, 12*(17), 7132.

Peng, T., Harris, I., & Sawa, Y. (2018, January). Detecting phishing attacks using natural language processing and machine learning. In *2018 IEEE 12th international conference on semantic computing (ICSC)* (pp. 300-301). IEEE. DOI:10.1109/ICSC.2018.00056

Peng, T., Leckie, C., & Ramamohanarao, K. (2007). Survey of network-based defense mechanisms countering the DoS and DDoS problems. *ACM Computing Surveys, 39*(1), 3.

Pereira, R. I. S., Dupont, I. M., Carvalho, P. C. M., & Jucá, S. C. S. (2018). IOT embedded linux system based on Raspberry Pi applied to real-time cloud monitoring of a decentralized photovoltaic plant. *Measurement, 114*, 286–297. doi:10.1016/j.measurement.2017.09.033

Peter, A. F., & Meelis, K. (2015). Precision-Recall-Gain Curves: PR Analysis Done Right. NIPS.

Peter, G. (2022a). *Histogram Shifting based Quick Response Steganography method for Secure Communication* (Vol. 2022). Wireless Communications and Mobile Computing.

Peter, G. (2022b). *Design of Automated Deep Learning-based Fusion Model for Copy-Move Image Forgery Detection* (Vol. 2022). Computational Intelligence and Neuroscience.

Pettersson, E. (2018). *NLP for Historical (Or Very Modern) Text.* Uppsala University, Language Technology: Research and Development. https://cl.lingfil.uu.se/~nivre/master/fou-historical.pdf

Phinyomark, A., Ibanez-Marcelo, E., & Petri, G. (2017). Resting-State fMRI Functional Connectivity: Big data PREPROCESSING pipelines and topological data analysis. *IEEE Transactions on Big Data, 3*(4), 415–428. doi:10.1109/TBDATA.2017.2734883

Phishing Activity Trends Report. (2020). Retrieved from https://docs.apwg.org/reports/apwg_trends_report_q2_2020.pdf

Ping-Chen, X. (2011). SQL injection attack and guard technical research. *Procedia Engineering, 15*, 4131–4135.

Poonam, Y. M., & Mulge, Y. (2013). Remote temperature monitoring using LM35 sensor and intimate android user via C2DM service. *International Journal of Computer Science and Mobile Computing, 2*(6), 32–36.

Potharaju, S. P., & Sreedevi, M. (2019, June). Distributed feature selection (DFS) strategy for microarray gene expression data to improve the classification performance. *Clinical Epidemiology and Global Health, 7*(2), 171–176. doi:10.1016/j.cegh.2018.04.001

Powell, B. M., Kumar, A., Thapar, J., Goswami, G., Vatsa, M., Singh, R., & Noore, A. (2016). A multibiometrics-based CAPTCHA for improved online security. In *2016 IEEE 8th International Conference on Biometrics Theory, Applications and Systems (BTAS)* (pp. 1-8). IEEE.

Prakash, P., Kumar, M., Kompella, R. R., & Gupta, M. (2010, March). Phishnet: predictive blacklisting to detect phishing attacks. In 2010 Proceedings IEEE INFOCOM (pp. 1-5). IEEE. Doi:10.1109/INFCOM.2010.5462216

Priyadarshini, K. M., & Ravindran, D. R. E. (2019). Novel Two Fold Edge Activated Memory Cell with Low Power Dissipation and High Speed. *International Journal of Recent Technology and Engineering*, 8(1), 1491–1495.

Priyadarshini, K. M., Ravindran, R. E., Krishna, S. V., & Bhavani, K. D. (2021, February). Design of Compact and Smart Full Adders for High-Speed Nanometer Technology IC's. []. IOP Publishing.]. *Journal of Physics: Conference Series*, 1804(1), 012152. doi:10.1088/1742-6596/1804/1/012152

Provost, F., & Fawcett, T. (2013). Data Science and its Relationship to Big Data and Data-Driven Decision Making. *Big Data*, 1(1), 51–59. doi:10.1089/big.2013.1508

Putra, M., & Nazaruddin, Y. (2019). *Development of Virtual Firefighting Robots Using Breitenberg and Fuzzy Logic Methods*. Academic Press.

Qin, B., & Li, D. (2020). Identifying Facemask-Wearing Condition Using Image Super-Resolution with Classification Network to Prevent COVID-19. *Sensors (Basel)*, 20(18), 5236. doi:10.339020185236 PMID:32937867

Quinto, B. (2018). Big data visualization and data wrangling. *Next-Generation Big Data*, 407–476. doi:10.1007/978-1-4842-3147-0_9

Radev, D. R., Hovy, E., & McKeown, K. (2002). Introduction to the special issue on summarization. *Computational Linguistics*.

Rahim, Murugan, Mostafa, Dubey, Regin, Kulkarni, & Dhanalakshmi. (2020). Detecting the Phishing Attack Using Collaborative Approach and Secure Login through Dynamic Virtual Passwords. *Webology*, 17(2).

Rajakumar, R. (2017). GWO-LPWSN: Grey wolf optimization algorithm for node localization problem in wireless sensor networks. *Journal of Computer Networks and Communications*.

Rajeswari, M., Amudhavel, J., & Dhavachelvan, P. (2017). Vortex search algorithm for solving set covering problem in wireless sensor network. *Adv. Appl. Math. Sci*, 17, 95–111.

Ramesh, Tilak, & Prasad. (2012). Efficient Implementation of 16-bit Multiplie Accumulator Using Radix-2 Modified Booth Algorithm and SPST Adder Using Verilog. *International Journal of VLSI Design & Communication Systems*, 3(3).

Ramzan, Z. (2010). Phishing attacks and countermeasures. Handbook of information and communication security, 433-448. Doi:10.1007/978-3-642-04117-4_23

Rani, R. R., & Ramyachitra, D. (2018, January). Microarray Cancer Gene Feature Selection Using Spider Monkey Optimization Algorithm and Cancer Classification using SVM. *Procedia Computer Science, 143,* 108–116. doi:10.1016/j.procs.2018.10.358

Rao & Manikonda. (2019). CSRR-loaded T-shaped MIMO antenna for 5G cellular networks and vehicular communications. *International Journal of RF and Microwave Computer-Aided Engineering, 29*(8).

Rao, S., Verma, A. K., & Bhatia, T. (2021). A review on social spam detection: Challenges, open issues, and future directions. *Expert Systems with Applications, 186,* 115742. doi:10.1016/j.eswa.2021.115742

Rathinam, R., Govindaraj, M., Vijayakumar, K., & Pattabhi, S. (2015). Removal of Colour from Aqueous Rhodamine B Dye Solution by Photo electrocoagulation Treatment Techniques. *Journal of Engineering, Scientific Research and Application, 1*(2), 80-89. http://www.dsecjesra.com/

Rathinam, R., & Govindaraj, M. (2021). Photo electro catalytic Oxidation of Textile Industry Wastewater by RuO2/IrO2/TaO2 Coated Titanium Electrodes. *Nature Environment and Pollution Technology, 20*(3), 1069–1076. doi:10.46488/NEPT.2021.v20i03.014

Rathinam, R., Govindaraj, M., Vijayakumar, K., & Pattabhi, S. (2016). Decolourization of Rhodamine B from aqueous by electrochemical oxidation using graphite electrodes. *Desalination and Water Treatment, 57*(36), 16995–17001.

Rathinam, R., & Pattabhi, S. (2019). Removal of Rhodamine B Dye from Aqueous Solution by Advanced Oxidation Process using ZnO Nanoparticles. *Indian Journal of Ecology, 46*(1), 167–174. http://indianecologicalsociety.com/

Rath, M. (2017). Resource provision and QoS support with added security for client side applications in cloud computing. *International Journal of Information Technology, 11*(2), 357–364. doi:10.100741870-017-0059-y

Ravi, N., & Shalinie, S. M. (2020). Learning-driven detection and mitigation of DDoS attack in IoT via SDN-cloud architecture. *IEEE Internet of Things Journal, 7*(4), 3559–3570.

Ravi, N., Subbaiah, Y., Prasad, T. J., & Rao, T. S. (2011). A novel low power, low area array multiplier design for DSP applications. In *2011 International Conference on Signal Processing, Communication, Computing and Networking Technologies* (pp. 254-257). IEEE. 10.1109/ICSCCN.2011.6024554

Rawat, A., Jha, S., Kumar, B., & Mohan, V. (2020). Nonlinear fractional order PID controller for tracking maximum power in photo-voltaic system. *Journal of Intelligent & Fuzzy Systems, 38*(5), 6703–6713. doi:10.3233/JIFS-179748

Raza, M., Iqbal, M., Sharif, M., & Haider, W. (2012). A survey of password attacks and comparative analysis on methods for secure authentication. *World Applied Sciences Journal, 19*(4), 439–444.

Razavi, M., Alikhani, H., Janfaza, V., Sadeghi, B., & Alikhani, E. (in press). *An Automatic System to Monitor the Physical Distance and Face Mask Wearing of Construction Workers in COVID-19 Pandemic*. Academic Press.

Rehman Javed, A., Jalil, Z., Atif Moqurrab, S., Abbas, S., & Liu, X. (2020). Ensemble adaboost classifier for accurate and fast detection of botnet attacks in connected vehicles. *Transactions on Emerging Telecommunications Technologies*, *4088*. Advance online publication. doi:10.1002/ett.4088

Rinker, T. W. (2019). *sentimentr: Calculate Text Polarity Sentiment version 2.7.1*. https://github.com/trinker/sentimentr

Ristoski, P., Bizer, C., & Paulheim, H. (2015). Mining the web of Linked Data with rapidminer. SSRN *Electronic Journal*. doi:10.2139/ssrn.3198927

Robardet, C. (2013). Data mining techniques FOR Communities' detection in dynamic social networks. *Data Mining*, 719–733. doi:10.4018/978-1-4666-2455-9.ch037

Robledo, H. F. G. (2008). Types of Hosts on a Remote File Inclusion (RFI) Botnet Symposium conducted at the meeting of the CERMA'08 Electronics. *Robotics and Automotive Mechanics Conference*.

Rodríguez, G. E., Torres, J. G., Flores, P., & Benavides, D. E. (2020). Cross-site scripting (XSS) attacks and mitigation: A survey. *Computer Networks*, *166*, 106960.

Roland, G., Kumaraperumal, S., Kumar, S., Gupta, A. D., Afzal, S., & Suryakumar, M. (2021). PCA (Principal Component Analysis) Approach towards Identifying the Factors Determining the Medication Behavior of Indian Patients: An Empirical Study. Tobacco Regulatory Science, 7(6), 7391-7401.

Ruwase, O., & Lam, M. S. (2004). A Practical Dynamic Buffer Overflow Detector. In NDSS (Vol. 2004, pp. 159-169). Academic Press.

Sabrol, H., & Satish, K. (2016). Tomato plant disease classification in digital images using classification tree. *2016 International Conference on Communication and Signal Processing (ICCSP)*, 1242-1246. 10.1109/ICCSP.2016.7754351

Saeidi, M., Zarei, J., Hassani, H., & Zamani, A. (2014). Bearing fault detection via Park's vector approach based on ANFIS. *2014 International Conference on Mechatronics and Control (ICMC)*, 2436-2441. 10.1109/ICMC.2014.7232006

Sahingoz, O. K., Buber, E., Demir, O., & Diri, B. (2019). Machine learning based phishing detection from URLs. *Expert Systems with Applications*, *117*, 345–357. doi:10.1016/j.eswa.2018.09.029

Sahoo, D., Liu, C., & Hoi, S. C. (2017). *Malicious URL detection using machine learning: A survey*. Doi:10.36227/techrxiv.11492622.v1

Sahoo, K. S., Tripathy, B. K., Naik, K., Ramasubbareddy, S., Balusamy, B., Khari, M., & Burgos, D. (2020). An evolutionary SVM model for DDOS attack detection in software defined networks. *IEEE Access: Practical Innovations, Open Solutions*, *8*, 132502–132513. doi:10.1109/ACCESS.2020.3009733

Sahoo, S. R., & Gupta, B. B. (2019). Classification of various attacks and their defence mechanism in online social networks: A survey. *Enterprise Information Systems*, *13*(6), 832–864.

Sahu, B., Dehuri, S., & Jagadev, A. K. (2017, January). Feature selection model based on clustering and ranking in pipeline for microarray data. *Informatics in Medicine Unlocked*, *9*, 107–122. doi:10.1016/j.imu.2017.07.004

Saini, H., Bhushan, B., Arora, A., & Kaur, A. (2019). Security vulnerabilities in Information communication technology: Blockchain to the rescue (A survey on Blockchain Technology). In *2019 2nd International Conference on Intelligent Computing, Instrumentation and Control Technologies (ICICICT)* (Vol. 1, pp. 1680-1684). IEEE.

Sajja, G. S., Rane, K. P., Phasinam, K., Kassanuk, T., Okoronkwo, E., & Prabhu, P. (2021). Towards applicability of blockchain in agriculture sector. *Materials Today: Proceedings*. Advance online publication. doi:10.1016/j.matpr.2021.07.366

Sajja, Mustafa, Ponnusamy, Abdufattokhov, Murugesan, & Prabhu. (2021). Machine Learning Algorithms in Intrusion Detection and Classification. *Annals of the Romanian Society for Cell Biology*, *25*(6), 12211–12219.

Samanta, D., Dutta, S., Galety, M. G., & Pramanik, S. (2022). A Novel Approach for Web Mining Taxonomy for High-Performance Computing. In J. M. R. S. Tavares, P. Dutta, S. Dutta, & D. Samanta (Eds.), *Cyber Intelligence and Information Retrieval. Lecture Notes in Networks and Systems* (Vol. 291). Springer. doi:10.1007/978-981-16-4284-5_37

San Martino, A., & Perramon, X. (2010). Phishing Secrets: History, Effects, Countermeasures. *International Journal of Network Security*, *11*(3), 163–171.

Sangeetha, P., & S, H. (2019, June). Rational-Dilation Wavelet Transform Based Torque Estimation from Acoustic Signals for Fault Diagnosis in a Three-Phase Induction Motor. *IEEE Transactions on Industrial Informatics*, *15*(6), 3492–3501. doi:10.1109/TII.2018.2874463

Sani, A. S., Yuan, D., Ogaji, S., & Dong, Z. Y. (2020). Cyreume: A real-time situational awareness and decision-making blockchain-based architecture for the energy internet. Handbook of Real-Time Computing, 1–49. doi:10.1007/978-981-4585-87-3_48-1

Sarmah, U., Bhattacharyya, D. K., & Kalita, J. K. (2018). A survey of detection methods for XSS attacks. *Journal of Network and Computer Applications*, *118*, 113–143.

Sathiyamoorthi, V. (2017). Web usage mining. *Advances in Data Mining and Database Management*, 107–130. doi:10.4018/978-1-5225-1877-8.ch007

Sayed, S., Nassef, M., Badr, A., & Farag, I. (2019, May). A Nested Genetic Algorithm for feature selection in high-dimensional cancer Microarray datasets. *Expert Systems with Applications*, *121*, 233–243. doi:10.1016/j.eswa.2018.12.022

Schulman, M. (2021). Missouri vs. Holland [1920]. *History Central*. https://www.historycentral.com/documents/MissourivsHolland.html

Schweinberger, M. (2020). *Semantic Vector Space Models in R*. The University of Queensland. https://slcladal.github.io/svm.html

Schweinberger, M. (2021). *Sentiment Analysis in R*. The University of Queensland. https://slcladal.github.io/sentiment.html

Scott, P. (2019). Welcome to BMJ Health & Care Informatics. *BMJ Health & Care Informatics*, *26*(1). Advance online publication. doi:10.1136/bmjhci-2019-000010 PMID:31039116

Sehgal, P., & Chaturvedi, P. (2022). *Survival Strategies in Cold-adapted Microorganisms* (1st ed.). Springer Singapore. doi:10.1007/978-981-16-2625-8

Selvaraju, S., Ramba, V., Subbiha, S., & Dubey, P. K. (2019). An innovative system architecture for real-time monitoring and alarming for cutting transport in oil well drilling. *Day 3 Wed.* doi:10.2118/197870-MS

Semastin, E., Azam, S., Shanmugam, B., Kannoorpatti, K., Jonokman, M., Samy, G. N., & Perumal, S. (2018). Preventive measures for cross site request forgery attacks on Web-based Applications. *IACSIT International Journal of Engineering and Technology*.

Setiyani, L., & Rostiani, Y. (2021). Analysis of E-Commerce Adoption by SMEs Using the Technology - Organization - Environment (TOE) Model: A Case Study in Karawang, Indonesia. *International Journal of Science, Technology & Management, 2*(4), 1113-1132. doi:10.46729/ijstm.v2i4.246

Sharda, R., Delen, D., & Turban, E. (2021). *Analytics, Data Science, & Artificial Intelligence: Systems for Decision Support* (11th ed.). Pearson.

Sharma, A., Singh, A., Sharma, N., Kaushik, I., & Bhushan, B. (2019). Security countermeasures in web based application. In *2019 2nd International Conference on Intelligent Computing, Instrumentation and Control Technologies (ICICICT)* (Vol. 1, pp. 1236-1241). IEEE.

Sharma, A., Singh, A., Sharma, N., Kaushik, I., & Bhushan, B. (2019, July). Security countermeasures in web based application. In *2019 2nd International Conference on Intelligent Computing, Instrumentation and Control Technologies (ICICICT)* (Vol. 1, pp. 1236-1241). IEEE. DOI: 10.1109/ICICICT46008.2019.8993141

Sharma, L., & Garg, P. K. (2019). Block-based adaptive learning rate for detection of motion-based object in visual surveillance. *From Visual Surveillance to Internet of Things*, 201–214. doi:10.1201/9780429297922-14

Sharma, S. K., Jain, A., Gupta, K., Prasad, D., & Singh, V. (2019). An internal schematic view and simulation of major diagonal mesh network-on-chip. *Journal of Computational and Theoretical Nanoscience, 16*(10), 4412–4417. doi:10.1166/jctn.2019.8534

Sharnil, P. (2021). Covidsaviour: A Novel Sensor-Fusion and Deep Learning-Based Framework for Virus Outbreaks. *Frontiers in Public Health, 9*, 797808. Advance online publication. doi:10.3389/fpubh.2021.797808

Shernan, E., Carter, H., Tian, D., Traynor, P., & Butler, K. (2015). More guidelines than rules: CSRF vulnerabilities from noncompliant OAuth 2.0 implementations. In *International Conference on Detection of Intrusions and Malware, and Vulnerability Assessment* (pp. 239-260). Springer.

Shibata, M., Okamura, K., Yura, K., & Umezawa, A. (2020, December). High-precision multiclass cell classification by supervised machine learning on lectin microarray data. *Regenerative Therapy, 15*, 195–201. doi:10.1016/j.reth.2020.09.005 PMID:33426219

Shi, L., Jianping, C., & Jie, X. (2018). Prospecting information extraction by text mining based on convolutional neural networks–a case study of the Lala Copper Deposit, China. *IEEE Access: Practical Innovations, Open Solutions, 6*, 52286–52297. doi:10.1109/ACCESS.2018.2870203

Shinde & Patil. (2021). *A Review of IoT based Health Monitoring and Future Health Prediction System*. Academic Press.

Shivaprasad, G., Reddy, N. V. S., Acharya, U. D., & Aithal, P. K. (2015). Neuro-Fuzzy based hybrid model for web USAGE MINING. *Procedia Computer Science, 54*, 327–334. doi:10.1016/j.procs.2015.06.038

Shi, X., & Songlin, L. (2020). Design and Implementation of a Smart Wireless Fire-Fighting System Based on NB-IoT Technology. *Journal of Physics: Conference Series, 1606*(1), 012015. doi:10.1088/1742-6596/1606/1/012015

Sicari, S., Rizzardi, A., Miorandi, D., & Coen-Porisini, A. (2018). REATO: REActing TO Denial of Service attacks in the Internet of Things. *Computer Networks, 137*, 37–48.

Silge, J., & Robinson, D. (2016). tidytext: Text Mining and Analysis Using Tidy Data Principles in R. *Journal of Open Source Software, 1*(3), 37. doi:10.21105/joss.00037

Simmonds, P. P., McNamara, T. S., & Bracewell, P. J. (2018). Predicting win margins with sentiment analysis in international rugby. *Proceedings of the 14th Australian Conference on Mathematics and Computers in Sports*, 137-142.

Simpson, J. A., & Weiner, E. (1989). *The Oxford English Dictionary* (Vol. 2). Clarendon Press.

Singh & Misra. (2016). *Detection of plant leaf diseases using image segmentation and soft computing techniques*. Academic Press.

Singh & Saini. (2018a). Security for Internet of Thing (IoT) based Wireless Sensor Networks. *Journal of Advanced Research in Dynamical and Control Systems, 6*, 1591-1596.

Singh & Saini. (2018a). Security for the Internet of Thing (IoT) based Wireless Sensor Networks. *Journal of Advanced Research in Dynamical and Control Systems, 6*, 1591-1596.

Singh & Saini. (2018b). Security approaches for data aggregation in Wireless Sensor Networks against Sybil Attack. *2018 Second International Conference on Inventive Communication and Computational Technologies*, 190-193.

Singh & Saini. (2018b). Security Techniques for Wormhole Attack in Wireless Sensor Network. *International Journal of Engineering & Technology, 7*(2), 59-62.

Singh & Saini. (2018c). Security Techniques for Wormhole Attack in Wireless Sensor Network. *International Journal of Engineering & Technology, 7*(2), 59-62.

Singh & Saini. (2019). Detection Techniques for Selective Forwarding Attack in Wireless Sensor Networks. *International Journal of Recent Technology and Engineering, 7*(6S), 380-383.

Singh, A., Sharma, A., Sharma, N., Kaushik, I., & Bhushan, B. (2019). Taxonomy of attacks on web based applications. In *2019 2nd International Conference on Intelligent Computing, Instrumentation and Control Technologies (ICICICT)* (Vol. 1, pp. 1231-1235). IEEE.

Singh, A., Sharma, A., Sharma, N., Kaushik, I., & Bhushan, B. (2019, July). Taxonomy of attacks on web based applications. In *2019 2nd International Conference on Intelligent Computing, Instrumentationand Control Technologies (ICICICT)* (Vol. 1, pp. 1231-1235). IEEE. DOI: 10.1109/ICICICT46008.2019.8993264

Singh, M., & Shaik, A. G. (2016b). Application of stockwell transform in bearing fault diagnosis of induction motor. In *2016 IEEE 7th Power India International Conference (PIICON)*. IEEE. 10.1109/POWERI.2016.8077436

Singh, A., & Shaw, S. (2020). Optimizing approach of recommendation system using web usage mining and social media for e-commerce. *International Journal of Computers and Applications, 176*(40), 34–38. doi:10.5120/ijca2020920510

Singh, M., & Shaik, A. G. (2016a). Bearing fault diagnosis of a three phase induction motor using stockwell transform. *2016 IEEE Annual India Conference*, 1-6. 10.1109/INDICON.2016.7838972

Singh, P., Gupta, P., Jyoti, K., & Nayyar, A. (2019). Research on auto-scaling of web applications in cloud: Survey, trends and Future Directions. Scalable Computing. *Practice and Experience, 20*(2), 399–432. doi:10.12694cpe.v20i2.1537

Singh, R., Tanwar, S., & Sharma, T. P. (2020). Utilization of blockchain for mitigating the distributed denial of service attacks. *Security and Privacy, 3*(3), e96.

Singh, S., Gupta, D., & Chandhoke, A. (2014). Web Mining: Taxonomy and Survey. *Advances in Computer Science and Information Technology, 1*(2), 56–60.

Singh, S., & Saini, H. S. (2018c). Security approaches for data aggregation in Wireless Sensor Networks against Sybil Attack. *2018 Second International Conference on Inventive Communication and Computational Technologies*, 190-193. 10.1109/ICICCT.2018.8473091

Singh, S., & Saini, H. S. (2021a). Learning-Based Security Technique for Selective Forwarding Attack in Clustered WSN. *Wireless Personal Communications, 118*(1), 789–814. doi:10.100711277-020-08044-0

Singh, S., & Saini, H. S. (2021b). PCTBC: Power Control Tree-Based Cluster Approach for Sybil Attack in Wireless Sensor Networks. *Journal of Circuits, Systems, and Computers, 30*(07), 2150129. doi:10.1142/S0218126621501292

Singh, S., & Saini, H. S. (2021c). Intelligent Ad-Hoc-On Demand Multipath Distance Vector for Wormhole Attack in Clustered WSN. *Wireless Personal Communications*. Advance online publication. doi:10.100711277-021-08950-x

Sinha, K., & Verma, M. (2021). The Detection of SQL Injection on Blockchain-Based Database. In *Revolutionary Applications of Blockchain-Enabled Privacy and Access Control* (pp. 234–262). IGI Global.

Sinha, P., Jha, V. K., Rai, A. K., & Bhushan, B. (2017). Security vulnerabilities, attacks and countermeasures in wireless sensor networks at various layers of OSI reference model: A survey. In *2017 International Conference on Signal Processing and Communication (ICSPC)* (pp. 288-293). IEEE.

Siteefy. (2021). *How Many Websites Are There in the World?* Retrieved November 13, 2021, from: https://siteefy.com/how-many-websites-are-there/

Somesha, M., Pais, A. R., Rao, R. S., & Rathour, V. S. (2020). Efficient deep learning techniques for the detection of phishing websites. *Sadhana, 45*(1), 1–18.

Somoza Sánchez, V. (2020). Why users do not accept big data: Benefits and challenges of big data implementation. *Academy of Management Proceedings, 2020*(1), 20225. doi:10.5465/AMBPP.2020.20225abstract

Song, Y., Zhu, Y., Hou, J., Du, S., & Song, S. (2020). Astronomical data preprocessing implementation based on FPGA and data Transformation strategy for the FAST telescope as a giant CPS. *IEEE Access: Practical Innovations, Open Solutions, 8*, 56837–56846. doi:10.1109/ACCESS.2020.2981816

Soniya, S. K. (2013). A review of different type of multipliers and multiplier-accumulator unit. *International Journal of Emerging Trends & Technology in Computer Science, 2*(4), 364–368.

Spiekermann, S., Korunovska, J., & Langheinrich, M. (2019). Inside the organization: Why privacy and security engineering is a challenge for Engineers. *Proceedings of the IEEE, 107*(3), 600–615. doi:10.1109/JPROC.2018.2866769

Srikanth, I., & Arunmetha, S. (2021, February). High Level Synchronization and Computations of Feed Forward Cut-Set based Multiply Accumulate Unit. *Journal of Physics: Conference Series, 1804*(1), 012201. doi:10.1088/1742-6596/1804/1/012201

Sripada, N. K., & Mohammed Ismail, B. (2019). Challenges In Generative Modeling And Functioning Nature Of Generative Adversarial Networks. *Journal Of Mechanics Of Continua And Mathematical Sciences*, *14*, 83.

Srivastava, T., Desikan, P., & Kumar, V. (n.d.). Web Mining – Concepts, Applications and Research Directions. In W. Chu & T. Young Lin (Eds.), *Foundations and Advances in Data Mining. Studies in Fuzziness and Soft Computing* (Vol. 180). Springer.

Srokosz, M., Rusinek, D., & Ksiezopolski, B. (2018). A new WAF-based architecture for protecting web applications against CSRF attacks in malicious environment. In *2018 Federated Conference on Computer Science and Information Systems (FedCSIS)* (pp. 391-395). IEEE.

Steinhauser, A., & Tůma, P. (2020). Database Traffic Interception for Graybox Detection of Stored and Context-Sensitive XSS. *Digital Threats. Research and Practice*, *1*(3), 1–23.

Stolojescu-Crisan, C., Crisan, C., & Butunoi, B.-P. (2021). Access control and surveillance in a smart home. *High-Confidence Computing*, *100036*. Advance online publication. doi:10.1016/j.hcc.2021.100036

Sun, Yin, Liu, & Chai. (n.d.). A novel rolling bearing vibration impulsive signals detection approach based on dictionary learning. *IEEE/CAA Journal of AutomaticaSinica*. . doi:10.1109/JAS.2020.1003438

Sun, M., Chen, J., Tian, Y., & Yan, Y. (2021). The impact of online reviews in the presence of customer returns. *International Journal of Production Economics*, *232*(1), 107929.

Sun, M., Liu, K., Wu, Q., Hong, Q., Wang, B., & Zhang, H. (2019, June). A novel ECOC algorithm for multiclass microarray data classification based on data complexity analysis. *Pattern Recognition*, *90*, 346–362. doi:10.1016/j.patcog.2019.01.047

Sun, S., Cegielski, C., Jia, L., & Hall, D. (2018). Understanding the Factors Affecting the Organizational Adoption of Big Data. *Journal of Computer Information Systems*, *58*(3), 193–203. doi:10.1080/08874417.2016.1222891

Su, Z., & Wassermann, G. (2006). The essence of command injection attacks in web applications. *ACM SIGPLAN Notices*, *41*(1), 372–382.

Syed, A. B. A., & Kumar, M. (2020). Energy Efficient Routing Technique for Underwater Wireless Sensor Networks. *International Journal of Advanced Science and Technology*, *29*(11s), 859–868.

Sze-To, A., & Wong, A. K. (2018). Discovering patterns from sequences using pattern-directed aligned pattern clustering. *IEEE Transactions on Nanobioscience*, *17*(3), 209–218. doi:10.1109/TNB.2018.2845741 PMID:29994222

Tandel, J., Mistree, K., & Shah, P. (2019). *A review on neural network based abstractive text summarization models*. Paper presented at the 2019 IEEE 5th International Conference for Convergence in Technology (I2CT).

Tann, W. J. W., Tan, J. J. W., Purba, J., & Chang, E. C. (2021). Filtering DDoS Attacks from Unlabeled Network Traffic Data Using Online Deep Learning. In *Proceedings of the 2021 ACM Asia Conference on Computer and Communications Security* (pp. 432-446). ACM.

Teekaraman, Kumar, Kuppusamy, & Thelkar. (2022). SSNN Based Energy Management Strategy in Grid-Connected System for Load Scheduling and Load Sharing. Mathematical Problems in Engineering.

Teraguchi, N. C. R. L. Y., & Mitchell, J. C. (2004). *Client-side defense against web-based identity theft.* Computer Science Department, Stanford University. Available: http://crypto. stanford. edu/ SpoofGuard/webspoof. pdf

The Avalon Project. (2008). *Yale Law School Lillian Goldman Law Library.* https://avalon.law. yale.edu/default.asp

Tornatzky, L., & Fleischer, M. (1990). *The Process of Technology Innovation.* Lexington Books.

Trujillo-Guajardo, L. A., Rodriguez-Maldonado, J., Moonem, M. A., & Platas-Garza, M. A. (2018, June). A Multiresolution Taylor–Kalman Approach for Broken Rotor Bar Detection in Cage Induction Motors. *IEEE Transactions on Instrumentation and Measurement, 67*(6), 1317–1328. doi:10.1109/TIM.2018.2795895

Tsalis, N., Virvilis, N., Mylonas, A., Apostolopoulos, T., & Gritzalis, D. (2014, August). Browser blacklists: the Utopia of phishing protection. In *International Conference on E-Business and Telecommunications* (pp. 278-293). Springer. DOI: 10.1007/978-3-319-25915-4_15

Twardos, M. (2011). *Timeline of the United States Most Deadly Wars.* The Information Diet.

Tweneboah-Koduah, S., Skouby, K. E., & Tadayoni, R. (2017). Cyber security threats to IoT applications and service domains. *Wireless Personal Communications, 95*(1), 169–185. doi:10.2139srn.3170187

Umadevi, M., Rathinam, R. S., Poornima, S., Santhi, T., & Pattabhi, S. (2021). Electrochemical Degradation of Reactive Red 195 from its Aqueous Solution using RuO2/IrO2/TaO2 Coated Titanium Electrodes. *Asian Journal of Chemistry, 33*(8), 1919–1922. doi:10.14233/ ajchem.2021.23330

University of Groningen - Humanities Computing. (1994-2012). *"Documents" American History from Revolution to Reconstruction and Beyond.* http://www.let.rug.nl/usa/documents/

Uthayakumar, J., Vengattaraman, T., & Amudhavel, J. (2017). A simple lossless compression algorithm in wireless sensor networks: An application of seismic data. *The IIOAB Journal, 8*(2), 274–280.

Vajjala, S., Majumder, B., Gupta, A., & Surana, H. (2020). *Practical Natural Language Processing: A Comprehensive Guide to Building Real-World NLP Systems.* O'Reilly Media. doi:10.1145/2064448.2064475

Van Der Heijden, A., & Allodi, L. (2019). Cognitive triaging of phishing attacks. In *28th USENIX Security Symposium (USENIX Security 19)* (pp. 1309-1326). USENIX.

Vana, P., & Lambrecht, A. (2021). The Effect of Individual Online Reviews on Purchase Likelihood. *Marketing Science*, *40*(4), 708–730. doi:10.1287/mksc.2020.1278

Veena, K., & Meena, K. (2022). *Cybercrime Detection using C SVM and KNN Techniques* (Vol. 2022). Wireless Communications and Mobile Computing.

Verma, P., Goyal, A., & Gigras, Y. (2020). Email phishing: Text classification using natural language processing. *Computer Science and Information Technology*, *1*(1), 1–12. doi:10.11591/csit.v1i1.p1-12

Vicario, G., & Coleman, S. (2020). A review of data science in business and industry and a future view. *Applied Stochastic Models in Business and Industry*, *36*(1), 6–18.

Vijayarani, S., Ilamathi, M., & Nithya, M. (2015). Preprocessing Techniques for Text Mining – An Overview. *International Journal of Computer Science & Communication Networks*, *5*(1), 7–16.

Vilca, G. C. V., & Cabezudo, M. A. S. (2017). *A study of abstractive summarization using semantic representations and discourse level information*. The 20th International Conference on Text, Speech, and Dialogue, Prague, Czech Republic.

Vittoria, M. P., & Napolitano, P. (2020). Identifying localized entrepreneurial projects through semantic social network analysis. *New Metropolitan Perspectives*, 12–21. doi:10.1007/978-3-030-52869-0_2

W3C. (2021). *W3C standards*. Retrieved November 11, 2021, from: https://www.w3.org/standards/

Waller, M., & Fawcett, S. (2013). Data Science, Predictive Analytics, and Big Data: A Revolution That Will Transform Supply Chain Design and Management. *Journal of Business Logistics*, *34*(2), 77–84.

Wang, Z., Wang, P., Louis, P. C., Wheless, L. E., & Huo, Y. (in press). *Fast In-browser Face Mask Detection with Serverless Edge Computing for COVID-19*. Academic Press.

Wang, M., Shao, W., Hao, X., Shen, L., & Zhang, D. (2021). Identify consistent cross-modality imaging genetic patterns via discriminant sparse canonical correlation analysis. *IEEE/ACM Transactions on Computational Biology and Bioinformatics*, *18*(4), 1549–1561. doi:10.1109/TCBB.2019.2944825 PMID:31581090

WebsiteSetup. (2021). *How Many Websites Are There?* Retrieved November 11, 2021, from https://websitesetup.org/news/how-many-websites-are-there/#number-of-active-websites

WGBH Educational Foundation. (1995-2011). *People & Ideas: The Puritans*. PBS, WGBH Educational Foundation, 1995-2011. https://www.pbs.org/wgbh/pages/frontline/godinamerica/people/puritans.html

What is RFI | Remote File Inclusion Example & Mitigation Methods | Imperva. Learning Center. (2019). Retrieved 3 November 2021, from https://www.imperva.com/learn/application-security/rfi-remote-file-inclusion/

What Is S. Q. L. Injection (SQLi) And How To Prevent Attacks. (2020). Retrieved 4 November 2021, from https://www.acunetix.com/websitesecurity/sql-injection/

Wickham, H. (2016). *ggplot2: Elegant Graphics for Data Analysis.* Springer-Verlag.

Wickham, H., & Hester, J. (2020). *Readr: Read Rectangular Text Data. R package version 1.4.0.* https://CRAN.R-project.org/package=readr

Wickham, H., François, R., Henry, L., & Müller, K. (2021). *dplyr: A Grammar of Data Manipulation. R package version 1.0.6.* https://CRAN.R-project.org/package=dplyr

Wickham. (2019). Welcome to the tidyverse. *Journal of Open Source Software, 4*(43), 1686.

Wijaya, D. T., & Yeniterzi, R. (2011). Understanding semantic change of words over centuries. In *Proceedings of the Workshop on Detecting and Exploiting Cultural Diversity on the Social Web* (pp. 35–40). ACM.

Williams, J., King, J., Smith, B., Pouriyeh, S., Shahriar, H., & Li, L. (2021). Phishing Prevention Using Defense in Depth. In *Advances in Security, Networks, and Internet of Things* (pp. 101–116). Springer. doi:10.1007/978-3-030-71017-0_8

Wilson, T. (2021). *Barack Obama: 'A common dream born of two continents', Democratic National Convention - 2004.* Speakola. https://speakola.com/political/barack-obama-keynote-dnc-2004

Wimmer, H., & Aasheim, C. (2019). Examining Factors that Influence Intent to Adopt Data Science. *Journal of Computer Information Systems, 59*(1), 43–51. doi:10.1080/08874417.2017.1295790

Wiredu, G. O., & Sørensen, C. (2006). The dynamics of control and mobile computing in distributed activities. *European Journal of Information Systems, 15*(3), 307–319. doi:10.1057/palgrave.ejis.3000577

Witten, I. H., Frank, E., & Hall, M. A. (2011). Data transformations. *Data Mining: Practical Machine Learning Tools and Techniques,* 305–349. doi:10.1016/B978-0-12-374856-0.00007-9

Xindong, W., Xingquan, Z., Gong–Qing, W., & Ding, W. (2014). Data Mining with Big Data. *IEEE Transactions on Knowledge and Data Engineering, 26*(1), 97–107. doi:10.1109/TKDE.2013.109

Xu, G., Yu, Z., Yao, H., Li, F., Meng, Y., & Wu, X. (2019). Chinese text sentiment analysis based on extended sentiment dictionary. *IEEE Access: Practical Innovations, Open Solutions, 7,* 43749–43762. doi:10.1109/ACCESS.2019.2907772

Yao, Y., Chen, Y. H., Wang, Y., Li, X. P., Wang, J. L., Shen, D. H., & Wei, L. H. (2010, August). Molecular classification of human endometrial cancer based on gene expression profiles from specialised microarrays. *International Journal of Gynaecology and Obstetrics, 110*(2), 125–129. doi:10.1016/j.ijgo.2010.03.020 PMID:20471643

Yap, J. (2012). *450,000 user passwords leaked in Yahoo breach.* ZDNet. Retrieved 4 November 2021, from https://www.zdnet.com/article/450000-user-passwords-leaked-in-yahoo-breach/

Ye, Z., Zhao, H., Zhang, K., Wang, Z., & Zhu, Y. (2019). Network representation based on the joint learning of three feature views. *Big Data Mining and Analytics, 2*(4), 248–260. doi:10.26599/BDMA.2019.9020009

Yie, L. F., Susanto, H., & Setiana, D. (2021). Collaborating decision support and business intelligence to enable Government digital connectivity. *Research Anthology on Decision Support Systems and Decision Management in Healthcare, Business, and Engineering,* 830–847. doi:10.4018/978-1-7998-9023-2.ch040

Yılmaz, E. N., & Gönen, S. (2018). Attack detection/prevention system against Cyber Attack in Industrial Control Systems. *Computers & Security, 77,* 94–105. doi:10.1016/j.cose.2018.04.004

Yin, D., Zhang, L., & Yang, K. (2018). A DDoS attack detection and mitigation with software-defined Internet of Things framework. *IEEE Access: Practical Innovations, Open Solutions, 6,* 24694–24705.

Yue, C., & Wang, H. (2008, December). Anti-phishing in offense and defense. In *2008 Annual Computer Security Applications Conference (ACSAC)* (pp. 345-354). IEEE. DOI:10.1109/ACSAC.2008.32

Zainuddin, Z., & Ong, P. (2011, October). Reliable multiclass cancer classification of microarray gene expression profiles using an improved wavelet neural network. *Expert Systems with Applications, 38*(11), 13711–13722. doi:10.1016/j.eswa.2011.04.164

Zarei, J., Kowsari, E., & Razavi-Far, R. (2019, June). Induction Motors Fault Detection Using Square-Root Transformed Cubature Quadrature Kalman Filter. *IEEE Transactions on Energy Conversion, 34*(2), 870–877. doi:10.1109/TEC.2018.2877781

Zeileis, A., & Grothendieck, G. (2005). zoo: S3 Infrastructure for Regular and Irregular Time Series. *Journal of Statistical Software, 14*(6), 1–27. doi:10.18637/jss.v014.i06

Zeiler, M. D., & Fergus, R. (2014). Visualizing and understanding convolutional networks. In *European Conference on Computer Vision.* Springer.

Zetter, K. (2010). Hacker Sentenced to 20 Years for Breach of Credit Card Processor. *Wired.* Retrieved 4 November 2021, from https://www.wired.com/2010/03/heartland-sentencing/

Zhang, M., Fan, B., Zhang, N., Wang, W., & Fan, W. (2021). Mining product innovation ideas from online reviews. *Information Processing & Management, 58*(1), 102389.

Zhang, P., Du, Y., Habetler, T. G., & Lu, B. (2011). A survey of condition monitoring and protection methods for medium-voltage induction motors. *IEEE Transactions on Industry Applications, 47*(1), 34–46. doi:10.1109/TIA.2010.2090839

Zhang, P., Zhang, F., Xu, S., Yang, Z., Li, H., Li, Q., Wang, H., Shen, C., & Hu, C. (2021). Network-wide forwarding anomaly detection and localization in software defined networks. *IEEE/ACM Transactions on Networking, 29*(1), 332–345. doi:10.1109/TNET.2020.3033588

Zhang, X., Saleh, H., Younis, E. M., Sahal, R., & Ali, A. A. (2020). Predicting Coronavirus Pandemic in Real-Time Using Machine Learning and Big Data Streaming System. *Complexity, 2020*, 1–10. doi:10.1155/2020/6688912

Zhao, B., Chaturvedi, P., Zimmerman, D. L., & Belmont, A. S. (2020). Efficient and reproducible multigene expression after single-step transfection using improved bac transgenesis and engineering toolkit. *ACS Synthetic Biology, 9*(5), 1100–1116. doi:10.1021/acssynbio.9b00457 PMID:32216371

Zheng, X., Zhu, W., Tang, C., & Wang, M. (2019, July). Gene selection for microarray data classification via adaptive hypergraph embedded dictionary learning. *Gene, 706*, 188–200. doi:10.1016/j.gene.2019.04.060 PMID:31085273

Zhong, Y., Tang, Z., Ding, X., Zhu, L., Le, Y., & Li, K. (2017). An improved LDA multi-document summarization model based on TensorFlow. *IEEE 29th International Conference on Tools with Artificial Intelligence (ICTAI)*.

Zhou, W., Habetler, T. G., & Harley, R. G. (2008, December). Bearing Fault Detection Via Stator Current Noise Cancellation and Statistical Control. *IEEE Transactions on Industrial Electronics, 55*(12), 4260–4269. doi:10.1109/TIE.2008.2005018

Zhuang, Y., Sampurno, Y., Wu, C., Wu, B., Mu, Y., Borucki, L., Philipossian, A., & Yang, R. (2014). (invited) comparison of slurry film distribution between a novel slurry injection system and conventional slurry application method. *ECS Transactions, 60*(1), 625–631. doi:10.1149/06001.0625ecst

Zikria, Y. B., Yu, H., Afzal, M. K., Rehmani, M. H., & Hahm, O. (2018). Internet of things (IOT): Operating system, applications and protocols design, and Validation Techniques. *Future Generation Computer Systems, 88*, 699–706. doi:10.1016/j.future.2018.07.058

Zorrilla, M., Florez, J., Lafuente, A., Martin, A., Montalban, J., Olaizola, I. G., & Tamayo, I. (2018). Saw: Video analysis in social media with web-based Mobile Grid Computing. *IEEE Transactions on Mobile Computing, 17*(6), 1442–1455. doi:10.1109/TMC.2017.2766623

About the Contributors

Ahmed J. Obaid is a Asst. Professor at the Department of Computer Science, Faculty of Computer Science and Mathematics, University of Kufa, Iraq. Dr. Ahmed holds a Bachelor in Computer Science, degree in – Information Systems from College of Computers, University of Anbar, Iraq (2001-2005), and a Master Degree (M. TECH) of Computer Science Engineering (CSE) from School of Information Technology, Jawaharlal Nehru Technological University, Hyderabad, India (2010-2013), and a Doctor of Philosophy (PhD) in Web Mining from College of Information Technology, University of University of Babylon, Iraq (2013-2017). He is a Certified Web Mining Consultant with over 14 years of experience in working as Faculty Member in University of Kufa, Iraq. He has taught courses in Web Designing, Web Scripting, JavaScript, VB.Net, MATLAB Toolbox's, and other courses on PHP, CMC, and DHTML from more than 10 international organizations and institutes from USA, and India. Dr. Ahmed is a member of Statistical and Information Consultation Center (SICC), University of Kufa, Iraq. His main line of research is Web mining Techniques and Application, Image processing in the Web Platforms, Image processing, Genetic Algorithm, information theory, and Medical Health Applications. Ahmed J. is Associated Editor in Brazilian Journal of Operations & Production Management (BJO&PM) and Editorial Board Members in : International Journal of Advance Study and Research Work (IJASRW), Journal of Research in Engineering and Applied Sciences(JREAS), GRD Journal for Engineering (GRDJE), International Research Journal of Multidisciplinary Science & Technology (IRJMST), The International Journal of Technology Information and Computer (IJTIC), Career Point International Journal Research (CPIJR). Ahmed J. was Editor in Many International Conferences such as: ISCPS_2020, MAICT_2020 , IHICPS_2020, IICESAT_2021, IICPS_2020, ICPAS_2021, etc. (Scopus Indexed Conferences). He has edited Some books, such as Advance Material Science and Engineering (ISBN: 9783035736779, Scientific.net publisher), Computational Intelligence Techniques for Combating COVID-19 (ISBN: 978-3-030-68936-0 EAI/ Springer), A Fusion of Artificial Intelligence and Internet of Things for Emerging Cyber Systems (ISBN: 978-3-030-76653-5 Springer). Ahmed J. has supervised several final projects of Bachelor and Master in his main line of work, and authored and co-authored several scientific publications in journals, Books and conferences with more than 65+ Journal Research Articles, 5+ book Chapters, 15+ Conference papers, 10+ Conference proceedings, 8+ Books Editing, 2+ Patent. Ahmed J. also Reviewer in many Scopus, SCI and ESCI Journals e.g., CMC, IETE, IJAACS, IJIPM, IJKBD, IJBSR, IET, IJUFKS and many others. Dr. Ahmed Attend and participate as: Keynote Speakers (40+ Conferences), Webinars (10+), Session Chairs (10+), in many international events in the following countries: India, Turkey, Nepal, Philippines, Vietnam, Thailand, Indonesia and other countries.

Zdzislaw Polkowski is a professor of UJW at Faculty of Technical Sciences and Rector's Representative for International Cooperation and Erasmus+ Program at the Jan Wyzykowski University Polkowice. Since 2019 he is also Adjunct Professor in Department of Business Intelligence in Management, Wroclaw University of Economics and Business, Poland. Moreover, he is visiting professor in Univeristy of Pitesti, Romania, WSG University Bydgoszcz, Poland and adjunct professor in Marwadi University, India. He is the former dean of the Technical Sciences Faculty during the period 2009 -2012 at UZZM in Lubin. He holds a PhD degree in Computer Science and Management from Wroclaw University of Technology, Post Graduate degree in Microcomputer Systems in Management from University of Economics in Wroclaw and Post Graduate degree IT in Education from Economics University in Katowice. He obtained his Engineering degree in Computer Systems in Industry from Technical University of Zielona Gora. He has published more than 75 papers in journals, 25 conference proceedings, including more than 20 papers in journals indexed in the Web of Science, Scopus, IEEE. He served as a member of Technical Program Committee in many International conferences in Poland, India, China, Iran, Romania and Bulgaria. Till date he has delivered 24 invited talks at different international conferences across various countries. He is also the member of the Board of Studies and expert member of the doctoral research committee in many universities in India. He is also the member of the editorial board of several journals and served as a reviewer in a wide range of international journals. His area of interests includes IT in Business, IoT in Business and Education Technology. He has successfully completed a research project on Developing the innovative methodology of teaching Business Informatics funded by the European Commission. He also owns an IT SME consultancy company in Polkowice and Lubin, Poland.

Bharat Bhushan is an Assistant Professor of Department of Computer Science and Engineering (CSE) at School of Engineering and Technology, Sharda University, Greater Noida, India. He received his Undergraduate Degree (B-Tech in Computer Science and Engineering) with Distinction in 2012, received his Postgraduate

Degree (M-Tech in Information Security) with Distinction in 2015 and Doctorate Degree (PhD Computer Science and Engineering) in 2021 from Birla Institute of Technology, Mesra, India. He has Published more than 80 research papers in various renowned International conferences and SCI indexed journals. He has contributed with more than 25 book chapters in various books and has edited 11 books from the most famed publishers like Elsevier, IGI Global, and CRC Press. He has served as Keynote Speaker (resource person) numerous reputed international conferences held in different countries including India, Morocco, China, Belgium and Bangladesh. In the past, he worked as an assistant professor at HMR Institute of Technology and Management, New Delhi and Network Engineer in HCL Infosystems Ltd., Noida.

* * *

Rajasekhar Chaganti worked as a security engineer at Expediagroup Inc in security incident and response team. Currently, he is actively involved in security research and working towards PhD degree from the University of Cumberlands. Prior to joining Expedia, He served as a security analyst in procore technologies and possess knowledge on SIEM, vulnerability management, DNS, and endpoint security. He is holding the industry certifications such as AWS Solution Architect, Certified Ethical Hacker, and CCNA cyberops covering various aspects of security. He was a research assistant at UTSA performing software-defined networking security research and received MS in computer science focusing on computer and Information security from UTSA in 2018. His research interests are in machine learning/ AI for security applications, network security, threat detection in IoT, cloud and blockchain environments and social engineering scams. Prior to joining UTSA, he worked as a patent research analyst for Stellarix consulting services in Jaipur, India. He performed patent research related to patent novelty, invalidation, and landscape projects in electronics and computer science domain focusing on cybersecurity, machine learning, IOT security and cloud computing. He has been a reviewer for IEEE Access, Information and computer security, springer cybersecurity Journal, wireless communications and mobile computing, journal of cybersecurity and mobility, cybersecurity skills journal and volunteered for organizing cybersecurity symposium for smart cities and other security initiatives.

Santoshkumar Vaman Chobe has obtained his Bachelors' Degree in Computer Science & Engineering from D. Y. Patil College of Engineering and Technology, Kolhapur, and Masters' Degree, ME in Computer Science & Engineering from Walchand College of Engineering, Sangli. He is working as a Professor in the Computer Engineering Department at Dr. D. Y. Patil Institute of Technology, Pimpri, Pune.

He has published more than 40 research papers at the National and International Conferences and Journals. His areas of interests include Machine Learning, Data Science, Web Mining, and Compilers. He also has Patents and Copyrights on his name.

Mohammad Daradkeh is an Associate Professor of Data Science and Analytics at the College of Engineering & IT, University of Dubai. Prior to joining the University of Dubai, Dr. Daradkeh worked at Yarmouk University in Jordan and Lincoln University in New Zealand. His research interests are mainly in the areas of Business Intelligence, Analytics and Data Science. He received his PhD in Software and Information Technology from Lincoln University, New Zealand, and MSc. and BSc. in Computer Science from Yarmouk University, Jordan. He has published numerous research papers with reputed publishers such as Elsevier, Springer, Emerald and IGI. He has presented research papers at various international conferences. He is also a member of the editorial board of several reputed journals.

Mohamed Ali Hajjaji received his PhD in Electronics and image processing from the National School of Engineering of Monastir (ENIM) and Burgundy University (BU), France, in 2013. His current research interests include hardware implementation of image processing applications.

A. K. M. Bahalul Haque is currently appointed as a Junior Researcher at LUT University, Finland. He was a lecturer at North South Unversity Bangladesh. He has completed a Bachelor of Science in Computer Science and Telecommunication Engineering from Noakhali Science and Technology University, Bangladesh. He achieved M.Sc. in Information Technology from Fachhochschule Kiel, Germany. He is a research enthusiast and his area of research interest includes Blockchain, IoT, Smart City, Cyber Security, and Cloud computing. He has published papers in reputed international conference proceedings. journals and book chapters.

Abhijit Dnyaneshwar Jadhav is currently pursuing his research study in PhD (CSE) from KLEF, Guntur. He completed his M. Tech. (CSE) from RGPV in 2014-15, Bhopal and B. E. (Computer Engineering) from University of Pune in 2007-08. He registered 11 patents, 29 copyrights and published 14 research articles in reputed journals indexed in SCI, Scopus, Google Scholar and IEEE Explore. He is having total teaching experience of 13.5 years in engineering institutes. He is currently working as an Assistant Professor in Dr. D. Y. Patil Institute of Technology, Pimpri, Pune. His area of interests are Machine Learning, Data Science & Big Data Analytics, Data Mining & Data Warehousing, Database Systems, Data Structures, Software Engineering, Internet of Things, Cloud Computing and Network Security. He is the lifetime member of ISTE, IAENG, Annual CSI & ACM.

Saptadeepa Kalita is currently pursuing PhD from Sharda University in the Department of Computer Science and Engineering. Area of Research is Machine Learning and Cyber Security.

Avinash Kumar is an Assistant Professor of Department of Computer Science and Engineering (CSE) at School of Engineering and Technology, Sharda University, Greater Noida, India. He has completed Masters in Cyber Security, De Montfort University, United Kingdom. He also done Masters in Computer Science Engineering at Galogotias University. He received his Undergraduate Degree (B-Tech in Information Technology from SMU. He has worked as Security Analyst from more than three and half years. He has worked as Research Assistant in United Kingdom on IoT security over Cloud Foundry taking Content Centric Networking as medium of communication. He was a keynote Speaker at IEEE Day Celebration webinar at Sharda University. Delivered Keynote at IEEE International Webinar organised by NSU Industry Applications Society Student Branch Chapter. He earned numerous international certifications such as Certified Ethical Hacker (EC-Council), Cisco Certified Network Associate (CCNA-Routing and Switching), Cisco Certified Network Associate (CCNA-Security).

Seifeddine Messaoud holds a doctorate degree in the Electronics and Microelectronics from the Faculty of Sciences of Monastir, University of Monastir, Tunisia. Seifeddine Messaoud conducts research, at the Electronics and Microelectronics Laboratory, on SDN, NFV, Resource Management, 5G, IoT, Industry 4.0 (IIoT), Artificial Intelligence, Deep Learning, SoC Design, and Embedded Vision.

Abdellatif Mtibaa received his PhD degree in Electrical Engineering at the National School of Engineering of Tunis. Since 1990 he has been an assistant professor in Micro-Electronics and Hardware Design with Electrical Department at the National School of Engineering of Monastir. His research interests include high level synthesis, rapid prototyping and reconfigurable architecture for real-time multimedia applications.

Parma Nand is a PhD in Computer Science & Engineering from IIT Roorkee, M.Tech & B.Tech in Computer Science & Engineering from IIT Delhi. Prof Parma Nand is having more than 27 years of experience both in industry and academia. He had received various awards like best teacher award from Union Minister, best students project guide award from Microsoft in 2015 and best faculty award from cognizant in 2016. He had successfully completed government funded projects and spearheaded last five IEEE International conferences on Computing, Communication & Automation (ICCCA), IEEE students chapters, Technovation Hackathon 2019,

Technovation Hackathon 2020, International Conference on Computing, Communication, and Intelligent Systems (ICCCIS-2021). He is member Executive Council of IEEE UP section (R-10), member Executive Committee IEEE Computer and Signal Processing Society, member Exec. India council Computer Society, member Executive Council Computer Society of India, Noida section and has acted as an observer in many IEEE conferences. He is also having active memberships of ACM, IEEE, CSI, ACEEE, ISOC, IAENG, and IASCIT. He is life time member of Soft Computing Research Society (SCRS) and ISTE.

Joshua Ojo Nehinbe obtained Ph.D. in Computer Science from the University of Essex, UK in 2011 and M.Sc. in Computer Science (with research) from the University of Agriculture, Abeokuta in Nigeria in 2004. He has worked in the banking sector as a Software engineer; Globus support specialist, Head of IT and auditor of Information Systems. He also had cognate experience in IT consultancy with local and international firms. Joshua Nehinbe teaches Undergraduates and Post graduates students in the areas of Cyber security and forensics, database design and management, software engineering, Leading E-Strategy and data mining. He has published over 40 reputable journal papers, conference papers and co-authored book chapters with foreign experts in the areas of best industrial practices, security and forensics in Cyber Physical Systems. He is a professional member of the Institute of Electrical and Electronics Engineers (IEEE), British Computer Society (BCS), British Academy of Forensic Sciences (BAFS) and Nigeria Computer Society (NCS).

Tyler Soiferman is currently an undergraduate student at Stevens Institute of Technology in Hoboken, New Jersey, USA. He is pursuing a degree in Computer Science.

Safa Teboulbi is currently a PhD student in Electrical Engineering at the National School of Engineering of Monastir, Tunisia. Safa Teboulbi conducts research at the Electronics and Microelectronics Laboratory. Her current research interests include Deep Learning, Algorithms, embedded systems, and hardware implementation.

Index

X

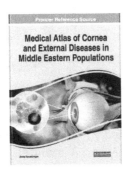
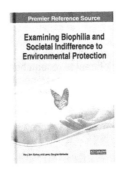
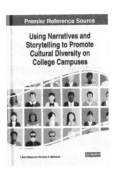

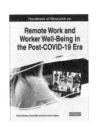

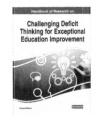